D0686686

Finding and Knowing

Psychology, information and computers

Finding and Knowing

Psychology, information and computers

Clare Davies

Routledge
Taylor & Francis Group

LONDON AND NEW YORK

Published by Routledge

Haines House, 21 John Street, London, WC1N 2BP, United Kingdom
(a member of the Taylor & Francis Group)

Copyright (©) Clare Davies 2005

ISBN 0-85142-454-6

Except as otherwise permitted under the Copyright, Designs and Patents Act
1988, this publication may only be reproduced, stored or transmitted in any
form or by any means, with the prior permission in writing of the publisher.
Enquiries concerning reproduction outside these terms should be sent to the
publisher at the address above.

The author asserts her moral right to be identified as such in accordance
with the terms of the Copyright, Designs and Patents Act 1988.

Typeset by Data Standards Limited, Frome

Printed and bound in Great Britain by MPG Books Ltd, Bodmin, Cornwall

To Calvin, for being still

Contents

List of illustrations

Preface

For this book, I've looked for research and views that fit within the structure I've defined and help to answer the questions I consider. In Chapters 2–6 this structure is the same every time: each chapter is named by a basic activity we do with digital information, and asks what or when we do it, how we do it, what goes wrong with it, and what we could do to improve things, before listing some further reading.

As the target audience is normal readers as well as abnormal academics, I've used informal language, explaining jargon and giving examples, and I haven't broken up the text with obscure academic references. However, as a researcher myself I do want to credit other people with their ideas and let fellow researchers trace them. So, the numbers in the text reference the numbered (but also alphabetical) list at the end of the book.

If you're not interested in names and publication details, just ignore the numbers. All my notes about the *content* are on the pages themselves as footnotes. Anything you see in **bold** is in the glossary at the end of the book, to help with the unavoidable jargon.

So, if you're a fellow researcher, you can still see if I've cited your favourite people because the Bibliography is alphabetical—so that numbers aren't consecutive when they're cited. If you're an ordinary person who just wants a quiet read but might also check up the odd reference out of interest, I hope this works too. As I'll discuss later, designing information for every audience isn't always easy!

Acknowledgements

The idea and commission for this book came while I was working for De Montfort University's then quite visionary (but sadly soon defunct) International Institute for Electronic Library Research. The basic ideas I formed there about the relationship between information science and cognition became the basis for chapters 2, 3 and 4.

More recently and crucial to this book, my ongoing Visiting Scholar status in the psychology department at Northwestern University in Evanston, Illinois, has given me access to a wealth of online scholarly sources that I could otherwise only dream of. The dedicated folk who run such fabulous IT and library resources almost never get acknowledged, yet all our torches are lit from the fire that they keep burning.

My two years at NU (for which I thank my former boss, David Uttal) not only gave me Chicago to play in—one of the world's greatest cities—but it also let me hear talks by some of the most amazing people in cognitive science and psychology, within and beyond the department. This book is much better for it. Many conversations with Norbert Ross, my then office mate, helped me to firm up my concerns about methodology and the role of context and culture in our cognition, and they also helped keep me sane!

My current colleagues in the Research and Innovation unit at Ordnance Survey, a unique and brilliant research environment, helped me cope with the final push to the finish. However, all views in this book are entirely my own, and do not represent those of any organisation I work, or have ever worked, for—or, for that matter, any other organisation. Likewise, I am entirely and exclusively responsible for any errors which may appear.

My parents handed down their curiosity, critical thinking, and a passion for knowledge which has always pushed me on. U2, Dave Matthews and WXRT Chicago all made dull editing a breeze.

Before I began this book the patience and kindness of my husband, Calvin, were already legendary. Having an anxiety-prone author in the house was a severe test of them, but he was not found wanting.

Writing a book while holding down three successive full-time jobs, moving continent twice and house three times is obviously ridiculous. I promise to behave more sensibly in future.

Chapter 1

Information, computers and people

This is a book about what happens when people try to find, look at and use information on a computer. While thinking about this, it romps through many ideas and issues. My aim is to try to shed new(ish) light on information use, by linking together many different sources of thought about how we and our computers behave.

Unlike most books on this sort of topic, the main aim isn't to persuade software designers to make easier programs that fit people's needs and behaviour patterns, nor to persuade website owners to change their design to make them clearer. Plenty of other authors are doing that better than me. However, some insights about good and bad design do emerge along the way.

The main target reader of this book isn't academics; it's any person who uses, or who could use, or who teaches, designs, studies or helps people to use, information on computers. That probably includes you. So why should you read it?

First, you might be curious to know what research has been done into information use, especially if you've ever growled in frustration when you couldn't find what you wanted in a database, or spent hours on the internet without achieving much in the end.*

Second, it might help to know about the things that can go wrong when we seek and use information. We might then be able to compensate, avoid them, or at least consider them, given the time we spend on such tasks.

Perhaps the best aspect of this book is that while we're thinking about this one small set of things that people do, it can be a 'test track' for some interesting insights about ourselves from psychology and other sciences. This book is a chance for the non-academic reader to learn a little more about them. Equally, researchers in information science and psychology will hopefully find a fresh insight or two, since nobody ever has the chance to read or think about everything.

As the author, I should also explain why I wrote the book, and why I felt qualified to do so. I work as an applied cognitive psychologist.

---

*Given that the net is rapidly becoming people's first port of call for every type of information, it won't surprise the reader that much of this book focuses on it. But many of the ideas I quote could be applied to any online information source, from a CD-ROM encyclopaedia to a digital map.

This means I focus on how people's **cognition** works in everyday settings. Cognitive psychology focuses on people's mental processes (e.g. perception, thought, problem-solving, language and memory). It has sometimes received a bad press from people who feel it's too remote from reality, doomed to isolate little things about our minds out of the big picture, and too dependent on assumptions that our brains work just like computers do.

This book isn't going to argue one way or the other about such attacks, but it is an effort not to throw out the baby with the bath water. I think cognitive psychology has learned some interesting and helpful things from four decades of research, and we can use some of them in real-life situations. However, other areas of psychology are relevant as well. We don't just sit in a corner mentally processing things without reference to the effects of social, emotional or organisational context.

In fact, I've written this book at a time when even the phrase 'cognitive psychology' is becoming obsolete. The 1980s and 1990s saw huge progress in techniques for studying the brain, and parallel strides in computing technology that have made computer-based modelling techniques much easier and more affordable to cognitive researchers. These went alongside hugely increased technical literacy among psychology researchers themselves. Computers became the main tool for every activity from running experiments to writing papers about them, to modelling how people had behaved in them.

As a result, *cognitive science* is the buzz-phrase of the moment. It implies that researchers don't just do experiments but *also* measure participants' brain signals during them *and* build computer-based models to simulate those signals. There is still a problem that these are lab-based studies of artificially simplified activities. Also, 'cog sci' is still failing to integrate the models together into a 'theory of everything', or even to agree about which type of model to build. Still, exciting working models of people's behaviour are starting to emerge, and I'll mention a few later in this book.

Steven Pinker, whose books are perhaps the best ever attempts to make cognitive researchers' ideas truly readable for non-psychologists, began his book *How the Mind Works*[228] with two crucial caveats which I'd like to echo here: first, we don't understand much about how the mind does work. Second, most of the ideas and work in this book come from other people, and are only interpreted (or misinterpreted!) by myself.

2

Disciplining disciplines, and following fashion

It would be stupid to relate psychology to a practical area like information use without thinking about other relevant sciences. A lot of the research this book draws on is from **information science**. This studies such information sources as databases and libraries (and more recently, the internet and the World Wide Web—referred to as 'the web' throughout this book). It tries to work out how to improve them for their users. Many people aren't aware of the mountain of research that lies behind the design, organisation, management and cataloguing of their local library, and especially its computerised catalogue (if it has one).

Librarians' expertise is in information, that is, deciding what people are looking for in it and offering the best ways to find it. Although that information traditionally lay in books, some of their expertise ought to tell us something useful about handling information from *any* source. This is why most universities link information science and librarianship into one department.

The third main research area that's important for this book is called human–computer interaction, usually shortened to **HCI**. This is where computer scientists, and some psychologists, try to work out how we can build computer systems with more **usability**.* HCI links with yet another academic subject, **ergonomics** (or, in the USA, **human factors**), which is commonly connected with the design of chairs and other work-related objects. **Cognitive ergonomics** focuses on improving the comfort and safety of objects that involve our mental processes, such as software and gadgets.

A few years ago, information scientist Gary Marchionini[186] implied some distrust of HCI research, and he doesn't seem to be alone within his discipline in this view: 'The objects of information seeking are ideas and their many representations. These abstractions are distinct from manipulating physical objects and typically are less well defined than is manipulating numeric or factual data' (p. 210). It's certainly true that in the past far too much HCI research has focused on simplified computer-based tasks, such as basic text editors and simple drawing or email programs. As in cognitive science, the motive is often to discover a basic underlying

---

*They use the term 'usability' and not 'user friendliness' because a 'friendly' computer could be very nice to you but still not help you achieve what you want. A friend told me of a certain Japanese businessman who courteously nodded and smiled at each suggestion my friend made, 'Yes, yes, yes...', then added, once my friend had stopped talking, 'No.' A polite response that doesn't move you nearer your goal is nicer, but no more use than a rude one.

principle through this simplified work, and then apply it to more complex behaviour as well. Unfortunately, many academic HCI researchers continued through the 1990s to talk about software design issues in quite simplistic and hard-to-scale-up terms. Yet they were actually using far more complicated and flexible software just to write their papers on it. HCI's restoration as a credible research area is partly due to inspired practical 'bibles' of web design like Rosenfeld and Morville's *Information Architecture for the World Wide Web*,[244] which brilliantly combines information science and HCI aspects.

And there are other sciences involved in this research apart from psychology, cognitive science, information science and HCI. Sometimes we're handling information specifically to learn from it, so research into education matters too. Sometimes the information is about images or real world places, so geography, cartography and graphic design come in. Mathematicians and physicists have also weighed into debates on how to model the internet and how human-like its computers could ever get. And because sometimes it's worth taking a step back to ask what it's all really about, this brings in a few philosophers.

I've been very lucky, over the past decade or two, to work alongside experts in most of these areas, so I'm able to draw on them as well as on psychology. Links across different areas of knowledge are still subtly discouraged by our education system, which makes my position rare indeed.* But even without this trend, psychologists seem to be particularly bad at taking time to learn from more applied disciplines. Sometimes this may be based on the notion that physicists would not expect to learn much from engineers: the 'purer' scientists' knowledge is supposed to help the 'applied' people to explain their work, but not the other way around. This is a shame.

This book is not the first effort by a cognitive psychologist to apply psychological knowledge to the 'real world'. Donald Norman's books on modern technologies and general design, the most famous being *The Psychology of Everyday Things*[212] (also published as *The Design of Everyday Things*), charted that famous cognitive researcher's gradual disillusionment with laboratory experiments and abstract theories. Norman seems to have felt it was almost his duty to immerse himself in practical issues of computer user interfaces, and

---

*In particular, the system that currently dominates British research still mostly rewards a mainstream lack of imagination, where people stay on one safe bandwagon within a single subject, rather than seeking collaboration with different disciplines.

even more basic artefacts like taps and door handles, as if to atone for the lack of practical uses of most cognitive psychology.

Edwin Hutchins expressed similar worries in his elegant 1995 book on naval navigation, *Cognition in the Wild.*[137] Based on his experiences while studying navigation teams on warships, Hutchins argued that cognition may be so dependent on the context, and on social interaction between people within any kind of group, that it was false to study any mental processes on their own. However, most cognitive researchers haven't followed Norman or Hutchins out of their labs; they feel (rightly in many cases) that their work to build a scientific foundation is also worthwhile.

To some extent, cognitive research was forced into the public eye by the rise of evolutionary psychology. It seems as if almost every month a news story tells us that researchers have claimed an evolutionary 'explanation' for a detail of everyday life, such as why women gossip, why we bother to be altruistic toward others, why we grieve or laugh, and so on. Suddenly every aspect of our supposedly sophisticated lives is fair game for being reduced to caveman ethics and concerns. Some of the ideas are intuitively appealing, others are ridiculously over-simplified, and some totally ignore the wide variety of human choices. All too often, an equally plausible evolutionary 'explanation' could predict the exact opposite behaviour just as well.

I'm not alone among psychologists in being sceptical of at least some of this research. I'm perfectly happy to accept biological evolution *in general*—I'm not a Genesis literalist like the Darwin-banning school boards in some southern US states—but I see its simplistic application to complex human behaviour as suspiciously trite and convenient. It can't account usefully for individual differences, or predict any one person's actions. The debate over this issue is ugly and often stalemated, as many mainstream researchers prefer simply to ignore the evolutionists or to pick out ideas that suit their own beliefs and interests. Meanwhile the evolutionists try to make us believe that our only choice is between their ideas and sheer superstition.

One of the world's best-known cognitive psychologists, Steven Pinker, in his bestseller *How the Mind Works,*[228] did try to meld evolutionary ideas with current knowledge of cognition. The resulting book is a classic and highly readable text, even if some people dispute its strong evolutionist flavour. Jerry Fodor,[97] another key writer on cognitive science and its philosophy, has suggested that Pinker went too far in his enthusiasm for evolutionary explanations. Fodor pointed out that there are alternatives to evolutionary psychology:

> It's common ground that the evolution of our behaviour was mediated by the evolution of our brains. So, what matters to the question of whether the mind is an adaptation* is not how complex our behaviour is, but how much change you would have to make in an ape's brain to produce the cognitive structure of the human mind. And about this, exactly nothing is known. That's because nothing is known about how the structure of our minds depends on the structure of our brains. Nobody even knows *which* brain structures our cognitive capacities depend on.

Fodor was exaggerating: we *do* have increasing piecemeal knowledge about how certain areas of the brain seem to be more involved in some tasks than in others. Some people believe we've got even further than that, but the theories often founder when people realise that a part of the brain isn't what it seemed after all, since very many of our behaviours seem to involve *lots* of bits of brain *at the same time.*

Still, Fodor gives us an alternative to seeing every aspect of our behaviour as specially evolved to help our hunter-gatherer ancestors. We could assume instead that the development of a bigger brain was the only big evolutionary step. If this is true, then with a bigger brain our behaviour could become more complex and varied, but not necessarily evolving 'Darwinianly' in itself. Since a bigger brain is bound to be able to do a lot more than a smaller one, in ways that we've only started to understand in the past couple of decades, it could be that this brain growth just *happened* to cause some of our current behaviours and differences, almost as side effects.

Fodor also pointed out that just because we can think of a neat 'evolutionary' motivation for people behaving in a certain way, it doesn't mean that that is the *only* possible motivation. And sometimes, according to Fodor, we may not need any explanation at all. We may like doing some things 'just for their own sakes'. Pinker had suggested that we might have evolved an attraction towards fiction (novels, films, plays, etc.) as a sort of information-seeking device. It gives us a chance to think about situations that we ourselves might face, and to ponder what we would do without (yet) having actually to face them. For example, we can weigh up the evidence and ask ourselves what *we* would do in Hamlet's dilemma over his uncle's murder of his father? Fodor ridiculed this:

> Good question. Or what if it turns out that, having just used the ring that I got by kidnapping a dwarf to pay off the giants who built me my new castle, I should discover that it is the very ring that I need to continue to be immortal and rule the world? It's important to think out

---

* By this Fodor means the question of whether everything in our minds was adapted for a direct evolutionary cause, such as helping primitive man's survival.

the options betimes, because a thing like that could happen to anyone and you can never have too much insurance. (p. 212)

In other words, a great deal of what we do, like and fantasise about is so far removed from the likely issues we face in our everyday survival, and even from those that our ancestors faced, that we *can't* find trite evolutionary explanations for it all. While Fodor's dismissal is frustrating for any psychologist who feels that ultimately we should somehow be trying to explain *everything* about human behaviour, it is still the case that information use on a computer, like magic immortalising rings and giants, doesn't easily fit with an evolutionary perspective. Nor, indeed, do very many situations in our modern lives.

The key point in all this is that evolutionary psychologists (along with current economic pressures on universities to be 'relevant', i.e. short-termist) are effectively forcing cognitive ideas out into the real world where they ultimately have to work. Until recently, information scientists had to work much harder to spot anything relevant in cognitive science jargon. But as some have found (and we'll see later), the deeper you delve into the research literature in cognition, and the harder you're prepared to work to overcome its jargon barriers and unusual points of view, the more likely you are to realise that it *does* have more to say about information seeking and use. In this book I've tried to bring up some ideas that information scientists may not have previously noted.

As we'll see, some of the most applicable ideas in psychology emerged some decades ago, often before 1980, particularly the whole concept of the human mind as an 'information-processing device' which underpins a lot of cognitive work. It was a lot easier to sit back and think of the 'big picture' back then, in the days before the discipline became so enormous and complex that we found it hard to see the wood for the trees. Also, it takes time for any theory to become widely known. Many of the more recent ideas in psychology are still unproven and subject to debate and revision, making their application in the real world risky and unclear.

Often, as we'll see in later chapters, cognitivists have laboured over experiments in which topics like attention and memory are reduced to a scattering of random letters, words or basic shapes, as if a small child's toy-box has been emptied onto a blank computer screen. It's pretty hard to know whether we can apply the millisecond differences in the times people take to select a red triangle out of a number of blue squares to the massively more complex task of choosing which text to click in a web page. A lot of cognitive work deals with such building blocks of perception and memory. Yet the things that tend to

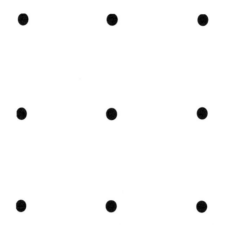

Figure 1.1. The 'nine dot problem' beloved of psychology textbooks. Draw four straight lines through the picture so that every dot is on a line, without lifting the pencil from the paper.

go wrong with our computer use are usually (though not always) problems with our 'higher-level' processes, like thinking, deciding and reading. These are actually less well understood, and less well modelled, precisely because it's harder to 'get at' them in the lab. Every writer on cognition is aware of this.

By the time I'd finished writing this book, I was more convinced than before that psychologists could learn, with information scientists, a lot more from studying real-world areas like information use. It could be a way forward to help us crack the mystery of our reasoning and decision-making processes. When you search for information on a computer, you are obviously using those processes in a 'real' and personally (maybe even socially) motivated way. At first sight, this may seem quite different from experiments where psychologists ask you to solve a 'trick' problem like the one above.[255] (The solution, and the reason why it's not obvious, is in the next chapter.)

Yet relative to many situations in everyday life, information use on computers is still *fairly* restricted and straightforward. Like psychologists' problem-solving studies, it can be studied in a controlled, semi-realistic (or **ecologically valid**) situation, as library researchers have shown again and again.* And it would be daft to imagine that you had *no* motivation for solving a problem if you did indeed try to solve it. However, the impact of different *sources* of motivation

---

*It's much less of a challenge than applying cognitive work to native non-Western cultures, as some psychologists and anthropologists are bravely attempting![247]

may affect people's responses in both situations, as we'll see later on.

One important distinction is worth noting, though. Psychology aims purely and simply to understand people's *behaviour*, to model it, and to predict it if possible. That's why, as a psychologist, I find people's information use interesting in its own right, when it goes badly as much as when it goes well. The other subjects I mentioned above have other goals: mostly they're concerned with building better *systems*. Their theories are designed to help come up with better computer software, better training for librarians and users, better user interfaces—a better world.

It can be frustrating to try to glean insights about human behaviour from the literature on information and computer sciences. Their user studies, models and books all intend to go just far enough to help the building of the next generation of systems, but not to really grasp what's going on in the mind (let alone the brain). To be fair, their researchers often try extremely hard to learn from psychology, even taking psychology courses themselves to deepen their knowledge, but still their motivation is at a different level and for a different purpose.

Psychology researchers are often asked what the *use* is of their research, but deep down many of us don't feel there has to be one. To us, the goal of understanding every nuance of the human mind is worth pursuing for itself for now, and in time we'll find uses for that understanding that we haven't even thought of yet. Theoretical physicists can get away with this sort of statement, and psychologists often feel that they should too. So, as we'll see in this book, sometimes the links between psychology and information science are less clear, less convincing, less well-tested, than we'd ideally like. Much work is still waiting to be done.

One aim of this book, then, is to give you broader knowledge of computer-based information use than a lone psychologist, ergonomist, information scientist or computer scientist would usually tell you. Of course no book can cover everything that even one of them can tell us, so this book is inevitably selective, and is bound to annoy some people whose favourite (or whose own) research has been left out. However, I've felt encouraged, in my efforts to bring these areas together into one book, by a much-overlooked suggestion by the famous cognitive psychologist Jerome Bruner.[38] As long ago as 1957 he suggested that combining concepts 'on the margins between fields' is what creates scientific progress.

Some metametametacognition

I've chosen to structure the remaining chapters of this book according to the things we do with information, and the most obvious order in which we think about using it (e.g. we generally have to find it before we read it in depth). The chapters focus on searching, browsing, reading and making use of information, in that order. This presents a few difficulties: as many information scientists have recognised, the lines between these activities are blurred. We may have a more or less 'formal' strategy for gathering information, [186] in which we may focus more on searching by typing words into boxes, or we may spend more of the time browsing and reading ('informal'). We're unlikely ever to run a search without browsing the results at least a little, although we're sometimes likely to browse or read without searching.

Nevertheless, since research has focused on these activities in different ways, it seemed sensible broadly to follow this scheme. Unlike most previous authors, I've tried to consider all the major activities of information use. Previous books have tended to focus on searching and browsing only, and research into reading has been completely separate, yet there are many links and analogies we can draw across these areas.

I've chosen to use a similar set of questions for each chapter:

- What, when, why and by whom is this activity done?
- How do we do it?
- What goes wrong with it?
- What can we do about that?

I'll reveal one possible answer straight away: the last question often comes down to improving our personal **metacognition.*** Metacognition is the act of reasoning about ourselves and our own behaviour patterns. When we're using a computer, we can become so involved in the task we're doing, and our interaction with the machine, that we find it hard to step back and observe our own choices and problems. As a result, these situations are probably familiar:

- We start browsing through the web or a database, thinking we'll go back and check a certain potentially useful item in a moment, but then forget it.

---

* 'Meta-' is a prefix indicating that something is referring to its own kind of thing. 'Metadata' is data that describes the content of other data; 'metacognition' is thinking about your own thoughts. This section explains how this book considers people's use of metacognition; hence the section title!

- When we obtain search results, we fail to stop and think about whether the results look too broad or too enormous, and wade into the list of items, quickly getting overwhelmed.
- We start reading something which isn't quite what we needed but which looks interesting anyway, and soon are so absorbed in it that we forget our original goals.
- We print out a document, optimistically assuming we'll read it later on, but then leave it on the printer or never take it from the bag we stuffed it into.
- We memorise a fact or figure or quotation we see on a web page, confident that we'll be able to recall it, but later we can't.
- We underestimate the amount of time we'll need to deal with some information, or we overestimate the amount of information we can sift through in the time we have.
- We stick to strategies that simply aren't working and allow ourselves to become frustrated and angry, instead of backing down and trying a different approach to the problem.

With more sophisticated metacognition, we would, in theory, be able to avoid many of these situations. Metacognition is not as big a research area as you might expect. Most metacognition work is in the area of problem-solving and in the study of children's development. Parents won't be surprised to hear that children frequently show very limited, or no, awareness of their own limitations, and often don't realise that they don't understand something well enough to act on it properly.

Yvonne Waern briefly reviewed some metacognition studies in her 1989 book on cognitive aspects of computer use.[300] She included studies showing that young children, when taught insufficient rules for playing a game, didn't realise that they didn't understand enough to play it properly. They confidently recited the rules that they did know to other children, without realising that they themselves couldn't follow them. Children don't predict accurately how much they'll remember of something they've just learned, and don't plan their learning in any organised way to make it easier to memorise items. Fortunately, most of us develop these aspects of metacognition as we grow up.

In adults, the extent to which metacognition is used constructively depends very much on individual personalities, and on specific situations and their emotional significance. However, sometimes it is hard to tease out metacognition from the bigger, all-engulfing philosophical issue of consciousness, and from the smaller, well-researched cognitive issue of attention. Once we bring in the emotional side as well, studies of metacognition tend to blur into the issues of over-confidence in our abilities on the one hand, and our need for **self-efficacy** (basically, self-belief or self-confidence), on the other. We'll see in Chapter 2 that both *too little* self-efficacy, and *too much* confidence in our predictions and probability estimates, seem to cause problems for some aspects of computer use. Maybe we should try to train our metacognition as a way to avoid both extremes. As the Temple of Apollo at Delphi was famously inscribed, 'Know thyself'.

Gary Marchionini, in his reflection on the role of metacognition in using information systems,[186] seemed to define it so broadly as to be our entire conscious self, describing its role as a motivating and guiding force as well as providing the thoughts that monitor our actions. It's true that we become aware of an information need by realising that we don't know something, and this is a metacognitive thought. However, that thought in turn comes from an event or requirement in the real world, so we need to look further than the metacognition to see what makes us want information. We don't normally think of metacognition as including the state of wanting, or the feeling of knowing we want something, because these are emotional states rather than cognitive processes—so the two are connected but separable.

If we talked about metacognition in the all-encompassing way implied by Marchionini, we would have to plunge deep into the murky world of consciousness research. Philosophers, psychologists, neuroscientists and even linguists have been arguing about the nature of human consciousness for over a decade now, and this book is not the place for that debate.

However, one relevant piece of evidence that's emerged from some of the studies of consciousness shows how poorly we monitor our moment-by-moment awareness of the world. We exhibit **change blindness:** that is, we fail to notice when something unexpected is added, replaced or moved in a scene we've been watching.[268] In other words, as we monitor a situation in what we think is a close and careful way, we still fail to memorise many details of it. While the change blindness studies generally involve psychologists pulling cute tricks on their experiment participants—tricks that are fortunately rare in everyday life!—the point they make is that we are *not* fully monitoring the world around us in as much detail as we think we are.

It shouldn't perhaps be so surprising, then, that we also fail to monitor ourselves. We can focus so hard on struggling with the immediate action, that we don't ask ourselves if that action is still the best way of solving our overall problem. Laboratory experiments show that our attention is excellent at focusing on one small thing to the exclusion of others, yet in real life that thing in itself is often a distraction from the main goal, or a dead end that impedes our progress. Distraction isn't always a bad thing—librarians have long recognised the value of **serendipity** in finding something that's not immediately relevant to their current task but will be useful for another project they have in the back of their minds. Serendipity was certainly crucial for finding many of the articles and papers I cite in this book, while I was working on completely different research projects.

Serendipity is usually a good thing in information seeking, so long as we maintain some memory of our original goal. We tend to be *aware* of a serendipitous distraction. It's a deliberate detour from our main route, and we know we still have to resume that route afterwards. More dangerous is the type of distraction that seems not to be a distraction at all. An example is trying repeatedly to search the web using particular words, when in fact those words are not the best ones to describe our topic, or when searching in this way is actually a less efficient method than browsing from a relevant starting point. We struggle, and so our minds pour greater effort and concentration into that struggle. We don't ask if the game is worth the candle, or if the candle can be bought another way.

Evolutionary psychologists would of course leap on the argument that this was a logical way for primitive man to behave when most of the problems he faced were in the physical world. He or she could overcome them just with extra effort and force. That may be so, but it doesn't help us to understand either why or how, in specific situations, we do or do not say, 'Hang on, is this helping? Am I getting anywhere? What else could I do instead? Was there another explanation?' I'll mention more about metacognition in later chapters. The point for now is that we should be able to monitor the task we're doing and the way we're thinking about it.

A computer, as many people have pointed out, is not a television; we expect to physically *act* on it as we view its screen. That interaction should therefore be much less *cognitively* passive than the way that we are often seduced into behaving, when we watch the computer apparently doing things for us. Marchionini pointed out that although computers allow us to discover things more quickly on one level, nowadays we have to devote more time than ever to what he called 'managing the personal information infrastructure' instead of to the problem at hand. We may even spend so much time focusing on the *process* that we never actually complete the *product*. We have to keep more information in our memory than we used to (partly because, as I'll discuss later, we're less likely to take notes). We also have to devote effort to understanding the computer and persuading it to do what we expect.

Any frequent computer user knows the feeling of wondering how much time they really save by using it, and how much they waste when things don't go to plan or need extra actions to work. Such a reader might feel that the last thing we need, as we already have to devote so much time and cognition to computer problems and failures, is to have to increase our *meta*cognition about the whole process. Yet the point about metacognition is that if we practise using it, it improves our problem-solving abilities and thus gets us out of the sticky mess sooner. Like all the healthy habits suggested by personal training courses and self-help books (many of which also boil down to metacognition about life choices and time management), it takes an investment of effort that achieves more and feels better in the end.

For now, it's simply worth noting that it is possible to seize the bull by the horns and become more proactive in your strategies as you grapple with online information. The many problems that I'll discuss in the following chapters show how much this is needed, if we're to cope at all with the ever more complex choices thrown at us from the computer screen.

Computers and selves

Of course, even if we did monitor our own cognitions so that we knew exactly what we were doing and thinking and why, the computer wouldn't. We'll talk in later chapters about the problems with this, using labels like '**pragmatics**', 'relevance' and 'shared assumptions'. At bottom, the computer's knowledge of us and our contexts is always very limited. It hasn't been through decades of growing up. It isn't a deeply complex brain that can learn from every social encounter and build up its understanding of other people. It isn't 'one of us', and hence doesn't know all of our social conventions. However, the situation may run even deeper than the issue of knowledge. Perhaps it comes down to the subtler question of how we decide, or know, whether or not the thing we're talking to has some kind of mind or 'self'.

Ulric Neisser, a well-known psychologist, wrote a controversial book in the 1970s called *Cognition and Reality*.[205] In it, he expressed his frustration with the reduction of our complex everyday experiences to the niggly, unrealistic, highly controlled experiments his cognitive colleagues performed in bare university laboratories. This was the start of Neisser's interest in a more 'ecological' approach to psychology. He later[206] developed the concept of five different 'selves'.

He saw these as the five aspects of our conscious, self-knowing being.

- The 'ecological self' perceives the outside world and its own body through the senses.
- The 'interpersonal self' lives in society and deals with other people.
- The 'conceptual self' holds beliefs about who I am and what roles and categories I fit into.
- The 'temporally extended self' has memories of a life history.
- The 'private self' has thoughts, dreams and emotions which are unique and unknown to others.

The computer's limitations on achieving any of these forms of 'selfhood' are obvious, so that's one theoretical problem when we deal with them. For now I'd like to focus on a slightly different issue: our *own* 'interpersonal self', i.e. the person who interacts with other people. Our understanding of this, according to Neisser, develops partly from what we learn from interacting with others, right from babyhood when an adult makes funny faces at us.

Neisser[206] linked this idea to those of certain philosophers, such as Wittgenstein, and theologians such as Martin Buber, who have argued that there is a basic difference between our understanding of our relationship to other *people* ('I–Thou') and our relationship with *things* and ideas ('I–It'). Which of these relationships do we have with our computer?

A more recent philosopher, David Jopling,[145] who was sympathetic to Neisser's point of view, argued that we don't even need to make a decision about whether another person has a 'self' like us, and then decide how to respond to it. We don't wait to draw conclusions from the hard evidence that the person is talking, responding to us, and making facial expressions and gestures, and so on, and hence decide that they must have a 'self'—we simply know (although possibly not if we're autistic[197]). We know that other minds exist simply because we've encountered them—our understanding of ourselves has come from what other minds have shown us. This idea is called **intersubjectivity**:

> The distinction between persons and things is the most fundamental way of dividing up the furniture of the world. We think of ourselves as essentially persons and only contingently as things, material objects, minds, mammals, reasoners, scientists, taxpayers, and so forth. Similarly, we think of other humans as essentially persons... We learn the distinction between persons and things at our mother's knee and rarely stray from it; it is part of the general framework of human life. (pp. 299–300)

Jopling added that we don't have to establish that a creature we meet is a person—we automatically respond to it as a person if we have any kind of dialogue with them, even an unspoken one. The fact that we are communicating somehow tells us, from infancy, that we have a self and so does each other person.*

This is all very appealing and direct, and would delight the students I've taught who hated cognitive psychology's obsession with concrete scientific evidence, ignoring personal intuitions. However, we don't *only* interact with other people, so we need to think about whether we can make sense of *all* our interactions this way.

Presumably, Jopling would say that our ambiguous relationships with animals—sometimes treating them as though they have minds and 'selves', and at other times not—is due to the extent to which we feel we manage to have a 'dialogue' with them, despite their lack of language. In this modern age, we have a further problem, which makes us mix up persons and things *much* more often than Jopling suggested. We **anthropomorphise**. In other words, we talk about machines as if they too have minds and 'selves'.

When we swear at the 'stupid' computer, accuse the copier of 'knowing' we're in a hurry, and yell "No, stop!!" at the printer as it churns out garbage, we're often only half-joking. It's only in the past 200 years of our evolution that we've developed machines sophisticated enough to do what animals do, making complex physical responses to our actions. Sometimes it seems like an even deeper 'dialogue' than the one we have with animals. In the past 60 years, we have developed a machine that responds not just with action, but with our own language.

If, as the above writers claim, we respond to things as persons just because we have dialogues with them, then our responses to computers are going wrong from the start. With a computer the lights are on, but nobody's home. Yet whatever objective, rational *knowledge* we hold that the computer can only do 'garbage in, garbage out', our instinctive equation of 'dialogue = person' will often make us *behave* differently. We may act as if the computer had learned from 'its mother's knee' to empathise with us, to want to help us, and to tell us what was obviously (to us) relevant to the situation at hand. Of course, with its parents actually being a Far East processor factory and a long line of time-stressed programmers, it hasn't learned any

---

*However, developmental psychology has found that our so-called 'theory of mind'—awareness of other people's minds—seems to develop at a certain point in infancy; we don't seem to be born with it. [197] Autistic children seem to fail to develop it, and the reason for that is still debated.

16

such thing. It then makes sense that we respond emotionally when the computer lets us down, just as when people fail us.

If we want, we can choose to stay sceptical about this 'inter-subjectivity', and to believe that we only judge something as a person from the evidence of its appearance and behaviour—that there is no 'magic selfhood' reaching out from soul to soul. This belief gives us the chance to convince ourselves that computers really *are* only objects (and perhaps to stay calmer when near them!).

Even then, we can still see that the use of language might make us expect too much, given the apparently 'custom' responses we get back. A person genuinely *will* try to fit their response to what they imagine you want to do with information, as I'll discuss further later.

Awareness of such limitations caused J. M. Brittain,[35] an information scientist writing in 1991, to cast doubt on the so-called 'cognitive paradigm' of trying to make computers model the knowledge of users and librarians, rather than just indexing documents regardless of their content. Brittain wrote that this aim 'may be regarded by many as a flight into fancy' (p. 101), and some other authors since have tended to agree with his pessimism. After all, they scoff, so-called 'expert systems' have got nowhere. Douglas Adams[2] made the fictional Deep Thought computer find the answer to Life, the Universe and Everything. We haven't even got computers reliably to handle basic problems in finance or engineering. What does 'artificial intelligence' have to show for itself apart from the odd robot, which can't even vacuum my house for me yet?

I think there are several different issues here:

- One is the aim of trying to put some semantics into a computer, some real linked-up knowledge which can be used to answer questions and to cross-reference related items, which is definitely *not* impossible (as we'll see later, it's already being done).

- This is different from the aim of producing an 'expert system' which can diagnose and solve problems in real-life situations as skilfully as a professional lawyer, doctor or engineer would. That would of course be a leap up from simply shoving in the facts, and we're nowhere near really achieving it, although in less sophisticated domains (such as insurance) computer-based decisions are now common.

- Then we need to distinguish both of these aims from the hope of getting a computer to take account of the *context* in which an individual approaches it to retrieve or use information.

17

- That itself, again, is much easier than making the computer respond like a real person with some awareness of its 'self' and a mutual 'cognitive environment'.
- Finally, all of these are separate from the possibility of making a computer really *understand* the *meaning* of the knowledge it stores—an issue which has caused enormous and fascinating debates among philosophers, psychologists and cognitive scientists, as I'll discuss in Chapter 5.

We *can* add more and more knowledge and intelligence to computer programs such as **search engines**, **browsers** and databases, so that their responses get closer and closer to people's needs most of the time. We're already doing this. And we can persuade users to specify their needs and intentions in ways that make the most of the computer's abilities. But the 'intersubjectivity' idea raises another interesting question. If we make computers more helpful and hence more 'human' in their responses, will it really help us?

Many novice internet users give up a search after their first attempt, thinking that 'nothing is out there' because some systems don't tell them that they misspelled a pop star's name. We'll explore this further in Chapter 3. But when a computer *can* spell-check, use a thesaurus and infer what we might mean by our input, it seems like a form of real intelligence, and we're quite impressed. Therefore, the more trustworthy a computer became, and the more it seemed to respond to me as a 'person', the more I'd trust that its search was the best that could be done, even if it wasn't. Our expectations would mislead us even though they were based on experience—in fact, *because* they were based on experience.

We must accept, as the technology moves on, that there'll always be room for wrong interpretations. The divorce courts will close forever before we make a computer behave with total understanding of our needs. We cannot make it even as sensitive and intelligent, and mindful of our needs rather than other goals, as our human partners. We know that they—and we—are unreliable enough.

Going out of style

When the web took off in the mid-1990s, whole shelves of books on information systems and information science immediately started to look outdated. Many things are predicted for the next internet, from ever-growing multimedia resources, accessed universally from miniature devices, to dismal predictions that business and government will turn the whole thing into a commercial exclusion zone and that the 'free lunch' of information is doomed. This book can't hope to stay up to date, since new techniques and technologies emerge every year. Yet its attempt to bring together what we know about human *behaviour* with information should date more slowly, as research takes longer.

Indeed, I hold a strong view on this issue, which will become obvious from the references I cite in this book (including Bruner's above[38]). The frequent failure of most academics to learn from other fields and from the historical developments of their own field, so that they tend to cite only papers from the past decade, is *itself* mainly a problem of information use.

Most of the common databases of research papers that scientists use routinely (except for those scientists who simply rely on whatever papers their friends have recently written—and yes, such people do exist) date back only to around 1980 at best, and often as recently as 1990. Many people simply ignore all the work done in their field before their generation, except when they fancy a 'historic' quotation for a review paper they're writing. In psychology this excuse is less allowable—the major psychology database goes back right into the nineteenth century. But in every field, the jargon has changed so much that you rarely see an older paper when you search on a current topic name. Sometimes the database is set up to assume that, by default, you'll only want the past decade's papers anyway, so you have explicitly to change that setting if you want to go back further.

Making matters worse, the new (and wonderful) habit of journal publishers to mount online versions of the full text of every article they publish, so that scientists no longer have to spend hours at a decrepit library photocopier, can give them not a broader but a *narrower* field of vision. The methods of access are currently so publisher-dependent that it's hard to get an overview, rather than just relying on your 'favourite' journals. Even as this improves, there is still the problem that only post-1997 papers tend to be online in this way. Few publishers seem genuinely interested in adding their earlier journal volumes (probably partly because, as I said above, few scientists seem to care about reading them anyway).

In the scientists' defence, the sheer bulk of published papers is rising almost exponentially every year, and it's becoming nightmarish coping with even a single specialism. And that is precisely why the areas of research I cover in this book are becoming ever more crucial. Even the scientists who are supposed to help us can't keep up with their own knowledge field or learn from its history, never mind helping you with yours. Perhaps this book will motivate a few more people to work on the research topics it raises.

Meanwhile, as an author I take comfort in the fact that it's still relevant to quote psychology papers from the 1950s, and information science papers from the 1980s, while talking about the web at the turn of the millennium. It suggests that the ideas *I* put forward, like theirs, may still have some relevance and use in the next phase of the 'information revolution', however it develops.

The online 'library'

Earlier I mentioned the importance of librarians' expertise in dealing with information. Of course, some people compare the internet itself to a giant library, since it holds even more information. People were in fact trying to build such an 'online library', one holding full text documents, as early as the late 1950s. They finally succeeded in the 1990s, thanks to better software technology. But how much is it really like a library?

Librarians choose the items they store, based partly on quality (except in copyright libraries that receive everything). Nobody stops you from putting the most trivial drivel, or outright lies, on the internet; it's more like an eccentric magazine shop than a library. Equally, librarians, who have only limited space available to them, only remove things from libraries when they deem them outdated or of too little interest to readers. Yet things disappear from the internet every day which other people wanted to see, but whose owners or website hosts changed their plans or ran out of money.

This is a 'library' whose donors and authors control the texts, and change or delete them at will. There is hardly any limit on the web's space—even where individual computers run out of disk storage, we can add more at an ever-decreasing cost—but the chief limitation is on human motivation to maintain it.

In one sense, we could even deny that the internet exists. There is no physical entity that *is* the internet, in the way that a building and its contents can be inventoried and called a 'library'. None of the items that make the internet work are even necessarily dedicated to doing that and nothing else.

The wires, fibre-optic cables and electromagnetic waves that carry signals, and thus transport a copy of a webpage from a server in Kalamazoo to your desktop computer, may also be carrying telephone and/or TV signals.

The computer on your desk is busy doing many things at once, and only the 'web **browser**' software application is doing anything internet-related on it (and we don't need that either as internet access becomes integrated into other packages, such as word-processors, and with the basic operating system).

The server at the other end (and the intervening computers that route your webpage requests to it) may again be doing other tasks. Its disks will store many programs and files, as well as those which can be seen on the website. It may even generate webpage data 'on the fly', putting together a different assortment of advertisements and options for different users at different times, rather than storing static pages.

So where's the internet? It is a dynamic process, not an object or collection of objects. Speaking of the internet as a single entity is like imagining that every conversation everyone has is part of some giant orchestrated piece of performance art. A library is contained in its physical walls; the internet can't be.

Yet another problem with thinking of the internet as a library is the chaos you find when you try to search it. Nobody has organised it. Hubert Dreyfus, a philosopher, wrote that this seems like 'a new form of life in which surprise and wonder are more important than meaning and usefulness. This approach appeals especially to those who like the idea of rejecting hierarchy and authority and who don't have to worry about the practical problem of finding relevant information' (p. 12).[82] I don't know where such people exist. Surely we *all* love to subvert authority, but we also *all* need to find information sometimes.*

In the past couple of years, malicious individuals have hit the headlines several times with so-called 'denial of service attacks' on high-profile internet sites. These tend to be the sites acting as the nearest thing to a library catalogue. They either hold a specially classified database of high-content and popular websites, or allow searching of a much wider set of pages that nobody has checked for usefulness, or both. Some hackers may believe that people depend on these sites to find anything on the internet, but we'll see later that this isn't true. In any case, if one stops then there's still at least a dozen others to try.

One of these sites, provided by the big companies and often filled with flashy graphics, commercial 'banner' advertisements and tiny prettily-styled text, will probably appear as a default 'home page' when you first start up your web browser. Many bewildered novice internet users look askance at that page, which for a usability

---

*To Dreyfus, the web has 'an all-American democratic ring' in ignoring order and tradition. I doubt that Thomas Jefferson, who classified his own 6,487-volume library before selling it to Congress in 1815, would have agreed. Modern US society is hardly disordered or subversive, either. Web inventor Tim Berners-Lee was a British scientist working in Switzerland.

specialist is a heart attack on a plate. From here, in theory, you can reach the whole internet, but where do you start?

The metaphors used when referring to this type of website usually don't evoke libraries but 'gateways', or 'portals', or 'your personal internet' (especially if some of the content can be customised to suit your interests). And indeed, I have helped several novices who believed that that packed single page of links and advertisements somehow *is* the internet, and that the only resources that exist are those that are searchable from it or linked to it.

Novice users also confuse the 'portal' site's small white 'search box', for entering words and phrases describing what you want to find, with their web browser's (identical-looking) box for entering whole URLs (addresses) to jump straight to other websites.* Then they assume that if they type something into either box but only receive a 'not found' error message, the thing they're looking for doesn't exist on the internet or has permanently disappeared. We'll look at some of the reasons why this happens in Chapter 3.

Again unlike a library, most of the databases that you search when you use those little boxes contain a huge set of arbitrary pages which nobody has rated or chosen, but which some 'crawler' program has simply 'sucked up' from scanning the internet. Contrary to what many people assume, the millions of pages whose contents are copied and stored in the database are usually only a small fraction of the real, whole, internet (although possibly an increasingly large one, as they become more sophisticated at finding sites[†]). This is because the crawlers aren't quite as clever as their developers would like them to be. They miss many sites with no links to the ones they do find, or that have some kind of security barrier placed on them.

There's no way of knowing for sure whether the resulting database includes the best and most relevant pages for you, although it's likely that something relevant will be included. The result can be bewildering and frustrating. Even a highly experienced computer user of a certain age can sometimes feel nostalgic for the sight and smell of those simple little wooden drawers filled with neatly typed, perfectly ordered cream and pink cards that they used in the libraries of their youth.

The program behind the little white search box is a **search engine**. Once you've retrieved a list of potential sites, you usually see a few

---

*Browser makers themselves eventually realised this and made the address box function as a search box too, but it took a few years before this need was recognized.
† Of course it's hard to judge this, as they are currently the *only* practical way of finding so many sites, but they can be compared with each other, or a set of known sites can be tested against them to see what proportion is in there.

lines of text from each one so you can judge its usefulness, and a single mouse click will take you to it. Chapter 3 will examine in depth the problems, assumptions and drawbacks of this process, and Chapter 4 will consider what happens when you browse through the results list or through actual web pages themselves.

The companies who run and advertise on those glitzy portal sites that I was just criticizing have been changing the direction of the internet's development. It's becoming increasingly difficult for the original public access spirit of the net (promoted by its English inventor, former academic Tim Berners-Lee) to prevail against the heavy-handedness of the marketers. They too often believe that the key to people's hearts and wallets is through glamorous bells and whistles rather than accessible information.

Libraries, as institutions usually acting in the public interest, try to ensure accessibility to their material for people with special needs by investing in large-print books, audio materials, books aimed at different levels of education and books translated into other languages. The internet's commercial pressures, the lure of 'pretty' graphics, the sophistication of development software that moves web designers' focus from information to presentation, and sometimes the tight deadlines or simple ignorance of the designers themselves, all obstruct a fabulous chance for true social inclusion.

It's possible to present websites in different languages, with the user's browser automatically choosing the version they prefer. It's also extremely easy to design a website that blind or movement-impaired people can 'read' using enlargement or read-aloud software, but many web designers are not asked to think about such social inclusion issues. Yet the large-scale 1998 GVU web survey[149] showed that 8.2% of its respondents had some form of disability, most of them impairments of vision or movement. In other words, at least 2 out of every 25 web users may be needlessly excluded from glitzy websites. Also, if designers use too many irrelevant graphic images and 'plug-in' features, the website simply can't be used through a less wealthy user's slow second-hand modem and non-current computer model.*

For these groups, some information providers include a 'text-only' alternative website, which may or may not be as up-to-date and comprehensive as the 'pretty' version, and access to it may or may

---

* One small thing still helps people with all these disadvantages. If you build a website, try to ensure that every image on it has a so-called 'ALT' tag, giving a brief description of its content/function. Then people who can't or won't see the graphics will still understand the page. If you can't think of a relevant and brief description, do you need the image at all?

not be clearly marked on the home page. It offers increased speed and accessibility, but at the cost of unnecessarily making its users feel like second-class citizens. Meanwhile, with so little limit on space or colour, more *helpful* graphics could be included in long online texts than in printed books. Yet often we miss *that* opportunity too.

Relative to a library, the internet is a 24-hour, year-round, facility (so long as your computer and internet server are working!). You can talk, eat and drink while using it. It's right there in your home (a liberation for many housebound people), and never in history have information and ideas of all kinds, for all interests, been so widely available. It's all there—but are we ready for it?

Information, society and the web

Even before the web boom, people wrote many concerned and worthy tomes about the growth of the 'information society'. It's easy for journalists and academics in sophisticated big-city circles to see this 'society' around them. We should be realistic about this, however. Society, as Margaret Thatcher famously overstated, is a collection of individuals, and the 'information society' mainly comprises individual members providing and retrieving individual pieces of information. This book is about that individual process, and what we know about it from many disciplines, but I would not make many broader claims about 'society' from those observations. Psychology, the study of human behaviour, differs from sociology, which studies society as a whole entity; this book's focus is firmly on the former despite bringing in the social and emotional motivations that influence our online choices.

Furthermore, it isn't clear that everyone, even in 'developed' countries like Britain, would agree that they were immersed in or dependent upon our vast information networks. An illiterate 16-year-old sleeping on the street might disagree, as might a bewildered immigrant struggling with English (and his neighbours in a run-down public housing estate), or an elderly lady marooned in a busless rural village. We are dealing only with the experience of the 'information-rich' in this book, and overlooking the 'information-poor' (those with no access to the resources I discuss). Fortunately, surveys suggest that these are now a minority in our country, but of course they are still a vast majority elsewhere.* Perhaps, in a small

* As the satirical paper *The Onion* headlined late in 2001 after extravagant fund-raisers for the New York terrorism victims, 'U.N. Report: 70 Percent of World's Population Could Use All-Star Benefit Concert'.

way, some of the suggestions in this book could also help to spread the 'information wealth', by making information access a little more straightforward once people do get hold of a computer.

However, as Gary Marchionini warned in his book on information searching, written before the web took off, the imagined wealth of computerised access to information is two-faced.

> On the one hand, computers have broken down interpersonal barriers of race, gender, age, and culture; provided new modes of expression; and opened up new levels of communication. On the other hand, computers have given bullies new avenues for intimidation and control, exposed many technophobics, and provided yet another excuse for obsessive-compulsive perfectionists to avoid finishing their work. (pp. 16–17)

We need to consider more than information 'wealth' when assessing the internet. The kind of wealth that jingles in your pocket is increasingly required too, even after you've gained access to a computer and a network connection. The web's inventor, Tim Berners-Lee, created the technology to link academic information and documents together. As the web became publicly accessible, there was a clear sense of mission, of freedom of information. Yet now big companies control not only the browser technology used to access the web (although there are still alternative, 'open-source', browsers available for those who like to rebel), but also an increasing share of its content.

As small site-hosting and access-providing companies collapse or sell out to larger corporations, it seems as if multinational globalisation is steaming into the huge 'public square' of the web, just as much as in other areas of life. The suspicious approach of successive American governments to the internet, despite the enshrinement of free speech and information in the US constitution, seems to favour the interests of commercial entities over the 'common man' (as indeed do many US policies, as citizen's rights groups are quick to point out). Paranoia can easily develop!

To be fair, though, the web is largely the same as any other area of human activity that is largely controlled by Western capitalist democracies. Where there is a public consensus that something is a Good Thing, and where that is expressed strongly enough by voters, our governments usually move to help protect it. Realistically, since the maintenance and updating of the millions of websites that make up the 'public square' is an activity that needs people's real-life time and resources, and hence must be 'funded' somehow, three models of useful websites emerge.

First, websites funded by commercial companies. These may be advertisers unrelated to the site's content, whose sales of products are allegedly boosted by those banners and flashy graphics that we all love to hate, but which allow the site to maintain free access to the public through their funding. Alternatively, the company may be the actual provider of the site, who uses it as a shop front for selling products. They may also choose to 'add value' by providing free information of some kind, in the hope that the visitor to the site will also buy their products while they're there. Sometimes that product itself *is* the website, and you must pay to access it, as with some specialist financial information providers.

Second, websites maintained by public-service institutions, government agencies and departments, and major charities. These include many of the best information resources currently available. Examples include the BBC,[22] Ordnance Survey,[219] the main UK[77] and US[94] government public information sites, and the enormous family history database provided by the Church of Jesus Christ of Latter Day Saints.[92]

Third, websites maintained entirely by voluntary effort, either from individuals or by collective organisation. In reality, these sites usually depend to some extent on the previous two sources of funding, since their online availability is only possible by somebody paying the telecoms provider physically to attach the computer and to have a working 'address' on the network. However, their content may be entirely created and updated by people working in their own, unpaid, time.

This threefold model is very similar to the situation in broadcasting, especially in the United States. In Britain, there is little volunteer-run or charitably funded broadcasting outside local hospital radio, but in the United States many broadcast TV and radio stations, especially in larger cities, rely on publicly donated funds and/or on volunteer staffing. The price for not sitting through hours of glossy, meaningless and manipulative consumerist propaganda (the commercial breaks on TV and radio, or the obstructive banner adverts and maddening pop-up windows on websites) is donating money or time yourself to the cause of public service.

Note the opportunity this gives for people with some spare time to contribute to the socially beneficial cause of free, well-organised information, without even leaving their seat at home. With the web it doesn't have to be about money; there are excellent initiatives towards free information provision which only require your time as a typist, cataloguer, scanner or proof-reader, sitting in the comfort of your home.

These include the 'dmoz' Open Directory Project,[79] a volunteer-run human catalogue of informative websites, with more than 65,000 registered volunteer editors, to help people find non-commercially biased information among the chaos that I'll discuss in this book. Another is the FreeBMD project,[99] whose volunteers are slowly digitising the historical registers of births, marriages and deaths in the UK so that people can search freely for the official records of their nineteenth-century ancestors.

The oldest and best of all is the venerable, 30-year old Project Gutenberg.[232] Hundreds of volunteers have digitised over 13,000 out-of-copyright classic books for everyone to download free, including an increasing range of audiobooks. (If you have a scanner at home it probably came with some basic **OCR** software that will help translate a scanned page into digital text, so anyone can help.) Despite being hosted in the United States the books include languages from Welsh to Yiddish, albeit mostly English. They cover subjects from philosophy to science fiction and romance, and are produced in 'plain vanilla' so that they can be rapidly downloaded, read online and printed out no matter how ancient or simple your computer.

For their success, all these projects depend entirely on we users giving back to the web community, as well as gaining information from it. It seems likely that they, and the publicly funded resources, will be enough to keep the web worthwhile as a massive public encyclopaedia of knowledge, despite the apparent power of the multinational corporations. Indeed, the latter mostly recognise that if the web became too commercialised and content-poor, people would simply stop using most websites altogether, just as a similar (but equally precarious) balance has been struck in broadcasting. It's also easier, with so much greater choice online, to vote with our feet.

Overall, then, it's clear that it used to be much easier to talk about information systems and their use: they used to be formal, rule-based systems set into specific contexts, e.g. companies with clear management hierarchies, or libraries guarded by rule-enforcing librarians. They could be easily distinguished from informal information systems, such as asking your friend for advice in the pub. Changes in systems and in society were already making that distinction less clear, but now the web has changed everything: it has no clear role or definition and operates with few consistent rules.

Within the web you still find bits that do operate formally. For instance, **search engines** have certain rules to follow about processing search terms and presenting the output (although the rules are different for each one). Large content-oriented websites are often very highly structured and based on clear goals and purposes, and might only be accessible to a select group of people. But mostly it's a free-for-all, and the only overall 'system' into which it's embedded as far as we, its users, are concerned, is the highly informal system that is our lives.

Chapter 2

Wanting

Who wants what from information?

When you switch on your computer or mobile device, what are you after? Information is sought for many reasons, and what's sought ranges from simple facts or predictions to emotional guidance or explanations of complicated ideas. You may want a simple Yes or No answer to a question—e.g. 'Is it going to rain today?'—or a downloadable copy of *Wuthering Heights*. You could be a school pupil, an undertaker or an astronaut. You might hope to be calmed and reassured, or to look for a new challenge. You could be in a forest, an office, a library, a bedroom, or a bus shelter.

There are still many people who simply haven't yet seen anything on a computer, or on the internet, that's relevant to their lives or work. They may have looked and failed to find precisely because of some of the problems discussed in this and later chapters. The internet probably has information on every single subject on the planet; it either has the answer to your query on a page somewhere or a pointer to a book or human being who has it. If you've ever given up, concluding there was nothing useful out there, it's quite likely that your ideal information source was lurking just beyond a poor user interface, a different set of jargon or an unsuitable **search engine.**

There are always alternatives, of course. We want to be able to browse in a library, meet with fellow hobbyists, flick through magazines, deal with real people, wander through shops and castles, confront enemies directly and study old documents. Real life doesn't all happen in front of a screen. The advent of the internet hasn't stopped people talking on phones, meeting with friends, taking up interests and courses, visiting the cinema, making music and love, or seeing the world.

Psychologists and sociologists seem to agree that basic motivations make us social, active, creative, physical creatures who will never all be satisfied with couchpotato lives, even if some are. Instead, ideally the net would make us better informed about what's available out there so that we can make the most of our days. In fact, as internet access on mobile devices becomes commonplace, we don't even have to leave the net at home.

Wanting it: am I 'hard' enough?

In theory, anyone who can read this, or who can understand it if it's read aloud to them, can get information out of computers and the internet. Even with special needs, such as physical disability, a way probably exists to get someone online; I once saw a really useful website whose author happened to be quadriplegic. But more commonly, leaving aside the 'information inequality' situation, which means many people in the world still won't have access to the internet for some years to come, there are many people who do have access but who feel afraid of, or anxious about, using a computer. The term we usually use for this is **computer anxiety** or **computer aversion**, although you also hear it talked about as '**technophobia**'.*

The literature on computer aversion tries to explain it in terms of various psychological concepts, of which the most important is **self-efficacy**. This is your level of confidence in your ability to do something successfully. Studies have shown that low self-efficacy for computing activity predicts people's avoidance of it, and performance when doing it, more strongly than gender, age, training, or even expectations of whether it'll work.

Low self-efficacy is not always obvious on the surface. You might hear people say that they won't use the computer because it probably won't do what they want if they try to use it, or that they won't search the internet because there's 'nothing out there'. But certain research has suggested that what they often *mean* is that they fear that they personally won't be able to make the best use of it.[37][†] People sometimes also think that successful computer use depends on absolute talent—i.e. that good computer users are 'born' rather than

---

*Strictly speaking, 'technophobia' isn't a good word for it, since to psychologists a 'phobia' is a fearful condition that needs some kind of therapy or treatment; most people who feel uncomfortable about computers aren't anywhere near that extreme.

†This isn't always true, however: one important study[138] showed no *direct* link between self-efficacy and people's judgement of the usefulness of computers. Self-efficacy seemed to be related to people's view of computers' *ease* of use, and that in turn did seem to affect judgements of usefulness. In other words, not 'It's useless because I'm no good at it' but the more complex 'It's useless because it's too hard for anyone to use effectively, especially me because I'm no good at it'.

'made' through training—but that belief also lowers their self-efficacy, and so it becomes a self-fulfilling prophecy.

However, it's rather hard sometimes to tease out the effect of fear of embarrassment and humiliation. You could be afraid of being seen publicly as a 'stupid' computer user (even if you know that the reason is lack of training rather than inherent incompetence), and expect this even more because you also feel low self-efficacy about mastering the machine.

The lesson from all this is to have faith—self-efficacy can be changed quite easily. You're more likely to get good results from a computer (like most other things in life) if you believe you *can* learn to use it well. It's worth noting, though, that too much self-efficacy can also be a problem: thinking you know everything about, say, searching a database can stop you from learning new 'tricks' for getting better results (see Chapter 3). Also, it's unclear whether self-efficacy is really a single, fundamental psychological quality: we seem to have different levels of it in different situations. It could simply be a pattern of emotional responses to a specific set of cognitive beliefs. More on this later.

Whatever the role or existence of self-efficacy, it's clear that people's desire to use computers, in situations where it is optional, tends to be predicted by their personal computer anxiety and their judgement of the usefulness of computer systems, along with certain other beliefs and habits. Research has shown that you're also influenced by the attitudes and behaviour of people around you, as suggested later in this chapter, and by the amount of support you can get from others. However, it's also been suggested that your own personal attitudes are much more important than those of others. [222] In other words, it may be what you feel and not who you're with that makes the biggest difference.

This, and much of the other research on the factors affecting people's use of information systems, has tended to focus narrowly on academics, journalists or other professional people choosing (or not) to use them for their work. This is a very different situation from people thinking of 'surfing' the internet for their own purposes at home or in their lunch break. So-called 'knowledge workers' in the media, research and education have known for some years that computers were becoming the accepted tools for finding things out and getting them done. Maybe their supposedly 'discretionary' use isn't all that discretionary anyway. It's possible that social influences could make more of a difference to people when there's a *real* choice about use of online information systems.

It's true that even academics, addicted as they are to knowledge, sometimes reject computer-based information sources as either 'overloading' (a problem discussed in later chapters) or else as being unreliable, unreadable or poor quality.[16] Quality is more important than quantity when you're trying to use information to spark off original ideas. Sometimes reading everybody else's versions of a problem or issue is the *last* thing you want to do.

Even when we do want to know things, computers can't really interact with our ideas in the way a person can. They can give us information relevant to the ideas, but they don't yet do much to help us to link them conceptually (apart from giving us graphical or textual tools to express those links). A computer can't (yet) say, 'Ah yes, now that way of thinking reminds me of the ideas of So-and-so in a completely different field . . .', and it also won't shake us out of our intellectual dead ends by chatting and buying us a coffee. Still, the information in a computer is produced by humans, so some of that content can be almost as enlightening as real conversation, especially if we find a colleague's or soul mate's email address and start an online discussion.

Professors are also notoriously bad at getting themselves trained on better ways of doing their work. Being the world's highest-qualified educators, who are independent and time-pressured, makes it hard for them just to trot along to an internet training session. They feel, even more than you might feel when faced with a computer, either that they somehow just *ought* to be able to do it for themselves, or else that they shouldn't need to. Never underestimate an academic ego. Much of the baffled tone of the information science literature describing academics' crude and frustrating database searches can surely be linked back to these emotional issues.

Abilities, gender and computers

But apart from attitudes and feelings, is it true that people with certain types of intelligence do better with computers? What if you've heard the common statement (for instance) that males have better spatial or mathematical ability than females, and so are bound to be innately better at computer tasks too? I would say this: don't let any newspaper or TV programme convince you that this is some proven universal law, because it's not that simple.

First, we have to consider the murky world of academic politics, in which experiments tend only to be published if they seem to show **statistically significant** results (i.e. a really big, consistent difference between two groups of people, or a really big effect of some variable in the way people were treated). Studies where no real gender difference is found (or effect of age, class background, etc.) tend either not to be published, or to be written up with an emphasis on some other effect that *was* noted, without mentioning gender/age/class/race at all.*

This difference in the level to which gender-affected and gender-unaffected results get publicised, and even reported at all, is made much much worse by the national media, who almost never run a story saying 'Men as Good as Women at Verbal Communication' or 'Girls Equal Boys in Geography Tests'. Just as the constant 'drip' of news, yet apparent lack of good news, gives us an inevitably gloomy view of the world and a sense of constant change, think what our vague impression of scientific knowledge is likely to look like because of these imbalances.

Even when we find an aptitude test which *consistently* shows higher scores for males, or whites, or youngsters, or for the rich or the better fed or the Mozart listeners, and even when this difference occurs consistently across many careful studies (as opposed to any single, potentially biased sample of bored university students), we still have to remember these caveats.[†]

1. Most people can improve their score on most aptitude tests, if they get appropriate training or experience on it (or on related skills). For example, the famous alleged 'spatial ability' differences between males and females are often easily removed, after less than a day (or even just half an hour) of training the women on the task in question, because they were apparently largely due to differences in expectation and in applying spatial experience.[261] What's more, the differences found in some highly specific paper-and-pencil ability test often fail to scale up to supposedly similar situations in the real world: many studies have failed to find gender differences in tasks involving knowledge of someone's town, or reading a map,[104, 261] despite the oft-trumpeted male superiority in 'spatial ability', which actually only applies to a couple of specific mental rotation and perspective-taking tests.[278]

2. Even when one group of people does tend, on average, to do better than another at something, that doesn't mean that *every* member

---

*To be fair, these days most papers do quietly admit it when they find no or little gender effect, in a sentence buried on page 23 or so. There is a great deal of pressure on researchers these days to say whether a gender difference was shown in the results, even if they weren't looking at that aspect. Yet the authors probably still won't bother to mention it in the summary ('Abstract') of their paper, which is all that many readers will read. So people will still note gender differences more often than they hear of equalities.

†Most of the example studies I mention in this section are taken from the area of alleged gender differences in spatial ability, which is one of which I have the most personal knowledge. But the arguments I make here apply also to most other areas of alleged group differences which could be linked to computing ability.

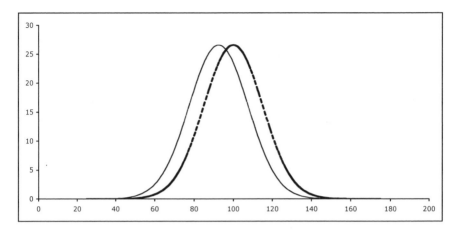

Figure 2.1. Typical graph of two groups' scores on a standardised mental ability test (e.g. grouped by sex or cultural subgroup). Along the bottom is all the possible scores on the test, centring on 100 (as in traditional IQ tests). The curve shows how many people in this fictional but realistic example get each score in each group. A lot more people are near the average than the extremes. Note how much the two groups' curves overlap: you can't predict anyone's score just from knowing which group he or she is in.

of one group is going to be better at it than *every* member of the other. Usually *lots* of people in the 'dumber' group score well above the average of the 'brighter' group because the score distributions overlap a lot. This is particularly important to remember regarding race and sex discrimination: there are plenty of fast white athletes, plenty of brainy black women, plenty of working-class quick thinkers. I've tried to illustrate this graphically in Figure 2.1.

3. Many scientists now argue that it is pointless to try to boil any real-world cognitive task down to a single measure, such as 'intelligence'. There are many individual aspects of abilities, and the supposed underlying *g* (general intelligence) factor tends to explain only about half of the variability in people's scores even on paper-and-pencil aptitude tests.[46] Computer use, and many other complex tasks, involve just as many skills that supposedly 'disadvantaged' groups (such as women or older people) are good at, as those that are supposedly harder for them. Handling information, since it's most often expressed in text form, uses women's sometimes-apparently-superior language skills, just as much as men's sometimes-apparently-superior spatial or logical skills. The wisdom involved in deciding among choices, and being self-disciplined enough to avoid distraction after many years of life experience, may be just as useful as youthful mental agility in

choosing the right resources and items, and in knowing when to give up one line of inquiry for another.

4. In studies of gender differences in some ability related tasks, such as reading a map or spotting shapes in complex patterns, women's performance was found to be as good as men's *if* the instructions were written so that they didn't *expect* to do badly. So if no mention was made of 'maps' or of 'spatial ability', and/or if they were told that a test was actually measuring some personality trait like 'empathy', their performance was fine. [264] Self-efficacy again?

Having said all of this, sometimes arguments like these simply won't be enough. Some studies, particularly regarding lack of confidence in technical tasks, have shown a 'we can but I can't' phenomenon. For example, even if a woman agrees that women *in general* are just as good as men at a technical skill, she'll frequently still say that *she personally* is no good. [37] If most females were to go around thinking that they're personally less capable than most others, then logically at least half of them *couldn't* be right, so it's an irrational attitude.

TV advertisements, PC salesmen and smarmy colleagues can give the impression that computer and internet use are as easy as falling off a log, and this leads people to think it must be easy, or, worse, it must be easy for everyone except them. Technology trainers complain, 'Our users have been led astray by the 'cyberspace for idiots and dummies' manuals. They come to us thinking that getting connected is a breeze'. [71]

Don't be fooled. Decades of research into people's behaviour with computers show that developing the right knowledge of the software you're using, and learning the best way to solve each problem or task, is a non-trivial process for everyone (even when the technology behaves itself, which, as we'll see, it often doesn't do if it's poorly designed). Each chapter of this book shows different aspects of what cognitive psychologists label **mental models**, and the need to have the right model of your task and tools to solve a problem successfully. However, this term is a metaphor for whatever really goes on in the brain: of course there is no labelled diagram or miniature toy computer inside your skull.

Thinking further about this point, you might already have found, if you're a computer novice, that sometimes even the local computer 'expert' will be unable to sort out your personal sticking point. The computer's way of doing things will have become 'obvious' to them, and what's confusing you will seem irrelevant to them. This can make you feel stupid or excluded, but it shouldn't. There are many deeply counter-intuitive things about using a computer to handle information, especially if you're used to physical information sources like books or papers.

Sherry Turkle, a sociologist and psychologist who's written well-known books about the social effects of computers and the internet, gave a beautiful example of this back in the early 1980s.[293] At that time personal computers were still a new craze, and were used mainly for programming, game-playing or word-processing, not for finding information (though that was already a major use for mainframe computers in the workplace). Turkle described a brave history professor who started using a personal computer for writing, a whole decade before many of her colleagues:

> When you use a word-processing program you become familiar with an environment in which there are 'places' analogous to files, 'objects' analogous to sheets of paper, and 'operations' analogous to copying, cutting, pasting, and filing. The analogies with physical reality helped Doris to get started . . . But Doris soon discovered that the analogies with the 'real' were not precise: what ruled here were the laws laid down by the programmer. Some simple operations produced results as if one were through the looking glass. If you give two documents the same name, one vanishes. If you display a document on your screen, it stays where it came from as well. Slowly, without any sense of a conscious break into a new way of thinking, Doris learned the ways of a formal system—she began to learn the peculiarities of a purely logical universe, one defined entirely by rules. (p. 190)

Computers can make things appear in two places at once, and vanish into thin air, because the things themselves are not concrete. But who would have expected a computer to act like that before they first used one?

The internet throws up similar conceptual puzzles. When people start to use it, they often assume that an overseas web page they read is still actually, physically, in the other country *as they read it.* People using dial-up modems worry that they'll run up a phone bill that's suddenly gone onto international rates.

In reality, the web works in a similar way to Doris's word-processor. When you tell it you want a particular 'page' to be displayed, your computer sends a message, split into tiny packets, out into the public packet-switching network, and that gets forwarded on between specially configured computers across the world in fractions of a second until it reaches the 'server' computer at the address you requested. The server sends a *copy* of the page back through the network to your computer, again splitting it into little packets, while the original file stays right where it is.

Even when a website uses so-called 'cookies' that let your computer send little packets back to the server to identify itself (generally anonymously, but individually enough to ensure that you get the right thing back each time), there is no real physical connection between the two. Despite the lazy metaphors we use for online access, there's just a lot of messages being sent to and fro, like two people frantically photocopying documents and mailing the copies to each other.

The only part of this amazing process that you or your employer may be paying for directly is the connection to the first node in the chain—your internet service provider (**ISP**), which sends the packets of data out onto the network and receives them back. If you use a dial-up modem, you've only dialled one telephone number, and that's all that you're personally 'connected' to. Beyond that, billions of packets of data are making their way through thousands of wires, but there's no open channel sitting there waiting for your personal 'packets' to come back. The routers and servers and cables are multitasking like mad restaurant chefs, preparing little bits at a time out of a hundred different meals.

Yet this conceptual weirdness that we have to overcome to use computers and the internet quickly becomes second nature for many people. There are many examples out there of good user interface design, making computers far easier to use for some tasks than they were when Doris started out. But not only that, like Doris people learning the internet often feel they've mastered a special new world—though we take that world much more for granted than people did in the early days. Turkle says of Doris that 'her pleasure in [learning the system] came from her belief that this universe is in principle totally understandable ... [As] time went on, its rules and hierarchy began to seem elegant, its patterns reassuring' (pp.16–17).

All this talk of a new conceptual world shows that when people fail to find or do what they want with a computer, very often the 'blame' lies with the unexpected way of doing it. When you're having trouble finding something that you know is in a database or a book somewhere, or is out there on the internet, the blame usually lies with an inadequate means of searching, e.g. a lousy index in the book, or a badly designed '**search engine**' on the computer. It doesn't mean that you're hopeless at searching, and it doesn't mean that the thing can't be found. It means that either you, or the software designers whose system is giving you grief, need to find a better way. There'll be more on this in Chapters 3 and 4.

How do we want it?

What kind of a question is that title? If we ask for a cheese omelette, we want a cheese omelette. Surely, if we ask for certain information, that also speaks for itself?

Well, another way to phrase it is: What do we know, think, and assume when we approach a computer to find information? Information scientists tend to think of your desire for information as a *problem* that you're trying to solve (even if it doesn't feel particularly problematic). Problem-solving, and what helps or hinders people when doing it, is also a major research area in cognitive psychology, and it's perhaps one of the most important basic issues in psychology as a whole. Helping people to solve problems better, by thinking through them in the right way, looking efficiently for the best information, and using it effectively, is obviously the essence of education and the key to human progress. The trouble is that it's not that easy, as we'll see later in this chapter.

Most of the research into people's starting points when they want information has, of course, been done by information scientists. It used to be the case that when you wanted information from an online database, you'd sit down with a librarian (often referred to as the intermediary) who'd discuss what you were looking for and translate that into a set of 'search terms' linked in particular logical ways. But the librarian couldn't read your mind, couldn't tell all the assumptions you might have about what was and was not useful, and couldn't tell what you'd seen before. So this so-called 'reference interview' didn't always lead to the librarian finding what you *really* wanted—and sometimes a lot of expensive charged-by-the-minute online time was wasted retrieving the wrong things.

Given the pressures on money and time that are always with us, a lot of effort was put into 'user studies' to try to help librarians work out exactly what the end-users really wanted, and hence to retrieve only what was relevant. This research effort continued, and was stepped up, after ordinary untrained people started doing their own searches on databases. The problem now wasn't what you told, or didn't tell, the librarian; it was what you did, and didn't, type into the computer yourself.

Meanwhile, since the 1960s a gradual sea change was sweeping through people's thinking in many areas of science, religion and business. The relatively clear, well-defined world of the 1940s and 1950s disappeared in most academic disciplines; art became even more abstract and education more creative; and even religious leaders began asking their flock to think for themselves. In psychology, clear black-and-white ideas about how we classify and describe concepts in our mind, that had held sway since the time of the ancient Greeks, gave way to theories of 'fuzzy' categories. These allowed for the way that we sometimes treat (say) a box as a table and at other times as a seat, and for the fact that abstract concepts are hard to define or classify at all. And in information science, the dream of defining clear measures of 'relevance' and clear statements of users' needs, so that search results could be exactly (and only) what was wanted, started to unravel.

Steven Pinker,[228] writing about fuzziness in human thinking, points out that we're by no means *always* fuzzy, even in everyday life. In legal and biological matters, we're very definite about things—as he says, we know only too well that 'you can't be a little bit pregnant or a little bit married'. Even though we feel that some birds, some women and even some prime numbers seem more stereotypical than others despite having precise definitions,[11] we can be very precise when we want to be, such as when a child tells us, 'I didn't *exactly* steal it . . .' But in general it's the fuzziness of life, the grey areas and the vague connections, that make things interesting.

'Interesting' can also mean frustrating, of course. If you've ever acted as an intermediary yourself and searched the internet on somebody else's behalf, you'll know how frustrating it can be when they reject some of the perfectly helpful-looking websites you find and start suggesting more criteria that they hadn't previously mentioned.

People's information need is often uniquely personal, and uniquely tailored to that precise moment in time. Even with something as simple as the time of a bus, you might need to know right now about a bus that goes after 3 p.m. and stops at the shopping centre, but you won't necessarily want that particular bus next time, and nor will the next person who looks at the timetable. If there isn't a 3 p.m. bus that stops at the shops, then maybe one that stops at the railway station will do because you know you can walk from there. So there are ways in which you can adapt your goal, which you might not make obvious when you first express what you need. This flexibility or 'wobbliness' in information needs is discussed further below.

Reasons for wanting information

Information scientists, whose major goal is to make information systems give people more of what they want, have spent many years wrestling with defining and classifying different types of information need. Some have come up with lists, i.e. taxonomies, of different reasons why people want information. For example, in the 1960s

Robert S. Taylor[289] suggested these: enlightenment, problem under-standing, instrumental needs, factual needs, confirmational needs, projective needs, motivational needs and personal/political needs.

The problem with a list as long as that, of course, is that some of those needs look identical in many situations (e.g. it's hard to separate 'enlightenment', i.e. trying to understand a situation, from a 'factual need'). At the same time, other items in the list don't help us to predict what information will satisfy the person. 'Personal/political needs' are aimed at helping you to feel you can control a situation. What exactly will help *you* to feel like that? And what about the person next to you? All the same, looking at these different types of need highlights the problem we have when we expect people to express their need exactly just by typing a handful of words on a computer, and we'll look at the effect of that inadequacy in the next chapter.

Bryce Allen,[9] another information scientist, tried to simplify such a list to just three main types of information need:

1. 'Perception and knowledge structure', by which Allen seemed to mean that people might realise that they have a completely wrong understanding of something, or no understanding of it, because it's different from any situation they've seen before. He cited the example of the Maori people in New Zealand, who reacted with complete bemusement when one of Captain Cook's men fired a musket and killed someone standing some distance away. We don't know what the new things are, so we're not sure what's going on or what we could do next. We need to build new knowledge structures. Cognitive psychologists have traditionally called such structures schemata or mental models. We'll see these concepts again in the next chapter.

2. 'Identification of alternative actions', i.e., working out what we might (not) be able to do. This creates the link between semantic knowledge (i.e. factual, descriptive) things that we know or have just learned (e.g. that guns are dangerous and likely to kill people unexpectedly), and procedural knowledge (about what we could do to avoid being shot). Another example for modern Europeans would be having a high phone bill, linking this knowledge to our understanding of the internet (knowing that it also depends on sending data down a cable network), and trying to find out if it's possible to make cheaper calls using the internet in some way.*

---

* Of course, given the increasing use of mobile cable-free technology, this scenario isn't as predictable as it used to be, but at the time of writing most UK residents still have a 'land line' telephone and also access the internet via the same underground cables.

3. 'Selection of alternative courses of action'. Supposing we find that there are two different ways of configuring our computer to take advantage of internet-based telephone calling. Which way works the best, or is cheapest? We want to compare alternatives to help us decide which procedural knowledge to apply, i.e. which thing we should do.

This shows that our different reasons for wanting some information will lead to two people wanting different answers altogether, even if they start off just by saying they want to know about (say) 'cheap telephone calls'. As Bryce Allen points out, if we have the first type of need, i.e. trying to find 'the answer' that fills a gap in our knowledge 'schema' or 'model', then a straightforward factual statement will do. In the second type of need, we have to identify what we could possibly do before we can choose to do any of it. We'll see later on that this, in the problem-solving jargon used by cognitive psychologists, is like identifying our 'operators', i.e. choosing the options and tools that we have available for solving a problem which we feel we have. In the third type of need we're actually trying to choose between two alternatives, so ideally we'd want some way of comparing the two alternatives. This may again come down to learning more facts about each, but also assigning positive or negative values to those facts to lead us to a decision.

If we don't expect to find that someone's already made such a comparison, or if our criteria are quite special and we don't expect anyone else to have felt the same way, we might want to create our own way of comparing them, e.g. by making a list of the relatively good and bad points of each alternative. Consumer magazines and websites frequently provide these comparison tables or listings for everyday products. Sometimes someone might still want to put together different people's comparisons, e.g. to look at *Which?* magazine[307] to find which washing machines are the most efficient, cheap and stylish, but also look at *Ethical Consumer*[90] to avoid buying it from a company that ignores environmental issues, animal welfare or workers' rights.

Brenda Dervin,[69, 70] one of the most influential researchers into people's information needs in all sorts of situations (not just with computers), describes all the above as 'Sense-Making', i.e., we're all trying to actively *do* things to make personal sense of our world. Rather than focusing just on reducing uncertainty, which is the main thrust of some researchers' concerns as we'll see later, her approach involves what she calls 'verbing'—focusing on what people are trying to *do*. So when we want information, such as the lyrics of a song, we're planning to *use* it for doing something (even if it's just settling

41

an argument or singing in the bath). We want information so that we can fill a 'gap' which is stopping us carrying on with what we're doing. It's as if you reached a wide ditch when you were out walking somewhere, and needed to find a bridge or a way around it.

Bryce Allen[9] interprets Dervin's 'gap' as if something is missing in our schema. Our current knowledge isn't enough to let us decide what to do next, so we need to add to it. It isn't clear that Dervin always sees it this way, and after all there could be times when it's not so much new *knowledge* that we need, as a new way of interpreting and using the knowledge we already have. Maybe it just hasn't yet occurred to us that we can use something we already know to deduce an answer or to take some action. We'll see some more examples of this later on in this chapter. Rather than adding an extra 'node' to our schema, we might sometimes just need to add a new 'link' between nodes. And the knowledge we need may be active procedural knowledge more than declarative facts.

Another way of thinking about wanting information was suggested by Nicholas Belkin[23] and his colleagues in the early 1980s. They argued that we need information when we have an Anomalous State of Knowledge (ASK): we realise that there's a problem (an anomaly) with what we know, and we look for information to remove that anomaly. This is slightly different from Dervin's 'gap' because an anomaly doesn't necessarily imply that there's a hole in our knowledge, but just that something seems to be wrong in it.

This is related to the much older idea in psychology of **cognitive dissonance.** Leon Festinger[93] first suggested in the 1950s that we try to avoid situations where knowledge seems to contradict other knowledge or beliefs, and to resolve contradictions between the things we already know, because such contradictions make us feel uncomfortable. A dryly cynical Dogbert, in Scott Adams's *Dilbert* cartoon, once used this concept to convince an overworked, exploited, underpaid and despised employee that his 'free choice' in staying in his job surely contradicted the way he was treated. The employee, in attempting to rationalise this, concluded that he must love the work and ended up blithely grinning. This type of rationalising can also contribute to the problem of **demand characteristics** in research, which we'll look at later.

However, cognitive dissonance theory, which, like Dervin and Belkin, would emphasise the emotional and action-driven reasons behind our information needs, does have its problems. Psychologists have found lots of situations where people seem quite happy to believe contradictory things at the same time (such as 'I shouldn't lie to my children or confuse them, and I don't want to teach them any superstitions or religions—but I'll tell them there's a Santa Claus').

If we never exposed ourselves to contradictory arguments, we would never change our minds, enjoy debates, or acknowledge the complexity of social and political issues, yet most educated people are prepared to do so. We don't and can't always avoid situations that contradict our current knowledge. In fact, much of our written discourse (such as this book) depends on making a 'storyline' out of contradictory ideas, so we might be looking for information to fill this 'storyline': we might need to find dissenting views, if only to have something to discuss.* The famous Danish physicist Niels Bohr is alleged to have said, 'We shall never understand anything until we have found some contradictions.' They are the challenges that make us improve our ideas.

Ultimately, though, we do usually feel better if we manage to resolve the situation by reaching a comfortable compromise (such as, 'Santa Claus is fun and it's only while the kids are little—I'll debunk it later'). And in daily life we don't tend to write books most of the time (thank goodness), so our motivations are different from those of the student or academic—an important point often overlooked in information science papers. Therefore, it's useful to bear in mind Belkin's idea that our desire for information can be fuelled by this need to *rectify the anomaly*.† It's also closely related to the more recent focus on 'uncertainty' by information scientists, though we'll see below that sometimes people don't *feel* particularly uncertain or anomalous when they decide to look for information on a computer.

Constructivism, emotion, and the Wizard of Oz

Carol Kuhlthau is another information scientist whose views on what we want out of information sources have been strongly influenced by concepts in psychology. In particular, she went to some lengths to link her ideas about searching, as a process of 'seeking meaning' (the title of her 1993 book [164]), to a movement by some thinkers away from fixed models of behaviour and towards 'constructivism', where the emphasis is on our constant construction of our own internal worlds and interpretations. Constructivists would argue that those internal worlds influence our behaviour much more than the actual reality around us, and for Kuhlthau this was the key to moving away from the old static views of information seeking.

---

* As any good dictionary will point out, the prefix 'dis-' itself implies that there are two sides, a negative as well as a positive.
† This uncatchy phrase was even the slogan of a trade union campaign a few years ago—an academics' union of course!

This thinking has been a big philosophical influence for a few decades now, in general life as well as in psychology. Yet in some areas of psychology it arguably *hasn't* been quite as influential, simply because many psychologists would find it hard to see how they can build a science of human behaviour, in which general laws can be identified to predict how people will act, if each individual is assumed to be governed by a completely unique internal 'world'. After all, there are many common patterns in people's behaviour, and those patterns are the major focus of the discipline.

Also, there's some suspicion about what we mean by 'internal representations' of the world: we know that actual pictures and words don't really exist in the brain. There are only complex patterns of neurons, and these don't generally fire in spatial patterns that fit the exact layout of a scene or object. Instead, somehow they produce the ability to think *as if* we were seeing the real thing, while not physically representing it at all. Furthermore, if we're not careful, we fall into the 'ghost in the machine' problem, where we find we're assuming that there's another little person within the head motivating and guiding its host. We then have to ask what guides that little person, and so on ...

However, the major aspect of constructivism that interested Kuhlthau was the idea that we constantly and dynamically build and alter our internal *knowledge*, and fill in its gaps by inferring and discovering new things. She picked out some psychology concepts which she felt especially applied to information seeking.

Cognitive psychologists since Frederick Bartlett in the 1930s have talked about how we seem to organise our memories into networks or webs of associations between things, with some things seeming more closely linked than others. As mentioned earlier, psychologists have traditionally called these schemas (or **schemata**) or **mental models**. When referring to schemas that tell us how to behave and what to expect in a given situation, such as eating in a restaurant, some work has also called them 'scripts' (although these emphasised the **procedural** side of knowledge—what you have to do and how). The way they're often simulated on a computer now is through **connectionist networks** rather than traditional 'box and arrow'-type programs.

Whatever word we use, everyday life has us constantly linking things together, both when we record them and when we think about them. Thinking about one thing often leads us into a 'train of thought', as the link between one thing and another sends us off to other topics, memories and ideas. In a given situation, or when thinking about a given topic, the structure of the knowledge in our memories gives us a basis for making decisions and inferences about what's going on and about what we need to know.

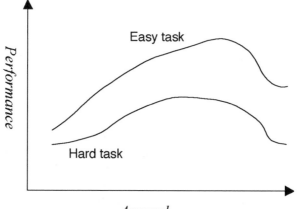

Figure 2.2. The Yerkes-Dodson law. As you get more aroused (stressed) about a task it makes your performance improve, up to a point, but beyond that you may fail, sometimes catastrophically. The harder the task, the earlier extra stress starts making things worse.

Kuhlthau drew on Jerome Bruner's writings about schema theory and its application to learning. In Bruner's eyes, we're constantly trying to construct and interpret information, and to build it into schemas that will help us to infer extra knowledge from what we already know. The extent to which we do this *effectively* depends partly on our emotional state. The well-known **Yerkes–Dodson law** in psychology, originally proposed in 1908,[320] suggests that when we have little emotional arousal or anxiety about a task, we don't try very hard and our performance tends to be low.* If we are more aroused (or anxious), performance goes up, but if we get too excited or panicky, it starts to drop again, so that in an extreme state we are just as bad at it as when we're utterly laid back and drowsy. For easier tasks, our 'peak' performance tends to need a higher level of arousal, and of course our performance will be higher in the first place than for harder tasks, but the same sort of curve is seen.

Later work has suggested that in fact sometimes high levels of arousal don't reduce the overall performance of some tasks, but only how efficiently we do them, and meanwhile the effects of arousal on easy tasks haven't always followed Yerkes–Dodson very clearly. However, the general idea that we can move from healthy motivation

---

*Actually, this was back in the days of **behaviourism**. Yerkes and Dodson talked only about how a stronger stimulus (e.g. a harder electric shock) would make an animal learn a habit more quickly up to a point, but would stress it too much beyond that point so that learning got harder. The generalising from this to all sorts of human situations is due to reinterpretation by later psychologists.

into counterproductive panic is one which makes intuitive sense in many real-life situations.

Following a suggestion by Bruner,[39] Kuhlthau picked up on this and related it to an idea suggested by George Kelly in the 1960s that we are naturally responsive to new information. When we see or learn something new, it can bemuse and stimulate us into learning and altering our knowledge constructs. However, if this disruption is too great, we'll feel too threatened by it (the way I was terrified as a child by the big display and booming voice put on by the Wizard of Oz in the film of the same name) and will reject it (dragging our mothers out of the cinema in the process). Kuhlthau likened this to the Yerkes–Dodson curve—again, if we want to find new information, but then too much information comes back for us to deal with, we won't be able to make the most of it. Yet if things are too unsurprising and safe, we tend to be bored and listless and find it harder to bother doing anything with the information we see. Thus you can't quite separate the emotional from the cognitive, even in something as mundane as choosing to look for information.

Users often suffer a dip in their self-confidence soon after starting to search for something, once they realise how complex a topic is or how hard it is to track down exactly what they want. Novice users, such as first-year students, tend not to realise that this is true for everyone, not just themselves! Kuhlthau linked this emotional response to her view that *uncertainty* levels are important as people work through a search process, echoing earlier writers like Belkin, although she didn't view the *removal* of uncertainty as the goal of the process.

This is all reasonable and certainly adds a new dimension to information needs and how we respond to them. Kuhlthau also used Kelly's distinction between **invitational** and **indicative** moods. In an invitational mood, we're open to new ideas and willing to run with a supposition to see where it leads us. In an indicative state of mind, though, we are more prescriptive and action-oriented—we know what we want and we're focusing on getting it. This rather broad-brush distinction is quite useful in the present context. (But do we know which state we're in from one moment to the next? Are we sometimes in neither?) As Kuhlthau pointed out, we need to be more 'invitational' when we first decide to search, browse or read information about a topic we don't know well. Later, once we've focused on what we want to know, we need to be more 'indicative' so we're less easily distracted.

According to Kuhlthau, if we try or expect to be 'indicative' quite early in the process, so that we expect to be able to be quite decisive and quick, when in fact what we get is a ton of new information to wade through, frustration results. Novice searchers tend to under-estimate the amount that they don't know and the complexities of the topic they're considering, so frustration is much more common with them than for the more experienced. Later, Kuhlthau[165] added that novice users of a system who have too much of an 'indicative' mood may also start out with some prejudice against the system's usefulness, and a lack of faith that it'll hold anything useful anyway. So they'll assume that any failure of their first search attempt proves this and will give up too early, in some cases never to try again. In my experience, many first-time internet users (especially older people) go through exactly this scenario.

Once again this is all reasonable, and George Kelly's work is still admired and used by many people particularly in social and clinical psychology. However, Kuhlthau's application of all these concepts was based on the assumption that when we do an information search, we're doing so for an *educational* purpose. Most of her studies focused on students trying to find information from search-ing a database when studying for an assignment within their courses, although she's also studied public library users.

Of course, we could argue that whenever we're doing something focused enough to be called a 'search', we're probably trying to *learn* something. But we may not always be starting from the same place as Kuhlthau's students. They started with a topic they knew little about. A crucial issue for a successful report was to reach a point where they focused on a specific aspect of the topic, and wrote explicitly about that rather than waffling around it. Thus, it was very important to be 'indicative' later but 'invitational' at first. The issue of needing motivation (and not having it spill into panic) was of course crucial too—remember your school homework?

Does this apply to us when we search a database or the internet in our everyday lives? Obviously, it depends on the context and reasons for our search. If we're trying to find a known item or establish a particular fact—two distinct types of information task—then we may do best to adopt an 'indicative' mood and concentrate on the issue at hand. (But, if the fact is likely to contradict our current belief, perhaps we need to be vaguely 'invitational' too.) However, if we're doing a 'subject search' of the kind that Kuhlthau's students usually had to do, obviously things are messier, as she described. The point here is that while we want to understand the ways in which human information use isn't straightforward, we have to hold in our minds that the ideal for some activities *is* quite simple.

From confusion to solution?

Kuhlthau[164] also reconsidered an old idea from information scientist Robert Taylor[289] that we go through four levels of need before we decide to search for some information: 'visceral' (vaguely sensing that we don't know something), 'conscious' (realising what we don't know), 'formal' (defining it verbally) and 'compromised' (reducing it to a few terms for entering into an information system or search engine). She likened these to George Kelly's suggested 'phases of construction', in which we deal with new information with initial confusion, deepening confusion as we're faced with unexpected results, hypothesis formulation to help us make sense of it (provided we don't feel so threatened or overwhelmed that we reject it altogether), and finally testing and reconstructing our knowledge constructs (schemas).

Kuhlthau lined up these two set of phases in parallel as if they were different descriptions of the same process. However, Taylor was talking about our realisation that we have an information *need* before doing something about satisfying it. Kelly was talking about the way we deal with the *results* of getting information. Taylor was describing the process by which, in his eyes, motivation gets turned into action. Kelly was considering how we respond to the action's result.

The similarity in the two authors' ideas, i.e. of mental confusion followed by resolution, aren't especially surprising. Yet the idea of a single emerging 'information need' that bubbles up and forms itself into a single one–off query is over-simplified, as the previous chapter suggested. Maybe Taylor would say that when our 'need' isn't clear, it's because we're still at the 'visceral' or 'conscious' stages of it. Fine, but sometimes we're at those stages for a long time while we stagger through information usage, trying to identify an answer we're barely able to recognise. As Kuhlthau seems to have concluded, along with other recent information scientists, it would be unhelpful to stick with such a simplistic linear model. It fails to account for the many motivations and complications facing an information user.

Of course, when we're in the middle of trying to make sense of a complex topic, especially as we learn something new and try to understand and write about it, both the 'what do I need?' and 'what does all this mean?' processes can be happening almost at the same time. The results of one enquiry make us decide to refine it *and* to start wondering about something else.

Kuhlthau's biggest contribution was not only to make us aware of this ongoing process, but also to remind us of the emotions involved. She also stressed, and continues to stress, that this means a need for careful encouragement and sympathetic handling, even (to use her word) 'counselling', when 'experts' (librarians, teachers and internet gurus) help 'novices' (anyone who doesn't know the subject, and/or the systems or resources, inside out). She also helped, like other authors in the early 1990s, to change the view of the library or database user from someone passively absorbing whatever they were given, to a busy builder and rebuilder of cognitive constructs and knowledge.

Harter[121] pushed this constructivist-based attitude even further. Drawing on the ideas of Sperber and Wilson, which I discuss further in the next chapter, Harter argued that the whole idea of an 'information need' was outdated, and that we might even want to drop the idea of 'information' itself.

To Harter, all we are doing when we look for knowledge is trying to achieve *relevance*. Yet this to him means trying to find whatever makes us *feel* we've got that. When we see some people looking at some information, according to Harter, there's no point worrying about how much of it is on-topic, and how much more there is that they haven't seen, because they will do their best to interpret the results in the most relevant way possible *anyway*. If somebody says 'I'm a green elephant' to us, we'll try to make sense of what they say by thinking of a way in which their statement would have meaning: they're trying to change the subject, lighten up, provoke an argument, start a joke, pretend to be insane, etc. Similarly, we'll take the results of an online database search and try to see what we can get out of it and why it's been retrieved by the computer.

Rather than seeing information use as a process of refining what your goal is, as Kuhlthau did, Harter instead sees it as a process of trying to *achieve relevance*. To him, *one* way to achieve that is by refining your goal, so some things become more clearly relevant than others.

Harter seemed to think that we labour under the delusion that the computer is *also* trying to achieve relevance, which (as we'll see) we can usually assume for human speakers. That may well be true for first-time computer users, who often attribute much more intelligence and much less diversity in the system than actually exists—like the Wizard of Oz, it might be big but it's not that clever. We've seen already that this anthropomorphism may well be a problem, and runs deeper than the 'relevance' notion. But it's also worth noting that experienced users know how 'dumb' the computer is and expect it to produce some rubbish along with the useful results. So Harter may have overstated his case regarding our efforts to see everything as 'relevant'.

It's hard to see how Harter's explanation could account for everything we do when we search. His interpretations also seem, like so many information science authors, to focus on academic and educational work where the users are searching for abstract ideas. For them, 'relevance' is obviously a looser concept than when, say, you're trying to find the time of the next train to Bristol or a cheese omelette recipe. All the same, Harter, like Kuhlthau and the psychologists she drew on, held a very 'constructivist' view of searching as a process of *cognitive change*, of something altering in our minds as we see information and learn from it, and that's surely true to at least a *small* extent even for simpler searches.

Another aspect of these 'fuzzy' views of people's information goals is the assumption that what you want is likely to change over the course of your quest for it. So if you start off by wanting to know if you're entitled to a welfare benefit, by the time you've learned about it you might realise you should know about some other benefit or government scheme instead. This assumption of shifting goalposts is the opposite of the robotic 'state need—do search—fulfil need' view of earlier information science, as we'll discuss later. We shouldn't overstate it, though. One study in America, observing people searching an online library catalogue system,[128] suggested that in fact people's goals didn't change at all while they were searching on a computer—in fact it was almost as if their overall view of the situation was 'frozen in time' while they were dealing with the computer itself.

One reason suggested for this finding was lack of opportunity to change the goals, because the computer system in question didn't give the users enough information (just the bare details of books) for them to learn anything that would alter what they thought they wanted. Another is that while using the computer, people are sometimes too busy coping with the task of using it to devote any attention to their real interest, so they don't manage to really *understand* it until they read the information in more depth (which we'll look at in Chapter 5).

A third possible reason, which may have been overlooked at the time, is that people taking part in studies like this, where they're being interviewed by an information scientist, might try to *seem* consistent and logical, even if in fact they've realised they've been approaching the task in the wrong way. Information scientists need to pay greater attention to an issue psychologists have had to face many times. People in research studies are always trying to 'second-guess' the purpose of the study and to 'perform' as well as possible in it. In other words, to borrow Dervin's phrase, they're always 'sense-making' about the *research* as well as about their own information needs and actions. We thus need to take extra care over the **demand**

characteristics and **experimenter effects** in our studies—the phrases used by psychologists for what a study's participants think we demand (want) of them, and how we subtly influence their responses.

Demand characteristics were first spotted in the 1960s,[220] yet psychologists themselves often still pay them only scant lip service. They just hope that so long as the purpose of their work isn't too obvious then participants in the research won't be affected by guessing it. It is true that it's best not to make your experiment or your hopes for its results too obvious, but this is only part of the story. The effort to 'perform as well as possible' and avoid embarrassment might mean that people are reluctant to, for instance, abandon a course of action, take a risk, refuse an unpleasant task, admit to distraction or disinterest, or tell the experimenter what they were really thinking when they chose an item.

So how do we know, in library user studies, that the participant's choice of an apparently irrelevant book wasn't just to impress the researcher by seeming more erudite? How can we be sure that the participant won't come back and redo the whole search again later when they're not being watched? Or end up borrowing a textbook from a friend and using that instead of all the wise articles we saw them download?

Experimenter effects, also known as experimenter-expectancy effects or Rosenthal effects, are slightly different. Here the emphasis is not so much on the *participant's* expectations as on the *researcher's*. Robert Rosenthal, a 'giant' of psychology, who has devoted decades to pointing out methodological flaws in experiments, first examined experimenter effects in the 1960s.[245] In one of the most stunning findings in psychology's history, he showed that even in an experiment with rats running through mazes, where student researchers had been led to believe that one group of (actually randomly selected and completely equivalent) rats was 'smarter' by breeding than the other, the 'smart' rats actually *did* somehow perform better in the maze task. The students' expectations were enough subtly to alter the responses of the rats. Rosenthal went on to show similar self-fulfilling effects of teachers' expectations in education, and to critique the self-selection biases of volunteer participants in many psychology studies. No research that ever examines human behaviour can completely ignore the possibility of our own biases influencing our participants' responses.

A final worry in information studies is that imposed tasks and self-chosen tasks may show completely different data. This was suggested by the work of Myke Gluck[109] studying people looking for information in broader settings. This difference between 'real' and 'requested' information-seeking tasks might help explain the differences among findings in some information science studies.

To summarise, it seems that goals can be fluid in certain situations, even where they seem less flexible, but we need to be careful when we observe people and make assumptions about their motivations.

It certainly seems that when using the internet, where the information you get back is usually much more than so-called **metadata**, it's much more likely that you will learn as you go along. You may either deliberately change or accidentally lose sight of your original goal.

Stress, health, and confidence

One of the most eminent information scientists in the UK, Tom Wilson, has been suggesting for many years, like Kuhlthau and Harter, that we need to take a broad approach to understanding people's so-called 'information needs'. He's pointed out that humans don't start out with a fundamental *need* for information in the same way that they need food, love, money and approval. However, in our quest to satisfy those more basic needs, information often plays an important part. Information use is then just as much to do with our *motivation*, i.e. our emotions and drives, as with our cognitive thought processes.

Wilson[314] has cited work from some psychologists arguing that we're likely to look for information when we're trying to cope with stress caused by a problematic situation in our lives (even if it doesn't feel terribly 'stressful'). The amount that we bother to hunt out or pay attention to information about our problem will depend on the coping strategy we adopt.

Some psychologists and psychiatrists [161, 225] have recently tended towards the view that there are basically only two strategies in real life. Emotion-focused coping involves trying to 'live with' the problem without trying to change it, and trying to think and feel more positively about it (possibly by trying to simply forget it, or by using therapies to improve your mood). Such a person would probably avoid seeking out more information on the problem. Problem-focused coping tries to change the situation we're in, and that type of coping is most likely to lead to a desire for information.

These notions of 'coping' and 'stress' sometimes seem a little extreme when we're just talking about going to a computer to look up something,* but emotion can have some influence even in more mundane situations. For instance, as we'll see later in this chapter, generally we're far more motivated to confirm what we want to believe than to disprove it.

Wilson also discussed studies of medical patients in various situations which have shown that people who are more educated, less prone to risk-taking, and less emotionally focused in their coping with an illness, are all more likely to want and to take note of medical information about their conditions or about the health risks of their behaviour (such as smoking). People who would rather cope emotionally than practically, or who are attracted to risk, or who simply would find all that information overwhelming and hard to read, are not so keen to know all the grisly detail.

This is not very surprising, of course. Perhaps we should avoid implying what most information science tended to assume until relatively recently, namely, that everyone should always want all relevant information in every situation. You may be someone who, like most researchers and journalists, tends to behave as an 'information junkie' addicted to truth seeking, but people often have good rational reasons for choosing to avoid information.

As we get older, we all encounter more and more situations in which ignorance seems like bliss, when the groan 'I wish you hadn't told me that!' becomes more real. The TV newsreader's suggestion to 'look away now' to avoid a sports result or a gory film clip is advice that we are sometimes very willing to follow. We can ask ourselves what do we 'need' to know, and what do we *want* to know? The danger lies in failing to distinguish the situations where ignorance is a fair and reasonable response from those where ignorance damages the individual, the society around them, or both.

Wilson has also suggested that self-efficacy, which we came across earlier, is a determinant of people's choice of whether to look for information to help them cope with a situation. While earlier we saw that low self-efficacy can make us think we won't be able to find information or use a computer effectively, at the same time Wilson suggested that we might look for information so we can improve our self-efficacy at coping with our current situation, whatever it happens to be. Alternatively, we could have so much self-efficacy, i.e. so much confidence that we could handle our situation anyway, that we might not feel we need information to help us.

---

* Some psychologists [81] have argued that 'stress' may not be a useful concept at all, and certainly needs a clearer definition, because it seems too broad. It's in every situation where we don't feel things are ideal in our lives, and every kind of possible response to them. Is there anything that is *not* stressful?

This isn't too helpful: we're then stuck with self-efficacy seeming like such a general concept that it could work either way in terms of whether or not we'll want information. It sounds like a Yerkes–Dodson curve again at best, and at worst just completely useless. If the concept is going to get us anywhere, we need more research to tease out self-efficacy about a *situation* from self-efficacy about *information use* within it.

Wilson's reviews of psychology work, which have brought important fresh ideas into information science, have focused much more on the emotional and personality sides of psychology (and emotional influences on cognition) than on cognition. It's perhaps not surprising, then, that he and his colleagues have recently developed a theory of information behaviour which focuses on the key idea of reducing *uncertainty*. Using university academics, they've tried to test whether people express more certainty as they progress through searches for and uses of information.[312]

Although the researchers did find that uncertainty seemed important, it seems people expressed a lot *more* certainty *right from the start* than the researchers had suggested. They often already knew many things about the topic at hand. They would also have had suspicions about the likely answer to the specific query. Our perception of our uncertainty level depends on the odds we place on such suspicions being true—we make a probabilistic calculation to decide how much we need further information, but that calculation is itself biased by emotional and contextual factors. That calculation alone doesn't seem to predict whether we'll actually go and look for information (since the confident academics, who knew a lot already, still went to look for more), but it may change our approach to the task.

In the 1970s and 1980s, psychologists discovered that people are often grossly overconfident in estimating their certainty about something which they actually can't know for sure.[177] They have even more overconfidence when considering something which fits their own beliefs,[246] so perhaps it's not surprising if academics express certainty. After all, one of their beliefs is that they themselves are experts! Yet the uncertainty-based view doesn't fit too well with this, because it isn't obvious why such 'certain' people would still be spending time on a search for more information.

One possible way to make sense of all this is to consider some research suggesting that we can influence experts' behaviour. If experts in a given field get rewards for accurate information, they will learn to self-monitor and to increase their caution and accuracy. When experts get rewards for merely inspiring (unjustified) confidence by making cavalier statements, they are more likely to show overconfidence bias.[95] We would hope that academics, like weather forecasters, would fall into the former category, but in reality the 'guru' or 'boffin' label can tempt them into the latter.

An alternative perspective is that academics are uncertain not about the *whole* search topic, but only specific gaps in it, e.g. 'Now, who was it who did that experiment which showed . . .?' or 'I need to quote one of the people who've argued that . . .' Their 'probabilistic calculation' about their need would then apply just to that fact or quote or named person or published paper. The context would be how much they felt they needed to justify something mentioned in their research papers or lectures—perhaps because other academics would be peer-reviewing their work and would need to be convinced.

For all that, it's not clear whether, in information seeking, this is true more for academic users than for other people who spend less of their time mulling over knowledge and justifying their work. It is true that in everyday life, as with the academics, we tend to be looking for very specific information (even if we can't express it coherently). Usually it's only when we want to learn about a completely new topic, e.g. as students or as someone newly diagnosed with an illness, that we have a vague uncertainty about the whole thing.

In any case, specific or general, it's worth noting that not everyone, even among those who focus on the emotional side of information seeking as well as the cognitive side, agrees with Wilson that the reduction in uncertainty is the main thing users want. Carol Kuhlthau wrote recently[165] that we should see uncertainty 'as a natural, essential characteristic of information seeking rather than regarding the reduction of uncertainty as the primary objective for information seeking'. Brenda Dervin has also seen uncertainty more as a motivator than as something that needs removing, as we saw above. Uncertainty is a useful thing and not something we necessarily ever lose.

What's more, Bryce Allen[9] has pointed out that we don't always worry about our uncertainty even when we have it. As stated above, people sometimes have good reasons for not wanting to know things. Even if we'd like to know, we might instead choose an 'emotion-focused' coping strategy, where we simply decide to live with our ignorance. Allen cited work by Kellerman and Reynolds[150] which showed that in some experiments where people had to communicate with other people to find information, they often chose not to seek information even when they were very uncertain about it. It seems that *motivation* to reduce uncertainty will vary with different situations. In other words, reducing uncertainty may not be the most basic motivation in itself, because even high uncertainty won't always lead to information seeking.

Certain personality factors may also be involved here—some people value certainty more than others, although the specific personality trait that causes this is open to some theoretical debate. Often, as Allen[9] puts it, 'There is a rule of parsimony of effort that seems to lead people to accept stock interpretations and automatic behavior whenever possible' (p. 65).

However we deal with the complexities, we should note the importance of this idea of ourselves. Except in a few limited situations, people cannot be seen as simple, knowledge-hungry creatures who can be taught to type some well-chosen words into a computer and get back a dozen or so well-classified references which can be neatly measured for topic relevance. By accepting that, we're on the way to better information systems already—in fact, the acceptance of it is already implicit in the way the web has taken off so successfully as a messy, choice-rich (but searchable) information resource.

The one thing we can say for sure is that our information needs always involve a lot of external circumstances, ranging from our background emotions to the amount of time we have spare. So the developers of such information resources as databases and websites can never define in advance the exact 'right' answer for every possible request.

What you know and what you want to know

Even if you have a large amount of apparent fuzziness and uncertainty about your topic, you're not coming to the computer empty-handed. Fortunately, when you look for information there are always things you already know, and other information you can draw on. A thoughtful consideration of these sources, by an information scientist called Dee Andy Michel[193] suggested three broad categories of knowledge sources:

- knowledge *internal* to yourself (e.g. your reason for wanting information, the beliefs you need to hold about it, the specific objective, knowledge of the general subject domain, and knowledge of how to do searching);
- knowledge *created by you* during the process (e.g. what you tell the computer you want, and how you tell it to look for it);
- knowledge *external* to yourself (e.g. online help, documents, feedback from the system).

To expand a little, the first category includes your world knowledge, which as we saw above is already stored within some organised, linked-up 'schemata' or mental models. It also includes your knowledge of the language you need to use to ask for what you want, and any constraints on what you want to find (e.g. things you *don't* want to find). And it includes what you know or believe is available in the information resource you're going to look at, and any experience you already have of trying to use such a resource. The second category is usually smaller and includes any notes or printouts you might be making as you go along, and also any stored sets of search results that some databases will let you save for further reference.

The last category, knowledge external to yourself, could include what you've already got from previous searching or browsing of some information source. That in itself may tell you more about what to look for next, if it's not exactly what you needed, or it may change your mind about what you need. And so it goes on. The process is often not like the straightforward cheese omelette request mentioned earlier, but an *iterative refinement* of it. It's a bit like stammering a series of descriptions to the waiter about what you really mean by a cheese omelette. ('It's an egg dish ... no, I mean a fried egg dish with cheese ... no, I mean a beaten and fried egg dish, with grated cheese ...')

Inevitably, the irony of the so-called '**Matthew effect**' kicks in: the more you know already, the more you're likely to find information that's helpful to you. (This concept, familiar in education research, is from a line in St Matthew's Gospel (13.12; 25.29), where Christ says, 'For to everyone who has, more will be given.')

You'll also have some awareness of the type of information you want. In an echo of the authors cited earlier, Large *et al.*[171] suggested that we do three types of search. These are known-item (I want So-and-so's recipe for a cheese omelette), factual (I want to know the number of calories in a cheese omelette) and subject (I want to know a bit about the history of omelette making). In the first two, we have a clear idea of what will satisfy our search. In the third, we might be satisfied with a variety of different facts and texts, and even different media, e.g. a picture of the oldest omelette pan in France, or the soundtrack of an interview with a specialist culinary historian. Our search goal then is fuzzy, but we do have some idea of what will satisfy it (or at least, we'll know it when we see it). If not, we're in trouble.

We'll talk more in the next section about how we deal with fuzzy, ill-defined goals, but of course it's still true that in general the more specific you can be about what'll satisfy you, the less time you'll waste while getting it.

However, sometimes our expectations of what we can find on the computer will be quite different from the reality. Kuhlthau's studies, discussed earlier, showed how students in particular move from unrealistic expectations to a greater understanding over time not only of their subject and the systems they use, but also of the value of doing such research for themselves. False expectations cause two types of problem in searching. While Kuhlthau suggested that prejudice against a system can create initial problems for a user, and cause them to give up too easily, some other studies (reviewed by Bryce Allen[8]) have shown many users *over*-estimating the likelihood of finding what they want.

In psychological terms, this probably links to the overconfidence bias I mentioned earlier. But in practical terms it's different. Novice users are often particularly overly confident of the system, but in academic studies they tend to be first-year students. These would have little knowledge of their topic (and so possibly a *lower* level of certainty about that, unless they've misunderstood its complexity, which Kuhlthau suggested was often the case). Your knowledge of and confidence in the system are quite separate from your attitude toward the information you want.

This overconfidence in systems can be true of relatively experienced users as well as novices. I tend to start from around 90% confidence of finding items on the internet, because I know how vast a store it is and how many organisations have put useful information online. When I then fail to find a list of staff contact details for a university department, or even a simple telephone number for a mail order company, I realise that I've overestimated the usefulness of their site. All too often (or not often enough, depending on whether you're a researcher or a marketer), websites are viewed as advertising hoardings, glossy product brochures, public relations exercises ... anything but true information resources. In the same way that traditional studies of library catalogue users have shown that relatively novice users expect far more books and journals than any provincial library could afford, I'm still more optimistic about the internet and people's information provision than the facts would sometimes dictate.

However, expert users do show different expectations and attitudes to what they find relative to novices. A 1995 study of experienced librarians[57] pointed out that experts have knowledge about what's likely to be available and why, and about how organizational policies and attitudes can subtly alter what comes up on the screen. They also tend to use their **metacognition** (awareness of their own thoughts, gaps in knowledge, and goals) more effectively to change strategy and to know when not to pursue dead ends. As mentioned in Chapter 1, this is a key skill in our efforts to handle information.

For example, Su[279] found that at the end of a database search, the scenario most strongly linked to user satisfaction was where the users knew a lot about using databases for the problem, could effectively communicate their needs to the intermediary (where used), *and* were confident that the results were complete. In other words, even online searches performed by librarians on users' behalf were better when the users were themselves 'expert'.

Su found that the other main scenario that seemed to make users happy, though it was less strongly linked to satisfaction than the 'expert' scenario, was where the user was less knowledgeable or experienced but wanted 'everything' about a topic. This type of user then felt pleased with the extent of what was found and thought it was *all* valuable. In other words, this is an easy-going novice with few demands. This isn't hugely surprising, but it does suggest that not only our knowledge, but also our criteria for what is a 'good' result, often change as we learn more about the information system.

This isn't to say that experts' expectations are necessarily higher. In fact, they're more likely to be more realistic, and in some situations experts will 'make do' with less than novices, knowing there's a trade-off between time and quality if they go any further. Gluck[108] suggested that this issue of user expectations could be the factor that links user competence (expertise) with the variations in relevance ratings given to the same items by different users. In his study, experts claimed that more of the items they found were highly relevant, whereas novices' less realistic expectations led them to express more disappointment with results which probably weren't all that different. Once again, we see the concept of 'relevance' being a movable feast rather than a straightforward measure. Of course, another aspect of expertise is knowing how to use and exploit the information you find; we'll look at this in later chapters.

Gary Marchionini[185] did a painful observation study of school-age students trying to use CD-ROM-based encyclopaedias. He noted that students who had the worst problems, with little idea what to do or how to use the features of the built-in search engine (even though they conceptually understood it), also had another problem. They didn't seem to really understand what their teacher wanted. They couldn't see what kind of information would directly contribute (by the logic applied by their teacher) to the topic of their assignment. In other words, their model of the *task* was at fault more than their model of the *system*. This of course would also lead to inappropriate judgements of the relevance of what they found. Again it's due more to expectations than to the actual process of searching.

At the other end of the scale of user expertise, Nicholas[208] studied time-pressed journalists accessing online databases. He pointed out that for anyone under such pressures (probably most of us these days), the key question often isn't 'What can I get that's relevant?' but 'What can I get that's relevant enough within a four-minute search?' **Recall**, the traditional measure of 'how much of the useful stuff we manage to retrieve', isn't helpful at all when we just want 'anything, quickly'. Rather than exactly satisfy our original request, we 'satisfice'—sacrifice accuracy for speed to reach a good enough solution.

Precision, i.e. how much of what comes back is relevant, is a similarly tricky issue in the light of users' expectations. Marchionini's most confused student seemed completely unable to decide how much precision was in the information he found. Even with more motivated and aware participants, Su[279] found that people's prior *expectations* of precision were a much better predictor of their satisfaction with the results than was the actual precision they got. If people expected it to be low, they weren't worried when it *was* low.

As with Nicholas's journalists, Su's users traded time and efficiency for perfect results, and tended to say that they simply wanted the 'right' articles regardless of how many articles they missed (recall), and regardless of how many 'wrong' articles also emerged (precision). Time pressures, and the need to just confirm a fact and then move on, seem to make recall and precision redundant.

These findings are important to bear in mind, since some in the information science community still persist in publishing papers where the alleged 'performance' of a hapless user is judged according to how a *librarian* or other 'expert' judges the results that their search produces. This, as studies have repeatedly shown,[129] tends not to correlate too highly with the *user's* satisfaction.

However, there's also a possibility that information scientists often seem to overlook: the participants in some studies may have assumed that the researchers' real interest was in evaluating the system's ease of use, *not* their own performance. So their ratings may have reflected the wrong aspect of their experience with the system. What's more, studies in which people chose the search topic *for themselves* show a closer link between system expertise, satisfaction with results and traditional 'relevance' measures, than when people take part in a study and do a search on a topic that the *researcher* defines.

As we've seen, Kuhlthau, like Gluck, focused on relevance from the user's point of view, and suggested that relevance to the user changes over the course of accessing information. At first you see a lot of *unique* (i.e. new) items: things that tell you a new, individual, fact or idea. Later on, as you learn what's available and what it's all about, you're likely to see more *redundant* (familiar) items: items telling you things you already (by now) know. She suggested that uniqueness versus familiarity would be a useful distinction to draw in the relevance debate, but it's difficult to see how we could measure this. If the transition from uniqueness to redundancy is something that happens moment by moment in every computer-based transaction, it's hard to see how it could help us to judge one system or search against another.

The problem for information scientists is how to evaluate their systems. As Rebecca Green[116] pointed out in a short but insightful paper in 1995, if a retrieval system responded perfectly—retrieving all, but only, relevant information—*we wouldn't be able to tell*, if we accept that the only valid measure of relevance is what the user chooses. We could never be sure that a system was perfect unless we could test it with every single potential user and all of their likely queries. It's impossible for information scientists to delve far into users' individual psychology every time they want to compare two different search engines. At least the older measures were relatively stable and repeatable (although even the subject-expert librarians, who judged relevance of results to help the scientists calculate those measures, varied much more in their relevance judgements than was generally admitted).

Green argued that we could improve on the traditional **recall** and **precision** measures by considering the different *ways* in which a piece of information could be relevant, i.e. its topicality, rather than just treating relevance as one-dimensional. She used some concepts from linguistics—yet another interdisciplinary gain for information science—to identify some of the 'yes this is relevant-ish, but ...' types of results when searching a religious scriptural database.

Green suggested that a retrieved record, webpage, or book might be 'topical' in three ways. Its relationship with what you typed might be a direct match, e.g. when typing 'Great Expectations' brings back something on the Charles Dickens book of that title. Or it's a hierarchical relationship, e.g. a website covering all of his books, or a page quoting a passage from that one. Or it's a syntagmatic relationship: one that brings back a different component of the same category, e.g. bringing back something about *Hard Times* with just a comparative mention of *Great Expectations*, which may or may not be of interest.

Anyone who has ever searched or browsed the web, for instance, can probably remember finding websites that, while vaguely on the topic we wanted, were too broad or too specific about it (hierarchical). Others focused on a different but conceptually similar thing (syntagmatic), such as a page mainly about a rock band we hadn't heard of whose music was vaguely similar to the band we actually wanted. Clearly, hierarchically or syntagmatically related items aren't a complete disaster—we might find them interesting and helpful—but usually we'd rate them as less 'topical' than exact on-topic matches. So if a system tended to retrieve a mixture of different types of topicality over the course of lots of test searches, we could judge that mixture according to the three types of topicality rather than just the one.

The topicality approach could help resolve the information scientists' dilemma, i.e. to help evaluate information systems. However, even the use of 'topicality' scales might still miss some of the subtleties in people's actions and choices. As we'll see later, sometimes being on-topic isn't what we need. We might want to see things in a different light, and we might even achieve this through drawing an analogy from a *completely different* topic.

What's more, Stephen Harter[121, 122] cited evidence that what seems relevant while searching or browsing, based on users' original expectations, can end up being dumped later as the users' context changes. We'll see in Chapter 6 that an item that a student or academic finds in a computer database, and thinks to be exactly on-topic, often doesn't end up being cited in their write-up some months later. So the ultimate problem with relevance judgements is that they only help judge the system against someone's needs at one snapshot in time. Most of the information may make little difference to the user's long-term development of ideas.

Of course, it has to be noted that the variations in relevance, in the relevance of topicality, and in long-term effectiveness, are all far more appropriate issues for academics and 'knowledge workers' dealing with complex intellectual matters than for someone who's just trying to find tomorrow's weather forecast, or therapeutic information on his newly diagnosed illness. Harter, like most information scientists, was concentrating his efforts on bibliographic systems rather than on wider information contexts. Topicality may be close enough to ideal for most real-world users most of the time, if the context is broader but the topic is less intellectually 'deep'. More non-academic information-seeking studies, looking at simpler information situations, might help us figure out the basic psychological variables that Harter hoped we could find through further research.

What goes wrong with wanting it?

We don't know what we want

Why are you reading this book? You could be a student in an area such as librarianship, information science, or **HCI**. You could be

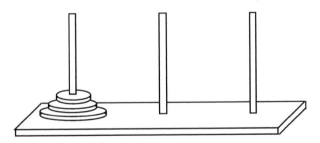

Figure 2.3. The famous 'Tower of Hanoi' puzzle: you have to move the three disks so that all three are stacked up on a different pole. But you can only move one disk at a time, and you are never allowed to put a larger disk on top of a smaller one.

someone whose work depends on finding information and who wants to do it more effectively. Perhaps you find yourself in an official or unofficial 'technical support' role to other information users, and want to know how you could give them better advice. Maybe you know a lot about information systems already, or maybe you're just generally interested in the 'information society' phenomenon. Maybe you're one of the half-dozen readers who know the author personally (possibly the only readers!), or someone who hopes to find quotations or ideas to use in their own writing or research.

Whoever you are, you probably *expect* something of this book. It's going to tell you something, and hopefully something that you didn't know or in a way that you didn't think about before. But do you know *exactly* what you're expecting? Stop a moment and consider that question.

Unless you're more goal-driven than most readers, you've just hit on the first problem of digital information use: knowing what you want to know. It's not just that we can be a bit vague about expressing what we want. Sometimes it's not even clear in our own minds.

As I said earlier, we can consider our desire for some information as a problem we want to solve. We solve problems all the time, and psychologists have studied our problem-solving for decades, so you might expect the results to be quite straightforward. However, the clearest, most consistent research results have come from looking at **well-defined problems**. Here you know exactly what you want to achieve, exactly what you've got to use to do it, and exactly where you're starting from, even though you don't yet know the actual solution or answer. One of psychologists' favourite well-defined problems is the 'Tower of Hanoi' toy puzzle, shown in Figure 2.3.

A well-defined problem in computer-based information seeking might be using a website full of film (movie) information, [140] to find out which railway station was used for filming *Brief Encounter* (1945),* because you'd like to go there and pose romantically in a raincoat. Great. But, as we saw above, many real-life problems are less well defined than that, sometimes much less. Often when you're looking for information, you really don't know exactly what'll satisfy you, what resource would be best to solve it, or even if such a resource exists, or what precisely you'll do with it afterwards. The computer will wait for you to type words into a small box, or to choose a website address to look at, but sometimes you don't even know what your ideal result would look like. What can the research tell us about such **ill-defined problems**?

First, as we saw above, our extra knowledge of other things outside the basic problem itself becomes more important. Developed between the 1950s and 1970s in psychology, Newell and Simon's problem-space theory [207] defined problems in terms of the *initial state*, the *goal state*, the *operators* (things you can use to solve the problem) and the *restrictions* on those operators.

With the *Brief Encounter* example above, all of these were clear. The *initial state* was a state of knowledge: you knew the name of the film, and that it *was* a film, and possibly some other things too, such as its being British, starring Trevor Howard and Celia Johnson, being written by Noel Coward, and being several decades old. The goal state was also about knowledge that would let you add the name of the place to your knowledge about the film. The main *operator* was the film database; its website includes a box in which you could type the name of the film. Then you could navigate through the information about it to find a section about 'Locations', and then read it. The *restrictions* on the operators could include the fact that the database only contains individual film information, so that it wouldn't help to type the phrase 'film locations' in the first place. It's expecting you to type something that will help it find one or more specific films.

In an ill-defined problem at least one of these things is missing, or is so broad that you have trouble deciding what's essential to the problem. In particular, when the goal state isn't clear (i.e. you're not really sure what will count as 'solving' the problem), you tend to spend a lot more time considering knowledge which could be relevant and testing it to decide whether it's what you need. Sometimes, this can lead you to getting so lost in all the information you're considering that you lose sight of the original problem altogether, or run out of time.

---

*It was actually Carnforth station in Lancashire.

For example, we might hope to find something to buy for lonely Auntie Ada, and have a vague idea that something like a pet could help. Then we spend so much time collecting and looking at different pet information, without a clear idea of our criteria for 'good' and 'bad' or even if it'll really solve the problem, that we still fail to make any decision. The longer we go on, and the more effort we've invested in the 'pet' idea, the less willing we may be to rethink the whole problem from the start, even though something needs to be done. The issue of unwillingness to give up on a line of action came up in Chapter 1 and will again in Chapter 3. The key point here is that ill-defined goals can be one reason for it.

Psychologists have had quite a lot to say about problems where the possible operators and restrictions aren't obvious, but the goal state is still clear. They have had much *less* success helping us understand problems where the goals themselves are ill-defined. This is hardly surprising, given that experimental psychologists need to control what you're trying to do to make any sense of the way you do it, and to compare your response to that of others. Problems with an ill-defined goal tend to happen spontaneously in real life.

What does seem to be crucial in ill-defined problem-solving, and in fact even with well-defined problems, is the solver's mental *representation* of the problem (once again, a type of **mental model**). Often we seem to be stuck at an impasse with no apparent way to solve the problem. This is frequently because we haven't yet really decided what the goal is. When I first started writing this chapter, I couldn't think what should go in this section of it. Although information scientists have attempted to classify people's information needs, I couldn't see much to discuss about what goes wrong. How can we *want* information in the wrong way, apart from the issue of confirmation bias (see the next subsection)?

Later on I remembered various types of research that didn't fit into the act of searching, browsing or using information, but still seemed relevant to people's ability to get there. I then realised that I'd been thinking only about wanting the wrong thing, which seemed like a non-issue. After all, you can want anything you like. But I also needed to think about not *knowing* exactly what you want, and holding different assumptions about what you feasibly *could* want from a computer. My representation of what might go wrong was itself wrong, or at least too narrow.

Classic psychology experiments, by a group called the **Gestaltists** who worked in the first half of the twentieth century, showed how crucial it is to be able to redefine the elements of a problem. Suppose I give you a candle, a box of matches, a hammer and some nails, and ask you to attach the candle to the wall and light it. You might spend a while trying to nail the candle itself directly to the wall, but then it can't be lit without burning the wall (and the nail probably won't hold it successfully). Maybe you'd try to work out how to make a bracket out of some nails and/or matches, so that the candle stays further from the wall.

What you might not think to do, unless you're unusual, is tip all the matches out of their box, nail the box to the wall, and then place the candle on it. Why? Because you've been thinking of the box only as something for holding matches, not as a potential shelf for the candle.

Similarly, in the nine-dot problem I presented in the previous chapter (see Figure 1.1), a crucial (unwarranted) assumption made by most people is that the four lines must stay *within* the space defined by the nine dots. Of course, when presented with the figure in a page of text, people are bound to assume they're not supposed to draw over the text, but in fact people still fail to solve the problem even when the dots are in the middle of a blank sheet of paper. In fact, however, the solution necessitates extending three of the lines to meet *beyond* the nine dots.

Here's how to draw it: starting at the bottom left corner dot, draw a diagonal up through the central dot to the top right dot. Now draw a vertical line down from there, through all three right-hand dots, and *continue it on* roughly to where a fourth dot would be. Now go diagonally upwards and left from there, straight through the mid-bottom and mid-left dots, and again *beyond the figure* until you're in line with the top row of dots. Then go across rightwards from there back to the top right corner dot.

Even the Tower of Hanoi problem (see Figure 2.3) has a kind of 'leap' within it: at one crucial point a disk has to be moved back into a position it's previously occupied, and the smallest disk has to sit briefly on the largest.

One of the Gestaltists, Karl Duncker,[84] called this inability to (literally!) think 'out of the box' **functional fixedness**. Other cognitive psychologists since have used other names for similar lack of flexibility in our thinking, such as Don Norman's **cognitive hysteresis**.[213] So-called 'lateral thinking' puzzles depend on this. Their solution depends on questioning one of your assumptions and altering it. This also seems to be important for solving many problems in life. When dealing with information, for example, functional fixedness could be demonstrated when somebody doesn't think of using a website for a different purpose from the searches they've done before. For example, if desperate, you could try using a map-producing website to check your spelling of a town's name (no map or wrong map = wrong spelling). To overcome our blockage we have to *restructure* our understanding of either the problem goal or of what we have and what we can do to solve it.

In fact, some psychologists[111] argue that even our sense of humour depends on this kind of 'leap' to a different representation of what's going on, and have even had some success identifying certain parts of the brain which are involved in doing it. Here are two typical jokes used in their studies:

> Q. Which side of a dog has the most hair?
> A. The outside.
> Q. What do engineers use for contraception?
> A. Their personalities.

(Apologies to any engineer readers!) Even if you thought those weren't funny, think how much less amusing they'd be if the two answers were 'the left side' and 'the Pill'. Riddles seem to depend on us having suddenly to see the whole situation in a new way, and the fact that we (sometimes!) laugh at them shows that we can do this. The best ones are probably too vaguely specified for us to discover the exact answer without being told. But it is possible to figure out some, such as this old classic:*

> What is greater than God,
> more evil than the Devil,
> the poor have it,
> the rich need it,
> and if you eat it you'll die?

Try that one on somebody else and see if they can solve it. Having dutifully learned my Catholic catechism as a child, my reaction to it was, 'But *nothing* is supposed to be greater than God, so this doesn't make sense ...' But then I struck lucky (or half-remembered it, perhaps). What if 'nothing' is the answer—after all it's a trick of some sort, isn't it? What about putting 'nothing' into the other phrases of the riddle? Does that fit? Yes! So the answer is actually 'nothing'. Here, the restructuring that's needed lies in realising that the solution isn't a concrete object at all but the *absence* of a thing, a negative state, which isn't an intuitive notion (after all, the number zero had to be invented; it didn't always exist in our number systems). Once again, we have to change an assumption before we can see the solution.

At other times, we solve problems by 'incubating' them: we put the problem to one side, perhaps sleeping on it overnight, and then seem to have an insight from nowhere by the morning. Psychologists

---

*At the time of writing, an internet rumour claimed that 80% of pre-school children, but only 17% of Stanford University students, could solve this riddle. I've been unable to track this to an authoritative source, like so many of these urban legends.

believe that this works by a kind of 'selective forgetting'—in effect, over time we happen to forget one of the assumptions which was getting in our way, so that we suddenly see a different aspect or possibility. An assumption was 'blocking' our awareness that a matchbox is something we can use as a shelf, not just for matches, that a dog has an inside as well as a left and right, or that conception can always be prevented by one partner refusing sex in the first place.

This suggests that it's important for us to question the assumptions we're making and the reasoning we're following if we find ourselves spending too long searching, browsing or reading information. It may be that we're fixating on one way of stating our problem when a better one is available. With Auntie Ada, we might suddenly realise that all she needs is company, not a creature that might shed too much hair on her sofa, and we could seek out the details of a social group for her to join. Or just visit her.

Can we learn to be better at 'losing' assumptions to see solutions, or is this based on some creative talent that we must be born with? Psychologists seem to favour the former—there should be a way to help everyone to think out of the box.* We *can* learn to question our assumptions more often, e.g. through the training in critical thinking which our education system is supposed to encourage (but sadly, often doesn't). It isn't straightforward, and for most of us the best we can do is to try to be more aware of how assumptions can get in our way. All the same, they make daily decisions and communications a lot easier.

Sometimes we want information to help us choose between alternative views of a problem rather than just to help us find one. Yet sometimes we might not yet know what those alternatives are, or even that there *is* a choice. Having started out with what seemed like a simple information need, suddenly we've made it a complex choice decision instead of a basic factual issue. We all know the exhausted feeling that comes from realising we have more choices than we really wanted. Some people actively avoid large supermarkets for this very reason. We'll see in later chapters that the internet very often feels like this—aisles and aisles of varieties of pasta when we'd only popped in for some macaroni. The trick is to be sure that macaroni *is* what we want, and then just stick to buying it.

---

*Mind you, if we were all perfect at doing this, most jokes would die a death since we wouldn't make all the wrong assumptions they depend on, so the world wouldn't necessarily be a brighter place. Perhaps humour is the compensation we get for the inflexibility of our minds.

Nor does the computer

Let's think some more about assumptions in communication. In some ways, with the huge amount of information available in a database or on the internet, saying what we want is a bit like ordering from a waiter in those helpful restaurants that offer to try to make anything we ask for. But with a computer, unlike a waiter, there is often no shared conceptual knowledge—you usually can't just say 'a cheese omelette' and expect the computer to know precisely what that is (or is not). Unless you're using that rare thing, an 'intelligent' or 'adaptive' system that already knows a little about what you're likely to need, it's all down to you.

A little-known branch of science called semiotics, the study of signs and symbols in communication, has defined different aspects of what we need in order to get information across to another person or thing. The first one, and the most relevant one to this chapter, is known as **pragmatics**. The pragmatics of a communication are the assumptions, context and motivations that underlie our attempt to communicate in the first place. They depend very heavily on our culture, which determines not only our use of language but also many of our desires and assumptions. Some philosophers would argue that culture even defines what we mean by 'truth' in what we communicate, i.e. that truth is a relative concept (a notion helpful to politicians since Pontius Pilate).

As well as the culture, which might be quite fixed or slow moving (although ours is not), there is the context in which we are currently communicating. There are restaurants housed under grass roofs in rural Zimbabwe, and in a formerly royal palace courtyard in St Petersburg, but the crucial aspect of the context is that they are still restaurants and, at a given moment, a customer is in them to order and eat food.

In conversation with people, the context changes from second to second as the talk continues, since each thing we say then forms part of the context for the next one, and other things might also be changing in the background. There are also norms for such communication (things that tend to be said in a certain way), and no communication occurs without some kind of implied intention. Often the intention also involves some emotions, such as the hope that you'll get your omelette eventually, or a feeling of gratitude towards a kind waiter. The communicator and the receiver are often both part of the same 'community of thought', even if that just implies that they share basic human experience and language in common (unlike, say, you and your cat). All of these help make up the pragmatics of the communication.

When we're talking to a computer, e.g. to ask it for information, there is often *no* context as far as the computer's concerned. The software programmer, very often, was trying to make as few assumptions as possible about what people might want from it. HCI writers have stated great concern with the importance of understanding users' real-life tasks and building software with that understanding in mind, but sometimes this is asking a lot of the poor software engineers. Ideally they'd like *everyone* to use their software for doing *everything* (and even if they don't, their profit-minded bosses might), so they may not feel they can rely on any pragmatics at all—nor even which language the user will speak.

Although novice users sometimes fear that the computer might 'know things about me', the reality is usually the opposite: it hardly knows anything at all. Nicholas Negroponte,[204] an MIT computing guru, has suggested that adding cameras and machine vision could help it to grasp *some* pragmatics. At present it doesn't even know whether you're still in the room and looking at it when it asks you for input. However, not everyone would make these pragmatic issues the priority in solving the human–computer communication problem.

Allen[9] pointed out an often-overlooked possibility: to some extent, we could *tell* the computer our context. We can imagine a system that established a dialogue with us, going through a quick question-and-answer session to check what we already knew as well as what we wanted to know, so that the information it retrieved and displayed reflected this. The 'online help' websites of many computer companies (e.g. Apple) are now increasingly trying this, although they can be frustrating to use when your query doesn't fit into the simple categories they suggest.

A compromise to this is a scenario where, in just one box, you type in what you want as a proper full-text question or sentence, which a computer then parses to pick out the meaning. In another box, optionally, you could say what you didn't want, or already knew, etc.—again in proper sentences rather than a bald **Boolean** 'word1 AND word2 NOT word3' statement. The computer can be taught to spot certain types of items, and to use a built-in thesaurus to match their *semantic* content to your request rather than their precise words. In other words, it abandons simple word matching and focuses instead on trying to achieve genuine relevance to what you seem to be asking.

In the late 1990s the search engine Ask Jeeves[15] became an increasingly popular choice for frazzled novice web searchers. It was a great first attempt to use natural language queries (letting the user type a question or other sentence) on the web, and to apply knowledge of typical things that people might want to know.

Personally, it often hasn't given me what I want. The number of topics and query types it's aware of is still tiny, compared with the huge and possibly infinite set of possible queries that people might ask. But it seems to be 'learning' from the things people type in and the results they then select.

To try to optimise its success rate, as well as trying to identify the type of query you're making, it also searches some standard web search engines in case none of its semantically based suggestions really fit your intention. The results page lets you see Jeeves's attempts to interpret your question, and separately the results from its general search engine trawl.

Unsurprisingly, Jeeves is a lot more effective when the search is for a straightforward general knowledge fact, or a basic explanation of a topic, than when you want to find something more esoteric or explore a subject in more detail. The more likely your request is to turn up in a pub quiz, or to be such a common query that someone will have written a help sheet especially addressing it, the more likely it is that Jeeves can answer it.

At the time of writing there are a number of such 'adaptive' websites which, if constantly used by a great many people, will gradually become better and better at diagnosing their queries and giving them what they need. In fact, the knowledge it will end up holding about the patterns of people's queries and what satisfies them should itself be a fascinating resource for scientists to study, in the same way that (but far more usefully and validly than) some psychologists have capitalised on 'reality TV' situations.

Things change extremely fast on the web, however, and people are demanding creatures. Other search engines are still by far the most used, despite their relative crudeness. While Ask Jeeves was evolving, people were learning too, and realising how to make the most of other more basic search engines. These, such as Google and Excite, boast a greater coverage of the whole internet and are often quicker to search. We'll look at the ins and outs of this more 'traditional' type of information search in the next chapter.

As people become more aware of what works (and what doesn't) with traditional search engines and develop strategies to overcome their shortcomings, they may feel that they'll do better out there on their own without bothering to express their context. In the process, they'll wade through a lot of rubbish and 'dead links' (where a page has been removed from the internet but search engines still index it; they don't update their databases half as often as some of us would like).

This is similar, of course, to the library users who never bother to ask the librarian anything: they feel they know enough about libraries to find everything they want for themselves, despite the annoying quirks of its classification system and the books that vanish when the catalogue still claims they're on the shelves. The self-confident computer user still needs to spell accurately if they use a search engine or database (still a cause of many failed searches). But some search engines now make suggestions if an input looks like a slightly misspelt version of a known word or phrase. This is just like your word-processor's spell-checker, but again learning from people's queries. Thus it's able to cope with words and names way beyond the official dictionary.

If a web search engine can attempt to interpret your context intelligently despite the vast range of possibilities out there, of course it's even easier for a more restricted system like a library catalogue to do the same. In the early 1990s a team at City University in London demonstrated, with the 'Okapi Enquire' system, [241] that building a kind of thesaurus into such a system gives it the chance to retrieve books not just with the words you typed in, but also other words which mean the same (synonyms).

The Okapi team had already also developed mechanisms of query expansion, whereby the system could look at the documents that the user judged most relevant and find other documents that contained similar words and phrases among their text. This way you would again see a focus on 'aboutness' and not on exact letter strings.

The benefits of including such automatic features were overwhelmingly demonstrated by the team at City, especially if the thesaurus is capable of learning and improving its knowledge of how *users* would link two words' meanings together (as opposed to similarities in strict dictionary definitions).

It's beyond the scope of this book to delve into recent advances in semantic reference systems in computer science (often based on so-called 'ontologies', basically formal semantic models linking up related concepts). At the time of writing none is yet a very impressive mimic of the subtleties of human meaning. However, one more point is worth making. Such a system is likely to be more *consistent* in its suggestions than a human librarian, as suggested by research by Mirja Iivonen in Finland. [139] When librarians suggested some suitable search terms for a given topic, and then did it again two months later, their suggested terms were different (it's unclear how much from the paper). They also differed greatly between people, although the underlying *concepts* suggested were very stable and similar—not that this fact would be of any use to an ordinary non-thesaurus-aided search engine.

What was more, people couldn't always see or explain the differences between their earlier and later suggestions. A computer, on the other hand, never changes its mind unless a programmer tells it to, and will do the same thing every time. Yet the web changes every minute. Any judgement of what's relevant out there would in the end be as changeable as a librarian's—and almost as hard to predict.

In the past ten years computers have become so immensely powerful, relative to their cost, that such a system is much cheaper to implement than ever before. Yet most systems still don't use any kind of semantic interpretation. Most library catalogues, even brand new ones being implemented as I write this, are still woefully limited—a painful irony when libraries sit cheek by jowl with information and computer science departments whose researchers already know a better way forward. Some day maybe every system will offer the dream expressed by Kuhlthau.[165] It'll be able 'to recognize an information need; explore information on a general topic; formulate a specific focus; gather information pertaining to a specific focus; and prepare to share what has been solved, learned or created'.

Such systems can never be perfect, but we're on the way there. The individuality of you, the user, would have to be included somewhere in the system's knowledge—hence there's been an increased effort to include 'user profiles' or 'user modelling' in computer systems. The recent growth in internet sites that expect you to log in so that they can track your usage and build a 'profile' of your requirements, means that the site providers themselves are recognising the value of individual use patterns as information for their *own* use. It isn't always for or to your benefit as a user, but often it does help you.

As discussed later, such websites as Amazon already keep track of your previous purchases and searches and try to make 'recommendations' based on your apparent interests. Yet these are a bare start. A really intelligent computer system, like Hal in the film *2001: A Space Odyssey* (1968), would know much more than that about you.

Let's imagine for a moment that we could obtain that information. For an academic or writer (assuming they use a word-processor, though it's surprising how many creative souls still prefer hand-writing or typewriters), it would be quite easy to gain great insight into their interests and tendencies, and the relative depth of knowledge they held in some areas. We would just get a computer to index the entire contents of their hard disk (and probably also the items in their filing cabinet, bookcase, and the piles of papers on their desks, the floor of their car, and . . .). An extensive interview with a non-writer might produce similar results.

However, all this knowledge of the sort of thing you seem to know about wouldn't help at all if a life-changing event caused you radically to shift your priorities and interests, as the most interesting people so often do. Nor would it be any use when you decided to check if something you *already* knew was available online (e.g. looking for references to your own work or organisation or website to check their accuracy, or just to boost your ego in a bad week). Since people are frequently mistaken about each other's intentions and meanings, even after decades of marriage or friendship, a computer doesn't stand a chance (at least at current technology levels). Intra-individual variations in behaviour have been largely neglected in psychology. Hence they are unknown variables to any would-be user modellers in computer science. But they are as much a problem as the inter-individual variety across the population.

So, as a rock singer once put it, 'You still know nothin' 'bout me'—no amount of information on a person seems enough to predict their intentions even in a simple search. Worse, probably no ethics committee would allow a psychologist to gather that much information about individuals, even if anyone was willing to participate, so we can't even be sure how far it *could* work. The best guess might come from looking at the work of secret services and spies rather than information science, since they gather far more detailed information about their subjects. How far do they manage to predict behaviour? Sadly, writing this three years after the terrorist attack in New York of 11 September 2001, with multiplying reports of intelligence failures (or rather failures to predict catastrophic human behaviour from the knowledge already held), the answer looks unimpressive.

Back in the more mundane world of the research lab, what can we do to help computers deal better with people's information needs? A start could be made, perhaps, if more researchers stopped treating inter- and intra-individual variance, often due to unclear motives, as an irritating source of 'error' in their data and started dealing head-on with its influence even in the specific, controlled situations of their laboratory studies.

Wanting the wrong thing

There are times when, unknown to either you or the computer, you may not really want the 'right' information anyway. As I've discussed already, over the past 40 years psychologists have shown repeatedly that people (including themselves!) look for information that confirms their existing beliefs. What's wrong with that? Two reasons.

First, according to psychologists who've researched this issue, philosophers such as Karl Popper and Bertrand Russell[91, 285] have argued that we can never decide that something must be true just by generalising from things or events that seem to support it. There may always be some evidence, as yet undiscovered, that *contradicts* it.

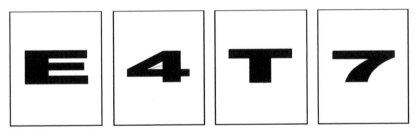

Figure 2.4. Wason's card puzzle. Which two cards do you turn over to prove that all vowels have an even number on the back?

Logically, if you refuse to believe that thousands of Americans have been abducted by aliens, it doesn't prove anything to find some other non-believers. Instead, you want either to find evidence that proves aliens *can't* have abducted those people, or at least devise a test which, if it worked, could *only* mean they *did* abduct them, and be totally willing to change your mind if it does work (and make sure that there's no way for you subconsciously to sabotage it!).

We don't usually do this, of course. Instead of looking for contrary evidence to challenge our ideas, we tend to show what the famous cognitive psychologist Peter C. Wason[303] called **confirmatory bias** when he first demonstrated it in 1960. Wason showed that if you tell people a rule and ask them to look for evidence to prove the rule, they do things that *couldn't* disprove the rule whatever happened, so they don't really help to prove it. In Wason's famous task, shown in Figure 2.4, most people choose to turn over the wrong cards. You're asked which two cards you should turn over in order to prove the rule 'If a card has a vowel on it, it must have an even number on the other side'.

Most people turn over the E and the 4, when they should turn over the E and the 7. The rule *doesn't* say that if there's an even number then there must be a vowel; it only says that the *reverse* must be true. If the 4 had an M on it, it wouldn't matter, but if the 7 had an A on it, it would.

Later experiments[50, 119] have used more realistic scenarios, such as what kind of stamp should be used on certain types of mailing envelope, or what diseases should be listed on the back of an application form for a visa to enter a country. They showed that although we often still fall foul of this task even with realistic items, we more often get it right than with the numbers and letters version. Sometimes, depending on the situation, we do know we should check that a rule or hypothesis isn't broken, instead of just getting evidence that's bound to fit it anyway. Specifically, we're much more accurate when we've been told that a rule must be followed before someone can *do* something (as opposed to being true just so that another abstract rule can also be true).

In other words, somehow we're better at reasoning about contracts and rules that allow or forbid *actions* than we are about states of things. However, other researchers, such as Pei Wang,[301] have argued that the question is not one of people being illogical, but simply choosing a different type of logic: non-axiomatic instead of axiomatic. Wang argues that the 'error' of inferring that people are illogical, on the basis of their responses to tasks where they may simply not realise which type of logic the experimenter wants them to use, is *itself* a logical error! Wang has developed a computer model of a non-axiomatic, 'reasonable' reasoning system which can be downloaded from his website (see the 'further reading' section).

This happens to fit quite neatly with the ideas of Brenda Dervin, who I mentioned earlier, that our 'sense-making' usually involves looking for information so that we can act. Under those circumstances, we should usually be able to apply logic correctly, and focus on checking for things that might either stop us or cause our actions to change. So before we book a holiday in the Caribbean, we might check that the island isn't dangerous or unpleasant in any way. But if we're only looking to confirm a belief (e.g. because we've heard some unpleasant remarks about a place we already like, and want to defend it), we'll probably look for positive aspects of the island and pass over any negatives. We seem to be 'poorer scientists' when we're dealing with belief than when we're deciding how to act.

So if we don't intend that the information will alter our actual actions, we're likely to look for what suits us rather than what challenges us. There will be some information that we *don't* want. This is especially true in a more complex situation. We saw above that some information scientists like to talk about users as trying to reduce *uncertainty* in a situation. Yet sometimes we choose to stay uncertain about some things so that we can focus on others, and avoid being 'overloaded'. We'll talk more about this issue of cognitive 'load' in later chapters.

The famous cognitive psychologist Steven Pinker,[228] discussing these and other evidence that we don't always make decisions based on objective logic, has pointed out that it's not fair to use this as evidence that people are stupid or irrational. We have enormously powerful brains, and we seem to survive and thrive incredibly well in the world, so the many pessimistic writers [105, 285] who've seized on our 'irrationality' are really too negative about human nature. There are often quite good reasons for thinking the way we do, and hence choosing what information to seek out or to notice. For instance, with Wason's card test above, Pinker argues that we're socially motivated to stop people cheating more than we care about logically verifying hypotheses. So we behave rationally when cheat spotting happens to go along with logical rule checking, but sometimes what *we'd* count as 'cheating' isn't strictly what the rules imply.

Pinker links this 'everyday rationality' idea to evolutionary psychologists' ideas about what type of cognitive bias would help us most in everyday human society, both in the past and in modern life. In other words, it doesn't usually matter if we're 'poor scientists', because most of our decisions need real-world knowledge more than strict deductive logic.

A lot of the time, this is true: the world, and especially human society, doesn't behave much like a science lab. However, personally I wouldn't rush out to buy a 'PROUD TO BE IRRATIONAL' T-shirt. We can talk about motivation often being stronger than logic, and avoid condemning individual people as 'stupid' just because of that, *without* having to believe that illogical thought is actually a Good Thing for social evolution.

Some people (though not everyone) would argue that there'd be far less violence if we behaved rationally for the good of society as a whole, rather than emotionally for our short-term satisfaction. After all, it seems rational to assume that rational behaviour would be socially advantageous. But then, evolutionary psychologists have their answers to that, too (e.g. favouring your own gene pool over others, removing rivals, etc.). They constantly turn up neat evolutionary advantages for everything from domestic violence to lottery addiction, so we can't expect much help there.

When these sorts of arguments seem to turn us into helpless creatures of fate, remember that while evolutionary psychologists can rationalize all the contradictory options in our lives through relentless Darwinism, they've got nowhere with *predicting* which ones you, personally, will follow. You can still choose to take a logical approach to using information, if you decide that you want to. Many people choose, rationally, not to buy lottery tickets; judges beg juries to weigh the evidence logically; rational consumer tests are highly valued. Wherever this book touches on evidence that people fail to follow scientific logic in their dealings with information, this isn't to imply that they can't do so, or that they're always wrong.

Whatever the cause, I have to add that even we trained academics are 'poor scientists' at times. When writing a paper we'll only look hard for evidence to support our ideas, unless we're very afraid of our peers rejecting them, but when planning an experiment we'll look out for anything that could make it 'go wrong', so that we can plan to avoid it. Ultimately, however, the experiment itself will aim to prove our personal suspicions, and usually it does. Several years ago I winced in (mildly hypocritical) horror at a psychologist on the television, who was ecstatic because she'd got some results that she'd wanted for years. She had demonstrated a very small, slightly bizarre, and apparently inconsistent, IQ-raising benefit of playing classical music to a group of young children (she had previously been a professional musician herself). I heard her say, 'You've got to have a dream, and then if you do the experiment the right way, the dream comes true!'

This may not be irrational, but it's also not science. Nor is the stubbornness shown by palaeontologists over historical fakes like the Piltdown Man, quoted by Bryce Allen[9] to illustrate group resistance to challenges of their pet theories. However, it's sometimes imagined that training in computer use, along with scientific training, will somehow make us more logical creatures, able to reason our way through problems more systematically and less intuitively than without such training.

Yvonne Waern[300] considered this possibility in 1989, in reviewing studies of whether programmers and computer science students were better at solving logic puzzles than, say, psychology students or people in other professions. The results are very hard to interpret. Computer science students, for sure, did solve such problems more often and more quickly than psychologists. However, they may have been people who were already more motivated towards deductive and formal logic, just as we might expect librarians to be natural organisers of their homes and lives (however true or untrue this might be!). Or they may have been great at logic in formal situations like tests and programming, but still as messy and emotional as other students in everyday life.

Waern also looked at studies suggesting that children develop better thinking skills if they learn to program computers with a simple language like LOGO. She pointed out that the evidence is ambiguous, and often has come from very evangelical researchers who are really hoping to see benefits for the children they study. Overall, it's hard to draw conclusions about whether the 'computer mindset' transfers to everyday life.

It would not be particularly surprising if it didn't. Laboratory-based problem-solving studies in psychology have often had people learn how to solve one kind of problem. They then see another problem which, while seeming to involve a different area, they could solve via the same strategy they've just been using, yet they often don't realise this without a big hint.[135] In other words, even when you bring the horse right to the water, it can't drink: people don't spot the underlying similarities in logic between one situation and another, and so don't reapply the solution that they've only just learned.

People usually only manage to draw analogies when the two situations look similar on the surface, i.e. when they both involve similar-looking objects, or both occur in the same domain of life (e.g. two medical dilemmas). It also helps if the problem's presentation is similar in both cases (e.g. the objects or people involved are introduced first, and the constraints of the problem are described in the same order). Unfortunately, computer programming and searching tasks look very little like most other situations we encounter.

Furthermore, the deductive logic involved in computer programming is only one strategy for solving problems, and tends to be constrained in very particular ways so that it's obvious that deductive logic is needed, and it's usually obvious which command or structure to use next. How often, in real life, do we find ourselves able to think, as a programmer might think, 'OK, this is an IF-THEN-ELSE clause because I need this to happen next, but only if a certain fact is true. So first I test carefully to see if the condition is true, and then if it is I'll definitely take this path rather than that one . . .'?

How likely is it, then, that the careful and rigid rational thinking needed to tell a computer the right thing, so that its entirely logically produced results are the ones we wanted, will translate into more logical problem-solving approaches in everyday life? It's a sweet hope, but an unlikely one. Theodore Roszak, in his consideration of the differences between human and computer thought,[248] wrote:

> Is the teaching of symbolic logic justified? Well, why not? It is intellectually substantial as a subject in its own right. Some would argue that it has a more general benefit: it can help train the mind to think clearly. That is a somewhat antiquated and dubious assumption. It is grounded in the creaky old idea of faculty psychology, which holds that there are certain mental muscles, like logicality, which should be developed for their general utility in life. For centuries Latin was doggedly taught in the schools on the same mistaken premise that it contributed to orderly habits of thought. (p. 55)

There seems to be little evidence that the classics, or computer programming, will change our patterns of thought in most of everyday life, but perhaps sometimes we might pick up ideas and strategies from both that can give us an analogy to ponder.

Bad influence

Maybe you could be more objective? Possibly not, since your approach to information also depends on where you belong. At school, I once raised an objection to a topic brought up by my history teacher, who loved provoking the class into argument by pretending to be an anarchist. She wanted us to discuss ways to create Utopia, the goal of some idealist groups in the nineteenth century. I said this was pointless—Utopia couldn't work anyway. As a sceptical teenager, I was completely unprepared for her reaction: 'But you would say that, dear, you're a Catholic.' Eh? 'You believe that heaven only comes in the afterlife, so of course you don't think Utopia could work here.'

I did? I didn't? For the first time, going pink in the face, I realised the inescapable influence of group membership.

Bryce Allen[9] points out, in his very thoughtful consideration of psychological aspects of information needs, that social biases can influence us just as much as our individual sense-making. Supposing we believe something in common with a group that we belong to (political party, church, family, friends, club, company). We might believe that our policy on welfare is the soundest, that God loves our country more than any other, that cannabis should be decriminalised, or that the product we make is the best in the world. If we intend to look for information connected with our membership of that group, it'll be even harder for us to 'think different' (as Apple, the computer company, recently asked us to do in an advertising campaign).

This has emerged even in laboratory experiments, where students at two quite prestigious universities watched a video of a football game between their two institutions. Afterwards both groups reported seeing more fouls by the opposite side than by their own.[91] This will be familiar to everyone who's neutrally observed any sports match while sitting beside an avid fan—'We woz robbed!'

Back in the innocent 1950s, 60s and 70s, psychologists were less aware of the power of social influence. They also had none of today's overprotective litigation-dreading ethics committees. Some famous classic experiments demonstrated the strength of social conformity.

- Solomon Asch[13] showed how easily people would agree to a visible size judgement that was obviously wrong, if they heard several other people making it.
- Muzafer Sherif's 'Robber's Cave' study[266] showed how easily young boys from identical backgrounds could be made to develop prejudice and hostility against each other.
- Stanley Milgram[195] showed how easily an authority figure in a white coat could persuade people apparently to inflict serious electric shock on others.
- Philip Zimbardo's 1971 'Stanford Prison Experiment'[321, 322] showed how two randomly assigned groups of top university

students (and their academic 'prison directors') could reduce themselves to utter inhumanity, conformity and helplessness.

Every basic psychology textbook has reported these findings for over 25 years, but we largely overlook the implications for our increasingly media-controlled social attitudes.

In theory, one of the beauties of the internet is its ability to absorb every shade of opinion, every freewheeling idea, so that we can challenge our own assumptions and social norms and avoid the dangers of conformity that led to the genocides and holocausts of the twentieth century. However, the research suggests that we'll rarely bother to do so unless we have some strong motivation. Even if we like to think of ourselves as free thinkers, we may feel socially obliged to avoid seeking challenging ideas, because 'alternative' is too often linked (especially in the United States) with more judgemental words such as 'hippy', 'tree-hugger', 'paranoid', 'drop-out', 'communist', 'fascist' or 'nutter'. We may feel such ideas could threaten the stability in our current way of life, and alienate us from our existing social ties.

If we've been delegated by a group in some way to find or produce information about something, we will feel highly constrained by what the others in the group will be prepared to accept, and we'll try to avoid damaging the consensus. If we do find anything that doesn't fit, then we'll have to choose either to challenge the group, or quietly to ignore it (even if we've managed not to overlook it ourselves, given our own strong expectations). So you can't expect a right-wing journalist or politician to show her or his colleagues, let alone their readers or voters, evidence that immigration causes far fewer problems in Britain than they've previously implied. Similarly, a left-wing journalist probably won't hunt out any figures suggesting that private companies sometimes run services better than public bodies. An ideally balanced news broadcaster or publication (or website) might dare to tackle both issues, but there are few such publications. Humans produce them all, and all humans have a complex social web of loyalties.

We can also be members of small groups which have particular roles and points of view within an *organisation*—that is, a bigger group which also might have other subgroups. Examples are a project team within a company, a year group within a school, or a committee within a voluntary organisation. Organisational politics could then be giving us another bias, maybe even conflicting with our personal and small-group biases.

Imagine a trade unionist trying to find evidence to help his colleagues to take action about something he doesn't personally see as a priority, but knows he must support. At the same time he worries about affecting the company's survival and biting too hard the hand that feeds them all. Given all the complications, it'll be much harder for him and his fellow shop stewards to think flexibly about the different courses of action they could take. He'll be even less willing than usual to get information that muddles the picture any further. Similarly with managers, combined loyalty to the 'management' and the 'workforce', both within the company, can complicate decision-making. The more complex the decision, the less extra information they'll want to see. In the jargon, they're trying to 'reduce the cognitive load'. In plain talk, they've got enough to think about already.

So, even when we're still just trying to decide what information we want, we're already strongly affected by our personal and social biases. Researchers have spent a lot of time studying particular groups of people, such as patients with particular kinds of illness and their carers,[311] or people in certain professions.[209] The researchers look to see what kinds of information these people tend to want. Then they can suggest ways of developing specific information resources that prioritise those things and organise them in the most useful way.

Contrast this with ELIZA. 'She' was a very early attempt (by ingenious computing wizard Joseph Weizenbaum) to make computers seem 'human' by making them use natural language. Easily simulating a non-directional therapist, much to the annoyance of the latter profession, ELIZA responded to every statement you typed by throwing it back at you, e.g. 'I'm feeling depressed today' led to 'Why are you feeling depressed?', and so on. ELIZA did not understand, in any real sense, anything you told her (we'll look more at computer 'understanding' in Chapter 5). 'She' simply parsed your statement and picked out a noun phrase to return within a request for further information. It is quite easy to make the program produce nonsense, but online recreations of her can still fool the unwary.

This is one reason why it's often better to look at a quality-checked internet medical directory or **subject gateway**,[218] than to try to look for, for example, 'cancer' with a general-purpose search engine. Of course, there'll be more results with the latter (tens of thousands!). But with the specialist information, a *person* has thought about why you'd be doing this search, what you'll probably want and how you want it.

However, in aiming information at a certain group or type of person, assumptions are made not only about what you want, but also what you *don't* want. You probably won't find links to the Humanist Society on a website written for Christians. This might seem obvious, but it means that you could easily hide within your own snug corner, even among the vast patchwork quilt of the internet, and avoid ever being seriously challenged. If it's true that we show confirmatory bias even when our membership of our social world isn't under threat, this could only be worse when it is.

What to do about wanting it?

For users

The best overall quotation I can give here, which is from Winograd and Flores's important book on computers and cognition,[315] is this:

> What is important is that people using the system recognize (as those duped by ELIZA did not) two critical things. First, they are using the structures of their natural language to interact with a system that does not understand the language but is able to manipulate some of those structures. Second, the responses reflect a particular representation that was created by some person or group of people, and embodies a blindness of which even the builders cannot be fully aware. (p. 124)

Those authors were partly thinking of systems like ELIZA, whose main 'duping' technique was simply using natural English. But the 'blindness' can always be there. As we've seen, it involves not just one 'builder' but many. There are the people who created the information resources you're searching for, the people who designed the web 'crawler' that recorded it (or the people who classified the resource into a database), the people who built the search engine that retrieves it, and the designers of the user interface that displays the results. Trying to understand *their* intentions and desires can sometimes help us.

I would add:

- Be aware of your own level of 'self-efficacy' concerning the topic, the information source you're using, and your ability to use it well.
- Be prepared for the unexpected when trying to build a 'mental model' of the way the computer is giving you information.
- If you're trying to be objective in your information use, for the sake of making a rational decision, watch for your own social and emotional biases.
- If you can't work out how to find what you want, check your current knowledge and your assumptions about your goal and the ways of getting there.

Regarding computer anxiety, hoaxes unfortunately heighten people's sense that online use is somehow risky. We have to learn to treat with extreme scepticism any email message saying that a new virus will 'wipe the hard drive' or 'destroy our files' the moment we look at a certain message or website. Try to ignore any message of *any* kind telling you to forward the message to 'everyone you know'. These are almost always hoaxes, exploiting the well-meaning and unwitting as a 'joke', and causing a massive waste of network capacity as they travel endlessly onwards, sometimes lasting for years.

For information providers and designers

Make it clear which and whose information needs will, and won't, be satisfied by the information you provide, and suggest appropriate strategies for different types of information goals. However, don't try to stratify your system into a limited set of options for each of your imagined user types, as many university websites unfortunately do. I often have no idea whether the information I'm looking for will be found under 'Visitors', 'Community', 'Staff' or 'Students' since I may not be any of those, or I may be two or even three of them at once. Even if I'm an outsider, the item I want probably won't be the bland and shallow marketing material of the first two categories.

It's good to offer (ideally context-specific) visual emphasis on the most likely options, so long as the user can also see how to go beyond those (e.g. via a site index or search field). There is a distinct feel in many, many websites these days of the users being corralled into a neat corner rather than truly having their information needs addressed. Fair enough for a profit making company perhaps, but disappointing for public service resources.

For researchers

We need more research into the following:

- What makes people in specific situations choose to seek information on the internet, or in other computer resources, in preference to alternatives.
- How 'self-efficacy' links to 'uncertainty', and how a person's self-efficacy about the situation and topic, about the computer system they're using, and about their ability to cope with the information might all *interact* in predicting their actual behaviour.

- Comparative studies of whether different types of information need differ in the ways that people should and/or do approach the problem.
- The possible effects of demand characteristics in information science 'user studies', where people are interviewed, surveyed or observed.
- Whether academics, students, journalists and other 'knowledge workers' differ from the general public (and from their own behaviour when not acting in a professional capacity) in the relevance of 'uncertainty' to their information behaviour.

Summary

This chapter has explored the factors surrounding people's desire to use information made available by computers and/or the internet. Starting with some barriers to people's decision to use such sources, it discussed these in the light of psychological research on attitudes and abilities, particularly the concept of 'self-efficacy'. From the computing standpoint, it mentioned the issues of mental models of computers' unexpected rules and behaviours, which don't fit our novice intuitions.

I explored the increased 'fuzziness' of recent years in considering people's concepts and information needs, along with the motivational aspects that influence people's choices. The next section described the ill-defined nature of many information problems and the ways in which we solve such problems, according to psychology research.

Finally, the computer's lack of pragmatic knowledge when we request information from it, and our own thought and social biases, were shown to affect the way we're likely to retrieve and handle information.

Further reading

Some of the points on computer aversion/anxiety arose from reading Mark Brosnan's thoughtful book: *Technophobia: The psychological impact of information technology* (London and New York: Routledge, 1998).

The discussion of social and organisational biases in information need, and some other parts of this chapter, draw on Chapter 3 of Bryce Allen's *Information Tasks: Toward a user-centered approach to information systems* (San Diego, CA, and London: Academic Press, 1996).

A fascinating book on the early (1960s–1970s) research into social biases, group membership and persuasion is P. G. Zimbardo, E. B. Ebbesen and C. Maslach, *Influencing Attitudes and Changing Behavior: An introduction to method, theory and applications of social control and personal power*, 2nd edition (Reading, MA: Addison-Wesley, 1977). Alternatively, any general or social psychology textbook will summarise at least some of this startling (and no longer repeatable) work.

Many of Tom Wilson's reports and papers on information seeking are available online at the time of writing: www.informationr.net/tdw

Pei Wang's 'non-axiomatic' reasoning model can be read about and downloaded from his website at www.cogsci.indiana.edu/farg/peiwang/papers.html

Issues of reasoning and learning about how things work, and transferring knowledge and logic from one problem to another (i.e. analogical thinking), are summarised briefly and readably in M. W. Eysenck and M. T. Keane's excellent textbook *Cognitive Psychology: A student's handbook*, 4th edition (Hove: Psychology Press, 2000). A more technical state-of-the-art account of the analogical thinking work is K. J. Holyoak, D. Gentner and B. Kokinov, *Analogy: A cognitive science perspective* (Cambridge, MA: MIT Press, 2000).

Internet hoaxes, about virus scares and others, are debunked at this indispensable website: hoaxbusters.ciac.org

Chapter 3
Searching

The human brain is a wondrously complex device, with so many thousands of links and cells that we've never figured out the limit to its long-term storage capacity. When we want it to have yet more information, we often turn to a much simpler thing, which humans themselves created—the computer. Sounds easy, doesn't it?

In the computer context, 'searching' refers to one particular type of action: asking the computer to retrieve information that matches something we've typed or selected. Other activities that we might think of as 'searching', such as looking down a list or across a map, clicking on links between web pages, or skim-reading a text document, aren't covered in this chapter. To the people who design and study computers, searching is data retrieval, i.e. a computing function, not a human action. To them, we don't do the searching, the computer does; like a helpful librarian on a quiet day. That often-overlooked difference in definition begins to hint at some of the problems that arise when we 'ask the computer'.

What do we search (and what do we get)?

Searching the web

Later on I mention the many issues involved in searching traditional databases, because they still have some relevance (and many such databases are still around). By the time of writing this, however, most people most often search through web interfaces and **search engines.** For this reason, this section will focus mainly on the web, since even older databases, such as library catalogues, are starting to have web-based user interfaces, and also to link on beyond their own holdings to other websites, much like the more generic search engines such as Excite and Google.

What people seem to do in web searches

Imagine you are typing a 'query' into the little text box of a web search engine. It's hard to say exactly what will happen when you hit the 'Return' key on the keyboard or click on the 'Search' button, because every search engine claims to work differently (and better than the others, of course!), and the technology behind them changes all the time. Our ability to catch up with them, though, is inevitably lagging behind. So it's worth looking at what seems to be happening when people search. One of the first large-scale studies of this was done by looking at a log of one million search 'query' records from just one such engine, Excite, by a group of American information scientists and computer scientists. [274]

These studies were among the first pioneering attempts to tackle the massive data source that is a search engine's usage logs, with its associated restrictions and foibles. Being first to deal with a new source of data means you have to work out for yourself the link between the data files and the human behaviour that seemed to create them. The logs tend to have a few peculiarities, based on the recording mechanism that created them, so this isn't always straightforward, but it's worth a look.

The researchers were mainly information scientists with perhaps a slightly pessimistic view of the expertise of the average user. Their earlier logfile analyses had concluded, echoing two decades of hand-wringing library user studies, that most people couldn't use search engines well. The near-uninterpretable strings that some people entered seemed to them to say that users were 'not up to' sophisticated search strategies, such as **Boolean** logic (even though many users were obviously trying these, but failing because Excite had an unexpectedly rigid syntax for them that needed upper case letters and particular spacing). The researchers had painted a stark picture of web users as impatient, unskilled souls who mostly typed only one or two words into the box, didn't browse beyond the first page of results, and didn't try to refine and repeat their search if the results didn't look good.

Fortunately, by the time of the 'one million' log analysis, either sober reflection or peer review comments seem to have made them tone this down. They also seem to have adjusted their calculation methods by then, which previously may have inflated the number of crude and brief searches. So this study gave more reliable results, which is why I'm citing it.*

The research group had earlier suggested that users rarely bothered to change and resubmit their search if the first results didn't look good. The million-query data contradicted this. It suggested that 52% of users changed and retried their query one or more extra times. In other words, users saw their first search attempt

---

* Both this and the earlier log 'snapshot' were taken in 1997, although the 'one million' results weren't published until 2001, so the difference doesn't lie in web use changes over time.

as not good enough, and did something about it, just over half the time. We can't tell if we can see the other half as a good sign. It could mean users got what they wanted first time, even with Excite's then quite crude search engine. Or it could mean that users gave up in disgust as soon as their first search failed and assumed there was 'nothing out there'. Realistically it's likely to have been a mixture of both.

The most emphatic point made by the researchers was that people generally only typed one or two words into the search box. In their sample 26.6% had just one term (i.e. a word or another string of characters without spaces). 31.5% had two, 18.2% three, and 23.7% more than three terms. Less than 1.8% entered more than seven.

The authors,[274] still fixated on the idea that most people do searches that are too simple, wrote, 'Thus, close to 60% of all queries had one or two terms, with most of them having the "magical" search length of two terms' (p. 230). Yet there's nothing 'magical' about something that happens less than a third of the time. What seems odd is the relatively *low* number of *one*-word queries—perhaps people realise that one word is rarely enough, or perhaps they tend to be entering double names or common phrases (Jane Smith, Manchester weather forecast, nude sex). The rest follows a pre-dictable falling-off (logarithmic) curve (see below). We scientists must be careful not to stereotype our subjects.

The researchers also worried about people's post-search browsing through results. They analysed the number of 'pages' of results (listing ten sites per page) that users browsed through after a query; 71% of users had gone beyond the first ten listed, to look at at least the next ten as well. To me, bearing in mind that web searching is not like trying to find every possible relevant book in a library, this was surprisingly high. We surely couldn't seriously expect users even to contemplate browsing more than a few dozen of the thousands of results which, even back then, could emerge from even a very specific search. We could put it this way: almost three-quarters looked at more than ten listed results, and half looked through more than 20!

It wasn't enough to impress the information scientists. They wrote:

> ... about one in every four users looked at ten or less sites. Another 19% looked at two pages only. That is, close to half of the users looked at two or less pages ... Were a few answers good enough? Is the **precision** of Web search engines that high? Are the users after precision? ... Or did they just give up? (p. 229)

Citing these and their earlier Excite study (which had suggested much less page-turning, but had still put it at around 42% of users), the authors concluded, 'The public has a low tolerance of going in depth through what is retrieved.'

People did often search with more than one or two words. They did view a reasonable number of results.* Yet they often did also try to improve and resubmit their search terms. What more could we ask?

As I discuss elsewhere in this chapter, it turns out that the issue isn't precision or lack of it—on the web you usually just want the most likely looking site to help you answer your question. You're not searching **metadata** anymore but real data, so with well-chosen search terms and a none-too-choosy attitude you will probably find some very fast. And, as I explain below and in the next chapter, the nature of the web is such that you usually don't need to browse very far to get what you want within a few clicks. So, although the researchers probably couldn't have known this, the users seem to have followed the same 'many small, few very big' trend as many other phenomena on the web, [136] as shown in Figure 3.1.

Excite, and other search engines in 1997, were still doing quite crude word-matching trawls of web page text. Later, Google started drawing on people's tendency to link from their site to others that were useful to them, so that sites that were linked to by lots of other sites were treated as more popular and useful (very like Amazon's 'other people who bought this book also bought . . .').

Teoma, my current personal favourite, builds on this. It identifies 'communities' of sites that seem to link to each other as a group. Then the 'How many sites link to this one?' criteria is based on sites that are in its 'local community', i.e. on the same subject. The focus is on what seems *to the relevant* to be relevant. It's a bit like asking my friends if I'm worth knowing. You don't ask everyone in the country, who mostly don't know me and would have more to say about, say, a pop star. Their ignorance and celebrity interests don't make me less likeable to *those who know* me.

Yet strangely, despite their ignorance of me, they probably know someone who knows someone who . . . and the likely number of someones needed to get back to me is the famously small 'six degrees of separation' (from the unproven theory that anyone on the planet can be connected to any other person through a chain of acquaintances). Websites work the same way: they cluster in groups in the way that people do. [136] If Teoma returns a well-linked site from within

---

*Why 'reasonable'? Because library database studies had criticised users who browsed through too *many* results, instead of refining their search, arguing that such browsing was inefficient and too cognitively tiring. By 'too many' those older studies had usually meant more than a couple of dozen. So these web users were behaving quite optimally by those standards.

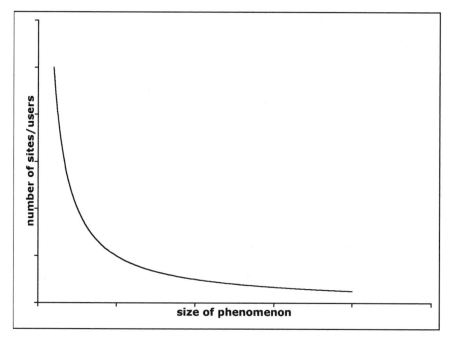

Figure 3.1. The type of 'power law' followed by many phenomena on the web (and elsewhere in society), and apparently also reflected in the research on people's searching and browsing behaviour. Lots of websites have only a few pages while a small number have thousands; lots of people's homepages include links to a few friends, while a few have very many links; etc.

a group that all talk about the same kind of thing and link together, then that site will be close to its 'centre' and hence very close to what you want.

As with Amazon's use of other people's multiple book purchases to suggest which books might complement the one you're viewing, this bypasses the rumbling computer science debate about how to put semantics into systems. Never mind the concepts, use people's *behaviour* (here linking their sites to others) as a guide. Don't do what they'd say, do what they do. Until we have something better to go on, this seems like a sound basis for any system where lots of human-based data can be adapted for it.

Our future networks may not involve keyword searches at all. Could we just get an agent to learn what we like and then keep bringing it back by itself? Yes, up to a point. But as I chased up ideas, references and interesting scientists for this book, I'd still have had to pat my agent on its head and tell it the things I was looking for, just as I'd go into a library with those words and names in my mind.

A lot of our information preferences might be about routine interests and hobbies. An agent could prepare information for me for catching up on current affairs and weather forecasts (with quite stable provider preferences). It could help me follow my favourite film genre or soap opera, and figure out what to have for dinner tonight (especially if it had helped order my groceries online too). This is why, for instance, the TiVo is a boon to people with reasonably predictable TV tastes. Even so, Nicholas Negroponte[204] has pointed out that even with adjustment for personal taste, an agent or 'personal filter' would also have to know (as editors do) about timing. When Negroponte reads a newspaper on a weekday, he just wants brief news that interests him (which he called *The Daily Me*). On a Sunday he'll browse open-mindedly through more general features (*The Daily Us*).

But searching is about proactively looking for something *new*, often in contexts we've never been in before (e.g. this is the first book I've written, and if I got cancer it would be my first serious disease). Unless the agent was so all-pervasive that it monitored every conversation and event of my life, I'd still have to specify new questions sometimes, and turn to computers to answer them.

What people *say* they do in web searches

Once again using Excite as the search engine of interest, a study by the same research group[273] surveyed users and asked *them* how they used the search engine, and what else they did when searching. The results showed greater persistence and effort than the researchers had previously assumed, although of course they were dependent on people's honesty and accurate self-observation. They also reflect a self-selecting group of people—those who had the time and inclination to complete the online survey. If these people were less rushed and more co-operative than others, perhaps we might see a slightly optimistic picture of their searching habits. However, the results are very interesting, not least because you can ask people questions which a single search engine's usage log simply can't answer.

Of 292 respondents to the online survey, 42% claimed to use Excite every day: 39% were trying out their first search on their current topic, but 31% had done 2–5 searches on it already, and 30% had done more than five searches for this single thing! Some 54% reported changing their search terms over successive searches, but 46% said they did not. However, when asked what query terms they were using, a third of respondents apparently didn't understand the question (a typical case of researchers forgetting that users don't speak the same jargon—we all do this sometimes). So we can't really trust the responses regarding how often they changed those terms.

Those who did respond to the question about query terms reported using on average 3.34 terms per respondent. Unsurprisingly, this was more than the previous log analyses had suggested. These respondents may have been the relative experts, of course, since they appeared to be able to understand what 'query terms' meant, so the average across novices could be lower.

Another survey was published around the same time in 2000 (but it's apparently now unavailable) on the excellent 'Search Engine Watch' website.[283] It involved 33,000 users of 13 of the major search engines on the web. Here 44.8% of respondents claimed to prefer using more than one keyword when searching, as opposed to 28.6% who said they tended to type just one word. The researchers contrasted this with some earlier data they'd collected at intervals since 1997, which had previously suggested that the number of people preferring to type more than one word, although always higher than the number typing only one, had been dropping from over 60% to just 40% by 1999.

The researchers suggested that the search engines were by then 'doing a better job of educating their users to be more specific with their queries'. It could be that the temporary rise in single-term searchers and decrease in multiple-term searchers was over the period of the web's most massive expansion in use, when very many new novice users were coming online and struggling to learn the best way to handle the search tools they encountered. In any case, although the researchers didn't tease out how many terms were implied by 'multiple' (two? seven?), it seemed that on the whole the users they surveyed were well aware of the need to tell search engines more specific descriptions. The number of people typing a complete question into the engines, probably prompted by the popularity of AskJeeves.com, had also risen to around 10% during that time, and the researchers commented that this was probably a good thing since most engines would give better results from the multiple words in a question, even if they didn't parse the question properly.

This survey also asked users what they did if they didn't find what they were looking for from their search. An overwhelming 76.9% said they did a different search on the same site, 19.0% said they tried a different search engine, and 4.1% chose to do something else. This suggests, as I did above, that the Excite log file analyses *had* underestimated people's willingness to change their search terms and try again.

Meanwhile, at the Georgia Institute of Technology a team in the Graphics, Visualization and Usability Center (the GVU) have been performing online web use surveys[149] regularly since 1994. Their tenth survey, conducted in 1998, was their most ambitious yet, with a range of questions on the 5,000 respondents' demographics, technology experience, everyday lives, online shopping habits and views about web privacy and security. There was even a special section for **webmasters** to complete.

GVU go to great pains on their website to explain that their sampling of web users isn't, and couldn't be, completely random, but is likely to be biased towards the more frequent and more experienced users (which is also true of the other surveys discussed in this section). Arguably, though, their surveys are the best we have of web use, since they are enormously detailed, build on long experience on the part of the survey team, remain unbiased by commercial concerns, and cover people from many countries. They didn't ask directly how people used the search engines, although they did ask how often their web use involved looking for specific information. Of the users, 69.7% said 'most of the time', although the question is a little ambiguous: 'specific information' could include 'a particular website I've heard about', in order to browse that site's content. Nevertheless, searching seems to be a crucial activity in people's internet information use, at least for those who respond to surveys.

What people search for on the web

Of course, the massive breadth of content of the web is the factor that really separates it from traditional, limited databases. People *can* look for absolutely any topic at all. What do they seem to go for?

The above Excite logfile study[274] attempted to classify the apparent search topics based on the words people typed. These, of course, are almost as prone to misinterpretation by another human as they are by the search engine itself, so we can't always know the real intentions. Certain sex-related terms were among the most common (including 'sex', 'naked', etc.). However, before we start to assume that most web searchers are the sad obsessives portrayed in the media, it's important to put this in context.

The misleading impression from simple term rankings partly happens because the people searching for sexual content use an extremely narrow vocabulary, which they will reuse endlessly, pushing those words up the rankings. A glance at the multi-volume Oxford English Dictionary in a library should convince the reader that that vocabulary is vastly outnumbered by the rest of the language, and a glance at the other query terms that rank alongside them in the logs also makes them seem less dominant. Among the other most frequent terms in that initial sample were 'university', 'free', 'music', 'software', 'home', 'college', 'games', 'school', 'jobs', 'american' and 'diana' (the log date was two weeks after Princess Diana's death). These aren't nearly as exciting as 'nudes' or 'erotic', but all selected more often than those (albeit less than 'sex'). So looking at people's topics simply by seeing which words are most often repeated is misleading when you realise what a small percentage of *queries* actually contain those words. 'Sex' appeared about ten thousand times in half a million one-off queries, i.e. around 2%.

The researchers also tried to classify 2,414 of the queries via human judgements. They found these results:

    16.9% = 'Entertainment, recreation'
    16.8% = 'Sex, pornography, preferences'
    13.3% = 'Commerce, travel, employment, economy'
    12.6% = Computers, the internet'
     9.5% = 'Health, the sciences'
     6.7% = 'People, places, things'
     5.7% = 'Society, culture, ethnicity, religion'
     5.6% = 'Education, the humanities'
     5.4% = 'The performing and fine arts'
     3.4% = 'Government'
     4.1% = 'Unknown, incomprehensible'

Again, sex may be one of the largest single categories but it's still small—around one in six queries in this 1997 sample. (Bear in mind that male internet users have always outnumbered females, although women have been catching up. Also, at that time most of our older and perhaps less hormonally charged citizens had yet to go online.) Sex was still less popular than entertainment information, although it's hard to say if this is healthy! Most crucially, we can't tell what percentage of *users* this is; it may be that the sex searchers would search more repeatedly and obsessively than other people, so they could be a much smaller minority.

Leaving the sex issue to one side, unfortunately the researchers' other categories seem so vague that we can't really tell what's going on. It's possible that the researchers couldn't either: e.g. if a user types 'city of London' are they interested in 'Commerce, travel, employment, economy' or 'People, places, things'? Once again we get more information, albeit biased, from turning to the online surveys, since these asked people to describe their topics.

In the online questionnaire survey of Excite users,[273] the researchers again classified people's stated topics. The most common concerned people (12%: these included searches concerning family members, friends, public figures or family tree tracing, which is a massively popular internet topic). These were closely followed by computers (12%), business (10%—but it isn't clear what counted), entertainment, medical information, then politics/government, then news, then hobbies, general surfing, science, travel, and then the rest were all under 5% (including arts and humanities, education, shopping, graphic images and employment).

In that sample, *nobody* admitted to doing 'adult' searches! Perhaps the sex searchers don't bother to complete surveys, or perhaps they do but they prefer not to mention their sex-related searches. Maybe they didn't call their searches 'adult', but saw them as a vaguely defined 'hobby' (e.g. looking for 'photographs'). We can't tell. In any case, the rich variety of the other topics, and the seriousness of most of them (other than entertainment), shows that web users are not merely 'surfing' but are really trying to use the web to help with their everyday life.

Similarly, in the tenth GVU survey, 73.6% of respondents claimed that one of their primary uses of the web was for 'gathering information for personal needs'. This was higher than the 65.9% who claimed to use it for their work or business, the 61.4% who said they used it in connection with education, and the 60.1% who looked to it regarding 'entertainment'. The figure for shopping online was 52.4%, but only a minority of users clicked the other suggested uses ('communication', 'time-wasting' and 'other').

Backing this up, only 33.4% of GVU respondents said (in answer to another question) that they used the web mostly 'to have fun and explore'—for most people, web use is serious—and 77.7% claimed to access online reference materials on at least a weekly basis (although it's not clear what people might count as 'reference'. Would a site giving the weather forecast count? The TV listings?). A similar frequency of use for 'research materials' (a harder category to misconstrue, presumably) was claimed by 49.9%, and by 44.0% for 'financial material'. Medical information was used at least weekly by 19.2%. Note that this doesn't mean that such material is less highly valued. Other research has shown that many people now turn to online sources for health advice (sometimes with poor judgement unfortunately, since not all such sources are authoritative or clearly written). We would be a literally very sick society, however, if we needed to access such information on more than an occasional basis. It's probably also a relief that only 13.9% were reading online job listings weekly or daily, for similar reasons.

Regardless of these bald statistics, on an individual level the topics you search for will alter not only with your life circumstances, and with the known availability of relevant items, but also with your level of access to the technology. With a monthly charged, always-on connection in my home, my most common uses of the web are nowadays checking the day's weather forecast, news and commentary, the weekly cinema schedules and tonight's TV programmes; I wouldn't have wasted money on any of these when I only had dial-up access. People who have to go to their public library or local college to search will probably only do so for personally significant activities, such as searching for employment or education courses. These important differences in search patterns are not likely to show up in general surveys like those above.

Searching for images

So far, when I've mentioned graphics and images on the web, it's only been to condemn their overuse for glamour, and their underuse for genuine information provision. Since pictures *can* convey so much information—probably far more than the 'thousand words' of the proverb—it's worth looking at what happens when we try to search for them. By definition, they usually don't contain words. So how can you tell a search engine what picture you want? Wanting a picture of a cheese omelette or a tea set is easy enough (but see below), but what about wanting a picture to illustrate an article on poverty? Or a cartoon that your father will laugh at for a birthday card you're creating for him? Some elegant and thoughtful work has gone into image storage and retrieval, and the results are starting to bear fruit on the web.

Inspired by Rudolf Arnheim's classic book of the 1960s, *Visual Thinking*, [12] in which Arnheim discussed the value of imagery in people's thought as well as in education and art, Peter Enser at the University of Brighton wrote a thoughtful paper in 1995 on the situation we find ourselves in now. [87] As he suggested, the web is only the latest in a long line of technologies that have filled our society with more visual imagery than ever before. We travel more and buy international products, so we rely on pictograms and icons at the airport and on the car dashboard, and the watch-those-details-or-it-won't-fit diagrams in the instructions for our Swedish furniture. The twentieth century saw cheap cameras and colour film, television, increasingly image-filled magazines and newspapers (due to cheaper colour printing methods), video recorders and camcorders. By the end of it, cheap scanners and cameras were letting us convert our visual imagery collections into an online kaleidoscope.

Yet when all of these images and videos are online, how can we find what we want? Arnheim, although he couldn't foresee the web and the development of massive image databases, pointed out that since computers didn't have our mechanisms of perception, they had enormous trouble processing even the most basic interpretation of shapes in simple diagrams.

This is still mostly true. These days computers are extremely sophisticated at handling maps, images and even complete three-dimensional worlds, and items (such as map features) within all of those can have text 'attributes' attached saying what they are. These are most often stored as **vector graphics**. But ordinary pictures and photos still tend to be **raster graphics**, where the computer just knows that a range of pixels is a certain colour. Scan in a copy of one of Monet's water lily paintings, and the machine won't have much of a clue.

At best, you can feed the image into a program using an **algorithm** for image-processing, which itself would probably have been derived from Marr's pioneering work in the 1970s on modelling the basic edge-detecting processes of human vision, [187] but probably adding some intelligent interpretation of the colour variations. Such a program may pick out the bridge and the individual lily pads. It may decide from the predominance of green that the picture was an outdoor natural scene (if it had been programmed to look for this), and it might be able to retrieve other scenes with a similar preponderance of green (but these could well include a St Patrick's Day party).

If it was *really* well programmed, it might realise that the out-of-focus edges and blurry blobs it was trying to detect were typical of Impressionist painting. However, it probably could not assign any abstract descriptions such as 'dreamy', nor identify the lily pads as such (unless it deduced their identity, somewhat riskily, from the presence of the bridge and the blue background). So most of the meaning of the picture would be lost on it.

If we asked it to retrieve the image, we'd probably have to use words to do so (unless we were excellent sketch artists), but the words, which to us have the same meaning as the picture, are the very words which the computer couldn't grasp for itself. If this is true for a highly stereotyped painting (and we can only shudder at what an algorithm would make of Cubism or abstract art), how much more is it true for the subtly different blobs of, say, cervical smear samples or other medical imagery? How can we ever make computers handle images in a useful way?

Arnheim also discussed that problematic link between words and pictures. He stressed the limitations of language, particularly its 'linearity'. As linguists and psychologists are well aware, language is sequential, i.e. you can only say one word at a time, so you utter a stream of them, a little like drawing a single line on a page. Obviously, this 'line' of words is rich in content, but it still constrains our description of, say, Monet's paintings to a very limited and syntax-dependent string. Arnheim considered situations where language can be more than one-dimensional, e.g. in concrete poetry or in opera duets. However, it is still true that our attention only allows us to notice one stream of words at a time even though we can occasionally pick up the odd word (such as our name) from another conversation going on in the room.

In fact, our ability to listen to just one conversation when others are all around us, the famous 'cocktail party phenomenon' studied in psychology since the 1950s, is generally an asset rather than a drawback. [124] Yet in Arnheim's view, this made language an 'overrated' medium of communication compared to imagery. We have to build up a mental picture of what's being described rather slowly, whereas a picture can have an instant and rich effect on our understanding. (But Arnheim was careful to distance himself from the idea that pictures are always necessarily helpful, e.g. bad diagram use in education.)

So, returning to the present day and our online searching problem, what can we do to help a computer with the translation between word and image? The answer seems to lie, at least for the present, in human classification (since, as the dmoz Open Directory Project website claims, [79] 'Humans do it better'). Yet classification of images is also a tricky topic: is the Monet painting to be classified as such, or as a mainly green image with some pink and blue bits, or as an outdoor garden scene, or as an image of tranquillity, or as a useful inoffensive graphic for a chocolate box lid? On this, Enser quoted Panofsky, an expert on art, who suggested as long ago as 1955 that we can classify images via two major classification schemes:

(1) the four simple questions Who? What? Where? and When? or

(2) within each one, the *pre-iconography* (the primary subject matter, i.e. what's actually depicted e.g. 'two old people', 'rocky landscape'), the *iconography* (the interpretation to be placed on the image, e.g. who the person is, where the actual location is), and the deeper *iconology* (intrinsic meaning i.e. abstractions and emotions).

Even if we just look at the level of the pre-iconography of a picture, we start to appreciate the trouble pictures can give us. All pictures, as Enser emphasised, are both 'of' and 'about' things: the former is an objective perceptual judgment, while the latter is more subjective. Of course, cultural differences and subjectivity affect the icono-graphic and iconological aspects even more than that. Iconology is especially problematic, since cataloguers can never quite predict what someone will ask for. Enser cited examples of people asking photograph collection curators for photographs of Europeans 'being colonial', or for 'Edward VIII looking stupid'.

So, like texts, images have different meanings to different people. I talk a lot in this book about the struggle to find text information that fits our needs and answers our questions, and how librarians' assumptions about those needs are often different from ours as users. Images raise the bar higher still. Fortunately, very clever technologies are developing to help us. Companies have produced excellent software which lets you ask for pictures that are more or less *visually* similar to a presented one in different ways, e.g. colour, brightness, shape or texture—all things that a computer can easily assess for you.

An example of this technology, at the time of writing this, was Convera's online demo of its Visual RetrievalWare™.[58] It seems to work quite well: click on an image of a rock with waves crashing over it and you get other seashore pictures to choose from. Great when your search is largely about visual similarities. For databases of medical images, matching such visual characteristics can mean the difference between normality and cancer, although they may be a less common focus in everyday life, as I suggested above.

More helpful from a semantic point of view are attempts to adopt classification schemes along the lines originally suggested by thinkers like Panofsky (who, it should be remembered, had never seen an online image database). Museums and libraries are keen to put 'meaning' into their categorisations of images, and a great deal of standardisation work is creating this **metadata.** Such work is extremely tedious-sounding to anyone outside information and computer science, but quite important to help us search more effectively in the future.

So, say I'd like to find an image of an expensive tea set. I search for an image, using a search engine's image-searching option, and I search for 'teacup'. The first few images I see are all of cups with no saucers, so I try searching for 'saucer' and instead see images of spaceships and children's toys. Fortunately 'cup and saucer' does much better, and 'porcelain cup and saucer' better still, bringing me some highly individual designs. Yet 'expensive tea set' brings back pictures of horses (with the tagline 'Expensive decision'), balance sheets and dollar signs, as well as (thank goodness) one or two actual tea sets. This is overall a poorer result than 'porcelain cup and saucer', even though I specified exactly what I really wanted (some tea sets are not porcelain).

The moral: searching for images on the web, at least at present, involves almost exactly the same techniques as searching for text. In other words, you need to type words that will match the description that somebody else has created in the image's metadata. That's the best we can realistically expect for now. Another thoughtful image retrieval researcher, John Eakins,[85] has suggested that any attempt at automatic indexing of image content by computers, beyond the basic level of recognising simple shapes and pre-iconographic identities, is likely to remain crude and unhelpful for years to come. So we still depend on communicating with fellow humans, indirectly through the computer, to find what we want, just as we always have.

How do we search?

Librarians 1, Computer Scientists 1

First, a little politics. The endless ability of librarians and computer scientists to underestimate each other has been a constant unspoken theme in information research. Librarians (often rightly) subtly critique the technology-centred systems that big commercial companies foist on them, and express despair at end-users' failure to use them well. Their literature is full of insistence on the need to redesign the technology (although often their suggestions about how are too vague to be useful to a programmer), and further insistence on the continuing need for their own existence as intermediaries. It almost goes without saying that they have very strong personal motives for these attitudes, as described back in 1986 by Marydee Ojala:[217]

> 'Librarians fear that their operations will be transformed from research facilities to warehouses for document delivery to online searchers. Some fear that the arrival of widespread full-text databases will make even the warehouse function obsolete. What will be left will be a training function.' (p. 201)

Ojala felt that the rumours of libraries' death had been exaggerated, and people would always still need intermediaries who could find information effectively on their behalf. And, as she pointed out, many people are excluded from the 'information revolution' by being too poor to afford a computer, or by living in places where none were available. All the same, you can read that sense of professional threat between the lines of many, many library and information science articles about end-users searching on a computer. This should be borne in mind when reading the research reviewed in this chapter.

On the other side, computer scientists seem to have little confidence in librarians' ability to beat the machines and find better information. Hence this quotation a few years ago from Brian Pinkerton, the founder of WebCrawler (one of the clever automatic programs that move from website to website, attempting to index the whole internet), comparing an internet search to a chat with a librarian:[282] 'Imagine walking up to a librarian and saying "travel". They're going to look at you with a blank face.'

Of course Pinkerton wanted to 'talk up' his software, but this statement couldn't be further from the truth. Most librarians' first reaction, if such abrupt rudeness got you anywhere, would be to point you straight to their carefully indexed section of travel books. Some search engines, by contrast, will bring you everything they've ever seen with the word 'travel' in it, although like the librarian they'll helpfully start with the items whose title or metadata contain 'travel', followed by the other items which mention the word most prominently. This approach, though, could still mean you'd miss many sites which described a place and/or how to reach it without using the word 'travel' anywhere in the text.

Similarly, the librarian could fail to lead you to, say, Bill Bryson's *The Lost Continent*[40] if it had been shelved under humour instead of travel writing. There is no perfect helper, either human or digital. But we have to use one, because we can't trawl item by item through every shelf, file, database or website. So searching for information is a case of the assistant you choose, and how you interact with it.

Searching is messy

When information scientists first started trying to compare different database mechanisms in order to see which ones tended to bring back the best search results, they relied on the assumption that users would go through a sequence roughly like this:

- defining the topic they wanted
- typing in appropriate search terms that fitted the exact topic (or getting an expert intermediary to do it for them)
- picking all *relevant* items out of the results that came back
- stopping and leaving

The 'relevant' items were deemed to be those which, in the eyes of an expert, were exactly on the topic previously defined. All others were assumed to be *irrelevant*. So the traditional measures of **recall** and **precision** were quite easily defined: recall was the percentage of all the database's relevant items which the system had found and displayed (i.e. an inverse measure of 'How much has this search missed out?'). Precision was the percentage of the found items which were relevant (i.e. the inverse of 'How much unwanted rubbish has the search produced?').

Over the years, in fact starting immediately back in the 1960s, many problems emerged in this approach. As we saw in Chapter 2, experts differ greatly from each other on what they decide is 'relevant' to a given topic. Users don't actually care much about recall in some circumstances, or about precision in others. The whole question of defining 'relevance' was pulled apart. What's more, in the past 20 years it's become hugely obvious that people just don't search in this nice simple way at all.

The 'messiness' of people's real-life searching behaviour with a computer only became obvious once non-librarians gained mass access to online databases. Until then, almost the only online searches were of specialist databases of particular types of literature, where you'd find articles on academic or professional topics. You had to ask a trained librarian to do your search, as an **intermediary**, and she or he would stick to the proper procedure. There wasn't much chance to mess around with it. Librarians are busy people, and it was intimidating and time-consuming to ask one to do a special search for you. There was also the cost to consider, back in the days when databases sat on big computers in a single place, dialled up through a modem on special phone lines, and charged by the minute for access. However, as Gary Marchionini has pointed out, [186] at least the process forced you and the librarian to sit down and define the problem you wanted to solve, and to plan the search strategy carefully, something which we nowadays rarely think to do.

Once people started walking into libraries to find that a computer had replaced the card catalogue, and had to sit down and try to use it themselves, it was obvious that reality is *very* messy.

- They don't always know what the exact topic is at the start.
- Even if they think they know it, it'll often change as they learn things from the items they find.
- They won't all just do one straight search and then go away; they may try again with a slightly different search term to get slightly more focused results, or even to 'zoom out' and get some items that give the bigger picture. However, many *will* do a single search when the librarian would have done more than one.
- They won't agree with librarians about what's 'relevant'.
- Sometimes the things that are most *exactly* relevant to the search terms will be of no interest to them whatsoever (they'll already have those, or know the content of them).
- Sometimes they'll be frustrated and confused for some time, and will do repeated searches that don't seem to satisfy them, before finally focusing on what they really want.
- At other times, they'll only be looking for one thing that confirms what they already believe, and won't care about any other search results (especially ones that contradict it).

So much for neat measures of recall and precision! Some information scientists rose quickly to the challenge of finding different models of the search process, abandoning attempts to focus on system measurements for indicating search 'success'. As we saw previously, some authors, such as Tom Wilson[312] and Nick Belkin[23] suggested that reducing uncertainty, or removing some anomalies in our knowledge, was the goal of searching. Others, like Brenda Dervin[69] and Carol Kuhlthau,[164] acknowledged this but also emphasised an emotional (also known as 'affective') and a active dimension. To them, we can't just look at knowledge without bringing in the way the user *feels* about it and *acts* upon it.

What's more, although most of the authors trying to model the search process suggested several 'stages' or 'phases' that people move through as they perform the search, some like Kuhlthau and Stephen Harter[122] acknowledged that in real life there often isn't a simple sequential progress through those stages. There's lots of backtracking and cycling through with each further search, and people change their idea of the goals and their knowledge of the topic.

As Harter pointed out, if we're looking for a change in our knowledge or thinking, then the last thing we want is something which just says *exactly* what we typed in. That's the equivalent of the computer parroting 'Next train to Bristol from here?' without giving us its departure time! That won't make any change in us at all—it's what we already know. Nor do we want the basic standard textbook about a topic if we're already familiar with it. Off-topic items are of course more important in some academic searches than in everyday factual or known-item searches, precisely because the academic idea of the 'topic' is broader and more abstract to start with, and the goal is to learn more or to elaborate.

However, sadly, while what we type in is exactly *not* what we want, most systems still simply match that exact input to some documents, instead of trying to infer what we really want from it. If we take the above point of view, almost every search engine we use is trying to give us the wrong thing.

When it gets it right, therefore, it's for one of these reasons:

- Someone programmed the system to provide certain information, and that's all it does, instead of searching a database of text records for the exact words you typed. It matches the words not to documents containing them, but to information which has to be calculated and assembled before being displayed (e.g. a rail timetable database).
- The words you typed *do* in fact appear the most in the very items you want, i.e. the ones that do contain the extra information

you're looking for. Typing the name of an obscure disease into any internet search engine will probably retrieve relevant medical and self-help information, for instance, although typing 'heart' won't.

- The system has some crude 'intelligence' programmed into it, that spots certain types of query and treats them as 'special cases' by bringing back predefined 'top' results.
- Some real *semantic* matching is going on, so that the system bothers to get you to a comprehensive cinema listings site when you type 'entertainment', or to a site on wildlife when you type 'animals'. Once again, though, if you really wanted the 1960s pop group, this is more likely to annoy or amuse than actually to help.

The first two of the above success scenarios are, of course, limited to specific situations which just don't always fit our information needs. However, the third and fourth show that even with a system which actually does, like a human, try to achieve relevance and infer what we want, we will always need our own wits about us too, and will still need to interpret critically everything we're given. Our cognitive armoury needs to include an awareness of the choices that somebody else would *like* us to make, as well as the ones we were aiming for.

Searching in a 'context'

In the last chapter, I discussed the differences between our communications with people and our attempts to interact with computers in terms of semiotics. I suggested that the computer isn't able to share the assumptions, or **pragmatics,** that underlie our normal communication with people.

Not everyone agrees with this view of pragmatics, though. In a sophisticated series of arguments in a 1986 book,[272] psycholinguists Dan Sperber and Deirdre Wilson rejected the idea that we can identify a list of shared assumptions for any communication between any two people. They argued that theorists had underestimated the amount that we *infer* from what we hear, about the implicit thought as well as the explicit meaning of the words. How, they asked, could we know which assumptions we do, and don't, share with the other person? How could we quickly mentally process so many possible assumptions, each time we spoke? And, if some of those assumptions were about what the other person assumed about *our* assumptions, things would become very circular and confusing, like the old 1970s Kursaal Flyers song 'Little does she know that I know that she knows that I know she's cheating on me . . .'

Instead, Sperber and Wilson argued that rather than a long list of assumptions, we operate in a *cognitive environment* which includes our knowledge, our intentions, and the context of what we're saying. In any given context certain aspects are obvious and other things are less so, but above all some things seem particularly *relevant*. The context would include the current topic of conversation, as well as the physical environment that both people were in and the means by which they were communicating. In fact, the relative relevance of anything that someone might say depends on this context.

So, for instance, 'What was that noise?' would not seem irrelevant to the *people* in the room, even if it was irrelevant to the *topic* of their conversation. Nor would 'Are you feeling okay?' if said to a participant who was unusually quiet or aggressive. Certain tangents leading off from the main topic, as well as certain niggly details that seemed trivial to an outsider, would be seen as relevant under some circumstances, as might analogies with completely separate situations. This social context surrounding our cognitions and utterances is increasingly recognised in psychology, linguistics and even computer science,[315] although it still stays on the sidelines in most lab work.

What has all this got to do with searching for information on a computer? Well, if we are to build more intelligent, effective search support, we need to build something which works a lot more like a human listener than a dumb matching device. We also need to talk to it in ways that help it to infer the context we're working in. Rather than just saying 'travel' we should elaborate our requests as much as possible; i.e., we should use more words.

Attempts to build better information retrieval systems have generally found far better results by 'expanding the query' (going beyond the set of items originally found that was based on the first word that people typed). Either the computer can use an internal thesaurus or other mechanism to relate the items to other, similar, items, or it can ask the users which of the various types of retrieved item is the type of thing they want. Michael Lesk[176] reviewed several major attempts to build more effective systems and added, echoing Sperber and Wilson:

> Note the importance of expanding the queries; nearly everyone found this useful in getting better performance. This models the reality that librarians do better if they can get their users to talk more about what they want. Too much of a conventional question is implied rather than explicit, and making it explicit helps. (pp. 171–2)

However, Sperber and Wilson's analysis implies that the *computer* should also expand on its assumptions. It shouldn't (though most still currently do) act as if it was just playing Snap, stupidly matching up anything that contained the words we told it. Instead, ideally the computer would take account of the context in which we're working:

- The other information we've just been looking at, and searches we've previously performed.
- The other things we're trying to do with the computer at the time (such as writing a document with a word-processor).
- The country we're sitting in at the time, and perhaps the institution or internet domain we're in as well (all of which is automatically detectable from our computer's network address).
- The level of sophistication in the language we use as we ask it a question.
- Our tendency to make spelling errors (or pronunciation errors, when using voice input).
- The level of technical expertise we seem to possess, based on the functions and features we've used.
- The alternative possibility that some or all of the above actually *doesn't* affect what we're looking for right now.

We want a computer whose cognitive environment, in other words, is richer than a simple matching algorithm to a big database. We need this because what we want is not a simple match, just as we don't want *Travels with My Aunt*[117] when we say 'travel?' to a librarian. We want what Marchionini,[186] quoting earlier work by Wilson, called 'situational relevance' as opposed to 'logical relevance'.

In **HCI,** the research area which attempts to build in more knowledge of the user's context is called 'user modelling', and the efforts that have been put into this area could well be refined by application to information seeking. Yet most have only considered how to improve the user interface to match the user's *skill* level. This is another important aspect, as we'll see, but one that avoids considering the *content* of people's tasks.

As I said above, there's a limit to what we can get the computer to know, and privacy is also an important issue here, but there's still room for more systems that would use context knowledge much more than in traditional computing developments. As mentioned earlier, the online retail shop Amazon[10] keeps track of the items you buy. When your computer next accesses the Amazon website, a list of tempting 'recommendations' is displayed, retrieved from quite refined product categories based on what the system has learned about your tastes. This strategy works with me and leads me to a 'serendipitous' purchase around one time in every four or five visits.

Of course Amazon's suggestions become more accurate with more use, but it often displays items I've already obtained from other sources because of course it doesn't know this. Its knowledge of the 'context' is limited to what I've previously done with the computer, since it doesn't come with me when I shop downtown. Nevertheless, if a retail site can show this much context knowledge concerning its customers, surely more information services could do the same. Amazon shows that money talks: commercial websites are leading the way in user-centred information provision. Users' relevance never translated so directly into cash for developers of traditional databases.

The key to Amazon's success is by using humans' choices to define what are really semi-**semantic** links between items, so that the site links related ones to each other rather than using quickly outgrown classification schemes, although it does have those for browsing. It seems to learn from its customers and so it can tell you, 'Other people who bought this book also bought these ...' just like an old-fashioned shopkeeper.

Another suggestion made by Sperber and Wilson is that the context isn't something which we decide about *before* we hear someone speak. Instead, once we've heard what they've said, we try to decide what context it's relevant to, and some possible contexts will be more likely than others. So, if we've just been talking about the weather, that's a prime candidate, as would be a noise we've both just heard, or the overall task that we're engaged in at the time, such as shopping or travelling. We don't just have one, static, context, but many possible ones at any given time.

Similarly, a computer that responded to our information requests would have to be prepared to pick among a number of relevant interests that we had shown in previous searches, with the latest and the previously most frequent topics being more likely than others. Amazon does the same, keeping track of my blues albums as well as my psychology books, but not suggesting a B. B. King CD when I'm hunting for a book on attention. Many other commercial sites are trying to build in this adaptiveness to users' interests, but most tend to thrust off-putting registration forms and all-too-forgettable password logins at us to do so. The only alternative at present is the less mobile option of **cookies**. New ways of personal identification may remove the 'password overload' phenomenon, but pose additional risks to privacy and civil liberties, as illustrated in a 2002 sci-fi film, *Minority Report*, where the patterns in a person's eyes are computer-scanned for every transaction in the same way as driving licences or passports.

Models and metaphors of the system

This notion of adaptive computing brings us back to the issue of how *we* mentally characterise what's going on with the computer—our **mental models**. Bryce Allen[8] has discussed some of the ways that the user's assumed mental models of both the task they're doing and the system they're using are relevant to searching information systems, and it's worth drawing on his discussion.

I talked in the last chapter about our model of the task we think we want to do (i.e. find and use some information), so let's consider our model of the system. As Allen pointed out, the *metaphors* used within a system's 'user interface' (which usually consists of the bits you see on the screen, and the ways you can respond to them) make a big difference to the user's attempt to make sense of what's going on.

This has long been recognised in HCI research, although software engineers still sometimes carelessly apply metaphors. We wince or laugh when we hear somebody mix metaphors in speech or in print. We ought to worry more when the metaphors picked by software designers don't fit either with each other or with users' likely ways of seeing the system.

The most famous example of this is the so-called 'desktop' metaphor used by both Apple's and Microsoft's windowing environments, where the 'trashcan' (or in British English waste bin) sits on the desktop. In Apple's case you eject a disk by dragging its image into this bin (although nowadays the bin magically becomes a strange-looking arrow symbol as we do this), causing many novice users to worry that they might have deleted the files on the disk in the process.

It's not just the bin, either, as shown in Figure 3.2. Software developers ask us to believe that alongside it on our fantasy desk sits at least one windowpane, some packages, an arrow, some folders stuffed inside each other, some tools, a set of menus, and occasionally a palette, a few buttons or an entire dock. It's not an office but a seaside restaurant undergoing refurbishment.

Similarly, as we saw with Sherry Turkle's observations earlier (p. 36), the inconsistent way that 'files' and 'documents' work in a computer can bewilder new users. On the other hand, a good metaphor can help users to cope with the new sequence of actions and the set of possibilities that they could use. The idea that information on the internet forms a 'web' of links and threads is one reasonably successful example.

Figure 3.2. Your desk, as seen by a user interface designer.

It isn't just metaphors, though, that help or hinder our interaction with systems: more subtle aspects of the language are also crucial, as we'll see later on.

While systems remain so far from perfect, we need to help people to cope with them, and to do this it would help to understand how their mental models are formed. Christine Borgman, an information scientist who's written perceptively about the difficulty of using information systems, has drawn on ideas from cognitive psychologists on mental model formation.[30] Taking a similar line to the constructivists we discussed earlier, she argued that the main way we establish a model is by acting as a scientist, making hypotheses about what might work, and how and why, and then testing them.

Cognitive psychologists have argued a lot about mental models and their formation in the past 20 years or so, but their studies have taken various different approaches based on exactly what they are trying to explain. There have been studies of people's mental models of how things work, e.g. how a ball falls, or what it is about the earth and the sun that makes winters colder than summers, or how a central heating thermostat controls temperature. These studies have been quite separate in their approach from other work on people's use of models during deductive logical reasoning (which not everyone sees as based on 'models' as such).[91]

The former type of study is probably more relevant to people's models of what the computer is doing and how, and so we'll discuss these further below. The 'models for reasoning' work is of more interest when we consider people's problem with the *task*, and their decisions about what to do next and what the results of their search imply. This, as we saw in the last chapter and will see again later, can fatally damage their chances of getting worthwhile results. As considered elsewhere in this chapter, we should always bear in mind for both types of study that the 'model' idea is to some extent only a metaphor for patterns of knowledge and thought.

The studies on how people think things work have sometimes seemed to show that even for basic physical concepts, such as the direction a physical object would take when dropped by a plane or a moving person, people have naive and mistaken ideas. Given a paper-and-pencil test in which different possible movements are shown and one diagram has to be chosen, most people choose wrongly. [44] There are many other studies along those lines, e.g. people think that their central heating thermostat makes the system put out a higher rate of hot air/water/steam when set to a higher temperature. [151] Most of them actually don't do that, yet *behaving as if* they do will save you money, as you'll probably adjust the thermostat more often instead of leaving heat pumping out when not needed. People think that winters are colder because the Earth is further from the sun in its elliptical (though actually not very far from circular) orbit, forgetting that winter in the northern hemisphere is summer in the south so this model can't be correct.*

Are people stupid? Are we living in a dream world of naive physics? Not really. As I just said, the inaccurate thermostat model is a more fuel-efficient one, not because of its accuracy but because of the resulting actions. More fuel is consumed if you leave the thermostat at a high setting, but this is due to heat loss from the house, so that the boiler stays on longer to keep it hot, not to a higher per-minute heat output from the boiler. You can do the right thing for the wrong reasons, but because it works, you have no need to question those reasons.

You could draw a comparison here to novice computer users, who tend to muddle up a computer's *memory* (a set of electronic circuits that act as small temporary 'stores' of key commands and data only while the computer's switched on) with its *hard disk drive* (which continues to 'store' data when the power's off). But their confusion

---

* It's actually because of the *tilt* of the earth: the northern hemisphere's angle to the sun between September and March makes the sun appear lower in the sky, allowing less heat energy to reach us as well as giving us shorter days.

over this often does no harm: it makes them take care not to waste disk space, and not to run too many programs at once, both of which will ensure that the machine continues to run smoothly.

Again, people searching the internet sometimes wrongly assume that they can only type one word into a search engine box. If the word they choose is highly specific, which is quite likely, then they'll still get what they want. Those with the alternative model that several words are best (which is usually correct) can sometimes type in too many words, making the search engine give up.

Furthermore, and this is crucial, often people's apparent 'models' are different if you test them in different ways. Asking people to walk past a bin, and drop a ball or scrunched-up piece of paper at the right moment for it to fall in, shows no intuitive problem with the curved forward arc the ball will take. Yet the same people will choose the wrong diagram in the paper-and-pencil-test version of the same problem.

Somehow when we have to *interact* with reality, instead of facing abstracted diagrams of it in lab tasks (or on a computer?), we tend to perform better. We also saw this with the studies of Wason's card-choosing task in the last chapter. People can behave more rationally and realistically when asked to consider *actions* to take, than when following the same reasoning simply to 'prove' a rule. So mental models aren't set in stone, and don't always predict what we'll choose to do.

Borgman[30] suggested that computer users need 'conceptual' rather than 'procedural' training to make them search more effectively. In saying this, she seemed to include as 'conceptual' the need to make people aware of synonyms and related words, such as not just typing 'brain' in a search for psychology books when not all of them would explicitly mention the brain in their title, even if they focused on the neuroscience side of the subject. She also suggested teaching people to devise a strategy. For instance, first try searching for this, then go back and try searching for that instead. Then combine the two searches (something which traditional database systems often let you do, by using Boolean logic; 'fuzzy' systems like most internet search engines don't need to give you this option, as you could type the whole thing in at one go).

This isn't the same as teaching the 'conceptual' *workings* of the system: Borgman's recommendations were really for action-oriented training, rather than deeper educational enlightenment, and this focus on learning how to *act* is likely to produce better results sooner than a course in the underlying mechanisms. Think more about your *concepts* and how to apply them, but you shouldn't have to think much more about the *machine*.

Another implication of this is that people don't need to worry too much if they don't understand how the computer (or the internet) really works. Obviously those who do understand can apply that knowledge usefully to some extent, as I discussed earlier. However, with the internet and many other information systems, the most crucial thing is understanding the types of content that people have put out there, *not* the bells and whistles of relational database technology or packet switching telecommunications. Here is another sense in which 'conceptual' knowledge is more important. But even a novice user can be shown, by demonstration ('procedural'), the sorts of things to type and not to type, the things worth clicking on and those likely to be dross, the search engines in which to try Boolean logic and those in which more words are better. You don't need the rocket science.

Similarly, in Yvonne Waern's book[300] on cognitive aspects of computing tasks, she pondered what we actually mean by a 'model'. She pointed out three major aspects of what we know about a system: WHAT it does (its functions), HOW it does it (the processes), and WHY it does it that way (the underlying structure and rationale of the way things work). We can, she points out, understand the WHAT and some of the HOW of a system, and be able to spot its similarity to another (e.g. two online search engines), and yet we might not understand their underlying processes or rationale (HOW and WHY). So we might mistakenly assume that the processes in one are the same as in the other.

There are many examples of the latter happening. The big study of people's queries with the Excite search engine, discussed elsewhere in this chapter, showed for instance that people often tried to include symbols such as '&' to mean the **Boolean** 'AND' operator, because certain other search engines used it as such, but unfortunately Excite didn't.

Waern argued that when we talk loosely about users' mental models of 'the system', we have to remember that most users neither know about *everything* the system does, nor care—they only 'model' what they need to know. Somehow we have an internal representation only of how *this* bit works, how it fits in with *that* bit, and how much it's similar to the similar bit of that *other* software. She suggested that when we find that our model isn't good enough, we become curious enough to start exploring in our own right in order to build a better mental model of what's going on in the system. She may be right—some of us become interested enough in a piece of software to 'play' with it—but most of the time, as she herself said at another point in the same book, people don't 'play' enough and so don't develop a perfect model.

Alan Cooper's recent book on the software industry, *The Inmates Are Running the Asylum,*[59] put this more forcefully. Cooper is a hugely well-connected and experienced former software developer who is now a user-centred design specialist. He describes what programmers imagine as the 'user' as *homo logicus*. This odd species, who looks something like themselves, likes control and therefore puts up with complexity so that he (it's inevitably a he) can do *exactly* the cleverest thing. He also wants to understand the system inside out, and therefore is prepared to fail and mess up his work while learning. As Cooper puts it, most people cease to be novice users who need hand-holding 'wizard' tutorials, but never make it to expert level: 'When people achieve an adequate level of experience and ability, they generally stay there forever ... users take no joy in learning [the system], so they learn just the minimum and then stop. Only *homo logicus* find learning complex systems to be fun' (p. 183).

There's no need to spend ages developing encyclopaedic knowledge of a system when it's only there to use as a tool. We just need the practical knowledge to get us through the job. We don't want egotistic product designers assuming that their product is so interesting that we'll want to read all about it in a long and badly structured manual before we do any work with it. As users, we're so much more impressed if we can just get on and achieve something straight away. Having achieved that something, though, two things may happen: either we are misled by our success into thinking we have no more to learn, or we are so motivated and pleased with the system that we decide it's worth seeing what else it can do, and learning its HOW and WHY as well as its WHAT.

Anyone designing any tool more complicated than, say, a hammer should want to lead us gracefully into the latter situation, where we learn to use their product properly because we want to. We would do so gradually while achieving our tasks, rather than investing a large amount of our valuable time beforehand (and then forgetting half of it).

The user interface people at AltaVista, another popular search engine, clearly had this idea in mind a few years ago when they implemented random 'tips' (which have since been removed). These let you learn single searching tricks in a drip-feed way each time you went back for another search, and so they were more likely to succeed (for a user who wanted to learn better strategies over time) than any number of long help pages. Nevertheless, when we do want to know how to narrow our search, we should be able to find more extensive help quickly in every system we use.

In a 1996 study, Nahl and Tenopir[203] found that when users could ask questions of a real human being while they were searching, 46%

of the time those questions were not technical but *emotional*: nervousness about whether they were doing it right, surprise at things that they found, and so on, thus echoing Kuhlthau's concern with the emotional aspects of searching. People need reassurance just as much as knowledge.

Nahl and Tenopir's study struck at the most obvious, and most often overlooked, feature of online searching: usually *nobody tells you if you're doing it right*. So it's not surprising if you're uncertain and frustrated. This is an activity where you gain no feedback about your efforts, except from a computer which doesn't know what you're trying to do. If it's designed according to good HCI practice, the system would not blame or criticise you for errors anyway, but would assume responsibility for them; yet failing to find what you want *isn't* an obvious error, so most systems will have nothing to say.* Maybe you could seek advice from a librarian or internet guru, but you may be too embarrassed to ask, even if one is nearby.

Yet given the chance, with a database designer standing beside you, wouldn't it make sense to ask, 'Is this the best way to do this? ... Is that really all that's in there? ... Is it meant to work this way? ... Is it okay to type that character?' and so on?

However, partly because you can't easily ask a person, you can easily forget that such questions are *worth* asking. Perhaps it doesn't occur to many users to question their mental models, because after all computers are meant to be easy, and people usually have to learn their use all by themselves. What's more, many people still tend to feel quite shy about asking for help, and most of us are afraid of apparently wasting time in 'training' when we have so much else to do.

Problems with the 'model' approach: rats and apple pie

In the late 1980s Waern studied people learning to use word-processing software, and showed that people develop their own models even if you've already given them an analogy to base them on. They will immediately start noting where the new system differs from the analogy, and this critical approach is necessary for them to appreciate the best way of doing things. When asked to describe how the system worked, her users found it hard to describe their models, and in fact many HCI studies have struggled to define what a person's system model would actually 'look like'.

---

*Some, though, will make a brief suggestion if many hundreds of results, or none, are retrieved, about how you might revise your search. This hint can be irritating to the experienced user, but may help a novice.

Perhaps it's best to see our 'model' not as a clear or easily accessed mental picture, but as a 'toolbox' of procedures and deductions about how one bit might work the same way as another, which we can retrieve from memory only when we actually need to use them (or imagine using them). As Theodore Roszak[248] wrote in the 1980s, it's not just our mental models of using computer systems, but of *every* accomplishment, which are often more about actions than pictures:

> Computers 'remember' things in the form of discrete entities: the input of quantities, graphics, words, etc. Each item is separable ... Unless the machine malfunctions, it can regurgitate everything it has stored exactly as it was entered ... That is what we expect of the machine ... [Humans] remember things as no computer can—in our muscles and reflexes: how to swim, play an instrument, use a tool. These stored experiences lodge below the level of awareness and articulation so that there is no way to tell someone how we drive a car or paint a picture. We don't actually 'know' ourselves. In an old bit of folk wisdom, the daughter asks her mother how she bakes such a good apple pie. The mother, stymied, replies: 'First I wash my hands. Then I put on a clean apron. Then I go into the kitchen and bake a good apple pie.' (pp. 96–7)

Roszak wrote that therefore the way we store information in our brains is quite different from the representations stored by computers themselves. This is true to some extent, in so far as the circuitry of the brain is very different from the centrally controlled binary 'on' and 'off' of standard electronic circuits—but it is not fair to say that we just store 'actions' (what psychologists call **procedural** memory) while computers just store 'items'. Every time we start an application, such as a web **browser,** or select a command within it, we tell the computer to run a 'program' of 'instructions'.

Ultimately that is all they have—just millions of instructions to the central processor to change a 1 to a 0 (i.e. to switch a tiny electronic circuit between 'on' and 'off') or vice versa. It's true that on one level all we have ourselves is firing and non-firing neurons, while a computer has a disk that stores data even without power. But like that disk storage, our brain can change what and how it retains information: some brain areas actually change shape and configuration as we learn particular types of knowledge. The way the brain can reorganise its links and structures to adapt to new situations and knowledge is called *plasticity*.[113]

Various evidence has suggested that our knowledge of the world can't just be procedural. Philosophers and psychologists have considered this very carefully: it's very tempting to imagine that our minds are entirely action-based, with all those endlessly firing neurons. As we've already seen, people do seem to reason more logically and solve problems more effectively when focusing on actions rather than abstract facts. However, there's plenty of

116

evidence that we must also cope with those facts and concepts somehow, and that this type of memory is separate from our procedural knowledge of how to do things.[41]

Therefore, most cognitive psychologists try to distinguish this procedural memory, of what to do next and how, from our **declarative** memory of facts, images, associations and events, and within the latter we tend to distinguish the **semantic** or conceptual (memory for things and their meaning) from the **episodic** (past events).

The HCI literature often discusses a 'mental model' as if it was purely semantic, declarative knowledge, that has been put together by abstracting from the episodic (i.e. from individual experiences). Yet as Waern pointed out, the key aspect of a mental model of a computer system is the procedural. With the right procedural knowledge in our mental model, when we sit down in front of the machine we almost automatically solve the problem of using it, just as we solve the 'problem' of tying our shoelaces without conscious fact-juggling effort. This will be the case even if, as we saw above, our declarative knowledge of the underlying system would turn out to be wrong if tested on paper.

For much of the twentieth century, when **behaviourism** held sway in psychology and wouldn't let us worry about what went on within the 'black boxes' of our minds, this learning and reapplying of procedures was called **conditioning**. Rats learned to run around mazes to find food, Pavlov's dogs salivated to the sound of a bell, and people learned to repeat actions that had given them what they wanted the first time.

Some behaviourists still exist.* If you come across a psychologist who seems to mention the word 'behaviour' more than average, they may be one. They are almost invisible to the mainstream community, and form an odd parallel universe with separate journals, websites, conferences and societies.[1] They no longer rely so much on rats to test theories of human behaviour, but they're ultimately still trying to explain behaviour in terms of linking stimuli with responses, without conjuring up complex mental constructs in between the two.

There are times when, tired of research that seems to lead to no coherent predictions or overviews in many areas, I can see their point. The models and distinctions we come up with in mainstream psychology are largely metaphorical, and in the past they were often too vague to be useful in *predicting* behaviour (although that's changed with the growth of computer models). In one sense, Roszak was right that action is all that is really 'in there'. By focusing more

---

*They tend not to call themselves 'behaviourists' these days, but 'behaviour analysts'.

on what we expect people to *do*, and testing how often they do what we predict, maybe we can make more progress in some areas where we often only seem to produce broad *post hoc* explanations, such as much of social psychology.

Behaviourists face many problems and prejudices, but they carry on regardless. They have struggled for many years with problems like the fact that we seem to associate together things that we've never seen or experienced together, once they're both associated with something else we know about. This is hard to pull off without coming up with some kind of mental structure! The stimulus-response relational theories [125] that they have developed to explain this end up vaguely resembling the cognitivists' **schema** theory of the 1960s and 1970s, i.e. a network of associations which are strengthened by exposure to related items. This makes it too easy for mainstream cognitivists to treat them as merely 'backward'.

However, the behaviour-analytic researchers, in their laboratories where nothing exists until proven, are doing us a great favour by showing what our theories would look like if they stuck to pure evidence-based logic. There's real hope in this. As the behaviourists continue to develop their theories, perhaps their work will merge with the findings of neuroscience and mainstream experimental research, and we'll manage to build some truly predictive theories of cognition that don't depend on vague concepts and metaphors.

Mainstream cognitive researchers have wrestled for years with almost the *opposite* problem to the behaviourists' patterns of association. As we saw in the last chapter, we *won't* always manage to transfer the problem-solving knowledge or 'mental model' that we've developed in one situation, e.g. with one particular piece of software or search engine, to other systems, especially if they look very different on the surface. We won't apply the procedures to one that we applied to another. Sometimes it's almost as if we don't have any permanent 'model' or 'schema' at all, but just repeat old actions and rules arbitrarily without any sense of a 'picture' of what's going on. Yet at other times, as I showed above, we do transfer our knowledge, but incorrectly. So we may not realise that systems tend to differ in minor but result-transforming ways, e.g. on how they interpret a phrase such as 'fish and chips'.

In some important recent work, psychologists are pulling these findings together into a more coherent picture. They are developing predictive models of the situations where we do, and where we don't, transfer knowledge from one problem to another. [135] These and other cognitive science models are far more specific and interesting than the traditional, vague, everything-links-together, schemata ideas, although one worry with them is how well they can cope with the 'messiness' of everyday thought and action. It may be a while before they can predict every situation (in fact, it may never happen, given the context-specific effects of emotion, fatigue, personality, intelligence and motivation), but their predictions are worth considering by information scientists and system designers alike.

To sum up, the least we expect of ourselves is to be able to use the same system repeatedly without suddenly 'forgetting' what to do. To do this, we have some way in our minds (a 'model', 'script', 'schema', or 'series of stimulus-response associations', depending on your favourite theory) to link together the different kinds of memory that we seem to hold, and turn them into tools to solve a repeating problem. As psychologists have long known, this learning process isn't observable by introspection. However, to some extent we can use our metacognition consciously to probe it—to ask 'why did I think that would work?' questions—in an effort to force our 'weakest links' to improve or be discarded.

Expertise

I mentioned expertise above when I considered the effect of users' expectations and system knowledge. Obviously, it's very closely linked to the idea of mental models that I was just discussing. What can psychologists tell us about expertise? Can they help us identify how some people seem to be better at searching than others? Is it just a case of knowing more about the task, and the websites and databases? Probably not; expertise also lies in choosing between strategies, and spotting patterns. Psychologists' studies of chess players' expertise can help us to see how this works.[110] When people play chess, their goal is to win, or at least to avoid losing. However, this goal is quite **ill-defined**, in that there are many ways of getting there. Chess masters and grandmasters, on careful observation by psychologists, are better at achieving this unclear goal than mere novice players because of three things:

1. They recognise particular groupings of pieces in a board arrangement, and think of those groupings in 'chunks' rather than looking at the queen or a pawn on its own. This helps them build an awareness of the 'deep structure' of what's going on across the board, and what can or can't be done next.
2. Unlike early chess computers, they *don't* appear to consider *more* moves, or look further ahead, than novices. (We know this because they still win even at 'speed chess'.)
3. They've probably learned from their mistakes, and therefore have a better idea of which kinds of strategies tend to be more

successful. Based on this, and their awareness of the rules, they won't even consider some moves which novices might ponder.

The grandmaster sees the 'big picture' of the current game position and what it means. Similarly, studies of expert physicists show that they look at the 'deep structure' of a physics problem by realising which strategies could work, based on a real understanding of what is, and isn't, relevant.

It isn't immediately obvious how we can apply this to the issue of telling a computer what information we want, but we can. The reason expert internet searchers may sometimes be better than you at searching a database to find, say, the 'Lumberjack Song' featured in the 1970s BBC comedy show *Monty Python*, is because:

1. They spot and 'chunk together' the logical structure in what you're saying you need: e.g. the search results ought to contain 'python (but NOT snake) AND lumberjack AND EITHER song OR 'suspenders and a bra" (a phrase from the actual lyrics). Similarly, when they see a listing of search results, they can categorise and reject with a quick glance the items which are real lumberjacks' home pages, the python-related wildlife sites even if they don't say the word 'snake', the 'adult' sites about women in scanty underwear, and the Monty Python fan sites that look like raving drivel rather than authoritative information.
2. Like novices, they still may only consider a handful of possible sources and strategies—but they'll be a good choice. An authoritative site about British comedy that's been included in someone else's index, or perhaps a specialist search engine for comedy song lyrics, will probably be better than a general-purpose engine that'll turn up lots of individual fans' websites.
3. They base the way they do the search, and the sources or search engines they choose for it, on their experience of what tends to work for a given situation, and what doesn't. For instance, they'll already know that current search engines on the internet are more comprehensive than they used to be, but still tend to leave out thousands of sites, particularly if they're based in the United States but you want something European. And they'll know which search engines let you specify the search more carefully, so that you'll cut out more of the rubbish.

What goes wrong with searching?

Pedantry and pain: old-style searching

To return to my well-worn metaphor about waiters and cheese omelettes, why don't we always get what we want, even if we have the right model and expectations and so on? When we ask humans for something, they can let us down because they fail to comprehend or relay our requests reliably and accurately.

Computers don't have this problem, but sadly they do have others. They often seem to behave more like a school playground joke crossed with Marvin the Paranoid Android from *The Hitchhiker's Guide to the Galaxy*.[2] Too often, what you get returned is precisely what you specified, which isn't at all what you wanted, like the old joke question about arachnophobia being a very long word but how do you spell it? Answer: I-T. Alternatively, you might see an error message stating that the poor system can't cope right now, and perhaps you could try again later. Pedantry and pain. The information science literature has been enlivened for years by sometimes hilarious observations of people's struggles with systems that sometimes seemed wilfully badly designed.[31, 142]

As users, we can't do much about internet sites and databases sometimes crashing from overload (although fortunately, with the ever-decreasing cost of processing and storage, this is becoming much rarer). Instead, let's look a bit more closely at that pedantry issue. What exactly is the problem?

Until only a few years ago, the major issue *seemed* to be the limited and logic-bound way you had to specify search terms when using a database. With the old-fashioned systems we had back then,* if you spelt a word one way, then that spelling and only that spelling would be used. If you asked for 'cheeses', the computer would never find an item that only contained the singular word 'cheese'. If you wanted to find both omelette and cheese, but not necessarily in the same phrase, you would have to type 'omelette AND cheese', though that wouldn't find any items that only contained one of those words. To find those as well, you had to type 'omelette OR cheese'. This forms part of the logic system known as **Boolean logic**. When it got more complicated and you wanted, say, anything by Delia Smith that was either a cheese dish or an omelette or both, you'd have to use

---

* I've optimistically described rigid record-based, Boolean-search-only databases in the past tense, but in reality, at the time of writing I'm still having to use such systems every day in my academic work since most bibliographic databases still work this way. There are probably thousands of other people out there also still using such systems.

brackets like this: 'Delia AND Smith AND (cheese OR omelette)', like in school arithmetic.

On top of all this, in those days you had to choose which 'field' of the database you wanted the computer to look in, e.g. the title, the date or the author of a book. But you might have wanted both books *about* Delia Smith, and ones written *by* her. Or you might have wanted any items which mentioned 'cheese' anywhere. And if you said you wanted 'cheese' in the title, some systems would even be stupid enough to think you only wanted things that were *just* entitled 'Cheese' (or in other systems, only titles that had 'cheese' as the first word). It was more complicated to do a broad search than to do a narrow one, unless you chose a vague term that would be in lots of things and wouldn't help you distinguish among them. It caught you between the proverbial rock and hard place.

With the English language being so rich with synonyms and shades of meaning, even that one vague term might not be enough if some of the records had used a different word, such as 'logic' instead of 'rationale' or 'affective' instead of 'emotional', or even 'canine' instead of 'dog'. Even librarians, trained in the importance of consistent standardisation in classifying things, vary enormously in the words they choose to describe items,[56] so a system with no thesaurus or concept-linking won't stand a chance of retrieving everything relevant.

Since AND and OR have more flexible meanings in English than they do on computers, many people made mistakes with this distinction. If they wanted items connected with a set of words, but *not* necessarily containing *every* single one of them *every* time, it would be incorrect to enter the words with AND between them. But people would often do so, because in English we often use 'and' loosely in this way. Similarly, in English OR might mean 'this or that but not both' or else 'this or that or both, I don't mind' in different contexts, but on computers it always means the latter. Also, sometimes people would forget to put any Boolean term between the words, so the computer thought they meant a complete phrase with the words in that order, e.g. 'cheese omelette Delia Smith' (which works on most modern search engines, so people are probably now even more likely to make this mistake when they encounter an older system).

Christine Borgman[31] attributed people's problems with Boolean logic to the classic 1970s psychology findings of Amos Tversky and Daniel Kahneman[148] that people are biased in their application of logic to decisions, and pay too much attention to the context, following 'heuristic' intuition rather than careful rationale. Actually, most of Tversky and Kahneman's work on people's biases did not focus on our use of Boolean logic, but on the context-based biases people show in more typical (and arguably complex) everyday scenarios, mainly those involving judging the probability or risk of an event given knowledge about similar events. Their work was fascinating, and important for our decisions about health risks and financial choices, but it doesn't directly connect to people's use of Booleans with computers.

Other cognitive psychologists have pointed to people's problems with Boolean-type logic, [183, 228] but several have pointed out that we don't need to accuse people of being irrational in this particular situation. The ambiguities in the English language cause the problem, and people are of course likely, quite logically, to expect AND and OR to mean similar things (i.e. to continue to be ambiguous) in computer languages as well. Whether they will assume OR to mean 'inclusive OR' ('this or that or both, I don't mind') or 'exclusive OR' (XOR: 'this or that but not both') probably depends on their most common use of it in ordinary life. Much of the time, of course, we don't even think consciously about whether to choose AND or OR in a sentence we're uttering or writing, so we won't be prepared for their effects on the hardwired, ambiguity-eschewing computer.

With these older systems, people would also forget the possibility of shortening or 'stemming' the terms they typed in, even though they usually were allowed to do so using a so-called 'wildcard' character (e.g. 'chees$' to find cheesy, cheese, cheeses and cheesemaker). And, since this 'wildcard' was a different character in different databases (maybe a question mark, an asterisk, a dollar sign . . .), they could enter the wrong one accidentally.

Like many of the problems ascribed despairingly to human error in the information science literature, this one is easily avoided with a little system intelligence. Applying linguistic rules and running through lists of their exceptions are bread and butter to a computer after all: they're exactly the sort of task it was designed for.

As for specifying specific 'fields' to search in older databases, people would make such mistakes as asking for 'cheese' in the title without realising how much that restricted them, or asking for 'Delia' as a keyword when that was too specific for a librarian to have entered as a special category. Finally, even if they did each search correctly (or well enough), they would forget, or not bother, to combine a series of searches to improve the 'recall' and 'precision' of the search.

Although for years librarians and information scientists were dismayed by people's alleged incompetence with searching, and argued that only trained 'intermediaries' (themselves!) should do the actual searching for their users, they also knew that this was ultimately the system designers' fault. Most library users aren't stupid, but they are busy, and they're not interested in the nuts and bolts of search engines. As Bryce Allen[9] commented in 1996, if you needed a training course to use a bank cash machine (ATM) you'd soon change bank, or start carrying huge wads of cash about with you.

With old, unfriendly information systems, it wasn't *completely* irrational to just do one overall search with a really vague term, get far too much irrelevant rubbish back, and print off the whole big list to scan through visually for yourself. It felt quicker overall and let you feel you were in control of your selection, even though it often took more time and involved just as much potential for missing your ideal items. It was the quickest way to ensure that the search at least found *something*—probably lots and lots of somethings—even if most of the results were unwanted. As we saw earlier, there's some evidence that people do learn to add more words when searching the web, e.g. 'Delia Smith recipe ingredients cheese omelette eggs', but if they also do this when they encounter older systems they'll run into trouble.

It was mostly librarians and information scientists who studied the problems people had with old-fashioned search engines. It was academic computer scientists who invented 'fuzzy' algorithms to replace them. Yet ironically, as I write this most libraries, even academic ones, still have computerised catalogue systems based on old-style databases, which may tell you stupidly that no books have the precise title 'Cheese' just because their title search is set up to be more pedantic than you'd expected. Many such catalogues (often termed OPACs, short for Open Public Access Catalogues) expect you to know which field of the database will hold the term you're looking for, and make it difficult or impossible for you to do a more flexible search.

This probably comes down mainly to lack of money – most universities are cash-starved, as more students are crammed in and managers expect more research productivity for less income all the time. But also, I sometimes suspect that librarians quite like the precise classification and logic of traditional search engines. If you can use them well, rigid record structures and Boolean conditionals (AND, OR, NOT, etc.) are more precisely powerful than fuzzy searching, which is why most search engines still allow you to use Booleans even on their sprawling database of webpages. Of course, trained librarians *can* use them very, very well, and the whole essence of their job focuses on cutting through clutter in neat, systematic ways, so Booleans have a certain appeal.

However, as Bryce Allen also pointed out, there are more subtle problems than the Boolean issue. Most library catalogue systems label the types of search you can do, not by what you want to *find*, but by what you *already know*. An 'author search' doesn't return authors: it asks you to type an author's name. These systems are now so familiar to librarians and regular users that we never notice the strangeness of their demands. Somehow, users have got used to specifying one tiny piece of what they know, rather than what they want to know. We could see this as an example of a system trying to match the context and knowledge the user brings to the task, which we promoted earlier as a good idea, but that would be overstating it. The computer only offers to match one tiny part of your knowledge, not the overall picture.

Users' mental model of such systems tends to have *inconsistencies* within it, but they may have a 'mental model' of a more consistent or a more flexible system than in fact exists. In certain common library systems still in use in British universities at the time of writing, you can type just the surname of an author on 'author searches', or type any words you like in any order for 'keyword searches'. Yet, as I mentioned above, 'title searches' often still expect the entire, perfectly spelled and ordered, title of the work you're looking for.

Of course, the title is the thing people will be most likely to *expect* to use to judge a book's relevance to them. They know that the system will usually display a list of titles in response to their input, even when that input *isn't* title-specific. They also know that books (at least textbooks) about a given topic are likely to have its name in their titles (though of course this is too simplified). Having been encouraged to focus on this not just by other parts of the same system, but also by more flexible search engines on the internet and in other computer systems, users will see a 'title' search as the most obvious thing to try. But typing only one or two topic words will make this search fail, where a keyword search would have worked. Not fair! How have we put up with this for so long?

Similarly, if they select a 'subject' search, thinking that that means they can type any words that they want to describe the content of the book, they can easily fail if the system is actually expecting them to enter one of a limited set of subject *headings* or *classmarks*. And when the hapless user tries an 'author' search, Christine Borgman[30] described evidence that all too often people enter the author's name in the wrong order, such as 'William Shakespeare' instead of the required 'Shakespeare, W'. (Note the comma and space, which are crucial in some library catalogue systems, while others demand a space with no comma, and so on.) Surely, you might think, a system could cope with the name in either order ... but no.

Astonishingly, I have yet to see a library catalogue with a built-in spelling checker, though I'd like to think that one exists somewhere by now. Studies have been demonstrating for 20 years that up to one in four failed searches are due to misspellings,[30] so surely it's worth the effort. Gary Marchionini has pointed out[186] that the built-in spelling correction option in word-processors is making us lazier typists, so this is likely to have a knock-on effect on database use too.

The result is that many library users still fail to find relevant information, either by using inflexible search options which they believe to be flexible, or by mistyping. We might wonder at such a situation arising in the twenty-first century, after around 40 years of relevant research in both HCI and information science. To compensate a little, the technicians who install such catalogue systems often try to warn you of their inadequacies. They often add a line of text on the title-searching screen, warning the user to try a keyword search instead if they don't know the whole title. But to the hapless user, what's a 'keyword'? To some novice users it will be an unfamiliar piece of computer jargon, not a promising way of solving their problem.

In any case, users' tendency to ignore on-screen text when rushing to perform an action is unfortunately all too well known.* Similarly, we don't stop to reflect on the many ways that our search may have gone wrong, when we don't find what we expected. Instead, we grab at a hypothesis ('Maybe I need to add "William" as well') and alter the search accordingly, without noticing that we actually misspelt 'Shakespeare'. We try a different version of the same word ('emotion' instead of 'emotional') without thinking of possible synonyms (e.g. in psychology, emotion is often referred to as 'affect'). We continue to add to a query which was incorrect in the first place, so that errors snowball and we still don't find anything.[142]

The old research figures from the 1980s, showing that up to one in eight user sessions consisted entirely of obviously incorrect queries, are probably still true today. They may even have worsened. Failure is more likely when the design of systems rarely considers our expectations.

The answer lies once again in employing more intelligent searching programs, which don't expect the user to learn strange conceptual and procedural distinctions just to find a book. Software developers

---

*Donald Norman[212] described this most neatly when he considered the irritating warning 'Do you really want to delete MyMostImportantFile.doc?', and how impatiently we tend to hit the 'Yes' button before immediately crying 'Oh, no!' ...

often dismiss users' problems as 'just a user interface issue', but in this case they're wrong. As emphasised by Christine Borgman,[31] this is a perfect example of how the *underlying* system enforces certain mental models which don't fit the users' needs, and which can't be glossed over with a user interface redesign. Yet let's face it, a library catalogue is a simple piece of software (compared to, say, certain huge word-processing packages, and even web browsers). It shouldn't be so hard to design it well.

However, the problems of information seeking are not restricted to computers. Gary Marchionini's painful 1989 study[185] of high-school students struggling with information seeking showed that the same students who had trouble searching an online encyclopaedia also made 'errors' when using printed sources. They didn't make proper use of the books' indexes, and once again didn't think to look for synonyms or related concepts when they couldn't find the term they wanted. To be fair, often book indexes are nonexistent or poor to the point of hilarity (my husband once studied from a physics textbook, full of mathematical proofs, whose index included the entry 'shown, it can be'). Training in information skills, which should ideally start in primary school, is and will always be the best weapon against search failures.

Pragmatics and problems revisited

Even with fuzzy searching, and even when you know how best to use it as above, things can go wrong. The computer can bring back too many irrelevant items (and put them much higher up the list than you expected). We thought we'd got the searching problem licked, but we haven't. Why? Because there are other problems with talking to a computer.

Donald Norman, a famous cognitive psychology and HCI guru, once summarised the conventions and assumptions we use when talking to other people, to show how different they are from the logic used by computers.[213] We tell people only what we think they need to know. We don't usually need to set the context of the topic we're talking about, because they've usually got some awareness of this (except in psychology experiments). We don't usually 'play games', saying trick things or using language in literal and unconventional ways. We assume that people will take the most usual, everyday meaning of what we say, and will believe it to be true. If there's some special condition or circumstance, we mention it, but if not, the listener can assume that everything's normal. And things that are obvious, unimportant or unlikely won't usually be mentioned either. When they are, it means something quite special is going on.

In **semiotics**, the study of signs used in communication, I mentioned earlier that people's background assumptions and motivations form part of the **pragmatics** of a communication. The meaning of the communication itself is called its **semantics**; the way it's said is the **syntactics** or **syntax.** Obviously these are both crucial too (the Boolean confusions above being good examples of syntactic problems). You can see from Don Norman's list, however, that the success of your communication still depends primarily on the pragmatics.

With a computer (at least a web search engine), we have to make a little more effort, partly by using more words, or rather more descriptive words, since obviously we don't need all the 'excuse me' and 'could I have' and 'please' of social interaction. We also need to think consciously about the relationships which we'd assume a person would know but a computer doesn't. We don't have to be as precise and pedantic as we used to be in telling the computer *how* to do the search, but we do still have to put thought into *what* we tell it to retrieve.

We've already seen that the two concepts in information science that describe this desire to get the search right, but without losing the chance to see relevant things, are **recall** and **precision**. If you wanted to get examples of a particular thing, say pictures of teapots, you'd be hoping for high precision but you wouldn't care about the recall: you don't need *all* the teapot pictures that are out there on the web. Someone doing a PhD won't get their dissertation passed if they don't know pretty much *everything* that's been written about their topic: they need high recall. In real life, precision is usually the more important of the two. Nevertheless, you wouldn't need precision to be perfect either, so long as you could easily pick out the two teapot pictures from all the saucepans and coffee pots, but it would help if those weren't there.

With the fuzzy search engines we now see on the internet and elsewhere, the amount retrieved is massive, because the computing power is there to bring back thousands of items if you want them. So the 'precision' issue becomes the issue of what appears *first*, most prominently, most accessibly, out of those thousands that you're probably not going to look at, although you can look at them all if you really want. So if you don't enter enough terms to help the computer to rank the results to suit you, you may find yourself sorting through thousands of irrelevant items (often listed only 10 or 20 to a page), with just the odd useful item scattered here and there among the list.

What's more, you often don't know exactly how the search engine *does* rank the results it retrieves for you. Large *et al.*[171, 177] suggested, 'Indeed it must be open to question whether or not searchers are willing to place total faith in "black box" search engines whose retrieval mechanism or impact on their search output they do not understand'. It's becoming increasingly obvious that many of those engines retrieve commercially sponsored results first whenever they can. Even without this bias you sometimes wonder whether the engine has prioritised a site because of some criteria you just can't see.

The upshot of all this is that the reasons for a given site appearing early in your results listing will rarely be obvious, and the site may look completely irrelevant to you. There can also be quite bizarre results occasionally. Just as MapQuest[184] used to have a delightful default if it misunderstood an address, plunging you into the middle of Kansas like an inverted Wizard of Oz, search engines seem occasionally to retrieve results that don't seem to say *anything* like the words you typed. If you find it fun, you can spend hours trying to 'confuse' search engines, although this is getting harder to achieve as the technologies improve. However, the growth in clever subversion of your search by companies, so that you see increasingly commercial results instead of truly useful sites, sometimes seems to counteract this. As with any information activity, we need to keep our critical faculties sharpened.

As was said above, to improve your search results you may have to learn a little about how the system itself works, and this isn't always as easy as it looks. We can see similar difficulties in searching as in many other computing tasks. For example, Yvonne Waern, in her thought-provoking book,[300] reported on some studies of novice computer users trying to master a word-processor. The 'space' character (' ') is simply a blank bit of the page to a user of a traditional typewriter, and therefore has no existence in itself. This caused an immense amount of trouble when former typewriter users were trying to learn how to line up columns of numbers, or to move around a page of text. The idea that spaces or tabs *make* space rather than skipping *over* some space was completely new. By now, most users old enough to have ever used a typewriter probably can't even remember when computers' space rules seemed strange.

Waern's users did their best, and mastered their tasks eventually. But Waern compared their struggle to develop a suitable **problem space** (no pun intended) for their tasks, and the way that many of them still hadn't really grasped what they could do with the system's functions to make their work easier, with the studies by psychologists of the famous 'Tower of Hanoi' puzzle discussed earlier (see Figure 2.3). This game is beloved of cognitivists precisely for its simple, well-defined nature.

Tower of Hanoi solvers usually pick up the 'tricks' quite quickly, such as, for example, moving the smallest ring temporarily on top of the largest to allow them to move the middle one. They can then apply those 'tricks' (operators) to a puzzle with more rings, more posts, or both. Why, Waern wondered, can't computer users pick up the 'tricks' so quickly when they learn a new system? She suggested these reasons:

- When learning a new computer system or program, you tend to do a number of slightly different tasks with it. Rather than repeating the exact same task, as in variations of the Tower of Hanoi, it's not nearly so obvious how the procedures you followed before can be reapplied to a new one.
- In the Tower of Hanoi task, the solver is in complete control. When she moves a ring from one post to another, it doesn't suddenly jump off that post and back to the previous one, or vanish completely. Yet, as we saw with Doris, the computer-novice historian cited by Sherry Turkle and discussed earlier (pp. 35–6), computers often do unexpected things which demand our attention and make us forget what we have just done. At other times, we don't even notice the unexpected results, so we fail to learn the consequences of some of our actions.
- The number of alternatives available in a computer-based task, especially where you can type what you like or select from a number of menu options, tends to be much larger than in a basic rule-constrained puzzle like Tower of Hanoi. The amount of cognitive effort needed to choose between alternatives, and the load placed on our limited working memory by remembering these choices and decisions, give users a 'sense of exertion' in Waern's words. This doesn't encourage them to put yet more effort into general self-training on the system.
- People taking part in experiments on the Tower of Hanoi task usually have to try to solve it as efficiently as possible. Computer users are often simply not interested in discovering the most efficient ways to do their tasks. They just want to get on with any way that works. So they aren't necessarily motivated to develop the 'ideal' problem space or mental model.

These problems of exertion and inefficiency are sadly familiar to anyone who has tried to persuade trainees or colleagues to create and apply a consistent set of formatting 'styles' for the headings and paragraphs of their word-processing documents. Some users will continue, for over a decade, manually and inconsistently changing lines of text into boldface or italics, which they'll later have to go through manually to smooth out the inconsistencies they created, *even though they know the software could do this better for them.* As a result, they also can't take advantage of further system features, such as outlining or table-of-contents algorithms. People seem very reluctant to learn a less direct way of doing things.

In another sense, though, the situation leads to too *much* consistency on the part of many users. People continue to try and try with an online search, instead of rethinking the problem. You'll recall that earlier, in the survey of Excite users, 30% of users said they had already performed five or more searches for their current topic, and a worryingly high (but possibly misunderstanding) number claimed that they didn't change their search terms (but did change search engine, apparently).

The crucial tactic is to rethink: maybe you're misspelling something. Maybe the websites that have what you're looking for describe themselves differently, e.g. using a synonym of what you're typing. Maybe they simply don't list your precise words anywhere because they expect you to go to their own site and *then* search a database *there* (e.g. 'flights Turkey' might be inappropriate when you really want to go to a generic flight-booking website and then search there for Turkey). You're not stupid, you could figure that out, but sometimes you might still persist fruitlessly with Plan A.

Some cognitive psychologists, such as Stuart Sutherland,[285] would label this persistence a form of irrationality. Sutherland summarised various researchers' studies of human choice and argued that the 'sunk cost error' often applies in everyday life: once you have invested a lot of effort or money into something, you become less willing to abandon or lose it. In other words, you allow the effort or money you spent in the past to affect your decision about the future. Sutherland cited the example of someone who loses a £15 theatre ticket, but refuses to buy another because they feel the play is not worth £30. Sutherland argued that this is irrational, because you have already lost the first £15 and will not recover it by staying at home and missing the play. If the play was worth £15 before, it's worth £15 again now.

Sutherland even likened this to General Haig's refusal to change tactics while losing thousands of men in the Battle of the Somme in World War I. He also believed this 'sunk cost error' to be related to Festinger's 'cognitive dissonance' which I mentioned earlier (pp. 42–3): i.e. people will attempt to portray themselves consistently, so they will make their future actions take account of their past behaviour even when it isn't relevant.

In reality, it may be unfair of Sutherland to brand the would-be theatregoer as 'irrational': if you are on a tight budget, you may not *have* another £15, or may not feel able to lavish the remainder of your spare cash on entertainment. In a sense this represents the *opposite* problem from that of foolish persistence: it is *giving up* due to past investment, rather than continuing mindlessly with Plan A. Meanwhile, General Haig's failure to change course probably had some political motivations too, such as not losing face. We need to be careful about applying cutely labelled 'irrational errors' to complex real-life situations. It is true that people often judge the present and future in terms of what something has cost them in the past, and it is also true that people persist with an inappropriate strategy when performing tasks. It is not clear that the latter is always due to the former.

There are two other possible elements to this problem. One is that we seem to have a notion that having been going for so long at this searching task, we must be getting close now ... but this 'journey' metaphor isn't the appropriate one, since we've actually made no progress at all. Perhaps we respond this way because in the physical world, and therefore in most of the tasks we attempt as children, things *do* progress over time if we keep putting in effort. As modern urban adults, however, we often seem to be plunged into a world of frustrating zero-progress situations, and the computer probably evokes more of them than any other artefact. Progress can be a complete illusion.

As well as adopting the wrong metaphor for the task, there seems to be an element of **cognitive hysteresis**, which I discussed in the last chapter (pp. 64–8). We seem to fixate on one version of the problem and be unable or unwilling to rethink it. This is of course also part of the problem with the users I discussed above, who didn't want to learn more efficient ways to use the computer, the difference being that for them Plan A was sort-of working.

This unwillingness to change is hardly surprising. We have already seen how difficult it sometimes is for humans to find a solution to an unfamiliar problem, especially an ill-defined one. We might expect that finding a *second*, different, 'path through the problem space' would be even harder, so investing that mental effort may seem less rational than carrying on regardless. Often, though, we're missing a simple and obvious solution by assuming this, and we will curse ourselves when we wonder why we didn't just go to a known travel agency website and search there for Turkish flights. We will realise this not by continuing to punch the keyboard, but by taking a break, putting the kettle on, going to the bathroom, asking someone else what they would do, or at least taking a deep breath and restating our goals to ourselves.

Related to this, of course, is the issue of 'how much is enough?', i.e. knowing when to stop your search and be satisfied with what you have found. With library catalogues and similar systems, at least one of the old measures of recall and precision is usually relevant. Nevertheless, it isn't always obvious when to stop, especially when your search goals were 'fuzzy' as discussed in the previous chapter. Gary Marchionini pointed this out: [186]

> Goals with very low specificity offer the greatest challenges to information seekers for they provide low levels of certainty about completing the task and require great efforts to develop confidence in the validity of one of possibly many interpretations. (p. 37)

With web searching, people are often hoping to solve their problem with one single site, because they are not performing in-depth research. In fact, we may naively assume that one site will be enough when in fact, due to the subjective and arbitrary nature of much material on the web, it may mislead us. Overall, however, for the web we need to rethink many of the worries that plagued information scientists about library systems and similar databases. There are no meanings to recall and precision when our ideal result is just one site which is the *right* one, but the search for the specific information is only just beginning once we find that.

Therefore, while the Excite researchers expressed concern that users didn't browse through many pages of results listings, we should not be surprised at all. The task is different because the user has to search effectively for an information source before searching (or browsing or reading or printing) that source, so new forms of assistance and training are required.

Finally, later in her book Waern pointed out another problem we have once we depend on a computer. Taking to heart Benjamin Disraeli's famous advice, computers 'never complain and never explain'. As I commented earlier, nobody tells you how well you're getting on with them. If the computer makes a decision of any kind— even if it's just the decision about which items to return when we've asked it to search—the decision is almost never justified; nor is it performed with any obvious degree of reluctance that could suggest we were barking up the wrong tree. When we see the results, we can't ask 'What on earth made you bring that up?'—we can only accept what we're given.

If we were unhappy with the service or decision given by a human, as Waern pointed out, we'd ask for an explanation. Of course, most search systems do hint at why they returned each item—perhaps in the summary listing they'll quote the part of the item that mentions the word you searched for. Some will provide a screenful of 'searching hints' if the search fails to find anything at all (or finds way too many items). However, these forms of basic, crude feedback don't tell us much about the way the system went about its search, so we don't learn a more appropriate mental model of it, and we don't know what to do to improve the situation. Most of us remain, as Christine Borgman put it,[31] 'perpetual novices'.

However, as both Waern and Borgman commented, explanations might not always be the best answer. They'd be quite important when the system was doing something more decisive than just returning search results from simple word matching. Waern quoted an example of a social security system in Sweden that used certain criteria to decide how to classify people, and hence how they should be treated, but didn't explain how it arrived at its conclusions (which often differed from those of its social worker users). Similarly, if search engines were deliberately holding back items from us or otherwise making inferences about what we wanted or needed, we'd want to see how they decided. But as Waern asked, 'Is it possible to provide explanations which people with little training can understand? Can we compensate for a lack in training by good explanations?' (p. 285) Even if the computer could tell you, in plain English, about its search algorithm, maybe there are only limited times that this would really help.

Nevertheless, the explanation issue reminds us once again that computer search engines are dumb, in both senses of the word—they say very little, and think even less.

The World Wide Wait

Back in 1995, when the web was still new to most people, computer scientists and HCI specialists were concerned with the new 'cyberspace' (or 'hyperspace' as they often called it then, referring to the way that 'hypertext' links within pages lead you along a 'path' through the 'space' of possible pages). Learned papers preached (and in fact still do) the need for spatial visualisation technologies, i.e. clever on-screen diagrams that would show you 'where you are' and what other documents and sites you might 'go to'. Academics worried about the hapless user wandering, lost in cyberspace.

Being at the time in the midst of a PhD looking into people's use of (really) spatial information, I was very interested in this possibility. I worked with a colleague, Dave Houghton, to brainstorm and circulate a detailed survey to staff and students at De Montfort University.[64] The survey included not only the 'lost in hyperspace' phenomenon, but also every other potential problem we could think of concerning web use, based on our own and others' experiences.

Sixty-two problems were listed—most surveys since then have restricted themselves to around half a dozen—and these were split into problems of access to web pages, and of reading them once they appeared. Respondents could also add their own, although few people did so.

The results, although only a small-scale survey, were resounding. Forget about the lonely vastness of cyberspace: almost nobody ever claimed to feel 'lost' on the internet, and even if they did, they didn't seem particularly worried by it. We'll look at the reasons for this in the next chapter. What people cared about overwhelmingly back then, and what people still claim to be most unhappy with in every online survey I see, is speed.

We saw earlier that in studies of journalists' and academics' searching behaviour,[208, 280] the pressures of deadlines caused them not to care about recall and precision, but only about finding the one thing that would be 'good enough' and *finding it fast*. Time is increasingly of the essence in our society, and yet time delays are the one aspect of computer use which seem never to improve. We used to have slow, low bandwidth networks that simply couldn't bring us much data very quickly, and those of us using a modem to 'dial' into remote databases or the internet faced even worse bottlenecks.*

Nowadays, as the network technologies improve all the time, unfortunately so do the technologies for adding 'glitz' to websites, and so you *still* have to wait, because the data itself has 'grown heavier' as if to compensate. I talked about the issue of commercial interest and web democracy in Chapter 1 (pp. 20–8), and at no time is it more painfully obvious than when we watch a dozen unwanted advertisements slowly take shape on our screens, just so that we can read the latest news or book a holiday flight. Meanwhile, the internet itself is a victim of its own success: at times everything we do runs into heavy network 'traffic'.

Studies some years ago on computer users' tolerance for delays[178, 300] showed that people generally expect a response in around 0.2–0.5 seconds, especially if they are in the midst of a complex, cognitively demanding task. Cognitive psychology suggests that when we're holding information in our working memory, it will decay in roughly this amount of time, so we will have trouble continuing our task if we have to wait longer.

---

* However, very often it is your internet service provider's level of traffic that determines how fast you receive information, not the speed of your own connection, which rarely runs to its full capacity. When people try to sell you extra fast domestic connections, often it will make only a small difference.

Some studies also suggested that if the users believe that the computer is having to calculate something before responding, or if they are only performing a simple task, they are prepared to wait up to two seconds (although most calculations that you could feasibly want a computer to do will take far less time than that). In those older studies, most users tended to give up waiting altogether after about 20 seconds. When I was supervising a student project in a British university in 2001, testing people's visual scanning of web pages, we checked the typical time taken to load a sample of commercial sites on my campus office PC (permanently online via the university's internal network, which in turn had a high-speed link to the wider internet). We found it to be well over 30 seconds in some high-profile cases. It's possible that if people were to give up as easily as they used to, many commercial websites would not be used at all!

Small wonder, then, that aggravated time delays are web users' biggest complaint. On the face of it, this might seem like yet another example of our allegedly 'irrational' behaviour. After all, waiting 30 seconds for a web page, when we are still prepared to wait 20 minutes for a meal or 10 minutes for a bus, seems like relatively small beer. Why should it matter so much to us?

Yvonne Waern[300] suggested that time delays are particularly important because of 'the brittle situation in working memory'. We are not in the middle of a problem-solving task when we stand at the bus stop or sit in a restaurant, but we are when we hit 'Search' or 'Submit' or 'Go' in a web browser. Although she was writing before the web even existed, Waern pointed out that the whole problem-solving process can fail completely, or at least need rethinking from scratch, if computer users unexpectedly face such a delay that they forget what point they'd reached and what they were planning to try next.

We also can't do anything else with the time we spend waiting—it's too short to make it worth picking up a book, and you can't keep putting on the kettle or going to the bathroom. The emotional frustration that builds up because of our desperate cognitive efforts to maintain concentration on the task isn't good for anyone.

Waern, and other authors in HCI, have stated the importance of feedback on how long things are about to take. But web browsers seem unable to calculate this with any accuracy at all. It would be an enormous help if, somehow, the internet could become more predictable even if it wasn't any faster, but this looks just as impossible as predictable journey times on Britain's overcrowded roads. Note also that, like the roads, building ever more and ever wider highways may simply lead to increased demand, bigger pages and just as much congestion, unless alternatives are found and used.

Waern found that expert users of a single computer system learn which processes will take a long time and roughly how long they do take, so they can plan and act accordingly. But with the internet, nobody is ever that kind of 'expert'. Every new site you access and every new search you request has an unknown, arbitrary wait.

Bernardo Huberman[136] has argued that when we give up waiting for a site and try again later we're following a rational strategy that depends on everyone else either continuing to try, or trying again at a *different* time from us so that the 'storm' in internet traffic dies down. He's compared this to game theory in economics: without knowing it, people are choosing whether to co-operate or defect. Such theories predict the overall patterns, but not your individual patience.

It will be interesting to see how internet users respond in the long run. I suspect that like car-addicted motorists, most of us will simply put up with it. We seem so dependent on computers nowadays that we never seem to mind the lack of improvement in speed, as extra functions and visual glamour counteract the improvements in hardware. Can we go on this way? Perhaps we can, but PC manufacturers may want to supply those squeezy 'stress balls' with each machine.

The Went Wrong Web

Imagine if the denial-of-service vandals I mentioned in Chapter 1 succeeded beyond their wildest dreams and knocked out every search engine and directory service on the web. How many of us would go on turning to the internet as an efficient information source, if all we could do was browse and rely on our bookmarks and other people's recommendations? Searching is the major way of handling the enormity of the web, as well as being (in theory) the most efficient way of finding something specific that we want. But the problems of searching on the web go beyond those discussed above.

Earlier I described some researchers' attempts to examine users' searching patterns with the Excite search engine.[143, 274] As so often happens with behavioural research in any field, the researchers decided to examine what goes wrong by trying to spot users' errors, and to do this they had to define what an 'error' would look like. With no knowledge at all of the individual users and their intentions this is obviously fraught with danger, but some results were clearer than others.

As with the 'number of queries' and 'number of words' issues I discussed earlier (pp.88–9), the original paper by this research team had some flaws in its calculations. Initially it seemed that only a tiny handful of users attempted to add some Boolean logic to their Excite searches, and that those few people mistyped certain operators up to 95% of the time!

Looking more closely, it was easy to see why mistyping could occur: e.g. to exclude websites with certain unwanted words, you could use either NOT in upper case or else the minus sign (e.g. 'cheese omelette NOT tomato' or 'cheese omelette –tomato'). In fact, of course, innocent users would often include the '–' sign *not* as a NOT operator, but as a hyphen. Knowing that hyphens would be treated as NOT, and that you had to type NOT, AND and OR in upper case, required making a special detour to the online help pages, which I (as an occasional Excite user) hadn't done myself before I read the researchers' paper.

The researchers commented loftily, 'It is easy to see that Web users are not up to Boole, and even less to rules. Redesign seems to be in order.'[143] (p. 11) While I would agree that Excite needed some redesign—at least by adding a quick summary of its syntax rules on the front page—the researchers were being quite unfair to the hapless users.*

It's true that less than 1% of users tried to use OR (understandably, since it simply isn't needed for fuzzy searching). Of the 3% who used '–' (although not always intending a NOT, as I said above) some 72% didn't do it with the appropriate spacing for its use as a NOT operator (in Excite's quite fussy syntax of the time). Around 5% of all users tried AND (but around half of them failed to use upper-case letters), and another 5% tried to use '+' (but with 30% of them getting the spacing wrong). Since these two strategies are unlikely to have overlapped much, this suggests that around 10% of users *were* trying to bring Boolean logic into their queries to some extent.†

So it isn't appropriate to suggest that users weren't 'up to Boole'— around 10% of them tried it, which is quite high for something that isn't always useful with a 'fuzzy' search engine. But it *is* appropriate to point out that the minus sign is a lousy choice of NOT operator, as people are bound to type hyphens when they appear so often in English.

Of course, if we tell people that search engines use 'fuzzy' searching, and encourage them simply to type words and phrases into the box, they aren't necessarily going to expect that Booleans are

---

*Of course, if the same people who mistakenly used lower-case were also likely to make errors with the meaning of AND and OR, as discussed earlier, perhaps it's best that Excite ignored 'and' and 'or' and treated the query as an overall OR.

†In a later paper that referred back to this study,[274] the researchers stated the figure for attempted Boolean and other modifiers to be 'one in nine queries'.

an option too. Less than 1% of users in the sample typed AND NOT, either in upper or lower case, but the researchers seem to have ignored people who typed simply NOT, so we can't even guess at the number of people who wanted to specify exclusions (as opposed to the accidental hyphens). I've heard novice searchers spontaneously complain 'I wish I could tell this thing what I *don't* want it to bring back!', expressing a desire for Boolean NOT clauses, without knowing that that's what they're called. If you don't know that you can do such a thing, you're quite likely not to even try. Thus, the more intrepid searchers in the studied sample, who did try entering 'and' or 'not' (but didn't dream for a moment that they needed capital letters), are probably a small fraction of the people who might have liked to do so if they had thought they could.

This is reinforced by the researchers' quotations of figures from earlier studies of search engine queries, which showed that up to a quarter of searches were using AND or NOT operators on those search engines (although the implications of using certain operators are different for different search engines, so we can't be sure of generalising across them).

Overall, then, it seems that while many people recognise the need to specify their searches precisely to improve the quality of the huge trawl of results, they don't always appreciate search engines' pedantry in interpreting their efforts. The Excite survey also suggested that people sometimes generalise, wrongly, from one search engine to another. I have found myself that when you try to find out just what a search engine will do with your input, you often find well-hidden help pages that are hard to scan through, so we can hardly blame most users for relying on their own assumptions. Search engine designers often seem to overestimate their users' knowledge just as much as the designers of older, traditional, systems.

This overestimation of knowledge is a two-way street. Novice users' first assumption about a search engine is that it somehow *is* the internet, and can search every page that's out there. This simply isn't so. There are currently many sites which one search engine will find but not another, even though the coverage of search engines like Google and alltheweb.com had reached well over 3,000 million pages each by the time I wrote this. And the ways that sites are generated, searched and ranked create many extra biases and omissions which novice users won't realise.

As I said earlier, for anything remotely research-related (including personal health concerns) you can choose to search one of the many excellent free and relatively impartial directories or 'subject gate-ways', listing websites classified by real people.[79, 237] These will be more likely to bring you something relevant and highly credible, albeit often less specific than you might get from a well-worded search engine trawl. In other words, put loosely, a generic 'whole-web' (though it isn't) search engine will usually give you higher **recall**, while a directory will give you better precision. Since **precision** is more relevant to most people in everyday life—they tend to be doing searches that just want one, or a handful, of answers—it often looks more logical to focus on directories to find information that experts are likely to have deemed useful to a reasonable number of people. Another alternative is to browse, which I'll look at in the next chapter.

The bottom line: satisfaction

Earlier, I mentioned two major surveys of web users. Having seen all the problems that occur in searching, we should consider what users themselves think about it. The (now unavailable) 'Search Engine Watch' survey asked respondents the crucial question: how often did they find what they were looking for on the web? Here, at last, is some good news: 59.8% of the respondents said they find what they're looking for most of the time. What's more, 21.2% said they were satisfied *every* time; 16.4% said 'some of the time'; 2.6% said 'never'.

Combining the 'most' and 'every' responses, the authors pointed out that this gave a rough 'success rate' overall of 81%. In the same researchers' previous surveys, this combined rate had previously been dropping slightly from around 87% in 1997 to 77% in 1999. The researchers cited the recent growth in using multiple keywords to explain the renewed increase. In any case, it seems that satisfaction with search results has always been high, at least among respondents to these online surveys.

Can we be sure that self-rated satisfaction is an accurate assessment of how well people are doing? Perhaps 'cognitive dissonance' plays a role here, so that people feel they need to say they are frequently satisfied in order to square with the amount of time they admit they are spending online? After all, information scientists have often remarked in the past on users' bafflingly high satisfaction with objectively quite poor results. The answer is that in the final analysis, people's sense of general contentment is all we have. The older information science studies demonstrated beautifully that there was no better measure of the 'relevance' of results than the users' own judgements of them. Even if we observed each user in person, we couldn't really be sure if they were truly getting the best thing for their situation, given all the constraints and motivations that might be involved. We simply can't *be* them.

The tenth GVU survey put the numbers a little differently: 45.4% of their respondents stated that failing to find new information when they needed it was 'one of the biggest problems in using the web'; 30% said that another major problem was finding information that they already *knew* was out there (which would usually suggest that the search engines were failing to return it at a reasonably high position in the results list when the user searched).

This means that in one survey, 81% of people seemed largely satisfied with their searching experiences, while in the other only 54.6% (at best) found no major problem with them. In both cases we have a satisfied majority, but in the latter case we also have a very large frustrated minority. How come?

Some likely reasons are: first, the 'not finding what I'm looking for' problem was the first one listed in the GVU survey, and thus was very prominent (and quite generically worded), and so it may well have attracted more clicks than some other options. Second, since the GVU respondents were allowed to click as many problems as they liked, it's worth noting that several other web-related problems were clicked even more often than this one (as we'll discuss further in the section on 'What goes wrong with searching', later in this chapter). Third, the GVU respondents may have included more 'novice' users than the Search Engine Watch sample, and so they may not yet have learned the best ways of handling search engines.

Fourth, and crucially, saying that you find what you're looking for 'most of the time' is *not* the same as saying that search failures are not a major problem. If that minority of failures ends up costing you dearly in terms of time, frustration or phone bill payments, it matters a lot despite its relative infrequency. Perhaps the cost of failure on the web would also seem high to users who, as we saw above, are often looking for specific information that they feel they really *need* for their everyday life, unlike the library-searching students and academics of most information science studies. Indeed, 92.6% of users stated that the web was an 'indispensable' technology for them. The stakes seem mighty high for a task which causes people so much apparent trouble.

What to do about searching?

For users

The first thing to recognise, perhaps, is that information seeking is itself a skill learned with practice. People say, 'Oh, I'm no good with maps ... with computers ... at navigating ... at writing ...' but almost *never* say ' ... at finding information'. This may be a good thing because it suggests that we know we can improve (whereas those self-dismissive comments suggest some sort of permanent disability, which is usually wrong), but do we assume there's no skill or expertise involved in information seeking itself? University librarians bemoan the students who, having never been taught to seek information for themselves while at school, have no idea where to start with a college library, and simply walk in and ask for 'that red book about economics'. We need to avoid making the same mistake with online sources.

Plan your search, and be prepared to change strategy. On the internet, be prepared also to change search engine, and to consider using directories or 'subject gateways' as well as the big generic engines. Remember that most of the time what you want is something that some kind of list-maker or specialist will have deemed useful enough to mention, whether it's patient information about a particular disease or florists' shops in Scunthorpe.

If you use one search engine or database quite often, find a one-off block of time (say, fifteen minutes) as soon as you can. Try to find the online help pages that tell you how the search works and what you can do to 'modify' your queries to make them more specific (e.g. Boolean logic, quotation marks around exact case-sensitive phrases, etc.). Make sure you notice the exact syntax for these 'modifiers', e.g. spaces and upper-case letters. Using these might save you hours of searching time later.

If you do use Boolean logic on search engines which allow it, try to be clear about the meanings of AND and OR, and remember to use brackets like these ( ) to make the meaning clearer.

Avoid 'snowballing' errors. Be suspicious if your second attempt at searching isn't any better than the first: maybe your first mistake was something more trivial or obscure than you thought!

Remember that just because something appears or runs on a computer which is restricted to deductive logic, it doesn't mean that what happens to you will be objective or fair: human beings put it all there and told the machine what to do with it.

Be careful about generalising from one database or search engine to another: the syntax will almost certainly be different, and the ideal number of terms to enter for a given search may well differ too. For instance, one word may sometimes, if it's unusual enough, be enough for searching a 'directory' website, but not a high-coverage search engine.

Try to develop your own 'metaknowledge' (because the meta*data* isn't always good enough). Be aware of how other people may have described and categorised the material you're looking for. As well as the type of site or record that you imagine will tell you what you want, could another type of site provide the information? For example, general travel agency websites also include the chance to compare different car hire deals for a certain location, which may be better than searching for the individual car hire companies. To give another example, a research paper written by a particular academic will probably be listed on their 'homepage' within a university's website, as well as in bibliographic databases, and you may even be lucky enough to find the full text online.

For web searching, read the excellent advice on the Search Engine Watch website.[281] You won't regret it.

The long list of suggestions made by Large *et al.*,[171] which in turn drew on recommendations by Tenopir,[290] may also be worth checking when searching databases and similar resources. However, in my view very long lists of Do and Don't warnings are liable to be forgotten in the heat of a search, so I haven't reproduced them all here.

More generally with computer use (and I think this applies particularly to searching), Waern[300] suggested that to develop a good mental model, or (casting our minds back to the problem-solving studies mentioned in Chapter 2) a good understanding of the 'problem space' (goals, possible operators, etc.), the new user of any system needs to:

- 'Play around' with different activities within the system, so you can learn new aspects of its functioning. Always sticking to the same few actions or commands doesn't let you build an understanding of how the system really processes information.
- Take notice of unexpected outcomes of your actions. If you didn't get what you expected, try to work out why, using any online help facilities if necessary. Once you know what's going on, you can use that knowledge next time. (And, let's face it, there probably *will* be a next time, and you won't necessarily have any more time available then than you have now ...)
- Reflect upon what you've seen. Discovering new things you can do, but not taking the time to work out how they could help you, probably won't allow you to incorporate them into your 'problem space' next time around (in other words, you'll forget you found them).
- Recycle, reduce, reuse, renew, as the environmentalists would say. Try to think beyond the current task to other tasks you might want to do, so that you build a more general, reusable, model of the system, website or search engine.

Based on our earlier look at the idea that we form our system knowledge by testing hypotheses, you could also try to be aware of your own hypotheses and assumptions about how the system is working, and challenge them: again this returns to the idea of **metacognition** discussed in Chapter 1.

For information providers

On the main screen that users see as they search, show briefly and effectively how your search works, perhaps by giving a couple of key examples. Make the online help very quickly accessible and browsable, for both experts and novices. They won't read long text descriptions, but they will read clear examples. Allow both Boolean and fuzzy searching if possible, but be prepared for people's mistakes with Booleans, and deal with them in an intelligent way.

Consider including either a thesaurus or a concept-mapping facility that can improve the relevance of the results, and the opportunity for users to browse to related sites. Automatic spell checking is a low-cost and helpful addition, too.

For research

We need more unbiased research into people's actual searching behaviour, and their intentions when doing it, especially when searching the web. Information scientists are already doing this. A focus on people's own queries, not ones suggested by the researchers, is crucial. An ideal study would probably record a user performing web searches, then play back the recording while asking the user to talk it through, i.e. to stop the playback and explain what and why they made each choice. This *post hoc* 'verbal protocol' work has been successful in HCI evaluations for years, and information scientists would probably benefit from more use of it too (although analysis of the qualitative results is hard work!).

It may also be useful to examine more large-scale log file samples, like the Excite studies. However, we need to treat the data very carefully. It can be hard to calculate statistics fairly to separate real queries and artefacts of the search engine's logfiles (such as 'repeat queries', which in Excite's case just meant turning the page).

There is more room also for the large-scale online surveys of web use to examine people's problems and choices in more detail, for comparison with the anonymous and unexplained logfile samples, since it's well established that people don't always give accurate descriptions of their behaviour.

As 'intelligent' agents are developed,[3] their ability to adapt to users' individuality and usage contexts will be crucial if they're to be any better than past crude 'crawlers'. Hopefully some of the above research concepts can help this.

Summary

This chapter has focused on searching for information. 'Searching' was used in the sense of a user specifying (usually typing) some input and the computer or website returning some content which is supposed to match it.

Since the most common form of information search is currently on the web, I reviewed some detailed studies of how and what people search there. Certain early studies seem to have downplayed users' skills to make them seem less competent, determined and adventurous at searching than they really were.

Searching seems to be very important for internet users. Most web use seems to be for purposes which at least its users see as serious rather than 'fun'. These purposes are probably changing as technology access improves. Surveys and logfiles show a great breadth of user needs and interests, with much less focus on sexual interests than some people might expect.

The many meanings that people can attach to images—even more so than text—remind us of the need for systems where people's contexts and linked-up **semantics** can reach better relevance than now. Although we don't yet have ideal semantic systems to achieve better relevance, we can often get close to them by drawing on records of what people do. Amazon and Teoma are good current examples.

Meanwhile the metaphors and the syntax used in systems often confuse novices, and are rarely consistent with each other. Even when people have the wrong model or metaphor of a system, often they can interact with it very well, and are not as irrational or mistaken as scientists like to make out.

The issue of **mental models** for searching isn't about 'correctness' or 'completeness' of the model, but usefulness. It should be driven more by what's best to do, and how, than by system design descriptions. If we could predict what people do and get them doing it better, we wouldn't need abstractions or facts. Experts seem to be able to move quickly from a 'big picture' assessment of the situation to well-chosen action. The key to this seems to be a suitable **problem space**, but this is hard to get right with computing tasks.

Old-fashioned, inflexible database systems still plague daily life, especially in libraries. People used to 'fuzzy' web search engines are probably struggling even more with older systems than earlier users did. Neither these systems nor the web tend to give much feedback to help users improve, and the web makes people wait for lengths of time which HCI studies had already shown to be incompatible with comfortable cognitive loads. Yet surveys show that most people persist and find what they want most of the time.

Further reading

For a deeper understanding of the current state of play with web search technologies, the best place is the Search Engine Watch website: www.searchenginewatch.com

Chapter 6 of Large *et al.*'s book makes many useful points: A. Large, L. A. Tedd and R. J. Hartley, *Information Seeking in the Online Age: Principles and practice* (London and New Providence, NJ: Bowker-Saur, 1999), ISBN 1-857-39260-4.

Any recent cognitive psychology textbook (e.g. Eysenck and Keane, cited at the end of Chapter 2) will supply readable background on the current views about mental models in cognitive science.

In the 1980s, Winograd and Flores wrote more generally about the problem of computers and cognitive context: T. Winograd and F. Flores, *Understanding Computers and Cognition* (Reading, MA: Addison-Wesley, 1986), ISBN 0-201-11297-3. However, their book may nowadays be seen as too pessimistic: although we haven't really built people's social context into most systems or search engines at all, we still seem to be coping better than they predicted.

If you're involved in any professional context in developing software, databases or websites, I'd urge you to read Alan Cooper's *The Inmates Are Running the Asylum: Why high-tech products drive us crazy and how to restore the sanity* (Indianapolis, IN: Sams Publishing, 2004), ISBN 0-672-32614-0.

For web design, this book is more sober, thorough and indispensable: Louis Rosenfeld and Peter Morville, *Information Architecture for the World Wide Web*, 2nd edition (Sebastopol, PA: O'Reilly, 2002), ISBN 0-596-00035-9.

Chapter 4

Browsing

When do we browse information?

To you and me, browsing is a loose variety of searching. However, at the start of Chapter 3 I had to dismiss the meaning of 'searching' that you or I would use, i.e. simply looking for information by any means available. Instead, that chapter focused on the specific use of the word 'searching' as something that a computer does for you, i.e. trawling through some kind of database in response to very brief input about what you want to find.

Browsing, on the other hand, is where we make choices among information items, based on what we see (or sometimes hear). We usually still have specific information in mind that we are trying to find, except in the situation where we are just killing time; even then we have certain interests and concerns driving our choices. So, of course, the motivation issues I discussed in Chapter 2 are still relevant.*

At the same time, browsing arguably includes all the activities of Chapters 5 and 6 as well—you are constantly reading, evaluating, perhaps noting down or bookmarking or printing or saving things, perhaps simply 'making a mental note' of something you hope to use later. It's a complex set of interactions. Yet there are certain aspects of human behaviour that are likely to be most relevant when you are browsing, because it has fewer constraints on it than continuous reading or computer-controlled searching. You're exercising a great freedom of choice, as discussed in Chapter 2, but this time at the more basic level of deciding where to look and click as well as the higher level of what sources to choose.

This chapter looks at some factors in your perception, **cognition** and personal characteristics that might direct that choice. Many of these haven't yet been applied to browsing in **information science**. Perhaps they should be, since browsing is (just about) the primary means of finding websites: for instance, in the tenth GVU web users survey [149] 88.3% of respondents claimed to come across websites by

---

*Unfortunately, information scientists often use 'searching' or 'using' when they seem to mean browsing, so the literature can be confusing at times.

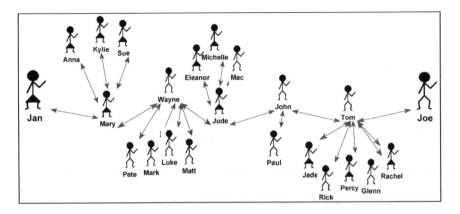

Figure 4.1. The 'six degrees of separation' between people and, allegedly, between websites. Note how you can be a party animal like Tom or a relative hermit like John, but you only need to know one person who happens to link into the chain between Jan and Joe. (In reality our population is massively bigger, but we also each know hundreds of people over the course of a lifetime.)

following links from other pages, a slightly greater number than the 84.8% who found sites using search engines.

Having said that, browsing isn't always casual or unfocused—sometimes it's the most efficient way to get precisely to what we want *after* searching, just as getting off the bus and walking the last mile will get us to the best picnic spot in a national park. Having searched to find a book or website which is *almost* where we want to be, we can use the information or links it provides to find the perfect source.

On the web, it turns out that browsing can be extremely efficient, for the 'six degrees of separation' reason I mentioned in Chapter 3 (on the web it may even be as low as four). [136] Websites cluster together into 'social circles' just like people do, and so you can leap across a whole cluster of sites in one click, rather than following hundreds in a chain (see Figure 4.1).

Until recently, this post-search use of browsing was not a big focus in research studies, except to check which items people selected and how 'relevant' they seemed to be. With older, quite boring library catalogues, few people would bother to browse for long through records about books. They'd probably rather potter around the physical bookshelves if they felt like browsing at all. Information science has also mostly tested time-pressured students and academics, rushing into the campus library to find one specific book before running off to class. Little browsing there.

Now that there are lots of other databases in libraries, however, we may browse through potential information sources and try to interpret their information in terms of our task *before* deciding which one to search.*

However, even for such restricted uses, it's oversimplified to see browsing as simply checking through, seeing the right thing and then stopping. That's the old-fashioned one-parse view of people's interaction with information systems, which previous authors have already rejected, as I discussed previously (pp. 102–5). In reality browsing and searching interweave together. We type some keywords for a web search, browse the results, find the ideal website among them (say, for cheap holiday flights), type in our destination to search for flight options, browse the list of results, change our minds, try a different site and then browse links from there, and so on.

From the psychological point of view, then, browsing is a very active type of interaction with information sources, where we both view information and make decisions to navigate through it. The first topic to examine is what happens as we view the screen (since most browsing involves visual information), and why.

How do we browse?

Made you look: attention and distraction

One of the oddest aspects of being a psychologist is that people take so much in human behaviour for granted. You can spend years investigating the mechanics of one of the many tiny miracles of human ability. People at parties will then simply say 'So what? It's obvious, isn't it?' or 'So—how is that useful to anyone?'

One of these overlooked miracles is visual attention. Somehow, out of the many colours and shapes that we can see around us every day, we select the things we want to observe and ignore the rest, yet stay subconsciously aware of some aspects of them. We can pay attention to a particular object even when we're not directly looking at it, although we may feel a strong urge to move our eyes to do so. We can move them in just a twentieth of a second to focus on something new.

Victims of certain types of brain injury[83] show that we shouldn't take these skills for granted. Some such patients fail to attend to anything that's visible on one particular side of them (even though they can *physically* see it), so that they draw half-complete drawings of scenes and objects without even realising anything's missing. This

---

*This possibility of browsing in order to define our search was pointed out by Cole and Mandelblatt, two Canadian researchers.[55]

is known is 'unilateral neglect'—the patient neglects one half of the visual field even though their eyes are processing it.

Other patients show 'extinction' effects: they can attend to one thing in any position in front of them, but if they're shown *two* similar things at once, then they'll fail to notice one of them (again on one particular side, e.g. always on the left), as if seeing the other one has somehow wiped it out. Yet others, with a rarer type of injury called Balint's Syndrome, can attend to only one object at a time no matter where things are; they report being unable to pour some tea because they can only attend to the pot *or* the cup but not both. These last patients also have trouble reaching accurately for objects with their hands, and with tracking a moving object, such as a ball or car.

Fortunately, such strange injuries are extremely rare. Most of us are astoundingly good at directing our attention while not losing our awareness of other items we can see. When we're browsing through information on a computer screen and deciding what to select for closer inspection, these attention mechanisms are crucial.

Often, when we're viewing some information, say the results of an online search or the front page of a complex website, we know what we're looking for and just need to pick it out from the array on the screen. Cognitive psychologists call this process of finding a known item among 'distractors' **visual search**. They've done many tedious-sounding but ingenious experiments to see what makes such searches easier or harder for us. Often these experiments involve very small, meaningless, abstract stimuli, displayed on a computer screen for just a few seconds while participants rush to pick out, say, the green triangle among the red squares, and at first it's not always obvious how such studies can help us when we think about complex real-world scenes and displays.

Still, the basic principles that come out of these experiments ought to tell us something about what we do, and don't, easily notice among the clutter. Some basic visual features, such as colour and motion, make it easy to distinguish one thing from others. For instance, looking for a single red item among blue ones is so easy that we don't need to scan through systematically in any way: the red just seems to 'pop out' at us, so that it seems as if we somehow processed the whole display at the same time ('in parallel'). When the features are less obviously different, though, or when we have to look for a **conjunction** of features, such as finding a big red square among a mixture of big blue and small red squares, we seem to have to search more slowly ('serially'?) through the display before we see what we want. Figure 4.2 shows such a conjunction.

Originally, the difference between the apparent 'serial' and 'parallel' types of search led psychologists to think that there were

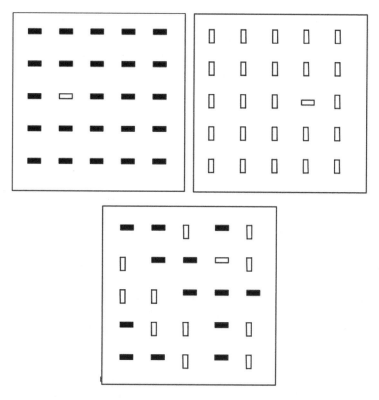

Figure 4.2. Searching for 'feature conjunctions' is harder than for single features. In the third square, finding the horizontal hollow bar is harder even though the other hollow bars are vertical, and the other horizontal bars are filled. So it's harder to look for an item which shares all of its characteristics with other things in a visual display, e.g. on a web page.

two different processes working in our brains. In recent years it's emerged that the distinction isn't so clear after all. Instead, some searches just seem to be more efficient than others, depending on the features manipulated. The efficiency level is a continuum rather than two separate processes.[317]

The basic features which, if the thing you're looking for is different enough from the distractors, make it instantly 'pop out' are these:

- Colour
- Orientation (i.e. whether lines are vertical, horizontal or sloping)
- Curvature (e.g. the letter C stands out easily among T, L, F and E, but not among O, G and Q)
- 'Vernier offsets' (i.e. slight kinks in lines that would otherwise be smoothly straight [an obscure but useful one for architects and

carpenters, which is also helpful when spotting accidental breaks in text or graphics])

- Size (of the objects themselves) and the scale at which you're looking (e.g. looking at parts of an object, or its overall shape)
- Motion
- Depth cues, that help you know what shape an object is in three dimensions
- Glossy versus matt surfaces
- Possibly other shape aspects, such as whether an object is complete, or has a bit missing.

How can we apply our knowledge of these to the problem of viewing complex information on a computer screen? After all, as Wolfe[316] pointed out, in the real world we don't conveniently have all the 'distractors' looking the same as each other and different from the 'target'. They have many conjunctions. A few points are worth bearing in mind.

First, knowing that the above features are the ones which stand out the most, we can be aware of how advertisers and webpage designers may be deliberately drawing our eyes towards things on the page which may not be what we want. In fact, on the portal site that you may use as your starting point on the internet there may be deliberate poor design to encourage you to stay on their site, seeing their banner advertisements and sponsored links, rather than 'search and go'.[136] This is, of course, not just true on computer screens, but in television, shop displays and posters as well. We'll see more about the issue of distraction later in this chapter.

Second, there are aspects of visual search experiments which make searching harder or easier even when there are no clear differences in the above features. One of these is grouping—if you have to find one thing out of a long list, it's faster to search if the 'distractors' are arranged into groups than when they're all equally spaced. This may be because we can to some extent view all the items within a small group in parallel and reject them all at one go. A similar issue is spacing—obviously, if the items to be searched through are spread all over the screen, you have to make larger eye movements to find your 'target'.

Finally, all of these can be borne in mind when we're designing or arranging our own information. If we know that one item will be wanted more often by users than others, or is more crucial for them to notice, we might make it a brighter colour, or larger. If we must have a large number of items listed on a display, we can focus on making them easily distinguishable and quick to scan through, and perhaps we can find a way to group items which reflect the same topic or come from the same source.

Naturally, as I said above, we're not just at the mercy of the colours and features presented to us because we normally direct our attention according to what we actually want to find. In the 'visual search' experiments that gave us the above list of 'basic features', people are usually allowed to move their eyes in any way they choose, so that in general the eye movements they make support their quick scanning over the field.* Another type of study by attention researchers makes people fixate their eyes on one spot on the screen, then tests to see what else they can attend to deliberately without being allowed to visually focus on it.[319] So what you're attending is not quite the same as what you're looking at.

Although experiments in laboratories don't tend to explore the broader effects of such findings, they may be quite important when we're using a computer. If, as we move around a website or use a database, the key information for our task keeps moving around from one screenful to the next, we're likely to waste time and effort looking initially at the wrong item on the second screen. Once we've realised it's the wrong thing, it is then mentally distracting to have to perform a special visual search to relocate the right information. Over the course of several minutes of interaction, this can become quite tiring.

Consistency from one screen to the next has long been a recognised principle in **HCI**. The roots of this principle lie in psychologists' findings that our tasks are quite disrupted when we're misled about where things are going to appear. If you find it difficult to make your way smoothly through a database or website, it may be because of poor consideration by the designer of where its users will naturally be looking from one moment to the next.

Here's another small miracle of vision: we can direct our attention to particular bits of the visual display *even after we've stopped seeing it*. In other words, if we've seen a set of letters on a screen, and then the letters vanish and we have to say what the third letter of the second row was, we can do this by scanning our immediate sensory memory. This instant photographic afterimage fades away within less than a second. Another visual trace then remains in our working memory for a while longer, but this is less detailed, more dependent

---

*Incidentally, our eye movements are in general much more varied than we realise because as well as those deliberate movements demanded by attention, they also move all over the place subconsciously in rapid movements called **saccades**. As a result, an individual fixture may mean nothing—we have to examine the overall pattern over time and the things which are fixated *most often*.

on what we had attended to while it was present, and easily interfered with by seeing new visual stimuli or remembering old images. Nevertheless, while these fresh traces last we can attend to different things within them almost as if they were still in front of us.

Musicians playing continuously while someone turns the page on the score they're reading, and videogame players realising that a monster appeared on the screen just after they'd turned away, both use this ability. Sometimes you see it used in a film where the villain appears on the screen just at the instant that the director cuts to another camera, and then you know that trouble is brewing. And so, when browsing through information, we often realise that there was another relevant item on the screen after all, just after we've selected something else.

All this knowledge about visual perception is easy to turn into advice for designers of human-computer interfaces. Web pages with flashing banners are annoying because apparent movement particularly distracts people. Trying to pick out your target item is harder if there are too many other items, and/or too many different colours and text styles, on the page. And, if we're trying to keep something from one page in mind while waiting for the next page to load, and if that loading takes too long, our visual memory trace will have faded away so we have to rely on some other part of our memory (e.g. by verbally rehearsing a word or number).

This kind of basic **ergonomics** advice has been around for at least three decades, and should be getting more and more precise as scientists churn out ever more accurate theories of how our visual system works, that are based on hundreds of psychophysical experiments. Getting the knowledge out of the lab and into the heads of website developers isn't easy, but things are changing now. Corporate websites are often being subjected to eye movement studies to see what users look at on them. Obviously, to some extent, this is more for their benefit than yours and mine, but it has to make the user experience a little better too. An annoying site doesn't get repeat visits.

Power plants and power users

However, we don't just look at the screen while browsing: we interact with the information on it. Our choices, and the reasons for making them, are considerably more complex when we deal with meaningful information, whether textual or in more detailed images, than simply selecting the right target on the screen. This is where such prescriptions from perceptual and cognitive psychology, and even from HCI research, can fail.

It's still the case, more than 40 years on from the first HCI studies, that most of the successful, clear results and suggestions from the discipline concern situations which are very simple, and most of its efforts to build models predicting people's problems with computers are tested only on basic tasks like text-editing or drawing simple shapes. In the 1990s the HCI research community developed a sudden obsession with designing the sort of collaborative software that lets two or more people edit and share information together (known at the time as CSCW—Computer-Supported Collaborative Work). Most of my tasks with a computer are things I do on my own, and only *want* to do alone, so I always felt that the vast amount of research money ploughed into collaborative applications was surely out of proportion to people's real needs (but see also later in this chapter).

While HCI folk agonised over these 'virtual whiteboards', the internet revolution happened almost behind most of their backs, with the exception of visionaries like Jakob Nielsen[211] and Ben Shneiderman,[267] who gained extra kudos out of everyone else's ignorance. By the late 1990s it could be said that programmers at games companies, writing death match games for Nintendo, knew more about the internet user population, and had more exciting ideas for interfaces for them to use, than most HCI experts did. Research was running way behind reality.

It had some important catching up to do. The web created a crucial shift in the way we use computers. Traditionally, there was an obvious separation between the *design* of the user interface—the menus, on-screen 'buttons', commands to type, etc.—and the *content* of the information you saw on the screen. You could design a library catalogue system without entering the details of a single book into it (except for a few test records), just as you could design an operating system or a text editing program without knowing what information your users would be handling with them.

The main exception to this was in the area of HCI known as **process control** or **complex systems**. The latter term is a little misleading. In terms of the variety of features, compared to the word processor I'm using to write this, most of them aren't actually any more complex. Yet what people are trying to do with them is often much trickier. These are the systems that help operators to control factories, warehouses and power plants—anything where some machinery is doing a lot of things at once in real time and needs to be monitored and directed, to regulate processes and prevent disasters. Thanks partly to infamous accidents, such as that at Three Mile Island nuclear power plant in the United States in 1979, and partly to the demands and funding of various industries, process control has been an important sideline of HCI research for many years.

In these situations the computer system tends to be built bespoke, i.e. for a specific use in a specific place, rather than off-the-shelf for retailing. The interface is built around the information it needs to display. Developers pay special attention to the visual design and to discouraging dangerous errors by the operators, e.g. by making risky actions harder than routinely necessary ones.

What does this have to do with you and I browsing a database or website? Well, it means that perhaps internet technologies have turned our web use into something like a process control system. Web pages started life as simple **hypertext** documents in which some bits of text were 'hyperlinks' that took you to other pages. Even at that stage, the gizmo used to navigate to another piece of information was suddenly *part of the information itself*. You didn't just pull down menus or ask the computer for a new file when you needed more information; you interacted with the information itself to change what appeared on the screen. Before long it wasn't just text that could be clicked on in this way, but also pictures, maps and little video clips.

As well as process control, this type of interaction also harks back to another pocket of HCI research. This was generally referred to in the 1980s and early 1990s as **hypermedia**. It examined the problems and potential of information systems that used embedded links to navigate around information, just as you do on a website, so you could expect to generalise the conclusions from hypermedia research to people's web use.

Unfortunately, many of their conclusions about such systems, which were mainly rather specialised and self-contained information systems used for education until the web took off in the 1990s, were hard to apply to the internet as it eventually developed. It doesn't even *look* like older hypermedia a lot of the time. Within a web page you can do a lot more than reading and clicking on text to move to another page. You can pull down little menus in the middle of the page, fill in forms, click on images and see them change, even drag the mouse to select how far to zoom in on a map. You can control the playing of a video clip, click on tabs and frames that make part of a page change but leave the rest on the screen, launch extra windows with other things going on in them, and even start a completely different application program.

Suddenly, what you can do and how you can do it is almost completely entangled with the information *content*, which is effectively created along with the rest of the interface.

So, you're no longer dealing with a predictable user interface (except for the menus and buttons in your web browser, and even those may become defunct within a few years of my writing this). You're dealing with a customised, constantly changing interface, and you don't even think of it as the interface because it blends in transparently with the information. In this way, the system is like a modern process control system, where you can control events by dragging bars or clicking buttons or selecting from menus. You interact with the information in many different ways to produce many different results, and the structure of the site is all tailor-made for its content.

At least, it should be. At present many sites, especially commercial ones, are instead designed and built using a 'shell' structure into which the information content is 'poured' later like concrete. **Usability** researchers[276] have bemoaned this approach. Studies show that people are much less likely to find what they want on this type of site. It just doesn't fit the natural shape of the information it carries. Hopefully this is a temporary phase in web development, based on an overly simplified use of object-oriented programming. Beyond this, technology trends are mostly towards greater intelligence and flexibility. It seems to be a safe rule of thumb that the closer the website developer was to its content, the better it's likely to fit.

Of course, even content-driven websites differ a little from a process control system because the latter does just that—it controls (usually physical) processes in the real world. Most websites don't, apart from oddballs like the famous drink-vending machine at MIT, hooked up to the internet in the early 1990s. Also, a process control system tends to be 'closed', i.e. it's usually built to be the one and only system that its operators have to look at, and it is integrated together by a single design team. An individual website might be like this: most commercial sites don't include any links to elsewhere. They want you to stay right there and shop! However, the web as a whole, as I've already discussed, is the product of *millions* of designers, most of whom do include links to other sites. The system is also 'open' in that new bits of it are added all the time, with no neat functional specification document directing this development.

For both websites and process control systems, there's a need to make sure that people can see how to act on the content and to understand the results of their actions. As a result, the difficulties of building up a **mental model** of a given website seem very much to mirror those encountered by traditional 'complex system' users.[240] For instance, people's understanding of the structure of even a very familiar website is often quite radically different from the actual pages and links it offers.[54]

The same process control research also showed (more than a decade ago) that we need to be very careful in studying people's problems with systems where the interface and the information are bound up together in this way. Being able to find one piece of information on a website, or to control one small mechanism in the factory, doesn't mean people really understand the website's structure well enough to do *every* possible thing that they might want to do with it, nor to use the best strategy for getting to a particular page. There's been a long-time hang-up about so-called 'hyperspace' among hypermedia researchers, which I discuss elsewhere. Process control research suggested years ago[240] that its users do *not* seem to develop an overall spatial mental 'map'. Instead, they tend to rely on **procedural** knowledge (i.e. habit) and on grouping similar items together in their minds.

It would not surprise those researchers that people's knowledge of websites also doesn't seem to form an overview 'map'. It also should not surprise the hypermedia researchers. A great expert in real-world spatial cognition, Stephen Hirtle, co-wrote a paper in 1995[155] about the potential relevance of spatial cognition to hypermedia. This cited research findings that even in the physical environments that we drive and walk through, it's hard enough to develop a coherent mental 'map', and it 'does not develop automatically in environments with confusing layouts' (p. 242). This implied that a system whose structure wasn't obvious, *and* that wasn't even spatially arranged, stood no chance of developing a spatial mental map.*

There can't be a less mappable environment than one where there is *no* kind of spatial layout to start with, and no reason to impose one artificially anyway. 'Cyberspace' is not a space at all: it is a metaphor that some computer scientists wish we'd use, but most users don't. Nevertheless, spatial metaphors do have their place, and I'll talk more about this later in this chapter.

Researchers have also tried to model people's use of process control systems generally more formally than is usual for hypermedia. Such modelling was explored, among other fascinating papers on people's mental models in everyday tasks which I cite elsewhere in this book, at a 1992 workshop in Cambridge.[29] Sadly, this workshop's proceedings have since circulated only as unpublished

---

*This paper came out before the web was in common use even within universities. It assumed the 'disorientation problem' did exist, and that people would get lost in hyperspace. However, as I discuss elsewhere in this chapter, people don't feel lost on the web.

photocopies or as online versions of its individual papers. Yet it seems (from the sheer number of citations since then) to have strongly influenced many researchers' thoughts about the cognitive side of HCI.

At the workshop one of the most distinguished researchers in both cognitive psychology and the process control aspect of HCI, Neville Moray,[198] pointed out the features that would typify a *truly* complex system. I believe that the web itself now fits his definitions. A complex system, according to Moray, is one in which:

- The system has too many parts for any one user to understand them all.
- It has some properties and variables which are never displayed or known.
- It may hold too much information for users to process effectively enough to make use of it all.
- It's decomposable into subsystems (just as the web is decomposable into separate sites), which in turn could also be decomposed further (into separate functions or mechanisms in process control, or into separate pages and databases on the web).
- Subsystems are closely coupled within themselves (as functions of one piece of machinery, or as pages within a site relating closely together), but are more loosely coupled between each other.
- The system is also dynamic, and could only be completely described *if* all the components could be listed *along with* their links and dynamics and their relationship to the users (which is impossible with the web, and often even with one website).

There is thus an obvious similarity between the web and the sort of system that Moray defined before most of us had heard of the web. The main difference is that process control operators must work in real time to use the system to change physical quantities and movements. Web users are usually only trying to alter their own knowledge or to perform tasks like shopping.

Although we should bear this distinction in mind, Moray's attempts to build and test rigorous formal models of operators' mental operations,[199] even building in apparently emotional factors, such as their personal level of *trust* in the system,[200] may well be adaptable to help us study online information browsing. It would be fascinating to apply Moray's work on people's trust in their systems[200] to websites and other information sources.

Learning from this well-established, elegantly researched real-world tradition could be an exciting boost for web use research, where the dynamism and complexity of the web sometimes seems an overwhelming obstacle rather than something that we can model and account for.

In the same workshop I mentioned above, where Moray outlined his criteria for complex systems, Simon Grant of City University pointed out[114] that an ideal model of people's use patterns would also model the *context* in which they were trying to do things (as I've already discussed in earlier chapters). Grant suggested that process control research could also shed light on how to model this. In this respect the process control analogy may let us down. The context of operators' tasks is inevitably much narrower than that of you or I as we approach the web in everyday life. But the similarities in structure (and lack of it) suggest that this could be a promising line of thought.

Beyond the information given

So far I've talked about the information we browse through, what we notice about it, and how the system presents it and lets us interact with it. Meanwhile, how are we thinking about it?

One of the most lucid and inspiring essays ever written in cognitive psychology (although this is not, on reflection, a stiff competition) was Jerome S. Bruner's 1957 book chapter[38] entitled *Going Beyond the Information Given*. Bruner, writing at a time when **behaviourism** still held sway to a large extent in psychology, discussed what it is that makes us do and learn more than just responses to stimuli (in other words, being more than Pavlov's famous salivating dogs). Quoting Frederick Bartlett (another eminent early cognitivist), he considered the 'bother' of the problem that we never respond simply to a sensory stimulus without also 'going beyond' it. As Bartlett had said,[18] 'people think whenever they do anything at all with evidence. If we adopt that view we very soon find ourselves looking out upon a boundless and turbulent ocean of problems.'

Bruner wasn't daunted. He said there was nothing for it but to 'jump right in', and he did. His paper started with some basic ideas, quoting William James, the grandfather of much modern psychological thought, who had commented that cognitive life began as soon as someone could exclaim 'Hello! Thingummybob again!' In other words, a lot of thinking is simply associating one thing with another, and generalising from one concept to another. In the decades that followed, the importance of concepts (and of comparisons between them for problem-solving) became a well-mined seam for research. But for our present discussion about dealing with browsing information sources, this later passage in Bruner's paper is perhaps the most crucial:

> There is perhaps one additional thing that is learned by an organism when he acquires information generically ... Once a situation has been mastered, it would seem that the organism alters the way in which new situations are approached in search of information. A mazewise rat, for example, even when put into a new learning situation, seems not to nose about quite so randomly. (p. 224)

In other words, the point when we start to be a master of a given task is the point when we develop an expectation of the patterns and categories within it. Yet we can only see those if we have experienced some different versions of the task, and learned to see what they have in common. Seeing always the same set of information won't help us to learn what underlies it, or to see a bigger picture. As Bruner wrote, quoting an alleged old proverb, 'The fish will be the last to discover water'. Once again, this is closely linked to the idea of **metacognition,** i.e. being able to categorise the cognitive artefacts and processes we've experienced just as we can categorise furniture or dogs. Metacognition, you'll recall from Chapter 1, is just cognition about cognition—going further beyond the 'going beyond'.

Novice users of some kind of product database or library catalogue, if they've never browsed through one before, might have no model to draw on about how it might be structured (usually in a hierarchy, leading from big categories to more specific ones). Then again, if they've seen the actual books on the shelves in a library, or the actual products arranged in a warehouse or shop, they might latch onto this 'thingummybob' and expect the database to have the same structure.

Like Bruner's not-yet-mazewise rat, novice web users have seen too few websites to realise the *types* of site that exist and decide what's best done with each one. Once they have tried a few search engines and realised their subtle differences and similarities, and once they have seen that many current websites have a 'Links' page listed near the end of the choices on the homepage, they are armed with strategies to try on their next session.

Similarly, once they've tried a few commercial websites and a few public service ones, they'll appreciate the different kinds of information given by each. Next time, perhaps, instead of starting by typing straight into a search engine's text box, they might go straight to a site that could provide a link to what they want. This is only possible because, after a period of randomness and confusion with any new situation, people automatically start to figure out how it all works— they go beyond the information given.

Note that this process *is* automatic. People aren't consciously taking information and mentally sorting it into differently coloured bins when they develop categories and concepts; the brain seems to create the 'bins' out of nowhere (although you can consciously think

Figure 4.3. Ad hoc categories: list some things you hate. Did this category exist already?

about it if you want to). However, the bins have very soft sides. Although Bruner thought that we could look at categories in terms of defining rules about them, we now know that many of our categories are fuzzy, so that sometimes it's convenient to classify a tomato as a vegetable rather than a fruit.[166] We can also group things together into arbitrary, temporary categories[17] (see Figure 4.3).

Based on an enormous volume of such research, work in cognitive science on concepts and categories has led to **connectionist models**.[189] In such models, simple exposure to lots of examples of a category tends to lead to an idea of what's common or 'typical' about it, without at any time drawing a firm line around some single bit of memory devoted to, say, 'breakfast foods' or 'travel information'. However, such models also need to demonstrate the speed with which we can show a completely different view of the same knowledge, simply by considering it from a different point of view. This is harder to model, but progress is ongoing.

Meanwhile, research also shows that some aspects of categorising are culture-dependent. Although everyone seems to share some common ground in the way we categorise such natural objects as trees and fish, people in rural native cultures may have a much more complex system of categorising specific fish or birds than people in urbanised Western cultures. Even expert fishermen among the latter will focus more on the catchability and eatability of different adult fish, while members of a native culture may be more aware of the fish's whole life cycle and its relation to the local ecology.[247] Furthermore, experts on something in any culture will classify things slightly differently to novices. And expertise is a moving target: expert librarians may have a different view about classifying anthropology books than expert anthropologists.

This should make us wonder about any classification schemes we ever use: my groupings may not be the same as yours, so what will happen when I browse your system? But much of the time, because of our shared cultural assumptions about knowledge, we may be similar enough to get away with it. I'll talk more about this later.

Bruner, and many researchers since, also noted something which the education system then took many years to catch up with, and which I touched on in earlier chapters. The patterns and strategies that help you to categorise are learned more permanently *through your own experience* than through instruction, because ultimately only you can embed the categories and associations in your mind. Although teaching can help you to solve a problem at one time, it is much harder for instruction to take on the same long-term role as experiencing the patterns for yourself.

So there's a limit to the extent that a book, say, could really help you to get the hang of what's out there on the web—even if it wasn't going to go out of date within a year. It can tell you how to find things, and how to interact with them, and give you some broad starter categories to help you spot what's going on, but in the end you have to get out there and wade in.

Personality

Another thing that could affect both browsing and searching is personality. Every so often, a researcher studying some aspect of information use tries to work out why the data they collect is varying so much between participants, even when they're all students on the same course, performing the same search task, and knowing the same amount about the system and the topic area. The most tempting and common strategy is to review some basic psychology literature, get hold of a personality questionnaire that sounds potentially relevant, and see if the students' scores on the questionnaire show a relationship to the way they used the system.

One such personality trait which has seemed quite appealing to information scientists is the notion of *need for cognition*,[43] which would mean that some people feel more of a 'need' mentally to process information than do others. Some researchers have found that a questionnaire measuring 'need for cognition' shows quite a strong relationship to people's searching behaviour—particularly the amount of effort people will put into searching even when it's not easy to find what they want.[299]

However, Tom Wilson[310] pointed out that if you ask people questions about how much they think they need information, and then look at how much time and effort they put into finding some, it would be rather odd if they weren't related. Even if the questionnaire was badly designed, people would probably try to behave in a way that matched their score. People generally do try to look consistent in front of researchers! This doesn't mean that it would be a stable predictor of a person's information seeking in other, less obviously connected, situations.

The main current theories of personality in psychology, based on analysing hundreds of studies to find the biggest underlying predictors of human behaviour, don't see this 'need for cognition' measure as a basic dimension—it seems to be out on a limb, along with many other imagined personality traits. This doesn't mean it's not interesting in the information science context, but it's difficult to see how valid or helpful it would be even if it was more widely accepted. Could we give people a quick test to judge their 'need for cognition', and then make the search engine behave differently according to how much detail they seemed to want? Even if we could, wouldn't it be easier just to let them choose the level of detail directly anyway? If this is the case, then can more complete theories of personality shed any better light on its role in information tasks?

It's worth admitting at this point that psychologists' knowledge of personality and its nature is still a complete mess. In the past century, hundreds of different personality 'traits' or 'dimensions' have been suggested by those psychologists who see such dimensions as the best way of describing people's differences. They usually 'measure' them via self-report questionnaires that depend on people saying how much they tend to behave in a certain way.

The idea is that for any given dimension (the most famous and common one is extraversion–introversion), every person sits, in a stable state, at some point along the continuum between two extremes. So you may be more introvert than you are extravert, but you're probably not an extreme loner. The assumption is that you will reveal your position along this trait 'dimension' by telling the researcher, honestly and free of any suspicion about how it might label you, the extent to which certain feelings and behaviour patterns apply to you.

The theories of the handful of major factors that might underlie all these traits are just as confusing, and depend largely on how the researchers choose to perform a certain process called *factor analysis*. Unfortunately, this modelling technique can be used in lots of different ways, depending for instance on whether you want your factors partly to correlate with each other (so that when one aspect of personality is strong in a particular person, another aspect tends to go along with it), or to be completely separate dimensions. This means that you can potentially see lots of different patterns in the data, very like a child's kaleidoscope.

After much analysis of the numbers, using data from many different populations to try to get a truly universal result, the current most popular theory has five major dimensions, known popularly as the 'Big Five Factors': [190]

- Extroversion–introversion: ranging from sociable and sponta- neous to reserved and self-controlled, as you might expect.
- Neuroticism–stability: ranging from impatient and anxious to calm and resilient.
- Agreeableness–antagonism: ranging from co-operative and trusting to sceptical and suspicious.
- Conscientiousness–undirectedness: ranging from cautious and persevering to careless and freewheeling.
- Openness to experience–nonopenness: imaginative and curious to conforming and narrowly focused.

Disregarding the obvious problems of value labels, consistency and accuracy in self-judgments, you'll notice that these dimensions all have a number of subtraits within them which may compromise your position along the overall trait: e.g. it's possible to see yourself as both co-operative and suspicious, and as both impatient and emotionally resilient. However, for now let's assume that we accept the theory, given that at some higher level psychology always seems overly simplified, and it's a price we're usually prepared to pay so that we can discuss implications without getting mired in detail. It's clear from the terms I've mentioned above that different placings along the dimensions would imply different strategies being taken when solving problems, including the problems of finding and processing information.

The most obvious dimension that could have a profound effect on people's approach to browsing is the 'openness to experience' factor, and I'll talk more about that below. Other factors have slightly more prosaic implications. If someone is highly neurotic and low in conscientiousness, you'd expect them to be very slapdash in their browsing, spending little time evaluating whether the site they'd reached was authoritative or whether other sites might give a fuller picture of the topic. You might expect somebody at the antagonistic end of the 'agreeableness' scale to be less willing to accept others' advice or information at face value. You might expect an extrovert to be more likely to ask a real person for suggestions about the best web site to try, rather than solving the problem alone, and so on.

A review of HCI studies invoking many different personality measures, back in 1991,[230] suggested that measures related to anxiety and self-esteem (which above would mainly measure 'neuroticism') were the ones most likely to affect people's effective use of a computer for any task, particularly in computer-aided instruction (learning) situations. We could boil this down rather simply. Apparently what most affects our performance with computers, in situations where 'performance' measuring is appropriate, is worrying about it!

All of these 'might expects', however, would only *predict* a specific person's behaviour to a certain (and quite low) degree of probability. How much use would it be to know, if we *could* know, that, say, most physicists tended to be introvert more than extrovert, and conscientious more than undirected, and so they might be more willing to use a complex and time-consuming information resource to find their key literature than, say, dance enthusiasts? The actual probability of a given user behaving in a way that was consistent with this might be too low to be worth considering.

Bear in mind, when reading literature on individual differences, that correlations of 0.4 between two variables tend to get most psychologists quite excited . . . yet such a correlation only explains (or predicts) 16% of the behaviour that they're observing. Would you want to redesign your system based on that?

It's also worth noting that a minority of personality researchers reject this whole situation of mutually related (or not) dimensions, and instead concentrate on classifying people into particular 'types' or 'temperaments'. In this group, however, unlike the 'Big 5' juggernaut, there is little consensus at the time of writing about the underlying theory, or the number of measurements, or the best questionnaires to use. This makes it impossible to apply practically.

Meanwhile, most researchers in both groups try their best to ignore the overwhelming evidence, built up since early studies in the 1920s, that no self-reporting personality trait questionnaire can 100% reliably and consistently predict someone's behaviour, at least where that behaviour can be scientifically observed.[47] Yet there seems to be little alternative: we still haven't found any reliable, efficient and ethical way of judging personality variables other than by either asking the people themselves or asking those who are close to them, to complete a standardised questionnaire. Finally, of course it's ironic in the first place that both sets of researchers—in the one area of psychology that bothers to recognise that people *do* differ individually—spend most of their time trying to herd us together into neat groups and labels via a bunch of simplified characteristics.

One possible way through all this, which is particularly interesting as we consider people's use of information, is a theory proposed some time ago by two researchers in Israel called Shulamith and Hans Kreitler.[160] They agreed that we can't ignore the *concept* of personality traits. After all, we have hundreds of words (at least in English) to describe people's traits, from 'impulsive' to 'dreamy', based on thousands of years of humans experiencing each other's behaviour.

The traits are not perfectly consistent across languages or cultures, and it may not be at all reliable to measure them by asking people to self-report, but we know that there are recognisable patterns in everybody's actions and moods. Yet we need to think in a more specific way about what each trait actually means, and what could be underlying it. They suggest that we look at how people interpret the *meaning* of words, things, events and concepts.

The theory works like this. If people tend to emphasise certain aspects of something when they describe it to someone else, it could reflect stable patterns of 'meaning preferences'. This focus on particular patterns of meanings could help to determine their response to a specific situation, because certain aspects of the situation would appeal to certain values or 'meanings' that were very salient to them. So those would influence the way the person behaved, and hence also their 'trait', i.e. tendency to behave the same way more than once. For example, people who tend to emerge as 'extroverts' on traditional questionnaires, when they're asked to describe things to other people, tend to place a big emphasis on aspects to do with 'action' and 'possessions', while introverts tend to define things more in terms of sensory qualities, concepts and ideas. But our 'patterns of meaning preferences', which the Kreitlers labelled 'cognitive orientation', can still be altered by life events and external influences, and sometimes the features of a particular situation make one aspect of 'meaning' seem more important than others so that the person behaves inconsistently instead of strictly 'to type'.

The theory has its limits and leaves a lot of things unexplained, and not every researcher in the personality area would agree with the idea that cognition (thoughts, memories and associations) underlies people's temperaments. Many have seen it almost as the other way around, and argue that our emotional and behavioural traits determine the way we choose to think about things. Unfortunately, solving such a 'chicken-and-egg' issue is beyond the scope of this book. I pointed out in earlier chapters that we seem to be influenced in our information choices by social, cultural and personal biases, but then where do these come from if not from a personal interpretation of what's meaningful? But what dictated those personal meanings? And so on. Clearly, our choices are an interplay of emotional responses to experience, and culturally induced values placed on it, with perhaps a smattering of genetic predispositions involved in both.

As well as being flexible and obviously applicable, the Kreitlers' theory nicely cuts across another tricky question: the annoying dispute about which set of traits is the 'right' one. The Kreitlers demonstrated how we can redescribe each trait theory and each associated questionnaire, quite economically, in terms of particular patterns of meaning preferences. Yet what's most interesting about the theory is its emphasis on the **semantic** associations we form in our minds.

We saw earlier that our memories are organised by networks of links and associations, often referred to as **schemata** or **mental models**. When we think of a word or object, we almost can't think of it in isolation without linking it to emotions, people, places, tasks we need to do, items in our homes, and so on. (At the end of the famous film *Village of the Damned* (1960), the heroic schoolteacher tries to focus his mind entirely on a brick wall and keep it there. It's hard!) So if we describe something, in the Kreitlers' 'meaning' test, the aspects of it that we mention obviously depend on our own, unique, mesh of associations, which is also what determines much of our other behaviour too.

When we browse through information and make choices about what links to follow, obviously that's also determined by our 'meaning preferences', as well as by the situation at hand. We might want primarily to find out a certain fact about our favourite musician, but different people may be more or less interested in, and distracted by, details of their personal life, or by the instrumental arrangement on their latest record. The way we go about the task, and the resources we choose to examine, won't just be determined by the situation, but by our own tendency to notice one word or image rather than another.

The Kreitlers' cognitive focus is particularly intriguing if we link it back to the 'openness to experience' factor of the 'Big Five' theory I mentioned above. Highly 'open' individuals tend to have an interest in the arts, in other cultures, and in learning many new things beyond what they may strictly 'need to know'. Such people may not only make different associations between concepts, but may actually structure their schemata or models more loosely so that ambiguity and uncertainty are tolerated, and associations can be revised easily when new knowledge comes along.[191] There would be no sense of threat to such a person in finding out more about a situation and changing their view of it—and that view would be less stereotyped or dogmatic in the first place.

Browsing for such people would be a rich experience, not just a time-consuming alternative to simple searching, but we might expect a loss of efficiency if they did not bring in self-discipline to focus the task and decide when they knew 'enough'. This area of personality theory should be particularly relevant to our efforts to understand people's browsing choices and strategies; perhaps more research could establish the exact cognitive relevance of the 'openness' concept.

Obviously, in less personal and more work-oriented or academic situations, there's less scope for our personalities to influence the results. But our individuality always makes *some* difference to our reactions and choices. With more research we may be able to pick out, at least in a narrow situation like browsing a library catalogue, the precise patterns of meaning preferences that alter the choices we make. We may see what common features they have across different users. We're in fact more likely to make progress with such research in the narrow area of information browsing than we are in broader, less controllable, life situations.

Some information science studies have tried to take a similar approach already, such as those by Brenda Dervin's 'sense-making' research group,[70] and by Myke Gluck.[108] It would be good to use such studies to build up a body of comparable data about people's real-world choices and meanings in information use, so that we can start to see common patterns across studies. For this it would help if similarly minded researchers collaborated and adapted a specific theoretical framework like that proposed by the Kreitlers. This could finally give us a chance (at long last) to make some theory-based *predictions* about users' behaviour. Perhaps we should throw away the personality trait questionnaires and give it a try. It's an exciting challenge.

Abilities and 'styles'

In Chapter 2 I talked a little about the idea of individual ability and the idea, which is likely to be false, that you have to be 'born to it' to cope with computer use or any similar cognitive tasks (pp. 30–7). This issue of ability is worth returning to now, because it crops up again in information science when considering individual differences in browsing and searching behaviour. We might expect to see that browsing, which involves more freedom of strategy than keyword searching, would vary much more with people's general approach to reasoning and information use, so we might expect psychologists' measures of these to help us distinguish what different people do. Yet, as we'll see, it isn't that simple.

In a thoughtful paper in 1987, Christine Borgman[30] suggested that individual differences in students' use of academic library catalogue systems (which in those days were the focus of most information science user studies) might be best explained firstly by the extent of experience the person had had with computers, and secondly by their choice of academic 'major'.

This might seem surprising. 'Major' is only the main subject a student chooses to focus on in their undergraduate degree, which in the United States, unlike the UK, tends to include a patchwork of unrelated subjects besides the main interest. Someone studying engineering might also be taking Russian literature, botany and sociology. Yet it was their major that marked them out.

Borgman had examined the possibility that the students' performance was actually related to a concept in psychology called **cognitive style**, which attempts to categorise people according to their different ways of thinking, but she found that academic major was still a better predictor overall. Scientists and engineers did best. Bryce Allen similarly concluded in 1991[8] that although studies of cognitive style suggested that information systems ought to be flexible, so that different people could find their own best way of handling them, this wasn't the biggest thing going on in the way people varied.

To Allen, the key variables were the kind of **mental model** that the system designers expected users to have, how obvious this model was, and how much their **working memory** would be taxed by having to juggle too much information at once. For example, it would be harder to juggle a book's author or title while accessing further details of it, if the screenful of extra details didn't include that information. Allen felt that overcoming these issues might depend on certain aspects of people's intelligence—their specific cognitive *abilities*.

The tussle between the style and ability perspectives on individual differences seems at times to be related more to politics than fact. Those who prefer to talk of people's differing cognitive styles or learning styles do so to put the emphasis on finding ways of making systems, education syllabi and information sources usable by everyone who might want to access them. Rather than assessing people and declaring some incapable, researchers attracted to the styles point of view simply suggest, non-judgmentally, that people think in different ways and that all ways are equally valid. Then they try to see how information tasks, or education programs, or computer software, can be adapted to make life easier for people who don't have the same 'style' as the people who designed it.

Their motivations and goals are fine, and there may even be some truth in the ideas that people are either 'holist or serialist', 'reflective or impulsive', and so on. John B. Carroll, in a massive life's-work analysis of hundreds of ability and style studies and tests that he finally published in 1993,[46] argued that it may not be possible to apply such mathematical techniques as factor analysis to decide whether styles exist separately from abilities. Two people with two different styles (if styles do exist) might find different ways to score just as highly on a given ability test, or may not, depending on the exact things you have to do in the test.

However, as Carroll pointed out, most measures of style seem not to be very consistently separate from each other. There's also a feeling, among psychologists who try to link people's behaviour with the way the brain works, that people don't fit into neat categories like 'serialist' or 'holist'. There's no obvious way of dividing a load of brains into different piles; instead, pretty much everything we observe about human behaviour and physical characteristics tends to range along a continuum. Although we have an urge to categorise things into neat boxes, and often speak of types of people that way too, we also are forced to admit that most of our boxes have fuzzy, collapsible sides, especially when it comes to classifying people.

Even the hugely popular 'left-brained versus right-brained' distinction, often touted in education, is severely questioned by the most widely respected neuroscience book on the differences between the two sides of the brain, Springer and Deutsch's *Left Brain Right Brain*.[277] In the fifth edition of the book the two authors stated clearly:

> Our educational systems may be deficient and may limit a broad spectrum of human capabilities. We question, however, the division of styles of thinking along hemispheric lines. It may very well be that in certain stages the formation of new ideas involves intuitive processes independent of analytic reasoning or verbal argument ... But are these right-hemisphere functions? We do not think it is as simple as that, and there is certainly no conclusive evidence to that effect ... Our educational system may miss training or developing half of the brain, but it probably does so by missing out on the talents of both hemispheres. (p. 299)

Meanwhile the most popular measure of so-called cognitive style, that of 'field dependence or independence', has shown itself time and time again to boil down to no more than some kind of basic ability test. Even the tests for this supposed style are just like standard ability tests: either you *can* find a funny little nodule within a bigger abstract pattern (in a series of patterns called the Embedded Figures Test), or you can't. You might find more patterns than your neighbour does, but that means you've done *better*.

There's obviously nothing good about a low score on these tests, although it may not reflect anything very troubling about you as a person. Researchers tend to find that field independent people have an advantage in various specific situations, while field dependent (couldn't find the nodule) people very rarely find situations where they are better off. When the occasional odd glimmer of usefulness of field dependence seems to come along, it can often be explained in terms of those people paying closer attention to a particular visual detail, in a situation where that detail happens to be briefly important. Yet even eminent, well-informed information science and HCI researchers continue to haul field independence into their studies to try to explain differences among their participants, or to suggest where to redesign systems or make them adaptive to different users.

After years of watching this in surprise, I've concluded that most researchers *know* that speaking of field dependence as a 'style' is bogus, and *haven't* accidentally missed the scathing scientific literature that wrote it off as a highly specific ability indicator of some kind. [46, 131] They just want to be able to make life easier for less-than-perfect students and workers (including academic professors in some studies), without having to damn anyone with a pejorative 'stupid user' label. There's nothing wrong with that, but it's a clear example of the delicate politics of applying behavioural science in the real world. It doesn't mean that there's really such a concrete entity as field independence, and it makes just as much sense to use a conventional IQ test (although I wouldn't recommend that, either). Allen and Borgman did better than most in avoiding this well-meant meaningless fudge.

What's a hapless 'field dependent' person to do? Studies have damned them so many times that you wonder if they can cope with computerised information resources at all. One study even suggested that they're less competent at learning to handle a mouse than the exalted 'field independent' among us. [288] The reader's overall impression from these studies is close to the reaction of the exasperated helpdesk operator in the famous urban legend, who told a user that there was nothing for it but to pack up their PC and send it back to the manufacturer because 'You're too stupid to own a computer.'*

---

* Incidentally this was never actually said, although the hapless user to whom it was *almost* said did exist: the alleged real story is readable on several 'debunking' websites. [194]

However, if you ever find yourself cursed in this way after a less-than-glowing score on the Embedded Figures Test, which I find pretty painful to do myself, you'll probably realise that this, like many self-confessed ability tests, depends not only on spotting the solution. It also requires *speed* to do so fast enough, which could be slower or faster than normal on that day and under those circumstances. A 1992 study[258] suggested that when ability tests like these correlate with how well we do retrieving information from a computer, it may be largely because of a basic speed-related element in both tasks, not some higher-level cognitive difference. Other studies in the area of ability testing have argued the same thing, although it's hotly controversial.[33]

It's possible that in this kind of experiment we confuse the *ability* to solve problems perfectly well, eventually, with the *speed* required in many ability-testing situations (either by imposing a fixed time limit on completing the test, or because the overall situation has a similar effect by making people feel pressured).

If that's the case, does it matter? I think it's less and less likely to do so. As our population ages and our technologies and tasks have to be adapted to suit this trend, this will mean computers will *have* to be usable by people who have slower reactions, learn things more slowly, and need help distinguishing the relevant detail out of overcrowded screens of information. These are exactly the features of both the allegedly 'field dependent' and *all* of us as we age.[305]

Research has also given us a clue about how to handle this problem. It seems to depend on some *choice* over the way that computers present information and perform tasks for us, e.g. by selecting different tools and resources within a multimedia program or a website. It seems that most of us can then handle computer user interfaces competently enough to avoid any serious impact on our task goals.[287]

Even where differences between groups of users exist, there are grave difficulties in interpreting what they really mean, as we'll see if we return to the information science research on this topic. Over the next few years after Bryce Allen published the paper I discussed above (p. 170), he did attempt some studies of the effects of specific cognitive abilities on information system performance, and found a few morsels of links between them.

There were problems, however. Like many other studies, Allen's non-significant results seemed to outweigh the significant ones, and even the latter were not of a kind to set the world ablaze, although he performed them with careful scientific rigour. For example, in a 1994 paper[7] he reported that tests of logical reasoning ability were related to a task in which students had to select some articles to use for an assignment. Some University of Illinois students saw the articles listed on the screen in reverse chronological order (most recent first). Others saw them listed in order of (previously humanly-judged) relevance to the essay topic. Students with low logical reasoning scores did unexpectedly *worse* with this relevance-ordered system than with the other one. They chose too many irrelevant articles. Students with high ability scores coped equally well with both systems.

While this seems odd, since the relevance-ordered system would in theory be easier for everyone, it was perhaps not all that surprising. The students seeing the relevance-ordered system only had to select items nearer the top of the list. A student with good logical reasoning and a reasonable state of alertness would work this out pretty easily. A student who perhaps wasn't paying much attention that day (hung over, distracted, or overly impatient), could score badly on the cognitive tests *and also* not be carefully selective with the system. After seeing some perfectly ideal papers at the top of the list, a student in this dopey state might continue selecting papers further down as well, after the more alert students had decided to call a halt. With the chronologically ordered system, however, all of the students saw relevant and irrelevant contrasting sharply together within the list, so this might alert even the tired, distracted or less bright ones to the fact that only a few articles were really on the topic.

Among other things this highlights the problem of using students in research, which plagues all the academic areas I've been discussing. I've sat in a lab myself plenty of times, waiting for a late-arriving student participant and then trying to make him or her focus on the task they're supposed to be doing in an experiment. Meanwhile they tell me how late they were up last night, how soon they'll be taking an important exam, how many other experiments they have to take part in this term, and/or how ill they're feeling. Performance varies wildly due to biochemical effects of the student's personal lifestyle, the effort they're prepared to put into the session, and the extent to which they try to work out the **demand characteristics** I discussed in Chapter 2.

Allen went to great pains to check test-rest reliability and validity of his measures, which were quite high. But a student who is half asleep on one day may well spend half the term in that state, so their performance on any task (including their own studying, which can also create severe fatigue in themselves) may depend more on their ability to pay attention in that state than on anything else. Alternatively, while such students may struggle to take seriously a typically abstract ability test (which often involves tasks like matching meaningless symbols or diagrams, or spotting the next letter or number in a sequence), some of them might muster enough interest to pay more attention to a more realistic and challenging task, and do it well. Then the correlation between the two tasks disappears simply because of motivational differences. Over a large enough sample, perhaps one of these two scenarios happens more often than the other—enough for a fairly reliable result to emerge if you're lucky—but what does it *really* say about your information system?

There is still, undoubtedly, a very real individual difference between the hard-partying student and the well-slept, teetotal, bright young thing who might follow them. But its effects may not be straightforward or reliable enough for the average researcher to have the time or resources to investigate. It may also turn out to depend more on complex and changeable social factors than on some innate cognitive style. Fortunately for the students, but not for scientists, ethics committees are reluctant to let us run biochemical tests on student participants to control for the effects of lifestyles and substances.

Indeed, students are arguably exploited enough already by universities, which often make them take part for course credit points rather than money or curiosity. Probably the only way truly to understand psychology research methods and their many potential pitfalls is to experience a wide range of experiments for yourself as they do, yet many departments fail to encourage the students to respond intellectually to the experiments. As a result, most students are just keen to get out of the lab and on with their lives.

On the optimistic side, it may yet be possible to design information resources to adapt to people's differences regardless of their cause. This remains the hope of the many applied researchers who seek psychology's help, but then find themselves presented with a psychometric test whose results seem frustratingly meaningless. A thoughtful psychology professor would probably warn them not to forget that cognitive style tests are *also* specific tasks devised by human beings with particular theoretical axes to grind, and that like the information tasks that the researcher wants to correlate with them, they're not a 'pure' scientific measure like a blood test.

The major danger, then, in studies of individual differences is that we can't tell the extent to which the differences between the two tasks (the psychometric paper-and-pencil test and the computer-based information task) might interact with the current state of mind of the participants. We don't know if the latter is a random enough effect simply to balance out across a large enough sample of exhausted, biochemically challenged teenagers, in one particular study in one particular lab, at one particular stage of the academic year. It's particularly ironic that very few studies in psychology, information science or HCI are ever replicated by anyone else. Yet in the more predictable physical sciences, great efforts are made to replicate exactly experiments in different labs before placing too much faith in them.

Furthermore, if we're interested in extending our *conclusions* beyond the student population (as most researchers are), we have to question the distribution of the sample data. Given a group of 18–23-year-olds, mostly middle-class and white, youngsters who have above-average academic skills and a chaotic just-left-home lifestyle, are their key individual differences well matched to those among the population even of that (usually rich Western) country, let alone of the human race? This doesn't matter when the only aim of the study is to help redesign systems that are mostly for student use anyway, but not when there's a more generic aim in mind.

Similarly, even where students are not used (which is rare except in studies explicitly looking at issues such as ageing), samples are often self-selecting. They may well be people who have lifestyles that give them the freedom, the motivation and the self-confidence to sign up for experiments in the middle of a working day, or people who all work for the same helpful employer, or residents of the same housing complex. And of course, people with enough self-confidence to try it.

The statistics that researchers usually use to test for differences or correlations in their data assume that each of their measures follows a **normal distribution** (also known as the **Gaussian distribution**): in other words, that the scores represent a sample from right across the type of 'bell curve' that I illustrated in Chapter 2 (see Figure 2.1). If something is normally distributed, then there's a better chance that it shows a representative sample, since most scores on most types of measure (from height to IQ) tend to follow the bell curve at least within Western societies.

More to the point, many of the statistical tests that we use to decide if anything is meaningful in our data depend on assuming that the sample does follow the curve. Despite the possibility of a real skew in the distribution where the sample is non-representative of the whole population, some researchers in applied behavioural studies fail to report, and possibly even to check, that this is the case. This means that even their few **statistically significant** results may be mean-ingless. That's even more likely given that many of the authors I've read ran so many statistical tests on such a very small sample that they were bound to find *some* apparent pattern just by chance.

So to summarise, cognitive styles seem not to tell us much, and are often just speeded ability measures with a prettier name. Both types of measure suffer from the same practical and theoretical problems when applied in research studies. Meanwhile, as I mentioned in Chapter 2, training people can often improve cognitive abilities, so they're not especially stable measures of a particular person (although some have more **test-retest reliability** than others). Finally, and most crucially, they don't seem to explain much of what really goes on when different individuals browse information.

This means that the only way to make sense of this question—as to whether individual differences can link to system characteristics—is to examine *exactly* what is going on. What are the *specific* cognitive activities and the demand characteristics of that *precise* situation? Any test is itself a peculiar cognitive task with a unique set of requirements. Some of these (but which ones?) might coincide with those of another task, such as scrolling, critically evaluating, or just selecting the right command from a menu, but which and why?

Picking apart what on earth they are in the first place in a given browsing situation, e.g. using a 'cognitive task analysis' method,[256] should be Step 1. Just as with the personality-related ideas I discussed above, we may need to come down to individual browsing tasks and contexts first, and then build up our tentative general ideas out of our understanding of those contexts and behaviours. We need more precision and thought, not more quick-and-dirty studies trying to find easy answers.

We do need the systems we develop and use to be more flexible and supportive of people with a different set of abilities and behaviour patterns than those of the programmer who wrote them, which is not an especially surprising conclusion perhaps, but one which even imperfect science reminds us to make.

Strategies (pre-web)

If we're asking when, why and how people *choose* to browse information, we might ask what we've learned from focusing on browsing *strategies*. Browsing, as I mentioned earlier, has become completely different now that real information content (rather than metacontent) is available on the internet. This means that most of the three decades of information science prior to the 1990s, and in fact most of the 1990s papers as well, predict little or nothing about people's browsing on the web.

Having said that, there are a few insights worth gleaning about strategy from the pre-WWW literature. An interesting 1995 paper by two Finnish researchers[42] looked at information seeking in the real-world setting of public administration (local government) work, which made a refreshing change from university libraries. They wanted to know how the type of information that somebody wanted to find out in the course of their job, and the complexity of the situation it referred to, affected who or what they consulted to help them find the answer. They persuaded office workers to keep diaries of work sessions when they sought information, as well as completing some questionnaires.

Although it may not seem earth-shattering, the researchers' carefully evaluated conclusion was that if a problem was more complicated it tended to require more varied information, and a higher proportion would be devoted to *problem-solving information*. Rather than following rule-based procedures to extract specific information from known specialist resources, a more complex information-seeking problem made the Finnish workers turn first to a more generic information source that might tell them how to tackle the issue. Then, when they'd formulated the problem, they could try to solve it. This is obviously an example of the **ill-defined problem** situations I discussed in earlier chapters, and a good strategy for solving them.

Generalising (riskily) from that study, it seems reasonable that browsing is more likely to occur in ill-defined problem-solving scenarios than in the simpler ones for which search engines are ideal. People will often be browsing because what they need to decide or learn is broad or hard to rationalise. A certain UK bank has, at the time of writing, been running some advertising based on the reassuring idea that they have magically simplified financial dealings 'because life's complicated enough'. People's real-world information seeking suggests that it is.

Even with the more classical library catalogue studies of traditional information science, it turns out that people changed their goals and actions during their trawls for information. As discussed in the last chapter, we've known for several years that people don't go through a simple, linear progression from define-my-topic to enter-my-key-words to select-relevant-results to get-the-book. Researchers like Carol Kuhlthau showed the backtracking and emotional shifts that happen during the course of information seeking.[164] Marcia Bates[19] memorably described searching and browsing as 'berry picking', and talked about the importance of browsing in picking out exactly what the user wants.

More recently, Hong (Iris) Xie of the University of Wisconsin[318] reanalysed some old data on people's searches, explicitly looking at the moments where they seemed to change strategy. Xie argued that we could understand these as changes in people's *intentions*, and hence their choices of actions. People shift constantly between their overall intentions, the need to find out how to fulfil them, and minor 'diversions', such as checking that what they've found isn't something they'd already got.

If this is true during relatively constricted bibliographic meta-information searching, imagine how much more true it is during internet-based browsing of real information. One of Xie's main conclusions was that information systems should support people's temporary 'opportunistic goal shifts' (such as going off to check something before returning to the main task), which traditional information systems simply couldn't do.

Here the web offers a great advantage, since you can always open a separate browser window or tab (*if* you've learned how to do this), while keeping the original screenful of information available at a mouse click or keypress. We can break the mould of traditional computer systems that made us do everything in fixed sequences. The graphical user interface, with its multiple windows, has of course let us do this to some extent for 20 years, but its importance in information seeking hasn't really been appreciated until now (and you can still come across traditional information systems that won't let you open more than one user session window at once).

This need was anticipated by an ingenious, but probably now redundant, prototype system called SketchTrieve, [126] which in the mid-1990s allowed an information seeker to jot down notes while searching for something, to drag words to online reference tools to check their meaning, and to reactivate earlier queries to double check something in the results. In other words, SketchTrieve allowed the user to shift strategy in the way Xie argues that people need to do. It tried to relieve the burden on **working memory** by encouraging you to do things immediately on the screen (instead of making 'mental notes' to check them but probably then forgetting to do so).

Some of the features of SketchTrieve are available, though much less elegantly, through the multiple windows and tabs, **history lists** and **bookmarks** of current web browsers, combined with standard computer features, such as copy-and-paste and multitasking applications. Sadly, though, making the best use of all these disparate, unintegrated tools requires a lot more conscious effort and skill than SketchTrieve did.

We have seen that the reality of browsing is so much messier even than the messy reality of searching that I discussed in the last chapter. A current successful browsing session might well involve two or three windows showing various web pages and search engine results listings, another one showing an online dictionary or currency converter, and a word processor window (and/or some graphical brainstorming software such as Inspiration® for making notes[141]). However, we can't see all of these bits of information at once, although sometimes it would be useful to do so.

Should we all invest in bigger screens? Possibly. In reality you and I choose to do some of the work on paper, e.g. by printing out key documents, scribbling on notepads or envelopes, and using reference books on the desk beside our keyboard. However, one of my hopes for the future is that as flat-panel screen displays become cheaper, much larger ones will become common to give us all a genuine 'workspace' for our multitasking.

Strategies on the web

Turning to studies of the web itself, early studies in the mid-1990s[48] showed that people's use of web browsers to get around the internet wasn't quite as the browser designers intended. People depended very heavily on the 'Back' button, yet did not really make much use of the **'history list'** that showed them all their recently visited sites. More experienced users made quite extensive use of the **'bookmarks'** feature (also known in some browsers as 'favourites' or the 'hotlist'), but novices took a long time to discover it. Once discovered and pressed into service, however, users never really got around to organising or updating the resulting huge, unwieldy menu of half-forgotten choices.

But how much do web users revisit any given page, anyway? According to those in-depth early studies, users would revisit maybe around 50–60% of pages, so the ability to easily backtrack seems important. If we tried to bookmark so many pages we'd soon run into trouble. Meanwhile a linear 'history' list tends to imply that we're interested in exactly backtracking through the sequence of pages we just saw, which is unlikely to be the case.

As a result, it was suggested by early web use researchers that users needed to see in the history list a sense of the hierarchy or the 'branching paths' that they had experienced, so that they could recall how the individual pages related to each other (e.g. which ones were from the same site). Recent web browsers try to do this to some extent: the history list in my current browser is organised by day, and within that by website (so that all the pages you looked at on one site are grouped together).

More recently, Nils Pharo[226] undertook an imaginative and thorough study of web users' work-focused browsing for his recent PhD at the University of Tampere, in Finland. In his thesis, Pharo drew on older models of information use, such as those I've already mentioned, e.g. the work of Belkin, Wilson, Dervin and Kuhlthau. However, with most such models being too old to have tackled the complexity and flexibility of using the web, he developed his own model as a framework for studying what people actually do in real-life situations.

By looking at each individual user's process as a 'story' of 'situations', 'transitions' and 'strategies', Pharo avoided trite categorisations of users. However, within the restrictions of a PhD project he could only go as far as developing the method and schema, and running a small test study with students to see how their browsing and searching could be classified with it.

Pharo placed a strong emphasis on the individual context of the task that's being done by each user. This has become an increasing concern of other researchers too in recent years. Paul Solomon wrote a thoughtful 1999 conference paper[269] on people's patterns of actions in people's information seeking which is closely linked to Pharo's points, and which took as one of its examples the task of planning some travel using web-based resources. Solomon wrote of contextual involvement in terms of what he called 'roundness', which is the way that the information source fits into the whole situation that the person is tackling. He took it further to bring in *all* the information sources (not just computer-based documents and databases, but also technical tools and social contacts) that we use to solve a real-life information problem.

Pharo's study, and common sense, are good indicators that whether or not we call it 'roundness', there's a whole lot more going on in web browsing than a systematic trawl through suitable information. Pharo recognised that people aren't always objectively rational and don't have full and perfect information to start with, as I showed in previous chapters. His study demonstrated that during web browsing people's non-systematic progress is altered *fundamentally* by what they happen to find en route. Their haphazard transitions from one temporary situation to another tend to follow an 'Oh well, given what's here, let's try it this way' strategy. Not only what they choose next, but also how they decide to tackle the overall task, may change when they reach a particular page.

Users' prior expectations and knowledge were crucial too, in Pharo's sample. This was demonstrated beautifully when some final-year information science students he observed, who had been thoroughly trained in bibliographic searching techniques for traditional databases, tried to search specialist literature websites by typing, for example, 'Shakespeare, William' instead of 'William Shakespeare'. This actually *lowered* the effectiveness of their search. It seems that browsing (and searching) on the web is a specific skill, for which 'expert' users of more old-fashioned information retrieval systems aren't necessarily well equipped.

We can't be sure just what expertise does mean in web browsing, however, because the few other studies done so far on the effect of expertise on web use have focused disappointingly on high school students rather than adults, and on extremely limited or simplified tasks. [153] Pharo, of course, was focusing only on university students working on research projects, so this may also limit his results, but he was extremely careful not to make simplistic conclusions about the notion of expertise.

The best comment on this issue, perhaps, had been made in an HCI conference paper way back in 1987 by Greutmann and Ackermann, [118] two researchers in Switzerland, who pointed out that expertise in computer use couldn't always be generalised between application programs and added the simple conclusion: '"Expertness" is bound to tasks' (p.149)

Whether expert or not, Pharo's users seemed to stumble unsystematically through their web browsing and searching, making apparently illogical decisions at times based on small aspects of what they saw. What can we say about this? Concluding that people aren't logical, and that their behaviour isn't predictable, wouldn't be particularly helpful even if it was fair. Yet if we assume that there's always a reason for people's actions, we can still seek out those reasons and look for patterns among them. For instance, why do people sometimes browse onwards to more resources, while at other times they make do with what they've already reached, if neither choice is objectively better than the other?

Solomon made one suggestion on this point:

> Continuity seems to be a critical thing in rounding. If the structure—resources and rules—works well enough not to cause much pain, then the thinking and focusing necessary to develop new patterns of action is not likely to occur ... Overall, it seems that roundness is the way that we simplify the world enough that we can accomplish what we need to accomplish. (p. 170)

Of course, it's easy to make observations like this, and this concept is closely related to the 'satisficing' concept suggested by other authors to identify when people make do with non-ideal search results. However, it reminds us once again of the role of motivation, and emotions like frustration and panic, in our information choices even at the level of small actions.

At the same conference as Solomon's paper, Heidi Julien [147] presented an almost vehemently critical paper about the failure of information scientists to treat users' contexts and emotions seriously. As a profession, she argued, they should have the humility to realise that people's information seeking difficulties are not a question of 'educating' those darned stupid users, but of drastically improving the tools and assistance on offer to them. She accused the discipline of seeing information seekers as 'children', 'patients' or 'bungling fools' (very much the opposite of the HCI mantra to 'never blame the user, blame the bad design'). She also, more constructively, highlighted some potentially important recent psychology research which suggested that people's information strategies even vary with their emotional moods. I'll discuss this further in Chapter 6.

Meanwhile, Solomon mentioned more aspects of the context of information seeking which are *always* overlooked in research studies, but which undoubtedly affect people's choices and eventual results in real-life information browsing, such as stopping for lunch or breaking off the task for other reasons. Indeed, speaking personally as a frustrated information seeker, I would love someone to investigate the effect on information seeking results of computers crashing, and of libraries mercilessly kicking users out at closing time!

How can we find out more about people's web browsing without losing sight of all these messy contextual issues? Using Pharo's schema and method, it should be possible to take our knowledge a lot further than the previous (often rather shallow or artificial) studies. For instance, we could 'sabotage' people's web browsing by creating a situation where they run into a site that we've systematically altered, to see to what extent and under what circumstances their strategy changes, i.e. what 'transition' they choose to make next based on what they see.

The classic experimental paradigm in psychology research has put people into a situation that we control to see how that situation affects their behaviour. Information science, on the other hand, has often tended simply to observe without really altering the system, except in extreme experimental studies where the whole system is a tiny false prototype and the whole task is rigged and highly restricted. We should be able to use a little more imagination with studies of web use, and find a methodological compromise between the artifice of the lab and the passive library observer. Then we can try to identify the patterns in the 'stories' of people's usage.

Often, it's partly local technical limitations that hold back such research. We need to take advantage of advanced programmers and tools, such as those taken for granted in computer science. The advantage of this has been shown by work at MIT in recent years, where for instance the famous MediaLab developed a simple tool called Cheese for tracking people's mouse movements while browsing the web. Just in their (unpublished) pilot study to try it out, they showed that people tended to hover the mouse over links that they feel very tempted to follow. People's second choices and confusions might be inferred from this, to add to our understanding of the actual links that they do click.

The researchers also suggested that when people use a website that they already know well, they immediately move the mouse straight towards the link they know they want to click. From this it would be easy to identify the choices which had become habitual to a user. Finally, a finding which should give many web designers pause for thought was that their sample of (web-experienced adult) users liked to have some blank white space on a page, not only to rest the eyes but also to 'park' the mouse, so that they don't accidentally click on a link or obscure any text. All this from a quick pilot test of a low-level computer program; imagine what could be achieved by more collaboration and larger-scale studies!

In other words, so many of the little, subconsciously driven movements and behaviours we exhibit while browsing could be studied to help build up a picture of what's going on with users, as well as more intrusive techniques such as asking them to talk aloud while browsing (what's known as **verbal protocol** data[89]). At present, we know very little about people's actual browsing patterns with the web; but with such tools and methods as I've described above, that should change very soon.

Thanks for sharing

So far I've been quite dismissive about the idea of 'collaborative' computing, since most people assume they would work best by doing most things with a computer on their own (provided they knew how best to do them—see below). However, if so many of us are browsing and searching the web, could we help each other, or at least learn from each other's experiences?

At one level, great examples of this are the commercial sites like Amazon.com and cnet.com. These use people's ratings and comments on items that they've bought to make recommendations for other would-be buyers. The BBC website's 'Talking Point' features often share highly perceptive and thoughtful comments on key current events and issues from users around the world. Those who worry that the internet reduces social interaction[159] may worry less about social disintegration as they see more and more such co-operative, voluntary 'information sharing spaces' appearing.

The concerns that we now do this at the expense of talking to family members and making face-to-face friends are still arguably valid. Yet if mobile phones make us even less likely to chat to the strangers around us on a bus or train, and *better* able to talk to our loved ones, perhaps our technology advances are cancelling each other out and merely changing the *ways* that we communicate?

Returning to the browsing task, what about choosing where to look for the information in the first place? Can people help each other with this, other than by emailing **URLs** to each other? In the mid-1990s this was a focus of a research group at Lancaster University, led by Michael Twidale (now at the University of Illinois at Urbana-Champaign, USA).[296] At first, given the timing of the research program, the focus was on whether users of library systems could collaboratively browse. They could draw on the choices and recommendations made by other users in deciding which books or journals to choose themselves.

Privacy issues were also considered: the researchers recognised that there was a balance between protecting individual identities and sharing meaningful user information. The resulting 'Ariadne' proto-type library system made users aware of others' activities, in a similar way to the later and more commercially motivated amazon.-com feature that tells you 'Customers who bought this book also bought these ...'

More recently, Twidale has continued to consider the general problem of using a computer for information tasks in environments where you're not entirely alone. People in a shared workplace tend to learn how to do tasks from each other, and one of Twidale's papers explored how the design of the user interface on the computer itself can help or hinder this over-the-shoulder process.[295]

It's hard to know how we can take account of this social context when we consider web browsing. Undoubtedly, people suggest sites to each other, and perhaps make suggestions about how to find the right page on a specific site. They might also help each other to understand how to use the features in their browser software. One obvious implication of this is that if items on your website aren't easy to mention aloud, e.g. because they have very long names or can only be seen when the mouse is hovered over a certain spot on the screen, it's much harder for people in a shared work environment to describe those items to one another.

Likewise, long URLs that seem meaningless to the user are simply impossible to communicate between users (even pasted into an email message, they often get word-wrapped onto two lines so that clicking on them won't work properly). Consistency and simplicity have long been watchwords in **HCI**, but their role in helping people to talk about what they're seeing and doing is generally underestimated. Papers like Twidale's are useful in reminding us that even when we might *prefer* to work alone on information tasks, in reality we often help or advise each other, and poor design can make this process needlessly hard.

Other researchers[294, 304] have also considered collaboration on the web in recent years, as a natural progression out of the decade of research into building collaborative tools for computing. There seems little doubt that despite recent setbacks, such as the demise of the 'Direct Hit' search engine that took users' selections of search results as an indicator of the value of those results for other people doing similar searches, the use of popularity and of people's considered evaluations of resources will continue to play a part. Indeed, the collaboration between content evaluators for **subject gateways**, and the users they serve, shows the importance of human help in sorting through the vastness of the web.

What goes wrong with browsing?

Lost in cyberspace: myths and realities

As I mentioned earlier, the first response of the researchers to the web's sudden take-off was to think of it literally as a 'cyberspace'. Surely people would get lost? Didn't they need some kind of spatial mapping interface to help them cope? How would they keep track of where they were, especially as they didn't seem to use the **history** list to help them?[48] To try to answer these concerns, while I was writing this book many beautiful creations emerged to try to create semantic 'maps' out of the web and/or its individual sites.[80]

However fascinating and artistic this is, most people don't seem to need to see such maps to deal with the internet. The tenth GVU survey of web users in 1998, although admittedly biased towards relatively frequent web users, suggested that some 88% of users reported finding new websites by following links from other sites.[149] Yet only a tiny 3.7% reported problems with knowing where they were and feeling lost. This is firstly because the web *isn't* really a 'space', as I discussed earlier. Our experience of it is not spatial: we see sequences of information appearing on our computer screen and can leap straight to anywhere, without having to perform any physical trudging 'round the block' to 'find our way home'.

If we must speak of it as movement through a space, then that movement is like a chauffeur-driven car where we're usually just looking through the window and telling the driver (in a variety of ways) where to 'go' next, but not how. Or, the web is more like the *Star Trek* film/television science fiction series, where our transporter device just 'beams us up' to the mother ship whenever we click on a little button with a housey picture. The operator of the transporter doesn't even need to lock onto our co-ordinates (i.e. 'know where we are') to get us there, which makes it better than the fictional teleport. We can't be lost, because we don't have to move *through* space to get somewhere. Portals and search engines give us a whole 'travel guide' of places to leap to—without making us aware of the 'journey' to get there. There's no need for an interplanetary map, route directions or shuttle pod.

So much for the 'space' metaphor. Browsing, in the sense of moving between websites by clicking on links and reading information to help us decide where to 'go' next, is in fact the only time when there is any semblance of moving step-by-step through a space. We can still leap around it without any sense of distance, but we do still have to know 'where' to leap.

Computers also let us leap around in some (represented) real spaces—e.g. within a **GIS** or a mapping website we can tell the computer to show the London bit of the map, and then the Manchester bit, just by selecting or typing the name and watching the map redraw itself. We don't physically have to drag the mouse up the motorway. But there, we are still looking at a geometrically defined picture which we *could* pan across if we wanted to—a map where distance is meaningful, based on the physical landscape. With the web we don't have or need this.

Indeed, if we tried to build such a representation, it would look different every time we switched on our computer, and we'd never cope with it. If the web is a 'cybercity', then it has a faster urban regeneration rate than a Sims videogame. Everything is changing, all the time. Every large organisation seems to rebuild its website at least annually. Specialist sites disappear or reorganise their pages with no notification, even to their chief users. New technologies demand endless upgrades and downloads of web browsers and 'plug-ins' respectively. During the time I've been writing this book, I had to throw away chunks of my original text, as they had lost all but historic value. Although I've cited stable, apparently well-established web addresses wherever I can, I don't expect to find them all still working two years after publication.

Never before in history have we thrown away the written word without archiving, so carelessly and rapidly. An academic who has explicitly studied the 'persistence' or lack of it in web pages, Wallace Koehler at the University of Oklahoma, has suggested[157] that there are particular characteristics of websites that predict how stable or unstable they will be, so that archivists can make decisions about how to treat their content. But this assumes we can even treat web pages as 'documents' in the first place, and predict how we will structure them in future. Jakob Nielsen, the perceptive web usability pundit, wrote in 1995:[210] 'The only certain trend on the Internet and WWW is that *there are no trends on the Internet.* It changes so fast that it is impossible to predict what will happen, and new trends may bloom and die overnight.'

As an aside, these rapid changes in web technology and design also mean that well-meaning design guidelines (for usability and information access, and for accessibility to people with special needs) have to run like crazy to keep up. Guidelines from the early text-driven days of the web[156] seem quaint in this time of applets and flashy animations. Most bland, corporate, deliberately anonymous commercial websites fail to live up to any design guidelines, even the most recent. But the guidelines are still worth using if you're building any website, and are updated to keep up with technologies.[51, 162, 181]

All of this implies that if we do build visual representations of the web, we can't rely on our visual recognition of their shapes and patterns, nor on using these to infer suitable browsing strategies, because the shapes and patterns themselves change constantly.

Without the use of such visual and geometric cues, there isn't really much reason to think of our interactions as spatial ones. For want of better language, we do still talk about 'going to' a site. But then in general computer use we often say 'go to this directory' or 'go into the database', and older computer users may recall that we sometimes did this even in the old command-prompt days when you only 'went' by typing a command, and the only response was a listing of names. We also say 'go to page 157' in a book, and it has been argued that this is reasonable since books do have a physical spatial reality,[76] yet few books supply a spatial map of their contents. Using spatial metaphors in speech doesn't necessarily mean that we need to represent our experiences on a map. Even in real-life space, such as a city, as I mentioned earlier, the procedural knowledge we get from following routes is often good enough without a complete mental 'map', let alone a physical one.

When are spatial metaphors helpful to people's 'navigation' through information, and when are they unhelpful? This has been debated for some time, with (for once) some early contributions actually coming from psychologists.[76] Even before the web took off, back in 1994, a conference workshop[73] for **hypermedia** researchers explicitly considered how information 'spaces' may, or may not, work. Various position papers suggested flaws in the 'space' idea. Simon Buckingham Shum, then at the University of York, suggested that the space in which one was 'moving' needed to have meaning in itself for a spatial metaphor to be useful. (The web, for instance, arguably has little meaning in itself for most users, and so does the average database.) Jolanda Tromp of the University of Amsterdam was in favour of spatial metaphors, but added that even in virtual environments that *look* like real spaces there are many inconsistent 'magic features' (beloved of video game players, but less comforting when you're trying to work). Keith Andrews at the University of Graz, Austria, pointed out that if you can dynamically restructure a 'space' (as you can on the web, e.g. by creating a new bookmarks list or set of search results), then the spatial metaphor is disastrous since you'll have to scrap any 'mental map' that you've started to rely on.

Finally, the workshop's convenor, Andreas Dieberger, who was then at Vienna University of Technology, wrote in the summary and conclusions that spatial metaphors

> ... might be useful in a smaller range of applications than is believed today. Like in all other user interface issues these evaluations will probably show that there is no universally valid spatial metaphor. This is especially true when we consider social and cultural issues. These issues are very complicated ones ... Spatial metaphors have to bring real advantages for the system: it is hard to sell a metaphor alone ... One of the conclusions of the workshop therefore was that we should stop talking, build something and evaluate it.

In the years since then, computer scientists have done just that, and we see some positive results among the many pretty prototypes and intriguing journal papers that vanished into obscurity. There is no doubt that when an organisation's website is vast and complex, a page showing a visual 'site map' (with clickable links straight to the different sections) can be a boon.[267] It is usually more like the **topological map** of the London Underground than the more familiar road atlas or world map (since geometric concepts like distance and direction are irrelevant and hence ignored).

For the web as a whole, meanwhile, one study of web users[234] suggested that as people gain more expertise, they become less likely to talk of the web in spatial terms, and more likely to use such metaphors as 'collections' of objects (such as libraries), or even in metaphysical terms such as 'co-operative chaos'. Perhaps these more experienced users have learned the hard way that spatial metaphors don't help, because there is no inherent structure out there.

The greatest value of any metaphor comes where it lets us infer a general **schema** that we can apply not only to the information we're examining right now, but also to other similar sources, without an attempt to impose a false sense of geometric quantities like distance and direction (which people are quite bad at handling in the first place). This is why contents pages work so well in books: everyone expects most books to be sequentially ordered with hierarchically related subsections, regardless of the physical thickness of each section. With website schemata, as with books, some aspects are about how the pages are related to each other (or, if you like, 'where' they will be), but these will also be mixed with expectations about *what* information is available. These have nothing to do with space as such.

Since websites can be structured in so many ways, and none, we can still relate to the comment made in 1994 by Andrew Dillon, Cliff McKnight and John Richardson, a prolific hypermedia research group at the then HUSAT Research Institute in Loughborough.[76] They wrote:

> Performing the hypertext equivalent of opening up the text or turning the page offers no assurance that expectations will be met since many hypertext documents offer unique structures (intentionally or otherwise). At their current stage of development it is likely that users/ readers familiar with hypertext will have a schema that includes such attributes as linked nodes of information, non-serial structures, and perhaps, potential navigational difficulties! (p.182)

Nevertheless, where websites share a common pattern experienced users can pick up that pattern and build on it, to help them find information on future sites. Less experienced users could be encouraged to learn the patterns, if they were shown obvious visual indicators and summaries of each site's content and structure. It is almost a moot point whether these patterns or schemata, or the indicators that suggest them, are worth calling maps.

Information overload and muddling through

Yet the motivation behind the well-meaning attempts to make 'maps' of the web does reflect a real issue: the possibility of information overload. Spatial or not, there is so much to see out there! Several years before the web even came into being, Theodore Roszak wrote:[248]

> One might argue that if the public took advantage of all the information the U.S. Post Office could deliver to its front door from public and private providers, it would soon be awash in data. In some of the world's totalitarian societies, the great political problem may be an official censorship that works to choke off the flow of information. In ours, the problem is just the opposite ... Here is a problem the Utilitarians never foresaw: that there can be *too much* information ... No data base will ever be invented that answers to the command: 'Show me everything that is true and relevant.' (pp. 162–4)

Nicholas Negroponte put it more succinctly:[204]

> Some of the world's most senior telephone executives recite the jingle 'Anything, anytime, anywhere' like a poem for modern mobility. But my

goal (and I suspect yours) is to have '*Nothing, never, nowhere*' unless it is timely, important, amusing, relevant, or capable of reaching my imagination. (p. 174, my italics)

Roszak went much further, arguing that information overload was 'a strategy of social control', allowing governments and big interests to dazzle us so that we couldn't see what they were really up to. Of course, it's not necessary to view the whole phenomenon as a conspiracy, whether or not there's any truth in Roszak's assertion. Most of the information on the web was put there by enthusiastic individuals who wanted us to know and care about *many* things, some of them highly politically charged, not by some CIA plot to keep us from knowing or caring about anything.

In fact, that's part of the problem: we can't move smoothly through a consistently presented, comprehensively marshalled series of facts about our topic of interest. Instead, we find one website that *almost* tells us what we want, and follow the link from that to another website that may be nothing like it but has another set of links which push us on to a site which seems more authoritative, but then ... This happens simply because there are so many different motivations and focuses for every topic, and most of them aren't quite the same as ours. Nowhere is our 'infinite human variety' more obvious than in the many different versions of the same tiny topic that can be found out there on the web.

For example, I once needed to know how to calculate the distance and the compass bearing between two locations on the Earth's surface, knowing their latitude and longitude. I had lots and lots of pairs of locations for which I wanted to do this, so I needed a formula that I could set up in a spreadsheet. The first website I found (via Google) gave me neat formulae for both.[227] Being an obsessive researcher, I wanted to be sure they were correct, and there wasn't enough source information or derivations to be sure.

Another search, with Ask Jeeves, found me a site which mentioned the problem, but just linked to a third site for the solution. That third site[49] had the most terrific, thorough, explanation of the different assumptions and formulae for calculating the distance, so I could see why the first formula I'd found wasn't accurate enough *and* avoid certain problems with my spreadsheet program. However, the page didn't explain how to calculate the compass bearing. Trying to trawl around that site didn't lead to any more help, but finally a new search (with alltheweb.com) led me to a great page which did.[298] I finally decided to use its distance formula, and to double-check a few of the bearings and distances by drawing them out in some mapping software.

While I was doing all this, I also uncovered various other sites which either relied unquestioningly on the first formula I'd found (because it was close enough for their needs), or else simply linked back to the site with the comprehensive discussion. In total I probably checked through at least a dozen web pages, not counting the search engines, and spent around an hour on the problem.

If I hadn't been doing this at home in the middle of the night, I could have gone to the library. If I'd done so, I might have followed the same kind of combination of searching the catalogue for books, browsing and following cross-references, double-checking and so on. It's possible that I wouldn't have done quite as much of the latter if the first books I found looked suitably authoritative—I'd assume they'd been proof-read very carefully, and they probably would have given the derivations of the formulae so that I could check it if I wanted. Whether I'm right to make these assumptions is debatable, as is whether the library would have been quicker than the web, but the main lesson is that there is rarely a simple, single website out there that'll either perfectly fit your requirements or link neatly to every other site that's relevant to them.

In other words, before we have a chance to get overloaded with the information we want, we could get overburdened with the complexities of just finding it, or rather, finding the exact version that we need. This is where the **semantic** links and agents currently envisaged by the World Wide Web Consortium[24] could come in handy, *if* they manage to link websites covering the same *ideas* and not just ones which mention the same words or refer to each other. As we've already seen, computers have trouble determining what a human would see as a relevant link between two sites.

Indexing by human helpers has its problems too. Although I've recommended **subject gateways** (web directories) as a means of finding good-quality resources on a given topic, often the rejected or overlooked sites are the ones that have the exact version that you want (which, to a cataloguer, seemed less generically useful and hence less worth cataloguing). Of course, a specialist personal 'agent' wouldn't be restricted in this way: it would be working to sift information just for *you*.

Sometimes the old information science distinction between '**precision**' and '**recall**' still has some relevance: occasionally we want to have access to every site on a particular topic, so that we can find among them the one that says exactly what we need (recall). At other times, we just want one good one; a list of a whole bunch of them will seem wearying (precision). In the former case semantic webs might help us best, to give us an easy way of checking out all the sites on a topic (so long as we can see which ones we've already visited, to monitor our own progress). In the latter case human-compiled directories might be more helpful, so that we don't face unnecessary choices. Until we have personal agents to do it all for us with a fabulous level of built-in artificial intelligence[3], we must choose horses for courses.

Faced with so much conflicting information, what do we do? Information overload is an endlessly mentioned topic these days, usually in a tone of despair by journalists trying to make a story out of the latest web survey. Yet really information overload has always been with us: how do we choose between a list of books in a computerised library catalogue, when we're only trying to source one single fact? How do we choose between brands of pasta in the supermarket? Is the web really so different from many other modern situations, and if not, surely we can apply most of the ideas and models already developed for other problems?

Just to mention one such idea: in 1992 Erik Hollnagel, a researcher in Denmark, suggested in a workshop paper[132] that certain principles apply to our efforts to 'muddle through' in a situation of information overload. Hollnagel cited a few papers from the 1950s and 60s about the 'muddling through' principle in public administration contexts, and used it to argue that people 'usually achieve their goals (solving a problem, making a decision, carrying out a plan) by actions which look more like stumbling than by the deliberate execution of a well-defined procedure' (p. 65).

Limits on human attention and memory, and ambiguity in communication, lead us constantly to compromise between goals, resources and demands. We just don't proceed logically or strategically, taking careful note of all that we've already seen and returning in due course to the parts that had the most relevance. Instead, when presented with more information than we can handle, our 'reactions range from a temporary non-processing of incoming information to abandoning the task completely' (p. 66).

It would be worth making a careful attempt to relate Hollnagel's ideas (which he developed further later in various publications[133, 134]) to the strategies that people adopt in open-ended information-seeking tasks. This might help us pin down the specific situations where so-called overload really occurs.

Citing earlier researchers, Hollnagel listed some ways in which people deal with this kind of 'overload' situation. He argued that cognitive science should explicitly study the trade-off between demand and capability, so that we can know what causes us to react one way rather than another. For many years, much of cognitive psychology has done this to some extent: studies of attention and of **working memory** in particular have shown us a great deal about people's ability to cope with large amounts of very simplified data.[91]

A problem with interpreting those psychology experiments, as I've mentioned a few times already, is that most of them use very artificial stimuli in lab experiments, or the sort of cognitive tasks used in intelligence tests, rather than meaningful *information*. Experiments on language that look at people's semantic processing of words, sentences and longer passages, may have greater relevance to the real-world 'information overload' issue. Yet they still tend not to include a realistic context or goal. Simply presenting undergraduate student participants with some text, without giving them a realistic goal for learning from it, isn't likely truly to simulate their links to real-world knowledge. There is increasing awareness of this in research, however, and experiments now do tend to try to use subjects that students will find relevant to them (such as graduate employment statistics, personal relationship stories, etc.). Meanwhile, the more basic and non-context-relevant findings can still be useful, as I've discussed at several points already.

There is also more awareness that we can't make simple statements about the limitations on human ability to deal with information without looking at the contexts in which those limitations kick in. For instance, a long-overdue article by Nelson Cowan at the University of Missouri[61] revisited the classic and much-cited argument by George Miller[196] in the 1950s that human short-term memory could only hold around seven 'chunks' of information at once. Cowan focused specifically on some conditions under which the limit might actually be as low as four 'chunks'. So much for the 'magical number seven'!

Cowan pointed out that it all depends first on what can be used to form a 'chunk' of information, and second on how other cognitive mechanisms interact with our working memory. In discussing this, he summarised a large number of cognitive experiments. Some of the peer commentaries which the journal printed alongside the article, where other researchers added comments or critiques of Cowan's paper, focused even more on aspects of the context in which people's limitations are studied, bringing in aspects of spatial visual arrangement, timing of presentation of items, and even theories about consciousness.

So, cognitivists are (now) very aware of this issue of context in measuring people's 'overload' limits. They can consider 'context' as narrowly defined within the bounds of highly controlled cognitive experiments, which is all the 'context' their own limited-capacity thought processes can reasonably deal with when considering complex and extremely precise theories of working memory.

Therein lies the problem: bridging the gulf between the very specialised research questions asked in such studies and their application in the real world.

We *can* apply our precise lab-based knowledge of people's information limits to everyday problems. Miller's original memory capacity limit of 'seven plus or minus two', and related research showing the effect of 'chunking' and of using letters rather than numbers, was borne in mind when the Royal Mail (taking direct advice from cognitive psychologists) developed UK postcodes. This led to a surprisingly easy system that used more easily memorable letters as well as numbers, giving fewer and easier 'chunks'. It is a good example of the sort of issue discussed in technical articles like Cowan's, showing how our capacity isn't just a set of equally memorable boxes. I tend to be fine at remembering the first (most important) half of a postcode, partly because the two letters tend to relate to a major city (e.g. BN for Brighton, CF for Cardiff). I'm much worse at recalling the second half, which is less meaningful.

But how can we apply these controversial and complex issues about 'chunking' in working memory to people trying to deal with information overload in browsing? As pointed out in one of the peer commentaries on Cowan's paper, by John Towse at Royal Holloway College (part of the University of London), sometimes an 'answer' like the seven-chunks or four-chunks suggestion is as useless as Douglas Adams's Deep Thought computer declaring 42 to be the answer to Life, the Universe and Everything.[2]

Indeed, as Towse pointed out, most research studies *assume* that people have a limited capacity and must get overloaded at a specific point in their task. So to some extent we design the research so that it *will* find evidence for that. This also seems to be true in the applied area of consumer behaviour and marketing research, where a debate on the relevance of the information overload concept to consumer preferences has run for over two decades,[88] and yet the notion still seems to be accepted without question in much of the field.[112, 262]

Towse himself is now involved in research focusing much more strongly on *what* people (in his research, children) remember and forget, for *how long*, and under *what conditions*, ignoring the idea that there could be any kind of fixed limit. This kind of research is important to get us away from studies where people's non-processing of information is lumped into an overall 'error' score. It's more useful instead to see exactly *what* people failed to take in and *when*, and what they did to compensate. There have already been some of these, e.g. studies in which the types of errors people made were examined, to see what really went on when people appeared to resort to 'guessing' at the point when they couldn't remember something.[170]

It is that level of thinking in cognitive research which tends to give us the most useful results, bridging the gap between 'hard' cognitivism and applied research. Luckily for non-psychologists, it's often (but not always) also easier to read than more technically precise papers like those of Cowan and his peers. However, to do such research means acknowledging that our longed-for 'general theory of human information processing' will be much more complex and conditional, and involve much more replication and co-operation, than we cognitivists would really like. But there's nothing for it, as Bruner said, but to jump right in.

The online 'library' revisited

When are two books, websites or bits of text similar? What kinds of links can there be between them? The problem of making conceptual links between things written by different people, with different purposes in mind, has of course been tackled before. Librarians have used classification schemes for printed books for centuries. Those librarians involved in online developments tend to argue strenuously for the relevance of their resulting expertise to tackling the internet classification problem.

I'd like to agree, but, on the other hand, as a lifelong library user, I'm not sure that I can. In the area I'm best qualified to talk about, psychology, I rarely see a library using a truly intelligent, up-to-date scheme for organising the many aspects of the discipline. The most common schemes have a uselessly outdated category of 'Experimental Psychology'. Into this is thrown all sorts of books from many different specialisms that all happen to do some experimental research studies (which is now almost *all* areas except psychoanalysis, though it was less universal a few decades ago). Other books about the same areas of human behaviour end up classified a whole aisle away, just because a librarian saw them as 'social' or 'cognitive' but somehow not 'experimental'.

I once tried, very hard, to persuade the people running an online subject gateway that included psychology to adopt a more realistic scheme for psychology that actually covered the way that *psychologists* split up the subject, so that sites on the same topics (say, language, or relationships, or visual perception) would all be together for once. For a while, they tried it. Then, after I stopped advising the project, they went back to the more easily defendable standard library scheme. Their funding came mainly from an organisation with a more library-oriented view of things, and perhaps their keenest users and contributors were fellow librarians too. As a result, I could only ever find anything useful by using the gateway's search engine, because browsing became as frustrating as it does in most library's psychology sections.

Of course, even (especially?) in non-ideal category schemes there is an occasional great moment of **serendipity**, when we find something we weren't expecting which is useful for some other task or topic in our crowded life. In library psychology sections such a serendipitous discovery usually requires a huge conceptual leap between two separate areas of the discipline, rather than simply gaining extra information about the current interest. This is not always, of course, a bad thing. Perhaps shelving the books randomly would make it even more fun.

This problem of forever-outdated shelving schemes isn't just my personal gripe as a psychologist, but a well-known problem in libraries. [168] Historically, libraries have been very slow to update their schemes even when better ones become available. To be fair, the librarians probably imagine that their users would protest if they suddenly reclassified and shelved all the books in a different order. More to the point, most libraries simply can't afford the time or money for such an exercise. But when it reaches the point when the books are so unpredictably organised that users have to resort to the catalogue database anyway, they can never use browsing as a reliable way of finding what they want. So they may never actually learn the current scheme anyway.

The parallel with the web is clear to this extent: if all of the websites on a particular topic contained links to each other (just like being close together on a shelf), then you could find everything on that topic simply by browsing. Because the links aren't coherent (some relevant sites aren't linked at all, as if they were stuck in a different area of the library), you always have to rely on searches as well.

Two underlying conceptual problems with the notion of 'cataloguing' the web were neatly summarised by Terrence A. Brooks of the University of Washington, in a 2001 paper. [36] Two false assumptions, in his view, needed to be demolished: the 'False Community Assumption' that there was 'a class of disinterested information workers to develop and apply subject cataloguing'. There are some, of course, but there's probably just as many unscrupulous website owners who will try any way they can to beat the system and have their websites appear when inappropriate, hoping to attract extra visitors (or just to 'beat the system').

Secondly, Brooks discussed the 'False Document Assumption', which I've also touched on already: the idea that webpages are documents or records with clear structures and physical existence. Actually very many of them are generated 'on the fly', and this breakdown into 'bits of resources' is likely to be become even more common. In theory, you could categorise the bits, but in practice commercial providers aren't even interested in having their bits classified anyway. On the brighter side, though, those web developers probably aren't developing the most useful information anyway, at any higher level than high street shops are information repositories.

Still, all of this concern about cataloguing may soon lead to something better. With the dream of the Semantic Web promised by Tim Berners-Lee, the web's original inventor, and his colleagues,[24] hard-and-fast classification may become less of an issue: the computer itself would finally take on some responsibility for relating similar things together, based on the real content of a page. At least, that's the hope.

There will still be imperfections, however. Studies of 'expert' attempts to assign keywords to database records, even in small sections of online library catalogues,[176] have shown gross inconsistencies between library 'subject experts' in assigning keywords to library items. Even with the use of built-in thesauri, context awareness and so on, it's hard to see how the W3C (the consortium that sets web standards) can make every website manager in the world apply even basic English vocabulary with consistency or thoroughness. It's even harder to link consistently to underlying *ontologies*—structures that link the meanings together. Nevertheless, the time to focus on dynamic, semantically based web links is long overdue.

Relevance, seduction and shopping

What happens *now* with these problems? Well, web developers are trying to help. Here's an imaginary situation: you're listening to somebody speak about a terrible crime, such as child abuse, when suddenly they say, 'Some years ago, I used to breed dogs.' What would you think? Your assumption would be that somehow, although it wasn't yet obvious, this statement was leading to something *relevant* to the situation at hand. You might come up with some (alarming) possibilities as to *how* it was meant to be relevant, because relevance was your automatic assumption.

In the provocative 1986 book[272] mentioned earlier, Dan Sperber and Deirdre Wilson argued that when we communicate with each other, we're not only saying whatever the *words* mean, but we're also implying that *we think it's relevant*. In fact, according to Sperber and Wilson, we usually assume that people talking to us are aiming at *optimal relevance* to us or to the situation. Even when they just have a need or desire simply to change the subject, the choice of new subject would still not be random but tailored to the audience. We tend to apply this 'principle of relevance' without thinking about it. We assume that we're hearing something because somebody believes it's relevant to us or to the situation at hand, whether that situation is making small talk, solving a mystery or learning a lesson.

As we saw in Chapter 3, computers, having no intentions themselves about what to tell us, just give information based either on what we have told them we want, or what somebody else has programmed them to present anyway. We've often told them too little for them to know our situation, so what we get back has quite poor relevance. This means that when, for instance, a novice database user gets back some records after a search and starts browsing through them, he is quite likely to assume that they must be relevant. As search engines and 'agents' become less crude by the year, he may be increasingly right, but read on.

A novice user may be more willing to accept that the advertisement banners and other peripheral items that are shown alongside her search results or on her allegedly 'personal home page' must also be relevant to her, when in fact they're based on advertisers' very crude assumptions about the type of person she might be. Using the knowledge I discussed earlier about the visual features that we most naturally notice in attention experiments, advertisers are quite good at placing the advertisements and links *exactly* where you'll most naturally be looking, and with *exactly* the combinations of colour, movement etc. that cognitive experiments have shown to be most salient. That doesn't mean that their content is relevant to you, but it could draw you in.

Yet the information providers, advertisers and website managers out there *do want* to be relevant. Sperber and Wilson's statement that we all strive after relevance is as true of them as of all of us. They do want you to see advertisements that you're likely to respond to (preferably with a credit card!), and they do want you to find their database or website so ideal that you come back and use it again and again.

There is now a whole industry of small consultancy companies that make money by helping website designers produce websites that work better. These companies realised very quickly the point I've made in this chapter about the interface and content now becoming one.[276] They swiftly abandoned old HCI guidelines based on hopelessly outdated user interfaces, and did some user evaluations of commercial websites to see what people were really up to. They then developed their own new guidelines for website designers to follow (including, as everywhere else in the consulting industry, lots of neat witticisms and funky words for simple ideas). Finally they set out to make money through seminars, training courses and reports for bemused and embattled—but often extremely well funded—commercial website designers.

There are two ways of looking at this booming consulting industry: on one hand, their efforts should produce sites which genuinely help you as a user reduce your frustration level and get you to what you want. On the other hand, their paymasters are largely commercial companies who, of course, want to sell you something, and usually assume that you too are selling something through your website. An example of this was an article by the very intelligent, pioneering firm User Interface Engineering (UIE), entitled *The Search for Seducible Moments.*[275]

Seducible moments? Seduction of whom, by whom? The example given in the article is of how two different companies go about trying to encourage you not only to buy their products online, but to use 'financing' (i.e. 'credit'). In a society wracked with individual debt problems and uncontrolled consumerism, I get an uneasy feeling when I see great usability advice turned to such a racket. But all tools are open to good and bad uses.

Maybe you and I, as users, should make ourselves fully aware of what 'seduction' techniques are being used on us. That flashing banner across the screen, or whatever its equivalent will be in a few years' time when technology has moved on, is equivalent to the way that large clothing stores often make men's clothing only accessible by first walking through women's clothes or luxuries. They (often correctly) assume that many men buying clothes will bring a more 'seducible' partner along with them.

Whatever tactics are employed to make money out of you, your main hope for sanity and solvency is to stay one step ahead and be aware of what they know, and perhaps try to stop them knowing it or using it. This is not easy: I used to use a piece of shareware which could block advertisements from reaching my computer screen. When I next upgraded my (commercially developed and advertiser-supported) web browser, it was mysteriously incompatible with the shareware program, so I was back to banners and popups again.

Providers of goods and services and government will all always claim to give us 'what the public wants', while blinding us to inconvenient alternatives. In my view, if the internet was taken over gradually by corporate greed and blandness, as has happened with some other media, we may all be less healthy for it (sometimes physically as well as morally). We may find it increasingly hard to even *find* the alternatives, the freeware and shareware, the small shops, the second-hand markets, the altruistic free information providers, the alternative news sources and protest movements, the non-profit assistance agencies. It's already a struggle to raise awareness of such sites to a typical web novice relying on a commercial portal as her starting point.

There is nothing wrong with making money. But we need to keep sharpening our own critical skills, and to keep questioning the source and motivation behind everything we see.

Pressure: motivation and stress

While on the subject of motivation, your own intentions are obviously relevant, as I discussed in earlier chapters. There is another way in which motivation is important, too. I mentioned earlier (p. 163) that Bruner[38] pointed out as long ago as 1957 that people learn better from doing than from hearing—a principle which is now well-established in education. However, it's not that simple either, as every teacher knows: people differ in the extent to which they will generalise a given experience to other situations, i.e. how well they will learn. People don't just differ from each other, but also vary in themselves from time to time.

Bruner suggested that motivation is a key issue in determining this. If you were under pressure when you got some online information, then you're less likely to have learned the generic patterns of the way you found it, and likely only to be able to follow *exactly* the same procedure again. You may have learned how to do (find) that one thing, but it seems to sit aloof in your mind instead of linking into broader ideas.

I said earlier that 'stress' is a difficult concept to define, and hence not popular among some psychologists. Bruner seems to have studied it in terms of 'tension due to immediate social pressure'. What effect did this have? Bruner himself performed experiments in which, in his own words, some participants were 'mercilessly badgered' by the experimenter for doing poorly at a perceptual task that was actually designed to be impossible. These poor souls were then unable to improve in their performance (now unbadgered) of another, manageable, task that they'd previously learned. People in a control condition (who'd been left in peace by the experimenter, and had been given an easier version of the perceptual task) gradually improved their performance at this other task.

The stressed participants seemed to veer between wildly extreme responses to the final task, as if they expected to have to make wild guesses instead of responding to what they actually saw. This, it has to be said, was probably partly because they'd been forced to make similarly wild guesses in the previous stress-loaded task. But when combined with the data from other types of experiment, from animals as well as humans, there was a clear effect of stress and motivation as well.

Most of us, at some time in our lives (in my case, in my first major academic exam at the age of 16), have experienced this blank inability to think properly when placed under great pressure, or when desperate to satisfy an important need. More recent research about the role of stress in decision-making in organisational settings (i.e. in the workplace) has again suggested that people will use different information and end up making a different decision if they feel under pressure.[253]

One moral of this is that browsing, while often the best way to find what you want online, is not going to work well if you are *both* unsure of the terrain you're wading through *and* also under pressure at the time. There might well be an argument for either sticking to search engines at such times, or just walking away for a while and having a nice cup of tea.

An interesting HCI study in the early 1990s by two American industrial engineers, Czaja and Sharit,[62] looked at the specific issue of stress, time pressure and cognition during office-type computer tasks. The researchers measured overall performance in different tasks, and people's subjective and physical responses to the work. The researchers varied the amount of thought needed for the task (contrasting a data entry task with one in which facts had to be deduced from browsing in an inventory database) and the 'pacing' (giving participants only a fixed amount of time to get each thing done). They also took such physiological measures as heart rate and breathing, and subjective ratings of how hard/tiring/time-pressured the tasks appeared, for women aged 25–70. The women had to spend an hour and a half on each task.

The results were a little messy and not always what the authors expected, which is not unusual for semi-realistic studies. For the information tasks there was apparently no effect of 'pacing' on participants' subjective sense of being under time pressure! However, this was partly because the extent to which the pacing was enforced was different for different tasks.

What can we make of this? The very fact that Czaja and Sharit chose to make the 'pacing' work differently for the two tasks shows that time pressure is a different kind of issue for more complex tasks than for the simple perceptual responses used by Bruner. Of course, unlike the real workplace, the whole thing was obviously just an experiment and there was no penalty for poorer performance, so there was no serious reason to feel stress in the first place. However, the vast majority of participants in experiments (especially non-student participants) do tend to feel a strong social pressure to perform well, since fellow human beings are closely monitoring them.

More specific research into the effects of task timing on computer-based information tasks[144] has suggested that the effect of time delays can vary greatly with the specifics of the task and the user interface. In some circumstances people change their strategies so that their behaviour fits around the predictable system delays, but at other times the delays simply cause frustration and no real changes of behaviour.

Be that as it may, Czaja and Sharit's main aim in their study was to examine the effects of ageing on performance and stress in computer work. Here's the good news. Their older participants, who generally got less done and found the tasks more tiring and difficult than younger ones (not surprisingly since the tasks were all of the type where speed of response and of thinking are of the essence, which is not where older people excel), nonetheless were not especially more (or less) stressed. They didn't consider their own mental workload to be any higher than did the younger women; their heart rate barely changed at all while working, although their breathing did vary a little more; and they apparently didn't respond any better or worse to the pacing than younger participants. Nor did older women feel under greater time pressure than younger women, even though they worked more slowly.

In other words, studies like these give us no especial reason to think that the cognitive impact of stress and time pressure gets any worse as you get older, despite the fact that you do things more slowly overall and that your body (e.g. heart rate) adapts less to the demands of the task. Perhaps older people simply refuse to be hurried. After all, they have greater experience of the proverbial trade-off between haste and speed.

Browsing, then, should still be reasonably workable even under time pressure, but people will often choose to search instead because it is quicker and involves less cognitive load.

Never going back again: retracing webpage visits

Earlier I talked about the increasing use of hierarchically organised 'history' and 'bookmark' lists in the web browser software used by most users as of 2002. How well this works for those users, many of them now with several years' experience while others are still discovering the new world of jargon and features for the first time, isn't known. My own experience, from regular web use over a decade and from observing and training other users, is that things may actually have been better when the history list was still a simple chronological backlog. It's still sometimes a real struggle to find again that page we saw yesterday about a particular topic.

One problem is that the title of a website is often used for every one of its pages, so only the full URL (and sometimes, with a frames-based site, not even that) changes between pages. Many URLs from the same site will only differ towards the end of their very long, frequently meaningless string of characters, so it's hard to tell them apart. Even the last few characters may not say anything that's meaningful to the user, especially on dynamically generated commercial sites. And if we get beyond all of that try to go back to a page we think we want and saw previously, we may find that it was dynamically produced by a program on the web server and no longer exists (because it never existed as a real entity in the first place). The web used to be quite transparent in its address system, but it's starting to feel as if the Royal Mail made half the people in Britain use random, often-changing strings of numbers and letters as their official postal address.

I have no doubt that this problem will be sorted out very quickly in the course of web evolution: something considerably more intelligent than the 'history' list will emerge. Individual pages will perhaps be visible in a 'thumbnail' display, to make the most of our visual memory.

Cognitive psychologists have been doing experiments for decades in which participants sit in front of a screen, seeing a long sequence of items or words, and then are tested under varying circumstances on what they remember. The most basic finding is that when people see a succession of items, their memory for what they saw is by far at its best when they *see the actual item again* (either the same visual image, or a strongly descriptive word describing or relating to it).

It's much harder to remember what you saw when you can't use simple recognition, so that you have to **recall** items with no help or with recognition cues that are less salient (i.e. less obviously relevant, which you may not have noticed or associated with the thing you saw). Recall and recognition are seen as such different processes that there are even separate theories about them, although it's been disputed whether they are really that separate.[223]

We'd get a much better shot at spotting the page we wanted to go back to if we had a chance to see again some miniature images of our recently visited web pages, or perhaps an extract of their text and/or their central image (perhaps intelligently extracted by the web browser). It could do this by looking at what appeared to be the key distinguishing features of a given page.

We can only speculate, based on the faltering progress of artificial intelligence research and its long-promised personal 'agents', how long it may be before things could be even better than that. Some cleverer ways of summarising the content of a page may soon become available, so that the browser uses observations of our behaviour to tell us something *really* relevant about each page. It would be just like a friend who'd been watching us surfing, e.g. 'and then you looked at this page from the Big Bargain electronics retailer, which told you their price was £123 for the XYZ-18 printer model'.

Would this involve impossible artificial intelligence? Well, no, but it would probably depend on a more standardised, meaningful use of **metadata** by website developers, as well as some imaginative programming in web browsers. The browser can't yet tell what it was about the page that was meaningful to you, especially as it may have been chock-full of advertisements and links to unwanted places, unless you tell it. We may have to wait a while, and maybe forever, for that day: metadata standards exist, but frankly nobody in the commercial world seems to take much notice of them at present— just like most voluntary standards in every aspect of life.

Web browsers are beginning to make it easier, with a few keystrokes, for you to record a brief note about a given page when you bookmark it. But this is unlikely to solve the whole problem, since the whole point of a history mechanism is to let you go back to things that you *didn't* bookmark because you didn't know you'd want to go back to them again.

Miscellaneous technical problems

Most of the remaining problems which seem to plague current web browsing are likely to sort themselves out before this book goes out of print. In the tenth GVU online survey [149] 57.1% of users complained of broken links that left browsing at a dead-end error message. To stop this happening, intelligent browser technology could check whether a link was going to lead to a real page.*

Other complaints in the same survey included having to register for sites unnecessarily (49.7%) or to pay for content (45.3%), or being slowed down by unwanted advertisements (62.3%). These are probably an inevitable part of the web's commercialisation. Sometimes I wonder if advertisers might decide not to bother anymore—perhaps market research will eventually show that the

---

*Sometimes we may still want to follow the broken link anyway: it's often possible to reach the page if it's just been locally moved. Systematically removing the last part of the URL after the final '/' and then hitting the 'Return' key, and then repeating with the next part if this wasn't enough, often gets you to a real page from which you can browse or search for the intended one.

banners and popups harm their image and attract little custom for the financial outlay—but I'm not hopeful. As with TV advertisements, we have our time wasted so that someone else's can be paid for. [136]

What to do about browsing?

For users

If you worry about wasting time browsing, try keeping something visual—a list or other reminder—in front of you to help refocus on your goals. Use bookmarks/favourites to keep a note of items that you'd like to go back to sometime later but aren't strictly relevant to the search (as well as the things that are directly useful, in case you need to check back to them later). But do take the time occasionally to organise these! There are also some cheap, clever software products around to help organise bookmarks more easily, and in recent years both Apple and Microsoft have started trying to incorporate 'Favourites' into the operating system to make browsing theoretically seamless.

I mentioned Bruner's insight into the importance of mentally categorising what we see, so that we can be less random in our efforts to be 'a mazewise rat' in future browsing. Here are some questions that apply when browsing websites (or any other type of information, including books and magazines). Based on these, we can categorise them and make more sense of the patterns we encounter:

- Who made this, and why?
- Who is their *target* audience?
- How hard might they have tried to make sure the information is correct?
- Who do they think they are?—How much of an expert are they, anyway?
- Are they likely to have included links to similar sites/books/ information sources, or not? (Yes for sites written by enthusiasts or academics; no for a retailer who doesn't want you to see the competition.)
- Are they trying to make any money from what they describe, or from you, and if so then how? Could that bias their choice of information to give you? (Remember, even academics often work on industrially sponsored projects.)
- Did you find what you wanted? Could you imagine this source ever giving you something else you might want?

As well as making you better able mentally to organise your information experiences, 'metacognitive' questions like these also encourage the development of a suitably sceptical 'browsing eye'.

For information providers

- Distinguish different items or webpages visually and by title.
- Give a 'site map', but don't try to get overly 'spatial' in it, as this is meaningless.
- Check out web usability guidelines and books, and bear in mind what grabs people's visual attention (which I outlined early in this chapter). Please try not to use this to annoy or unfairly mislead users.
- Evaluate your site with users, ideally looking at their eye and/or mouse movements.
- Use 'customer choices' (user histories) to help users follow the same choices and paths.
- Don't create information overload: place and format items consistently in terms of users' tasks and categories, and without too much clutter.

Further research

I would love to see someone adapt Moray's models and ideas on process control, to work on other non-process-control 'complex systems', such as the web. Hollnagel's ideas on cognitive work and information overload are obviously also potentially important for browsing and searching.

The Kreitlers' ideas on cognitive 'meanings' underpinning personality differences could be a real shot in the arm for the currently muddled individual differences area in information science. Coupled with intelligent ideas like Pharo's about how the browsing task changes while it happens, we might be able to find some real predictive measures, such as which types of 'meaning' cause changes in browsing decisions for people who hold them strongly.

For any research, I hope we can run more and more studies on real people outside universities, and replicate them! Clever data capture ideas like MIT's 'Cheese' can probably help.

Bruner, and Czaja and Sharit, managed to simulate pressure in the lab (Bruner's method probably wouldn't be allowed now by ethic committees, but Czaja and Sharit's 'pacing' would probably pass muster). A more careful look at the cognitive effects of time pressure in information work is badly overdue.

Summary

Browsing is as important in finding information as searching, and is even more likely to vary with your personal characteristics as well as those of the system. Browsing can happen before, after or even in the middle of searching, and is arguably the most 'active' form of interaction with the information source.

The basic principles learned from visual search and visual memory experiments in cognitive psychology should be able to help us learn what attracts attention on a website or other visual display, but more research is needed really to understand how the 'primitives' of visual attention apply in complex situations.

That complexity may be understandable by applying the same thinking that **HCI** researchers have used for **process control** systems in power plants, factories etc., where real-time interaction with a lot of information was already commonplace before the web was invented. Another area where HCI meets information science is in **hypermedia**, a strand of technical research and development which foreshadowed today's internet but involved much more controlled, logically related pieces of information. Both these HCI areas arguably involve the same kind of complex **mental model** as web browsing.

Efforts to apply **cognitive 'style'** and 'ability' measures to predict people's use of information systems have led to messy and unclear results, most of the time. However, in personality psychology the 'Big Five' theory is currently well respected, and may be worth considering in the light of complex information-seeking situations. An alternative approach to personality, the Kreitlers' focus on *meaning* (similarly to Dervin's sense-making work in information science), may be easier to fit to people's behaviour in information tasks. It's also more helpful to focus on strategies than on styles.

I argued against the near-myth that information networks like the web are 'spaces' (with a few reservations), and examined the well-worn concepts of 'information overload' and 'relevance' in the light of cognitive science ideas. I assessed some more contentious issues—categorising, privacy, commercialism, stress and recording previous browsing—for their effects on browsing behaviour.

Further reading

Guidelines for website design, including inclusive design to benefit those with special needs, include the following:

P. J. Lynch and Sarah Horton, *Web Style Guide: Basic design principles for creating web sites* (New Haven, CT: Yale University Press, 2002), ISBN 0300088981. www.webstyleguide.com

Wendy Chisholm, Gregg Vanderheiden and Ian Jacobs, *Web Content Accessibility Guidelines 1.0* (1991). www.w3.org/TR/WAI-WEBCONTENT/

Steve Krug, *Don't Make Me Think! A common sense approach to web usability* (Indianapolis, IN: New Riders Publishing, 1999). (I especially like the diagram about the reality of browsing or searching a website on p. 56.)

Visual attention is a highly technical scientific area, full of jargon. One clear, helpful introduction is in Chapter 5 of the Eysenck and Keane textbook cited at the end of Chapter 2. Any other cognitive psychology textbook that includes a chapter on attention will probably be almost as good.

Jerome Bruner's insightful essays and studies were compiled into a book, titled after (and including) the classic essay I've cited: Jerome Bruner, *Beyond the Information Given: Studies in the psychology of knowing* (ed. Jeremy M. Anglin, New York: W. W. Norton, 1973), ISBN 0-393-01095-3.

To gauge the breadth of current knowledge and consensus (or lack of it) in personality research, the following book is probably the best to start with: Lawrence A. Pervin and Oliver P. John (eds), *Handbook of Personality: Theory and research* (New York and London: Guilford Press, 2001), ISBN 1-572-30695-5.

Nils Pharo's work is summarised on his website, including the full text of his PhD: home.hio.no/~nilsp/index_eng.htm

Amazing widgets and creative research ideas abound at the MIT MediaLab: www.media.mit.edu

Mike Twidale's website (with his work on collaborative usability) is at www.lis.uiuc.edu/~twidale/

Lots of information on cognitive work analysis methods are summarised in this recent (expensive) 'bible', edited by Erik Hollnagel: Eric Hollnagel (ed.), *Handbook of Cognitive Task Design* (Mahwah, NJ: Lawrence Erlbaum Associates, 2003), ISBN 0-805-84003-6.

Chapter 5

Reading and making sense

When and what do we read?

To some readers, this chapter may need to justify its existence. If we're going to use a computer to obtain information, then we almost always *want* something. We most commonly (but not always) use a *search* mechanism to find possible matches for it. We almost always *browse* through what's presented to us. All of these involve interacting with the computer itself. But we often don't continue using the computer once it comes to seriously *reading* the information. People's preferred response when faced with a long piece of text is usually to print it out on paper (depending on how hard or easy it is to do that). The reading that people do on screen, so the argument runs, is just enough to make them decide that they've got what they want, and no more. So a chapter on computer-based reading might seem unnecessary.

However, the printing rule doesn't always hold. The amount that we read from the screen, before or instead of printing it, varies with the task that we're doing. Also, computer screens have become a lot more comfortable to look at, with high **resolutions** and more print-like **fonts**. There is less incentive to deal with printer mechanics and tree wasting. This is particularly true when we know that we only need to read the information once, and won't need to refer back to it again. As email becomes a more instinctive way of communicating with others, we know that we can attach an electronic document, copy or paste bits of text, or simply send people the **URL** of the webpage we want them to see, so print isn't needed to circulate information either.

Thus on-screen reading is more common, even while non-text forms of information output (such as images, video and animation) also increase. We read to make sense of information and to convert it into knowledge. We must also consider how we do that when the information we've found is in those less printable forms of output rather than continuous text.

It is important to be careful when reading shallow reports about the supposed non-reading of websites by their users. The BBC reported[20] in 2002 that 'most online viewers spend less than 60 seconds at an average site'. But averages are misleading, and this is a classic example of 'lies, damn lies and statistics'. Of course the average is around 60 seconds because at many sites you spend less than 10 seconds—they don't interest you—while at others a page that does interest you can take several minutes to read. Take an average across several instances of 10 seconds and one of several minutes, and you can easily get an answer under 60. It doesn't mean any more than the way you treat a magazine, flicking over the advertisements and only focusing on the articles that appeal to you.

Sven Birkerts[25] wrote in 1994 (before the web was in common use), 'We are in some danger of believing that the speed and wizardry of our gadgets have freed us from the sometimes arduous task of turning pages in silence' (p. 32). Is this true? Or have the rumours of the death of reading been exaggerated? If we do read, what's involved?

First, one good reason to try direct reading from the screen. When I was working several years ago at Loughborough University, the staff development group at the university distributed a list of tips for research students. Among such mixed pearls of wisdom as 'Your supervisor is a busy person—and if they're not, change your supervisor' and 'Remember, purple [the university colour] clashes violently with many other colours' was this classic tip: '*Photocopying is not the same as reading!*' If you've ever printed, copied or bought a paper or book, meaning to read it later but actually just shelving and forgetting it ... you'll know exactly what they meant. Keeping a printed copy makes dust grow, not knowledge. Reading it *now* increases the chance of learning from it.

Below I'll talk about the strategies and processes that we seem to use when we're reading, and how they partly link to the type and structure of the document. With the types of electronic documents we see nowadays on the web, however, it isn't always obvious *what* strategy we should use, since many of the physical and contextual cues aren't present anymore. If I click on this link I'll see a PDF document, which may take several seconds to load. But is it a report? an academic journal paper? a marketing brochure or an honest product specification? Will it have a clear structure, and will I be aware of how long it is so I can decide how to handle it? Since we do take a strategic approach to handling documents and don't simply read them word for word, ideally we would get appropriate meta-information about their structure and content before we started looking at them. This often isn't the case online, as I'll discuss later.

Even when we do decide how to read an online text, Andy Dillon's excellent 1994 book[74] on this subject argued that *manipulating* it can be more awkward than the physical handling of paper (although this isn't always easy either, as in his example of people reading broadsheet newspapers on trains). He devoted much of his book to considering how we should design electronic text to make this easier. Like most reasonable authors, Dillon argued that electronic texts would be used increasingly for some tasks, while paper would be retained for others. It's always nice to curl up with a book, and to leaf through an abandoned newspaper in a café. The more I surf the web and write about it, the more of a relief it is to potter around the quiet sanity of my local public library.

People have risen to defend paper books over the past couple of decades, although it's never clear why such people believe them to be so threatened. It's alleged that around 1,000 a day are still published in print around the world—more than at any previous time in history—although nobody can put an exact figure on it since many publishers are small independents. The self-appointed 'defenders of the book' sometimes even argue that the 'user interface' of a paper book is in some way more intuitive than a computer interface. Some people genuinely seem to believe that given a sheet of paper, or a bound set of such sheets, every human on the planet would know how it was meant to be used, even if they haven't learned to read or write.

Yet anyone who witnessed the news reports in the early 1990s from South Africa, when the fall of apartheid led to the first ever national elections, would know otherwise. Villagers in some remote areas who had never seen paper before, when handed a folded ballot slip and a pencil in the training exercises before polling day, sometimes didn't even realise that it should be unfolded first, nor how to do that. They didn't know which end of the pencil to use, how the paper was split into separate lines for each candidate, or the importance of lining one's cross up with the picture of the person one was voting for. We have to learn the skills needed to use paper. We *don't* have them from birth, and we don't instantly use them when we first see the stuff. Since paper is a relatively late invention in human history anyway, how could it be otherwise?

As pointed out wittily by George P. Landow of Brown University, [167] books are technology too, yet to some writers the word 'generally means "only that technology of which I am frightened"' (p. 27)! Landow suggested considering books as 'machines', as well as computers. They had to be invented and developed, and they deliver text sequentially using certain physical mechanisms and socially agreed conventions. For all that literate readers love them, they are not necessarily ideal.

Children may be more aware of the artificial, physical nature of books, from all the clever infants' books made with holes, pop-up models, sound chips, ribbons and textures. Boring grown-ups only care about the text.

Maybe we won't always need to use paper books at all. It's hard to imagine this, but then it's always hard to imagine future alternatives to present technologies. The myth apparently is not true that the US Patent Office almost closed at the end of the nineteenth century, assuming that everything had already been invented.[252] But such myths persist partly because we have the same trouble today thinking of the future and trying to imagine what else will come along. Who can blame us? My computer can listen and interpret both my verbal speech and my handwriting on its screen (although I never use either feature, being already half-trained to type). What else could they make it do, short of reading my thoughts?

We also have some beautiful and comfortable visual technologies for our text. With ever-increasing screen resolutions, and the advent of beautiful Apple computers consisting entirely of a flat screen panel, things are changing faster and faster. Some new displays are almost paper-thin, and almost as lightweight.[78] So we may not always need to make our text concrete by destroying years of natural plant growth, mashing it to a pulp and splotching it with ink. Of course we may choose to do that anyway, for the sake of artistry and tradition.

Yet serious reading is a separate issue from the ways that I interact with the computer for doing shorter tasks. When I'm trying to deal with complex and/or abstract knowledge, reading continuous text is still the best (only?) way for me to go through the *process of information*. What I mean by this is using the word 'information' in a similar way to Gandhi's oft-quoted comment when asked about Western civilisation. Gandhi replied that he thought it would be a very good idea. The pun here of course depends on '*civilis*ation' being seen as the process of *becoming* civilised. Thus *inform*ation could be the process of becoming informed, not just the stuff we pick up *in* that process. Bryce Allen used this excitingly active definition in his 1996 book.[9] Sometimes pictures, video, animations, virtual environments or even music can achieve this process just as well as text. Ultimately, perhaps we'll work out where to plug in the electrode to transmit knowledge straight to our brains, yet for now, text still rules supreme.

Those who feel the need to 'defend' the printed book obsess about problems of manipulation, such as the ones mentioned by Dillon. It's easy—once you've had enough practice—to flick through a book to find a particular passage, to check the contents and index pages and turn straight to the correct section, to mark your place with bookmarks, etc. Yet all of these features have been easily reproduced electronically, and even surpassed in some ways (electronic book-marks never fall out onto the floor; search tools let you check every word of the book in seconds). More to the point, all are *unnecessary* when you're simply *reading* a text from start to finish. They are only relevant when you're trying to get 'chunks' of specific information out of it, as I discussed in Chapter 4 (pp. 177–84).

To read continuously, in a bath, on a train, or at a desk, involves very little physical manipulation. All it needs is a text that is legible, coherent and instantly updated as you finish each visible page. Hypertext and interactive tables of contents can now change the order in which we read the independent sections of a text (if they've been written to *be* truly independent, which is an art in itself and often requires some repetition and reader-boring), just as you may have decided to read this chapter first (or alone). But within each section, most of the work is still done by our eyes and brains, and using a different medium for presenting the text doesn't change that work at all.

Above I mentioned Andrew Dillon's book on electronic text,[74] which he wrote just before the web boom. It aimed to help decide what designers of on-screen information should do to help people to read it more easily. This is just as important and relevant, of course, when the text is on a web page. Dillon emphasised the three simple questions of 'how', 'what' and 'why'—questions which had previously been considered by separate branches of research. These help a great deal in determining how a text should be structured and presented. If you're just reading to extract a simple fact, such as a telephone number or weather forecast, of course you shouldn't have to read whole sentences at all. Reading, as a process that takes time and concentration, should ideally be reserved for when the meaning can't all be conveyed more briefly.

It is still true that most information technology is not particularly geared towards this time-consuming reading process. Instead, it was mostly developed to give us facts, or quick 'how to' procedures like recipes, rather than deeper and longer discourses that might change our ideas. In one of his popular books on modern technology,[213] Don Norman returns briefly to a distinction which he and his colleague David Rumelhart (another famous cognitive scientist) suggested back in the 1970s. They argued that human learning might be of at least three different types. *Accretion* just builds up facts, vocabulary, and visual categories, such as bird species, etc. *Tuning* is learning and improving a skill or procedure. *Restructuring* changes our whole conceptual structure, i.e. our **mental model** or **schema**, concerning a situation or subject area.

Continuous text is often aimed at the last of these three, but some readers will choose to skim it to extract facts or procedural solutions. An academic website may painstakingly explain an academic theory or controversy (aimed at restructuring). But students may well mine it just to find out who invented something and then leave (accretion). The skills and technologies I discussed in the previous two chapters allow us to achieve this no matter how dense or long the webpage (or PDF file) happens to be. Spending minutes or hours reading, on the other hand, implies that you're looking for *understanding*. Presumably in order to understand you'll need to do some of Rumelhart and Norman's 'restructuring', but there may also be more to understanding than that, as we'll see.

How do we read?

What comes after ABC: going holistic

The first piece of **netiquette** learned by many novice email users is avoiding the temptation to put on their keyboard's caps lock and type everything in upper case, like an old telegram. There are two reasons for this. One is that capital letters are the social equivalent of SHOUTING VERY LOUDLY. Another is that upper-case text is physically harder to read. Why?

When we learn to read, initially we have to painstakingly link individual letters with specific sounds. In an irregular language like English, we also have to learn that the sounds of those letters change, sometimes quite radically depending on the other letters within a word. So a lot of our early efforts at reading involve focusing on this syllable-to-sound matching.

Soon, though, most well-taught readers stop having to do this for most words. Instead, we recognise a *whole group of letters* as a single meaningful **morpheme**. With the upstrokes (e.g. d, f, h, k, l) and downstrokes (e.g. q, y, p, g) of our letters, the shapes of the English alphabet form a much more distinctive set of these patterns as lower-case than upper-case. This is even more true for languages like French, which also include accents on the lower-case versions.

So the shapes of familiar words, and of the morphemes they consist of (e.g. 'spelling' has two, 'spell' and '-ing' where the latter has meaning in implying a verb), are much more distinctive when written in lower-case than in upper-case, and that makes us identify the shapes much more quickly. Over the course of a whole sentence or paragraph, the millisecond savings for each well-shaped word add up

215

to much less reading time, and much less physical movement by the eyes.

This also demonstrates that by the time we're fluent readers, we're *not* reading the single letters anymore (or their equivalent in other alphabets), but holistic letter *patterns*. When we proofread for spelling errors (a dying art, as computers take this over) we are looking for patterns which don't fit a known word, but we still don't have to assess each word letter-by-letter to spot that the pattern isn't right. This is why we are more likely, like primitive computer spell-checkers, to overlook typing mistakes that still make a different real word (such as the common typo 'form' for 'from').

However, this doesn't mean that learning to read is a simple matter of picking up those letter patterns. As Steven Pinker has pointed out,[228] it is wrong to leap from the idea that language develops naturally, even if we believe this (as Pinker apparently does), to the idea that reading develops this way too. Like the South African citizens mentioned earlier, we have to learn consciously to connect the letters to sounds and the patterns to meanings. This is a culture-specific, non-evolved, skill which our ancestors didn't have until long after they started speaking. It involves piece-by-piece linking of visual forms with the arbitrary sounds and meanings of our verbal language.

Threading through text

For some, of course, particularly people with seriously impaired vision (or with certain types of physical movement impairment), reading in the visual sense isn't realistic.* Also many fully sighted people also now listen to audiobooks when trapped in their car, although if they took a train instead they could read the text more quickly themselves. Speech generation technology was built into the Apple Macintosh over a decade ago, and can also work on other computers with an adaptor. This allows you to listen to any text instead of reading it.

Is the difference trivial? No. Listening involves quite different perceptual and cognitive processes from reading, partly because it is restricted to being almost completely sequential (you may think you read text sequentially, but you don't always, as we'll see below). You

---

*You may be assuming that people with impaired vision would use Braille. It's not widely realised, however, that only a small minority of people who have visual problems can read Braille – mainly those who have been almost completely blind from birth and so were specially educated. Most visual impairments start later in life, so people are more likely to turn to aids that either enlarge text or read it aloud, or both.

apparently have a small 'audio buffer' in your **working memory** which will let you mentally repeat the last few words if your attention wanders very briefly, but this only works for a few seconds. Beyond that the process is out of your control, because the words proceed in real time rather than just sitting on the page for you to explore at leisure. If your mind wanders when reading, you can easily reread the last sentence. To hear it again when it's being spoken you need to get the reader/player to stop and go back, which is a lot more effort than just moving your eyes.

Compare this to the rapid visual processes of reading. In the early 1980s[45] researchers concluded that we seem to retain between 7 and 17 written letters in our sensory 'store', in other words as a visual image in our minds that fades in around 90 milliseconds (around one-tenth of a second). However, this only applies to words which we've focused our eyes on (i.e. within about 2 degrees of angle from the central fixation point of our eyes). To move our eyes to focus on the next (or back to the previous) bit of the text, we don't have to move our heads unless we want to see something that's more than 30 degrees of angle from the current focus. Most reading involves very little head movement. Of course, if both the text and the book or screen were very large, this would change. So larger typefaces and pages are only helpful up to a point (as users of large-print books may know).

What did I mean when I said you don't read text sequentially? Surely it wouldn't make sense if we read sentences in any old order? Careful cognitive studies have revealed that yes, obviously we read most of the words and sentences in a text in the order they're written. But our eye movements and cognitive processes are constantly zipping back to the context of the previous words within a sentence, and of the previous sentences within the paragraph.[235] We apparently even manage to sense what's coming up next without being consciously aware or physically looking at it.[236] As we read through a paragraph, we might reach a sentence referring to something or someone mentioned a couple of sentences earlier. Our mental processing forms associations of the new information with the previously read knowledge about the object or person, while our eyes may flick back to check what came before.

Many of these eye movements (called **saccades**) happen too rapidly for our conscious awareness to follow, so we assume that we're simply ploughing through word-by-word like a small child. Other, more deliberate movements may consciously check back up the page to an earlier sentence or paragraph, particularly in texts that we're finding harder to understand.

The reason why this happens is that, as with every other type of information we encounter, we can't just pile snippets of information on top of each other in our memories – we have to take the meaning of the information and build it into complex networks or webs of knowledge. Our eye movements during reading reflect that web building. In a sense we're creating our own mental **hypertext**. The ability to do this so rapidly is unique to us humans. It's another of those miracles of human cognition that we rarely stop to admire.

There is already plenty of research literature on how all these mental processes work, and I can't hope to go through it all here. Decades of painstaking experiments and theories have thrashed out the process by which we interpret each word within the sentence, and interpret that in turn within the overall passage. Gradually, psychologists have come to accept that many of these cognitive processes must occur in parallel. Their models are now sophisticated yet clear enough to simulate on computers. There is great value in this work, especially in helping us to understand reading 'disorders', such as the various types of dyslexia. [238]

The difficulty comes, as with so many other much-studied aspects of cognition, when we try to apply all of this careful, isolated work to everyday situations. As Dillon [74] pointed out, psychologists have tended to focus only on the part of reading where you are settled in front of the text, simply looking at it and learning what you see. They have less to say about the messier issues, such as navigating through the text to find your place (which might be better defined as browsing as I discussed in Chapter 4). They also can't help much if you react with strong emotions that might make you choose to ignore, misinterpret or reject what you see.

Dillon was quick to add that information science couldn't help to fill the gaps in this topic either, as it had never tried to make reading part of its remit. It had focused entirely on helping people to find information, but not on what they then do with it. He found a beautiful quotation about this from a 1970s book on reading: [123] 'At the point where the reader and the book come together . . . it has been the librarian's habit to leave the happy pair and tiptoe quietly away, like a Victorian novelist.' [Hatt p. 3; Dillon p. 62]

Clearly, as Dillon and the authors he cited were well aware, reading online takes place only after a lot of other things have happened. What you choose to attend to in a text, what motives you bring and how hard you'll be prepared to work to absorb the author's full intended meaning, all depend on the context. Cognitive psychologists flap irritably at the word 'context', as if it threatens the credibility of all their tightly controlled lab experiments (which it sometimes does). A book like this one can't dodge it.

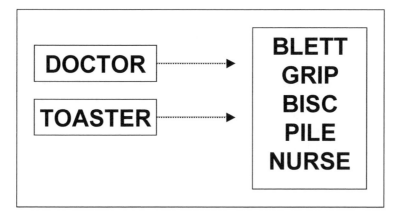

Figure 5.1. Semantic priming: as you go through the list of real and nonsense words, you identify NURSE more quickly if you previously saw DOCTOR than if you saw TOASTER. What we see creates expectations of meaning, even when we know that the meaning is irrelevant.

To be fair, reading researchers have studied context at 'micro' levels. For instance, a great deal of work on reading has revolved around the way that context *primes* us to expect particular things. Semantic **priming** appeared in experiments in the early 1970s. [192] You can ask people whether or not a string of letters is a word (when sometimes it is a real word like NURSE, and sometimes a nonsense word like BLETT). When it was a real word, people answered more quickly if a previous word had been semantically related to it (e.g. DOCTOR) than when not (e.g. TOASTER). Somehow hearing the related word had created a flicker of semantic context, that made NURSE easier to recognise. See Figure 5.1).

Similarly, syntactic priming means that a word is more quickly recognised when it is the type of word (e.g. noun or verb) that fits best into an earlier incomplete sentence. So our expectations make a big difference as we read even a small bit of text.

We also sometimes seem to skip words and sentences altogether, because we can so easily grasp the **pragmatics** of what the reader (or speaker) intended. Once again, this is shown by very neat, clever, but inevitably artificial experiments. Perhaps even those who dismiss psychology as forever 'proving the obvious' might be impressed to find that a sentence like 'Can't you be friendly?'—clearly suggesting a personal complaint—*doesn't* prime people to respond more quickly to a literally (but not pragmatically) similar sentence such as 'Are you unable to be friendly?' (which loses a lot of the implied criticism). [102] We don't seem to take the literal interpretation and *then* move from that to a more sophisticated inference about what the person really meant. Instead we seem to take the whole sentence and impute a certain tone and implication to it straight away.

We also make inferences that leap effortlessly from sentence to sentence, so that we can deduce that the 'he' in one sentence refers to the hero or villain mentioned earlier in that paragraph (this is called *anaphoric reference* or just *anaphors*). We even cope with *ellipsis* where whole phrases are missing from a sentence (e.g. 'I haven't learned any German but my husband has'—Has what? How did you decide that he'd learned German?).

If we're that clever while we're reading, it's perhaps not surprising that our models of the mental processes involved are still being refined.* There's a whole lot of thinking going on, and it happens much too fast for us to follow. For instance, we seem to need only a fraction of a second to decide which person or thing is missing from an anaphorical phrase or sentence, because we anticipate likely candidates in advance. In fact, it wouldn't be fun reading a passage that avoided anaphors. The text would actually be *harder* to read. It would be so wordy that the main verb would be drowned out, and the unnecessary words would repeat information that we don't need to see again and would waste time reprocessing. The sentence would also be a lot less elegant. Try imagining a rewrite of Philip Larkin's famous verse[174] which makes heavy use of anaphor:

> They fuck you up, your mum and dad.
> They may not mean to, but they do.
> They fill you with the faults they had
> And add some extra, just for you.

Here's my attempt at it. Bang goes the poetry.

> Your mum and your dad fuck you up.
> Your mum and your dad may not mean to fuck you up, but your mum and your dad do fuck you up.
> Your mum and your dad fill you with faults. Your mum and your dad had the same faults that they fill you up with.
> And your mum and your dad add some extra faults to you. The extra faults are just for yourself.

The types of inferences you made to interpret 'they', 'had', and 'extra' in the original version are necessary, automatic inferences. They let you grasp the basic meaning of each line quickly, while your brain sorts out what's missing from it. Other inferences we make are

---

*Another interesting thing to note, in passing: in a sentence like the one that references this footnote, you probably paused a tiny bit longer over the word 'are' than over the rest of the sentence. Why? Because 'involved' could have been the sentence's main verb, so 'are' was a surprise that made you change your idea of the sentence's structure.

optional, and depend on our situation and the way in which we choose to read. Cognitivists have had many years of wrangling over the extent to which people make different kinds of inference automatically while reading.[91]

Applying this research area to practical information use, Bryce Allen[9] cited some research suggesting that students who score high marks in college courses, and those who gain high scores on measures of creativity, seem to make deeper inferences from reading a text. Of course, it's not clear where the direction of causality lies. Are you more creative because you've learned creative modes of thought from your reading, and do you then score higher grades? Or is it some kind of basic creativity that lets you read 'beyond the text' to start with? Such correlations don't really help us figure out the exact cognitive processes involved, nor how to help more students to do better.

As Allen also made clear, and as various cognitive research has demonstrated, there's always a role of motivation. If we're really trying to get under the skin of a passage of text because it has some important personal relevance, and if we're reading at our own leisure, then we'll probably put more effort into making deeper inferences. This will differ from the strict 'call of duty' that results, say, from a student participant reading whatever's flashed on the screen in a timed experiment. As a cartoonist made one of his characters say, as he skimmed merrily through the day's new email, 'Reading goes quickly when you don't slow down to comprehend.'

Understanding understanding

So what's the result of all that clever processing? Allen[9] argued that the 'process of information' discussed earlier involves encoding and 'transmitting' the writer's cognitive structures to the reader, who 'interprets them, and learns from them' (p. 3). Yet, as Allen discussed, it's not always obvious whether the 'cognitive structures' that the writer intended are transmitted to the reader. Maybe a scattering of words and inferred concepts gets moulded into a completely different shape by the time the reader's long-term memory stores it away. If we wanted a computer to be able to 'read' a long-winded text and construct a simple summary or concept map for us, it would have to be able to do the same. But could it? It would help if we knew exactly what we take from text when we 'comprehend' it.

Until quite recently, simple and vivid stories were the most common type of text used in psychology experiments. This was an understandable choice. With stories, it's easy to test readers' comprehension by asking them questions and varying the amount of time you give them to infer complex situations. Then you see if they notice subtle changes in wording or meaning when they're shown sentences that almost, but not quite, match the originals. We seem to build some kind of **mental model** of the situation described in a text and throw away the original word order. This is important because our language allows us many different ways to order a sentence, but the reader has no reason to care or remember which order was chosen. It doesn't matter whether I write:* 'Nelly, the elephant who said goodbye to the circus, packed her trunk,' or 'Nelly the elephant packed her trunk and said goodbye to the circus.'

In both cases, if you're asked to say whether the word 'packed' was in the sentence, you'll get the answer faster if I first show you the word 'elephant' than if I show you the word 'circus'. This is true even if you saw the first sentence in which 'circus' and 'packed' were next door to each other[233]—they were close but not related, so word order didn't matter. Also, you might forget that the phrase 'said goodbye' was used at all, and falsely 'recognise' the phrase 'ran away' instead. What's more, if you'd seen the word 'unpacked' instead of 'packed', you would have more trouble with the later tests because the word you'd seen made less *situational* sense: why would someone unpack before going away?[107] You couldn't fit that into your mental model so easily.

All this clever research leads us to models of reading that focus on the *concepts* we learn about, *not* the exact words and sentences that we see. This is easy to believe when we're talking about simple stories involving concrete objects, but what about much more complex texts, about abstract concepts like love or politics? This is where we run into serious research problems.

When school teachers test children's comprehension of some topic, based on what they've read, they have to do so by asking them to recall facts, to make deductions that weren't actually stated, and to use the knowledge they've gained to solve problems. In other words, we make the children reconstruct the information because we have no way of seeing it in their brains. Unfortunately, this reconstruction is another cognitive process which not only can fail (you might just forget things), but also can be interpreted differently by the tester and the reader. Just asking a question in a certain way might subtly push readers to reinterpret what they thought they knew, in the same way that lawyers use leading questions in court. This is true even for scenes that have been witnessed personally, rather than just read

---

*This is my own example, not one used in real experiments to my knowledge. Obviously if you knew the old children's song from which the second sentence was taken, this would bias your responses in an experiment!

about, as Elizabeth Loftus demonstrated famously in her 1970s experiments. [179] When asking people how fast a car was going before it 'hit' or 'smashed into' another one, saying 'smashed' makes people estimate higher speeds than just weakly saying 'hit'.

In other words, sometimes looking at someone's comprehension, like looking at particles in quantum physics, actually alters it. We can study people's searching and browsing with some confidence because the results are visible, and can be judged by the users themselves, and those judgements are 'good enough' to help us identify where the process went right or wrong. They're probably not altered significantly by the *process* of the user saying, 'Oh yes, that's the sort of thing ... No, that one isn't.' But it's hard to judge the success of someone's *reading* without adding extra cognitive processes which alter it, by creating specific task demands.

In other words, one problem in studying reading is that the aim of the game is to get to certain 'higher' mental states which, in themselves, we don't yet really understand, i.e. understanding itself! I hinted at this issue in earlier chapters, because it's one reason why computers aren't so good at picking out things that have related meanings or topics—they don't (yet) assimilate the information they carry into some big, semantic net in the brain. Will they ever?

John Searle[259] is an American philosopher who, through the 1980s and 1990s, caused much head scratching in the community of researchers interested in artificial intelligence (AI). Searle argued that our efforts to build working computer programs that simulate human thought and language can *never* achieve a true human-like mind. His main argument was that they never have *intentionality* (something I touched on in earlier chapters—basically, they can't want anything unless they've been told to want it). He also claimed that they can never really *understand* what they're dealing with.

There are various versions of the story which Searle has told to make this point, but it usually goes like this. A person is locked inside a room. He or she neither speaks nor understands any Chinese. People outside the room can post written Chinese questions through a slot in the door. The person inside the room can create suitable answers to the questions by putting Chinese symbols together, following a rule book which is in there too. Every possible question is covered by the rule book (assuming this is possible, which some authors have rightly queried: see Figure 5.2). So if you're inside the room, you can always put together the right set of symbols to form an answer. You might even be good enough to 'pass' something similar to the famous '**Turing test**': an outsider actually can't tell whether it's a true Chinese speaker in the room, or just you with your rule book, or some computerized version of the rule book

So where's it all going, then?

Figure 5.2. Searle's Chinese Room: the first problem.

that can match up the symbols without human help. But according to Searle, no matter how long you're in there you never *understand* Chinese.

Hundreds of papers and books have cited this story. Writers from backgrounds as varied as neurophysiology, mathematics, psychology, computer science and even physics have weighed into the now 25-year-old debate. Searle, and other thinkers who partly agree with him, [101] argue that computer models of mental processes are always at this level: the model can put together the right associations and symbols, but never really *understands* what it's talking about.

He may, or may not, be right about computer models. Many writers[27] have argued either that he's wrong, or that his point rests on an unclear idea of what 'understanding' is anyway. Yet ultimately, nobody *else* seems to have a clear idea of what 'understanding' is, either (nor 'consciousness', usually mentioned in the same breath by writers in this area). Whole philosophy books have been devoted to this issue, but somehow it hasn't got any clearer. Until it does, we can't test Searle's claim one way or the other, but we can still build a lot of useful models.

Meanwhile you may wonder: what has all this to do with reading text on a screen? My point is that Searle's and others' worries about artificial intelligence have made us think much harder about what we *do* mean by 'understanding'. If we're to judge the success or otherwise of people's reading, we need to ponder this too.

What we obviously don't mean, as Searle stresses, is just recycling the words. Even though our education systems, at their worst, often only ask students to show that they have picked up the facts and can recycle them in the right context, at their best we expect much more than that. To be sure, the errors they make in their recycling can give alarming insight into their misunderstandings, as when a student wrote, 'Marie Curie won the Noel Prize for inventing the radiator'.[127] But more often, you can't distinguish comprehension problems from failures of expression, as when other students (quoted in the same book) claimed that Elizabeth I 'calmed her soldiers during a Spanish attack by assuring them that she shared a stomach with her father', and, 'Without the discovery of the flying buttock it would have been an impossible job to build the Gothic cathedral.' If you asked these students if they really thought Elizabeth I didn't have her own stomach, or to draw a flying but*tress*, they would probably get it right. Let's hope so, anyway.

Student essays aren't realistic of the rest of life. It's not enough in other circumstances (or in advanced education) for people to write a standard regurgitation of 'Everything I know about World War II'. We want them to use their knowledge to make *inferences*. Many studies evaluating student learning from electronic texts seem to have focused on recall for facts,[86] although others have also probed deeper.[6] Surely we must expect people not only to recall what they saw, but to use it to consider related questions like 'Do you think the war would have been avoided if Hitler hadn't failed as an artist earlier in life?'. Or, more mundanely, 'Given what I read in the online weather forecast, how crowded will it be on the roads this weekend?' Whether a factually correct, but non-question-answering, essay is allowed to pass an exam depends a lot on the brainwork *beyond* the rote learning.

In theory, a computer can be programmed to make inferences and select facts from what it knows about Hitler and people's responses to failure, and about what else might have caused the war. The program might then 'write' a much better essay than the human student. But would the program *understand*?

In Searle's eyes, presumably, the answer is no because the program still wouldn't really know what a war is like, what or who Hitler was, or what it feels like to fail at something. In other words, 'understanding' must involve associating concepts with the real, concrete, world of perceptions and the (not yet understood) internal world of conscious experience and imagery. But then what about, say, obscure aspects of particle physics, or mathematics? Can't they be understood mostly, if not completely, without relating them back to the outside world (even if this gives us brain ache)? Of course they can, but only some people are willing to juggle with so many abstractions. After all, experience shows that it's hard enough to keep some students interested in the 'abstractions' of cognitive science, which is about their own minds. Abstractions are hard work for us, but to a computer they're bread and butter—in fact, they're almost all it has.

For a student, just knowing how the basic ideas and arguments work—or making it seem *as if* she or he knows—is good enough. It's nowhere near good enough for the scientist who wants to take them further—to make inferences and links 'beyond the information given' and hence solve theoretical problems. For this moving on, we do need to know what the information means, at a level way beyond the Chinese symbol-arrangers in Searle's room. Even the most disinterested student has to have some idea about how each symbol or piece of information does, or doesn't, link to other knowledge. *That's* missing from Searle's experiment, but *not* necessarily from cognitive computer models. Also, ideally, that other knowledge would link back to perceptions of the real world in some way, not just to more symbols. Otherwise we'd suspect that our mathematicians and physicists didn't understand their concepts any more than we did.

On one level, we'd be right. Our need to link back to reality seems to be important not for thinking itself, but to give us the *motivation* to think. Its lack of importance for reasoning is why some authors have assumed that Searle is really talking more about intentionality, in the sense of motivation, than about computers' capacity for thought *per se*. He's written an entire book about that issue.[260]

However, computer models can, and do, make semantic links among the concepts they learn, just as we do. As I mentioned earlier, they can be made to form categories and to reason logically (and even less than logically, i.e. inductively) about real-life situations. Perhaps they don't have such rich imagery, ideas and emotions to associate with each concept, but how far that matters depends on us deciding how much of a big deal it is to have them, which philosophers and cognitive scientists still haven't cracked yet (and may never do). Roger Penrose, who broadly agrees with Searle, has argued that adding 'emotion' to a computer model wouldn't be good enough to make it really 'aware',[224] and he may or may not be right—but such a computer could still simulate a human pretty darn well if it had it.

Meanwhile Searle often writes as if he assumes[259] that computers can't even handle semantic meanings and link them together in the way I just mentioned—or at least, that their handling of them is somehow not good enough because it's not a *subjective* experience, e.g. of 'hot' or 'red'. If a computer had sensors that could experience heat or colour, and some kind of 'emotional' value judgement about how desirable they were, it still wouldn't be 'subjective' enough for Searle or for Penrose. But it would be a pretty convincing, intelligent and helpful robot 'mind'. It would go further down the road to 'understanding' than we often do when something looks complicated or irrelevant.

Research has suggested that for humans, our liking of concrete reality isn't always a good thing anyway. It can make or break our patterns of logical thinking, for good or bad, unless we train ourselves to ignore it. We saw in previous chapters that our attempts to solve logical problems go more or less awry if the problems are couched in different ways. Wason's cards are much easier to solve correctly if they concern permission to do something than if they just refer to passive states of being. But other realistic scenarios can have the opposite effect and make us less logical. Cognition is embedded in our everyday realities and strategies in this way, but that research showed that it isn't always *good* to try to 'understand' only by linking concepts to reality, because it can lead our thinking awry.

Similarly, when we read a continuous piece of text, such as a section of this book, our main aim is to link the ideas to things we already know, and preferably ones which excite some emotion in us, including the frustrations and excitements of sitting in front of a computer screen. Making more links to reality, and fewer to abstractions, *doesn't* always make us understand better. In fact, it can get in the way if we start being distracted by things we know which aren't related to the argument at hand (e.g. if a reader of a certain paragraph above was by now pondering Hitler's failed artistic career, instead of this tricky issue of understanding).

David Gelernter, writing[101] on creative thought and the potential for computers to develop it, called this distraction problem 'low focus' reading. By this he meant that the exact semantics of the text stop being the major concern of the reader, who is concerned about something tangential to it. Associations and ideas of our own could get in the way, when we should have focused on our knowledge of Hitler only for long enough to see the point being made. Yet these links to reality do give us a greater motivation to *try* to understand. Gelernter pointed out that 'low focus' can allow our imagination and emotions to enrich our response to what we read (e.g. with poetry). Where we want someone to learn important abstract concepts from our text, though, it might sometimes be counterproductive to add 'sexy' content that distracts their attention. This is particularly true for young students.[6]

In education, obviously there's a lot of concern about what helps and hinders students' understanding as they read a text, both online and offline. A thoughtful 1994 review of research studies about this by educational researchers Patricia Alexander, Jonna Kulikowich and Tamara Jetton[6] argued that there were many flaws in people's attempts to look at student learning from text. Shallow learning measures, and the common use of passages from sources which do not go very deeply into a topic, such as encyclopaedias, was just one of many problems Alexander *et al.* highlighted in research done at that time, and such issues still seem unresolved in this badly needed research area.[270]

Alexander *et al.* also bemoaned a tendency to compare different students studying different versions of a text, rather than designing studies to look at **within-subject** comparisons. Comparing different people, instead of comparing the same person doing one thing and then doing the alternative, always has the problem of a lot more **error variance**: the students differ from each other in many other ways, not just in what they were asked to do during the research. Comparing one person to himself isn't easy either, though, especially when you want that person to have *changed* in some way (such as learning something) during the course of the research. You can't 'unchange' them and then make them 'change' again.

Ways around this include having two different things to learn, and teaching the person one topic by one method (e.g. reading hypertext) and the other topic by the other method (e.g. printed text), to see how they compare. However, you'd need to hold steady, in your statistical analysis, the person's different levels of prior knowledge and interest in the two topics, so that they could be compared on the same terms, and this level of statistical sophistication isn't common in applied research. You'd also have the far trickier problem of matching the two topics in terms of the concepts you wanted the students to learn. What if one topic was intrinsically harder than the other? A lot more careful preparation would be needed.

Unsurprisingly, among the conclusions reached by Alexander *et al.* was that any educational text, whether 'linear' (continuous, like in most books) or 'non-linear' (such as hypertext), needs to be matched to the likely knowledge and interest levels of the reader. This must have been known at least since man first scratched letters on parchment, but somehow it can't be repeated enough to educational resource developers. More importantly, Alexander *et al.* suggested that some of the problems that occur when people are reading 'non-linear' texts (**hypertext** on computers) might not be due to the high-level 'conceptual mapping' problems that are often assumed. It may be that people with poor reading skills in the first place, who don't comprehend properly what they read in a single paragraph, have even more trouble when they have to navigate through a browser as well.

However, it's hard to be sure about such issues anyway when, as Alexander *et al.* complained, too many research studies reduce the idea of 'learning' to a test of shallow facts, rather than conceptual depth. This concern has also been expressed repeatedly by other reviewers of this area. As Stephen Weyer[306] wrote in 1989, 'Finding the facts faster will matter little in the long run if we don't understand what they mean, especially if they are isolated or they respond to the wrong question' (p. 295).

One good point about the increased use of 'non-linear' sources, such as web pages, is the encouragement it gives us to make extra conceptual links across subjects. Perhaps people will think more broadly and see new analogies between different situations as they read different information sources online that are linked by similar terms or ideas. Alexander *et al.* suggested that non-linear text encourages this, while traditional text-based learning leaves the reader to decide what else to look at and how it might be relevant. So perhaps online, 'understanding' takes on a broader (if shallower?) meaning.

Perhaps understanding also concerns whether we can apply the new knowledge beyond its original context of use. Searle's imaginary Chinese room captives, on their release, cannot reuse anything they've seen in the room, although if they did start to learn Chinese seriously then their visual memory of the symbols could come in handy. However, a robot that has sat in a lab for 20 years 'knowing' all about how things work in a restaurant, because it was programmed with the cognitive 'script' models designed in the 1970s by Roger Schank and his colleagues,[254] might make a reasonable stab at performing appropriately when finally carried out of the lab and down to the local curry house.

Given the right inputs in the restaurant, the robot might work out what was happening, who was eating the vindaloo, and how the bill should be divided. Its **procedural** memory would be perfect—it would never make a mistake about what to do. But the quality of its **declarative** memory would, just like a human's, only be testable by seeing what questions it could answer. It would still have no intentionality. Without intentionality, its level of understanding is almost a moot point: it could do what *we* wanted, but it's irrelevant whether it might still use that knowledge when it wanted something else, because it couldn't want anything else. It wouldn't even want the curry.

As I stated in Chapter 2, writers and teachers and website creators all assume that readers do have some intentionality, without being sure of what it might involve. We want people to be able to take what they read or learn, and benefit from it in ways that we haven't even thought of. That is another important point in itself. We can't think of all those possible benefits, partly because we have no idea what else may happen in that person's life, what other knowledge they might suddenly link it to, or what their needs and desires might motivate them to do. In other words, once their understanding belongs to them, and not to us, we can't easily assess it. We hope that their links will spread beyond the facts to other experiences, analogous situations, and new ideas. We don't want them to stop at *just* understanding—whether or not their computer could ever go that far in the first place.

Choosing what to keep

What can computers do to help readers to pick out the bits they, personally, need to understand and remember? They already have some useful features. Obviously the copy and paste functions are a great way to distil an online text. Many computer users I've met, however, still underuse this. The use of note-taking software should also help people to distil what's relevant to their current task. We can use clever box-and-arrow 'brainstorming' software, [141] sophisticated word-processors and simple text programs that create 'clippings' or 'sticky notes'. Current versions of Microsoft's Word software have a crude but sometimes effective 'Summarize' feature: sentences from a text that appear to be important are picked out and collated into a short précis (Word's criteria for picking them aren't clear—position within paragraphs seems to be the main one).

It seems, though, that people will only tend to take notes when they are preparing a text or presentation of their own, or need precise details to be transported elsewhere. In many everyday tasks, such as browsing a newspaper or checking the weather forecast, we don't bother to record the key facts or ideas, even though we know our memory is faulty. Young people tend to carry this carefree self-reliance over into tasks which are more complex and information-rich, unless they're shown the value of note-taking.

Even with everyday tasks, wisdom and self-awareness comes with age, as our memory faults worsen and our experience shows the problems that result. This tends to drive us toward more careful and habitual use of physical records—shopping and 'to do' lists, diaries and address books, and physical sticky notes, that truly wonderful invention which we can stick in obvious places where we won't fail to see it. In a recent complex research project, supervising students half my age, I used to sense them humouring me as I prepared checklists and scripts for us all to follow. I knew I wasn't the only one who would miss some details without those reminders.

A very common device used by students in reading is underlining or highlighting key phrases or sentences in the text. A small but in-depth qualitative study of readers by researchers at Rank Xerox's EuroPARC research laboratories, in 1997, led its authors[216] to argue that this was a useful thing. Although an infuriatingly selfish habit when applied to library books and not erased, underling/high-lighting does seem to enforce the concepts in some readers' minds. It helps them to do a second 'skim reading' of the text later that only bothers with the underlined items. The text highlighting feature in Word also allows this on a computer, but web browsers currently don't have any note-helping features like this.

The same researchers commented on readers' complaints about spatial crowding, or what has sometimes been called 'screen estate' (analogous to the term 'real estate' in America). With paper documents, you may have a desk or floor available to spread out the papers and sort them into piles, and perhaps to read bits from several at once while constructing a summary that links their ideas together. It's almost a joke that in contrast, the windowfuls of text that we may access online are piled up in a space smaller than a TV dinner tray. As cheap, flat, high-quality screens become as common-place as 'home cinema' TV screens probably will, we will be able to make the same use of spatially arranging multiple documents as we do with paper ones.

I mentioned above how Word can précis a passage of text. Yet this automatic summarising can really only work for either very simple or very predictably structured narratives. Authors rarely make it plain, in their prose, which sentences are the key ones that a computer should learn from. Even if they did, a reader with a different agenda might disagree. So even computers with some built-in semantic 'knowledge' would find it hard to know what to pick out from a new passage. It seems that 'literacy' can't be replaced by 'computer literacy' for a long time to come.

Of course, any humanities scholar would have told you that from the start, partly in defence of their own interests! This is also true, of course, for John Searle, the anti-cognitivist philosopher. His scope for pondering the nature of the human mind might *seem* (but not really *be*) under threat if it could clearly be 'reduced' to (extra-ordinarily sophisticated) computer programs. As this 'reductionism' *isn't* clearly proved, he can go on denying it. Any influence of this potential 'threat' is hard to spot, of course.

Samuel Taylor Coleridge will be revolving in his grave. Kathryn Sutherland[284] has pointed out that Coleridge, writing in 1817, condemned the newly fashionable circulating libraries. These let readers borrow and swap books for a small fee. Thanks to these, the novel and other forms of literature aimed at non-scholarly readers really took off. Coleridge was afraid they led to what would now be called 'dumbing down'. He felt that readers would simply graze through a novel, taking on board passively 'the moving phantasms of one man's delirium', instead of actively engaging with the material and critiquing it. Sutherland quoted him (p. 21) as writing 'I dare not compliment their *pass-time*, or rather *kill-time*, with the name of *reading*'.[284]

Modern doomsayers make the precise same point about the escapism of TV, movies and computer games, where one doesn't need even to conjure up the sights and sounds in one's own imagination. Philosopher Hubert Dreyfus has argued that internet use is the modern parallel to Kierkegaard's[154] decrying of 'the Press' back in 1846. To Kierkegaard the way that everything was reported simply for curiosity's sake, but nobody had to take any risks and commit to doing anything about anything, would lead to nihilism and despair. For Dreyfus, the internet user ends up the same way: 'Life consists in fighting off boredom by being a spectator at everything interesting in the universe and in communicating with everyone else so inclined ... Kierkegaard thought that people were addicted to the press, and we can now add the Web, because the anonymous spectator *takes no risks*' (p. 81).

Dreyfus is entirely wrong about risk on the internet—it is possible (though rare) to pick up a virus, have your browsing tracked by nosey cookies, have your credit card used fraudulently, upset your employer or parents, be targeted by a sexual predator or identity thief, and lose a lot of friends and credibility. His point about passivity and curiosity would perhaps be a potential problem if the internet was only about surfing, emailing and joining chat rooms.

With the press and other media, apart from the few who write letters or take part in programme-making, we do quite passively graze information, and discuss it with others out of curiosity (and sometimes actual concern, depending on the issue). With the web, though, we can also be active authors and artists, advertisers and publishers, buyers and sellers, cataloguers and writers. It's not clear how many people do bother to create their own website when they sign up for home access. But the huge number of blogs and personal homepages, the volunteer-created websites for all kinds of causes and campaigns, and the thousands of people buying and selling goods on eBay, make us much more active. We can choose and create what *is* meaningful to our lives. In fact, it's hard to avoid doing so, whereas with the traditional press we are stuck with someone else's choice of content.

Also, mainly *because* anyone can create web content, it's much more obvious to readers that what's out there is subjective and individual rather than objective and indifferent, so our critical faculties are probably sharpened, at least for some types of site, although we probably do still treat too much as credible and relevant (particularly on sites that ape the press that we're used to, that Kierkegaard savaged so bitterly).

It's nearly two centuries since Coleridge's remarks, and almost 160 years since Kierkegaard's, yet many of us do still find ourselves dealing with multiple texts, making critical judgements, and building complex mental networks of concepts from them. In fact, every chapter in this book has shown that the explosion of online information makes these skills *more* crucial now, for far more people. In Coleridge's day the curious, literate elite had simpler and slower lives. Fortunately, despite his fears, reading and critical skills have survived to help us cope with a far more complex world.

To summarise, in 'understanding' we can separate the issue of intentionality from semantic concept linking, critical thinking, and basic general usefulness. However, our and the author's intentionality (basically, the **pragmatics** of the text, which I discussed in earlier chapters) influences the *ways* in which we'll link the text with other things we know, and try to use its information.

When we loosely use the word 'understand', we normally assume all of these aspects. When we're trying to read text on a computer screen, we can achieve them all (so long as the language used in the text is familiar to us). The computer may only be able to help us with the semantic linkages, at best (and currently most of us don't have systems that can even do that). Even then, for it to know what kinds of links are helpful, we may first have to teach the computer what our interests are.

In a crude way, we do this when we perform a search for specific keywords. Some search engines highlight those words and phrases in the text they retrieve, so that we can quickly scan down to the relevant paragraph. The computer may, or may not, use a thesaurus to get to related phrases as well as the ones we typed in, and it may, or may not, also show some kind of conceptual mapping based on analysing the document's use of nouns and verbs. Yet at least until the Pentagon gets our whole lives taped,[239] the computer will still depend on *our* input about we're trying to 'understand'.

Painting a thousand words: non-text information

One of my personal research interests is in people's **spatial cognition**. It's been well noted in that area that in everyday

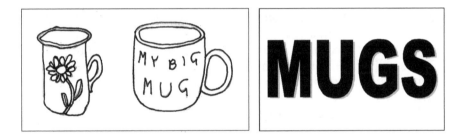

Figure 5.3. The picture superiority effect: even the simplest picture gives far more information and visual distinctiveness than the word that names it.

language, we tend to talk about *viewing* pictures, but *reading* maps. This is because maps, like text, involve symbolic representation: instead of looking like the things they're portraying, they have to be interpreted to some extent (although they match the originals much more closely than words do). Obviously, specialists who study the visual arts, or graphs, or scientific visualisations, will feel that there is plenty to 'read' in those images too—it's all a matter of how much depth you're seeking from the information conveyed. Back to that 'intentionality' issue again: even a painting has layers of pragmatics to consider if you want to.

This shows that things are a little more complex than you might think if you've heard of a once much-feted concept in psychology, the **picture superiority effect**. It's been known for a long time[265] that people are better able to say whether they've seen a picture already during an experiment than a word. Words which can be easily visualised (like 'elephant') are easier to recall and recognise than more abstract words (like 'language'). But we need to be careful here.

Even the simplest drawing contains far, far more information than the word that describes the same object. The drawing illustrates all sorts of spatial information about the relative sizes and positions of an object's parts, its overall shape, the way it's facing in the picture, and so on. Even the briefest glance at the drawing, as it's flashed up on a computer screen, gives the viewer much more to think about and link to existing knowledge (see Figure 5.3). This means that many different visual aspects of the picture might stay in the mind. The printed word has nothing on this. Furthermore, you've seen the noun before, looking almost the same, whereas this particular drawing may be completely novel. So it's hardly surprising that it has a richer and more memorable trace in our minds.

There is another reason why pictures are more memorable than words, and I'll talk about that in a moment. For now, the key point is that symbolising something so that it's 'read' instead of 'viewed', makes it less memorable than depicting its richer reality. A cross on a map to symbolise a church may not come to mind later, but a photograph of the church might, and so on. The important point here is not how good or bad our memories might be, but how much information we can 'read' from different representations, and how easily.

In modern life we often see an image alongside some text, or while hearing a verbal description. Images add so much extra richness, and can convey some things so much more simply than words, that it's a shame not to take advantage of them. The late Bobby Berman was a wise old don at Oxford, who once tutored Stephen Hawking, the English theoretical physicist. Berman's answer to students' struggles with abstract and obscure physics was always 'Let's draw a picture'. Sure enough, the pictures usually helped clear up the problem. We love to use words and images in tandem, and it's interesting to consider how this works. If images convey much more information than text, could they convey the *wrong* information? How does the text help or hinder our interpretation of the image, and vice versa?

To some extent, our focus of attention with a visual image is reflected in, and determined by, the language we use to describe the space it takes up—the spatial 'reference frames' that are implied by the things we say. The influence of these reference frames may be quite subtle, but important to our thinking about what we see.[65] If we focus mainly on the physical details in front of us, which is likely if it isn't well designed for its purpose, it can impede our **implicit learning** of the knowledge that the artist or cartographer intended to convey, such as the layout of a real town or the multiple agonies of Christ on the cross. Thus the way that the text directs our attention is important to avoid spending more time thinking about the irrelevant than the relevant aspects.

Nevertheless, whatever we're guided to focus on by verbal instructions, we still seem to quickly pick up some symbolic or **semiotic** aspects of most images. Even small children are able to do so, even with symbolic and unfamiliar images like maps.[26] We seem to come ready programmed for semiotics, determined to make a deeper interpretation of the visual array in front of our eyes.

This seems to be stronger for some people than for others, and may partly explain some people's impatience with abstract art even when they're given a description of the artist's intended meaning. They don't want to interpret the image for themselves, because its meaning is not *directly* clear from what's depicted. Often the artist is expecting the viewer simply to experience the image for a while, to see how they feel and what thoughts come to mind, and giving them the freedom of their own interpretation. Yet some people feel uncomfortable looking at something which doesn't give them an immediate link to familiar, recognisable concepts.

This leads us back to that issue of richness in 'reading' an image. I said earlier that there is another reason why pictures are more memorable than words, and why words that refer to concrete objects are more memorable than abstract terms. The reason is that we seem to represent both images and **propositions** in our minds. Propositions, loosely, can be thought of as information which can be described completely in words, like rules or facts. They don't need to be pictured, and we normally assume that they could be equally well described by any language or coding system. A description, such as 'the book is a bit to the left of the middle', is a proposition, despite describing something spatial which could also be pictured. But if it was pictured, that image would be more accurate in showing the book's *exact* position. A proposition is inevitably more vague when it's describing visual things. It's likely that we use both when we observe and record the visual world around us. [169]

A cognitive psychologist called Allan Paivio developed a 'dual-coding theory' of memory. [251] This suggested that we store images and propositions differently, but we can use both to help us remember something. When we study an image we seem to pull out propositions from it, as well as the visual look of it. When we hear a 'concrete' word, such as 'elephant', we picture an elephant in our minds as well as hearing the word. Later, the extra link to that mental image may help us to recall that yes, that was the word we saw. We don't have such help when we're trying to recall if we saw an abstract word like 'extra', so it's harder to recognise.

We can use this in everyday life. You've probably heard of the memory-enhancing tricks that draw on this imagery. An example is linking together the items on a shopping or to-do list by picturing some bizarre situation involving all the items. Similarly, some people learn foreign words by making a mental picture. The picture links together an item that the word sounds like in their own language with the thing that it actually means.

Like many theories in cognitive science, dual-coding theory may be an oversimplification. It isn't *only* imagery that can be used to help us recall words. Using other memory tricks, such as making up a sentence using the word that's being memorised, have similar effects. Also, when trying to remember pairs of words which were presented together, it helps to create a mental picture that uses them both together, but not to picture them each separately. In other words, what helps us to remember concrete words is the ability to make a link—any link—between things in our mind. Those things don't have to be images.

Nevertheless, images are something special. Decades of in-fighting among researchers about the role of mental imagery eventually concluded that images do have a number of useful functions in everyday life, and neuropsychology studies seem to show that some brain-injured people have specific deficits in particular aspects of processing images. Towards the end of this debate, Stephen Kosslyn, a very prolific cognitive scientist who was one of the loudest contributors to it, developed a 'computational theory' of mental images. The theory links them up to what happens when we see real visual images.[158] Kosslyn's theory also considers the role of propositions as well as images, as Paivio's did. It has a strong focus on what happens when we imagine an object.

Suppose we're asked to think of an elephant. We first recall our 'propositional' memory of what an elephant is. A lot of the knowledge we have about elephants is stored this way, according to Kosslyn's theory, so we could describe one even if we'd never seen one. Special processes check the links that run from that propositional record, to see if we do remember any images of elephants. If we do, we use another set of processes in the brain to recreate that image. Then we can study our mental image using the same cognitive processes that we used when we originally looked at the real elephant (or its photo). The advantage of being able to replay the image is that it gives so much more information (and that information is more immediately usable in the physical world, e.g. to help us to spot an elephant and not get trampled), that the imagery processes are automatic. We don't need to be told to picture the creature before it starts being 'visible' in our mind.

It's worth saying something at this point for people who think of themselves as 'right-brainers'. This distinction between propositions (or words) and images *doesn't* correspond neatly to the left versus right sides of the brain. It's clear that *both* sides (hemispheres) are involved in imagery in different ways: the left does a lot of the work, but, for instance, the right seems to help with things like rotating an image to 'see' it from another angle. So if somebody's told you that you're a 'right-brainer' and therefore shouldn't bother with imagery when trying to learn something, this is a bit overstated. Of course some people do seem to benefit from images more than others, and seem more or less willing to use imagery to help understand things. Kosslyn's theory shows how the visual-verbal distinction isn't a black-and-white category, and it isn't down to having a lop-sided brain. Once again, the more we understand about how we do things, the less easy it is to stereotype people into 'haves' and 'have nots' based on oversimplified ideas about brain function.

Of course, ultimately we don't have pictures (or words) in our brains; we only have millions of stringy neurons setting off electrical and chemical responses. But the issue of the 'phenomenology' of mental images—the fact that we *seem* to 'see' a real picture—is of course just one part of that elusive construct called consciousness, which I can't discuss further here. It has many books all of its own.

Games, learning and 'flow'

On a computer screen, images become flexible and powerful. Diagrams can be animated so you can watch machinery in motion. Maps displayed through a geographic information system (**GIS**) can show different 'layers' of space (like a pile of tracing paper with drawings on each sheet), so that you can choose whether to see only the road network, or also the buildings, rivers, etc. A painting or historic artefact can be 'zoomed in' to be viewed in detail, possibly more so than would be allowed in an art gallery. Details can be 'interactive', so we can click on them to see a popup window with text about them.

With our computers' current small screens, however, maximising our view of an image can cause us to lose such text from the screen, making it harder to switch between the two than it would be in a well-designed paper book. Also, we may not be able to see the *whole* of an image in full detail, as we could if we spread out a paper map sheet on the floor. So we have to sacrifice depth for breadth, or vice versa.

Still, computer imagery, and especially animation, lets us gain more information, more flexibly and interactively, from our 'reading'. Studies of schoolchildren suggest that when a procedure or technique is being learned, animations or images help the children to *reconstruct* the actions that need to be taken.[172] But they aren't needed for basic comprehension tasks where students will only be tested on their ability to *describe* the procedure.[173] Around the same time, it was shown that people can more quickly find and grasp the recipe or solution or fact they were looking for with **hypertext**, but they don't necessarily learn any more along the way.[175] So hypertext and images are both good for **declarative** information (facts), but animations help with **procedural** learning (the doing) and with deeper understanding.

There is still, even more than with printed imagery, a crucial issue of good design. When Edward Tufte wrote his first famous and beautiful books on graphic design,[292] computer graphics were less advanced than they are now, and used by far fewer people. But now that the web shows us clickable graphs and maps whenever we read the news, or check where someone lives, or find out today's weather, interactive graphics and their implication for our 'reading' are important. It isn't enough to worry, as Tufte did, about how the graphics *look*; we also have to ask more questions. Will users realise that they can click on a country to see more information about it? Will they then find their way back to the main image afterwards? Is their browser window large enough for them to see and use the map legend at the side? And so on.

With issues like these to consider, these should be exciting times for those interested in graphic design and in HCI. As the web integrates the user interface with the information, 'reading' becomes a physical activity that involves far more media than text, and far more of us than our eyes. It is also, of course, trivially cheap to put visual images into online text, whereas printed images have always been expensive to include and discouraged by publishers. Animation takes a little more effort, but again far less than it used to take to hand-draw each frame of old cartoons.

Over a decade ago Don Norman[213] suggested that such multimedia doesn't really go far enough in its attempts to help us learn. Norman was worried by multimedia software where clicking on an image brought up some trivial facts but no deeper conceptual knowledge. He argued that we were too bent on building resources that assume people have short attention spans and feed them small information doses. Instead, he said (as have others since, in more detail[100]), we should learn from videogame developers. They seem to know how to draw in the player and keep them absorbed in problem-solving and skill development.

Children are happy to experiment with different strategies to get around the magic doorway without losing their treasure. Supposing, instead, the game asked them to figure out the solution to two simultaneous algebra equations, or systematically to find the ideal combination of two chemicals to produce a reaction. It could even place these tasks in the context of the game itself (how many stones? which magic potion?). As Norman argued, games designers have a lot to contribute towards educational multimedia that, far from adding distractions and assuming bitty learning, draws in the 'player' to the same intensive 'flow state' as a good game.

To see this point we don't even need to focus on technology. Reading a good novel can easily produce the same 'optimal flow' as a good videogame for those with enough reading skills. We should bear in mind that most computer or videogames require certain cognitive and physical skills too, especially manual dexterity. To some extent the reading experience is less demanding (Norman labelled it 'experiential'). The readers don't have to solve any problems, although it's more fun if they do try to figure out what's ahead or whether the butler did it. In another way it involves *more* of Norman's notion of 'direct engagement', as the reader's imagination has to visualise each scene. But the reader makes no strategic choices.

It's possible to combine both genres. When I was a child I owned a couple of 'interactive' (printed) mystery storybooks, where my decision about the meaning of a clue, or about which tunnel to go down in a sewer system, led to a different page number and a different development in the story. In effect, this was a printed computer strategy game, but using text passages as well as (static) images. I had to read and picture the background events leading to the situation, but I also had to solve problems in the right way to reach to a happy ending. There's no reason why learning 'games' can't also include some reading, especially where text is still the best way to express an idea or instruct the 'player'. Indeed, the last time I tried to play an adventure game, it started with a long passage of text. It was supposedly a letter from a deceased wise old man, explaining the background to the quest, the likely dangers and the sad fate of the world if I didn't succeed. (As usual I couldn't find my way out of the first level of the game, so the world is doomed, but at least I enjoyed the story.)

As well as text an educational computer program can include video sequences, although in both cases there is a fear that these media are not 'interactive' enough. As Lydia Plowman discussed in a thoughtful 1996 paper,[229] in a group learning setting we can always intersperse such 'non-interactive' moments with periods of group discussion. Similarly a single learner can be asked to perform a task or answer a quiz to boost the 'interactivity' of a mixed-media tutorial. Plowman warned that in such situations, there may still be value in maintaining some sense of the 'narrative'—the overall story can be lost if learners keep switching between different subtasks and media.

We should also be careful about making things interactive for the sake of it. As Norman mentioned, all the modern buttons and flaps and wheels and flashing lights in museums don't necessarily make visitors learn more. Anyone who's stood in a modern museum as children rush through, turning every dial and pressing every button and then rushing on without even viewing the results (let alone understanding what ideas they represent) knows that 'manipulatives' are not enough. In the United States, research is now finding that children presented with pretty, fancily illustrated letter and number toys may find it *harder* to learn the abstract ideas that lead to mastery of reading and arithmetic.[297] Every Hollywood producer knows that if the special effects are too clever, there will be no need to worry about the holes in the plot or the deeper moral complexities, but viewers won't learn anything.

It isn't yet clear how much knowledge videogame players really absorb about the virtual world they temporarily 'inhabit', beyond basic recall of its problems and **procedural** memory for solving them. In a learning context, we would want users of interactive multimedia to remember the destination, the landmarks along the way and the wider picture, not just how to get to the princess and the glory.

What goes wrong with reading?

Structure: taming the big beast

As I mentioned earlier (p. 214), in his book on electronic texts Andrew Dillon[74] devoted a lot of attention to the notion of structure. In a formal document type, such as an academic paper, people may have built up one or more strategies for dealing with the content, based on knowing the kind of structure it has. There's a good chance with most documents that that strategy won't involve simply reading every word from start to finish, which would be the best strategy with a novel. If you're only in search of certain facts or ideas, as most of this book has assumed, you'll limit your reading.

As I said earlier, with electronic text it isn't always obvious what the structure is in a document you find online, so you may flounder around until a structure becomes clear. Being able to spot the structure is partly a matter of expertise: experts in the text's subject may use subtle cues that help them recognise where they are in a text, while novices rely more on serial reading.[75] We also mustn't assume that people can take advantage of the tools that let you leap around the document, circumventing its structure. A study in the mid-1990s[146] found that students didn't always fully understand the conventions of book indexes, so they didn't use the index in either a paper or electronic book as well as they might.

At present, the structure problem is most often solved by sticking to the same conventions as paper documents. Most of the longer PDF documents that you open on your computer will start with a largely useless title page, followed by a table of contents (often not matching the page numbers in the PDF version!) and a series of headed chapters. This is partly because such documents are provided as if every reader will print the whole thing before reading, but this is unlikely in the case of 200-page computer software manuals. However, since it's been known for at least 15 years that most modern library users seek specific information from non-fiction books and documents, rather than reading them right through,[231] this seems wasteful and inappropriate for most document types.

The main way in which this is slowly changing is by making tables of contents more interactive, and more hierarchical. As I type this, the well-known word processing software that I'm using has a 'document map' displayed so that I can leap back to the section on 'When and what do we read?' to add an idea. Software designed for reading documents often allows similar neat tricks. There is clear evidence that an overview—a 'hierarchical' document map or even just a straight list—does help people to learn from an electronic text. More structure seems to be more helpful when readers' initial goals are a little vague. This is often the case for students researching for an essay, for instance.[67]

In other words, if we are trying to extract ideas or facts from a large document with a complex structure, we want to be able to focus on the reading and not on the browsing issues I covered in the previous chapter. So navigation ought to be painless—*unless* the author really wants to force the reader to read thoroughly from start to finish. Then the structure may be deliberately obscured.

Recognising this, publishers are starting to present online scientific articles in a form which allows lazy or time-pressed readers to do exactly what they do with paper journals: read the abstract at the beginning, flit briefly over the main text and jump on to the results summary. There is an argument, however, that this is bad practice, and shouldn't be encouraged if science is to progress properly; readers should at least be encouraged to skim-read the middle pages so they can assess the quality of the work that's reported. So, arguably, publishers who still rely on unstructured PDF files are doing the scientific world a favour.

In this sense, the choice is not very different from that made by authors of books such as this one, which are meant to be read solely on paper. In the humanities,[68] scholars have contrasted two attitudes to electronic text, which tend to appear both in academic and popular writings. The 'modern' view contends that the technology is just empowering us to *access* texts more easily and better than ever before, but not changing *what those texts say*. The 'postmodern' view suggests that technology is changing the whole nature of our texts (among many aspects of society). Instead of being empowered we're confused, disoriented, and led into new ways of seeing things. By this view, the structure of what we read is likely to differ more and more, in the long run, from anything that went before.

So long as we're not expecting these changes to happen overnight, this seems quite likely. Technology tends to bring many changes and new possibilities, and some of these are always bewildering (as we can see in nineteenth-century authors' shock at the changes of the Industrial Revolution). The trick is to spot the baby in the murky water, so that we keep what we need and lose what we don't.

Skimming skills

Beyond the 'big picture' appraisal of the text is the physical need to navigate through each page of it. Often less text is easily readable on the screen than on a paper copy, so that the user has to scroll or to 'turn' pages more often. It's been known for some time[74] that this causes two problems for readers. First, it's harder to skim through the text to spot the bits we need, if we decide not to read in more careful detail. There are many more 'break' moments, when we have to move our eyes back up to the top of the screen. We can try to keep our eyes still while scrolling the text past them, but this gives us only a limited awareness of the context around the current focus point.

Second, it becomes harder to use your spatial memory to go back to a sentence or paragraph, based on remembering where it was within the page. We often use this with books, when we want to find a particular sentence again sometime after we first read it. With books the location of that sentence never changes.

That's fine for books. In webpages, line lengths and word positions can change just by reshaping the window, which means that the spatial position changes relative to the page as a whole. In this situation, and even in a less window-dependent situation such as a word-processor's continuous-view mode, there are no clear 'pages' within a text. The combined position within a paragraph and down the scrollbar can still be noted, but only if you're used to doing that. You probably can still use *some* spatial cues, such as whether the sentence was in a long paragraph or a short one, at the start of a section or at the end, etc. But you've lost the 'chunking' and the quick visual scanning that individual pages give you.

This isn't such an issue for a PDF or a similar 'page image' format, which usually has a fixed format for the text that the user can't change. Yet even there, if you can't see all of the page on the screen at once then your spatial memory ends up having to encode the two 'halves' separately. It isn't clear whether this gives us a harder job because we're recalling from more and smaller text 'chunks'. We might expect it to be harder, because we have to go through more chunks to find the right one. Then again, if we know the sentence was in a 'top half' chunk we can probably only look at those, making the job no harder than it would be with a printed book. It's definitely easier than the continuous-scrolling situation, unless the reader develops strategies for that (e.g. keeping an eye on the scrollbar position) to help them note where things were.

Page images are 'clunkier' in other ways, though. They can lead to a lot more clicking for the same amount of reading. With a document such as an academic paper or a very long instruction manual, people may well try to read on screen, so they won't be able to see the whole page at once. In such a situation it's pure idiocy to split the text on that page into two vertical columns. The reader has to view the page as four quarters (top left, then bottom left, then top right, then bottom right) instead of just two halves (top, then bottom). Yet some journal publishers and others still do this, at the time of writing. This worsens our need to commit more attention and working memory to navigating instead of pure reading. It also demands heavier use of our working memory, to keep holding a sentence or half-sentence in our minds while we're fumbling our way to the next one.

Navigation actions disrupt the 'optimal flow' state of reading. They distract us away from the concepts we were busy exploring and back to mundane physical actions. This is another strong reason why so many readers will choose to print a document before trying to read it through, but it's easily improved. Adobe's Acrobat software, for example, changes the cursor to a big hand when you click anywhere on the text, and lets you 'drag' the page so that a different area appears. This avoids having to move the mouse over to the scroll bars. By the time this book is five years old, I hope this tiny example can be read as a quaint historical precursor. By then we ought to have *much* more intelligent text interfaces.

In 2001 *Scientific American* reported that 'electronic paper' vision-ary Joseph Jacobson of the MIT MediaLab has an unexpected long-term dream. It's *not* a single, portable, electronic sheet whose 'window' would change to display each page of a book, as current screens do. Instead, recognizing the spatial and manipulation advantages of books, Jacobson dreams of 'the last book'. It would be several hundred bound pages of updatable, self-printing, hi-tech 'paper'. It could reconfigure itself from memory chips in its spine that stored the entire contents of the US Library of Congress.[78] The same physical object could be *Lady Chatterley's Lover* one minute and Darwin's *On the Origin of Species* the next. You could read each one page by page, or flick quickly through many pages, just as with a traditional book. Similarly, Robert Steinbugler of IBM, cited in the same *Scientific American* article, dreams of a sixteen-page flexible 'eNewspaper' which would contain the whole set of stories of a daily paper, updated each day. People could again benefit from seeing juxtaposed stories and physically flippable pages.

That would be great but by then, as now, much of our information would probably not be 'published' in that form. We are now so used to churning out searchable, editable text online. We can't just put the genie of the web back into its bottle and go back to relying on newspapers by the fireside. But we can use physical technologies to get us away from the current limits on what we can do online, and what gadgets we have to use to do it.

Several years ago a perceptive paper was published by Julie Foertsch[98] on the issues surrounding what she called 'e-text'. She suggested that all the scrolling and clicking and spatial shifting of current single-screen online viewing may change the way the texts themselves are written. If readers physically have to click the mouse to change what's on the screen, it's not helpful to use long-winded, complex structures in the wording of the text itself. They give the user more need to check backwards through the text. This happens, for example, when the current paragraph is making a point that's closely linked back to a previous paragraph. It's even more necessary when the point of that earlier paragraph was quite complex.

It's hard enough at the best of times to read text that's that complicated. It's even worse when you can't just quickly look upwards or leftwards to remind yourself what seems to be going on. Foertsch thought that perhaps e-text would encourage writers to try to avoid texts where both they and their readers would need to go back and forth to make sense of it all.

Thinking about email discourse as well as more formal electronic texts, Foertsch asked, 'Do authors say things more simply in electronic articles, or do they just say less?' (p. 319). She suggested future research should check on this. My personal hunch is that the issue here was the change from the typewriter to the computer, and it's now already past. It's harder for authors to look back up and over the page than it was when a half-typed page sat sticking upwards from the typewriter. It's also easier for them to edit the sentences to improve readability than it used to be with handwriting or type-writers. Moreover, their word-processor may nag them to simplify the text whether they want to or not. This is all true no matter how the text will be published and read. It's not about the text *staying* electronic, but about its having been electronic from the start.

For readers, we could just design our online documents to make the pages shorter, like a child's picture book, so that there was no scrolling within the page. This would please Jakob Nielsen, the web usability guru, who has been stressing for years[211] that web users don't want to scroll down a page, and usually won't bother. (However, he originally based this assertion on a lab study of Sun computer employees in America. They may not represent everyone's attitudes to online text.) One problem with this is knowing how big a 'screenful' *is*, though. One reader's full screen may be another's frustratingly small window, making them waste too much time turning pages needlessly. Meanwhile, some work in the early 1990s[106] suggested that presenting text online so that only short, paragraph-length chunks are visible at once makes people slower to comprehend it than with longer, whole-passage, chunks. The devil or the deep blue sea.

Of course, all of this assumes that we are in fact seeing less of a text on screen than we would have seen on paper. The e-paper visionaries (and sellers of big computer screens) would hope to avoid this. It also assumes that it is in fact harder to click a mouse to look back up/ across to earlier text than to turn paper pages. Screen resolutions are currently still improving every year, and large screens are relatively cheap compared to prices a decade ago. We are also, on the whole, a lot more skilled at mouse use (and the use of other, better, input devices—given its ergonomic drawbacks, I hope that the mouse will be redundant within a few years). Speech interfaces should make it ever easier.

Perhaps the issues that mar text reading on screens will just melt away. Meanwhile, there's no harm in trying to find the 'ideal' text format and layout for easy, comfortable, navigable, memory friendly reading. Yet that format and layout will probably depend on the type of text being read, as well as the situation in which people try to read it.

Cue overload and lost skills: 37 + 58 = ?

Foertsch wrote that beside the lack of stable spatial cues, the problem of remembering where you read something is made worse by the 'lack of contextual distinctiveness'. You're always reading on the same screen, and the texts all look similar to each other. Remembering where you were when you read the text may be a useless cue—you probably read most online texts in your office or study. But perhaps this is changing since Foertsch's paper, with the popularity of laptops, palmtops and 'e-book' gadgets.

Other aspects of the context of reading—such as distinctiveness of typeface and page format—can be made to vary in collections of electronic texts (as they do, enormously and luckily, between websites). This will happen only if the website producers or database designers *want* to do so. Most instead favour consistency. As a result, Foertsch argued that we have 'cue overload': the individual cues that would have helped us to remember ideas and their sources are linked to too many *other* ideas and sources too.

Foertsch was right to point out that when people deliberately collect a set of information texts together into a database, they're likely to make their appearance as similar as possible. Perhaps really what we want, when we're dealing with a collection of items, is for them to *not* be consistent.* Their authors might do better to be creative, making the most of the many different computer fonts and formatting options. Personally I'm still grateful when I have to find a paper within printed conference proceedings which were compiled by simply copying and binding the raw manuscripts from the authors. Generally the authors, whatever guidelines they had received, inevitably varied in their computers and typefaces (and sometimes, even now, used typewriters rather than a word-processor). It's so much easier to spot where one paper ends and the next begins. The publisher probably hated it.

If uniform online texts are harder to distinguish in our memory, at least they are easier for the computer to find again. There are many web search engines, and there's a search engine to check over my hard drive for the documents I've left scattered across folders. But I'm alone when it comes to figuring out how to locate a book or magazine among the piles in my home. Give me a search engine that works on my life!

However, Foertsch suggested that it isn't always healthy to rely on word-finding and document-indexing functions. She felt that it is often the cognitive effort that we put into mentally recording an idea or fact, and its context, that helps to make it memorable. This can be strengthened further by links to our **episodic memory** of when we saw it, and our **procedural memory** of how we found or handled it. When we read different texts at different times, Foertsch suggested that we can use our episodic memory as one way of **chunking** the information we're trying to integrate. Without that, we may suffer from at least a sense of that familiar spectre, information overload. More basically, we may just waste too much time repeatedly accessing the search facility, because we can't recall many specific bits of what we've already read.

This is, as Foertsch admitted, the same argument that makes people worry that they may forget how to do mental arithmetic, or even how to count, by coming to rely on calculators and computers. In both cases, the worriers may have a point. Even if we reach the stage when *every* arithmetic problem is *always* solved electronically,

---

*However, this contradicts the HCI guidelines for a good user interface, and as I pointed out earlier, the user interface and the content are all one in modern systems such as the web. It's not clear how to resolve these clashing user requirements, but it should be possible.

and *every* text has been digitized to be solely read online, we would still like to have those skills. Perhaps we should set ourselves mental homework to practise them.

However, we know that we tend to integrate the things we read into our **semantic** networks, or **schemata** or models, of things we already know, so that they're associated with those as well as with the context in which we read them. Steven Pinker[228] has pointed out that you don't need to relearn what an elk is, or what other concepts it's related to, just because you see the word written in a new fancy typeface. He wrote that 'this is how we know that your mind contains mental representations specific to abstract entries for words, not just the shapes of the words when they are printed' (p. 86). This is just as true for complex ideas as for single words, of course. We retain a vague visual image, and it has its uses, but the meanings are also lodged in our minds in their own, non-visual, form.

So there's a good chance that we'll still remember most of the ideas from an electronic text, even if we have more trouble navigating back to the sentence where we read them. Comprehension and memory tests of people reading online texts seem to support this. It's not as bad as we might think, possibly because we humans are so good at adapting to tasks and coming up with new cognitive strategies to handle them.

Truth and time-saving: 'that'll do'

'Factual Error Found on Internet' screamed the front page of the satirical paper, *The Onion*, in May 2002. 'The Information Age was dealt a stunning blow Monday, when a factual error was discovered on the Internet . . .' The spoof article went on to cite a website hosting company pledging, 'We will not rest until the Internet's once-sterling reputation as the world's leading source for 100 percent reliable information is restored.' Horrors!

Of course, such satire rests on people's understanding that the internet is actually awash with unchecked and even utterly fictional texts. I have heard people state airily, 'I never believe anything I read on the internet,' as if such total suspension of belief was even possible, in the same way that British readers of a sensationalist tabloid claim not to believe its news reports (yet strangely end up, after a while, sharing its prejudices).

In practice, even the lowest-credibility information source contains the inevitable tiny shreds of truth. Our recognition of these seems to open a crack in our armour so that some extra ideas are absorbed alongside them, since we so automatically form links and conceptual structures as we read. You can't stop that from happening without consciously evaluating each and every nuance of meaning implied by each word and phrase. To do that requires more cognitive effort, and greater use of our training in critical thought, than most of us are prepared to apply.

Naturally, this has implications for our democratic choices as well as our personal education. Just three months before the *Onion* article, BBC Online reported[21] that many protest websites are set up by disgruntled customers, political activists or former employees specifically to attack a company or organisation, without necessarily portraying any true facts about its dealings or policies. Nevertheless, as with any form of campaigning, most major activists are aware of the importance of credibility (and the avoidance of lawsuits), and so we inevitably take some of these organisations at their word because we assume they would not risk losing that credibility. Striking the balance is difficult, but no more so online than with any other medium.

Of course, we may also have personal reasons for our distrust. In 1991, an interesting study by Wesley L. Flake[96] looked at professional people's attitudes towards computer-based information. Flake found that among top-level university administrators, women were more likely to accept information from computer sources than men were. Women were equally happy with computer-based and non-computer-based information, while men in these senior positions were much more suspicious about computer-based sources. Flake linked this to the tendency for senior university managers to avoid using technology themselves at that time. Some older people feel intimidated by a new technology which they struggle to learn to master compared to their younger subordinates. Distrust in online information is a useful excuse for, but also a consequence of, those personal barriers.

Related to this, back in Chapter 2 (pp. 74–83) I talked about the biases that make us willing to want and choose information that fits our personal world view. Yet our biases, stereotypes and rigid conceptual categories also act as necessary cognitive 'brakes'. They stop us from musing endlessly about the interconnectedness and possible untrustworthiness of all that information. Then we can get on with making practical decisions about what we 'need to know'. Indeed, as Edward de Bono pointed out in the 1960s,[66] if we try to have a more open mind then our major problem is knowing when to stop:

> The dilemma is very real. When one comes to the end of an article in a scientific journal the following article always seems highly relevant ... When I was at Harvard I used to make a habit of picking up at random a

journal from the display shelf at the entrance to the library. There was never a time when a journal selected in this manner did not contain at least one useful article ... Unfortunately the matter gets worse as one goes more deeply into a subject. As the ideas grow more and more basic ... instead of narrowing, the field of relevance becomes even wider. (p. 163)

In other words, with reading even more than with browsing, the deeper one reads the more one sees links to other texts, other subjects, other ideas ... I found this relentlessly true while writing this book.

Of course, if our task is time-pressured or simply not very interesting to us, we will just want to get to the point of 'enough'. Such states of panic or boredom tend to resolve de Bono's problem. We simply won't bother to go any further than we absolutely have to, but this may lead us to exactly the opposite problem. Herbert S. White,[308] a veteran information scientist, summarised this eloquently (but, for academics, painfully), in a conference presentation back in 1993:

People with small and weak libraries who only get to see a half dozen journals in their field will insist stubbornly that this is all they need to see. What choice do they have? They can't admit that they don't know what they are talking about. I've never seen a meeting scheduled at 10am on a Monday morning cancelled because the presenter admitted that he had been unable to get what he needed from the library. Whatever he got just fortunately always turned out to be enough. Indeed, librarians know that if they later find information that contradicts what has already been said, they provide that information at their peril ... The information process is therefore, with or without technology, very susceptible to self-deception and self-delusion. (pp. 6–7)

At the time they were made, White's comments applied more strongly to searching and browsing than to reading. Now, however, we can incresingly access many different viewpoints and information sources on a given topic. Sometimes we're perhaps more likely to fall into the 'that'll do' trap when it comes to reading the results of our search. Rather than sitting down with one book and depending on it, perhaps we are more likely now to scan over several texts until we pick out the justification of the point we want to make. We won't have time left to read in depth the discussion that clarifies or even disproves it. We can go on cherry-picking from the papers in a field until we find the exact argument we felt like making, but the time we spend doing it can steal from the time we would have spent reading and thinking.

White's point is still valid: we often do find 'just enough' to say what we need to say. When we could only find one or two sources, like the deprived library users he described, we at least had to make the most of them to learn everything we could from one author's (hopefully) thoughtful and justified answer to our problem.

For these reasons, the book you're reading at this very moment might have been written differently ten years ago. I would have had less opportunity to make connections across different disciplines and lines of thought—less of de Bono's endless widening of 'the field of relevance'—and the book would have been finished far more quickly. I would have relied on more freehand discussion of fewer pieces of knowledge. In turn, you might have used this book as your main or only source of ideas about human cognition with computer-based information. Instead, you're holding a mixture of de Bono's relevance widening, with White's just-enough pragmatism whenever time panics took over. As for you, the reader, why rely on anything I say? Even if you've read the book right through this far, you can supplement or challenge every point with your own online research, without even leaving your seat.

Where does this leave the more specialised non-fiction, non-reference monograph? Who reads in depth anymore—and who has time to read?

In the humanities, where the deep study of texts is a traditional art, some[249, 250] have expressed misgivings about whether it's now too easy to 'decontextualise' bits of people's work. The computerised tools now let scholars 'smash and grab' the bits they want, to draw links between texts, while ignoring the author's more complex intentions. We all know the politician who moans about being 'quoted out of context'. Now we can commit the same sin with every text we access. But is it really a sin, or is it building richer associations among ideas?

We may not even need to see an original object (or book) at all now in order to research it: a 1995 paper[130] described a plant taxonomy database project in whose offices there wasn't one single plant, nor even a picture of one. This can be a good thing, not only to relieve tedious checking by researchers, but also to preserve delicate and rare items. The digitisation of historical manuscripts makes it far less necessary for researchers to handle and damage them.[34] Yet Sven Birkerts,[25] bemoaning his students' inability to cope with Henry James novels, felt that direct interaction with print was not a chore but an experience which lets us 'conceive of ourselves as souls' and added: 'I would urge that we not fall all over ourselves in our haste to filter all of our experience through circuitries. We are in some danger of believing that the speed and wizardry of our gadgets have freed us from the sometimes arduous work of turning pages in silence' (p. 32).

So does 'decontextualisation' mean that authors who have a single, but complex, idea to explore will get shorter shrift in modern society? Would anyone read the whole of *Das Kapital* anymore? Apparently not, but don't blame the internet. A *1988* study of library users showed that most readers of non-fiction books didn't actually read most of the text. [231]

We frequently hear (from inevitably harassed journalists, themselves the greatest 'smash and grab' thieves of all), that the issue is not technology but time. We're asked to consider the speed at which our society currently operates, and the impossible efforts we make to cram too much achievement into too few minutes and years. Then there's the alleged 'dumbing down' that supposedly makes people prefer TV and cheap novels to 'serious literature', which is said as if everyone had previously plumped for Dostoevsky. These still echo Coleridge's concerns, two hundred years later.

The fact that modern technology make all these things easier and faster certainly helps, but doesn't by itself cause these changes in society. We're also asked to believe that it 'shortens our concentration spans'. That's a common phrase which is, however, scientifically unproven in terms of people's actual cognitive abilities: lab studies and intelligence tests don't show a negative shift over the past 40 years, let alone the past 10. Nevertheless, pessimists see evidence in the way that information is presented in small doses on the tops of soft-drink bottles, in multiple-choice questions on game shows, and in the punchy headlines of news websites.

Whatever its genuine effect on our minds, this 'speeding up and dumbing down' situation is really *parallel* to the new phenomenon that, since *Das Kapital* is frankly an unattractive prospect for reading material, we are able to skip a lot of it by skimming quotes from a computer-based version. We do this even more easily than we might once have used a printed concordance or edited précis to achieve the same thing. Yet we can still turn off the TV and the web browser and *choose* the calm discipline of in-depth reading. Nobody is stopping us, and most of the classics of literature are now freely downloadable for us to try without leaving home to get them. [232]

Perhaps we have greater social pressure now to rush things, and less time to read further and think more deeply. Our choices and situations do determine how far we choose to read. If we actually care about living in a literate and thoughtful society, we will make sure that deep reading does still happen. This means not crowding our 'leisure' time so much that books are only read on beach holidays—a situation when we may not have the taste for Birkerts' beloved Henry James, anyway.

What to do about reading?

For users

- If you like or want to read more online, you'll probably feel subtly more willing to do so by having the best possible screen. A modern flat panel is much more comfortable and visible.
- Try to get into the habit of using bookmarks, note-taking, highlighting and 'sitemaps' (tables of contents etc., to help pick out the structure and key points of your reading. It's easy to forget to do this when reading on a computer.
- Make the most of images, maps and other multimedia. But don't be distracted by their 'glitz'.
- For key texts, take the time if possible *really* to read and follow the author's arguments and concerns. It's still worth it sometimes.
- If an electronic document (e.g. a PDF) is especially badly formatted (e.g. when at a legible zoom level, each page is longer than a screenful but split into two columns), give up and print it out.
- Try to notice visual cues—scroll bar position, fonts and colours, closeness to a heading, etc.—to plant extra memory links (retrieval cues), and also to help you find your way back to an earlier passage.

For information providers

- Design online texts to be visually navigable and memorable.
- Use multimedia for relevance, not play.
- Make the structure obvious.
- Help users to grasp quickly the type and conceptual content of a document.
- Think about what users' intentions and interests will be.
- Work on adding usable *semantic* links to your information items.
- Do not format a document for print and then expect people to read it online, unless they will really want to see the same format (e.g. academics may want to see a journal paper exactly as it was printed, so that page numbers etc. tally up).

For research

In-depth online information reading and learning, as opposed to browsing and finding quick answers, are still in their infancy despite at least two decades of hypermedia research. Knowing as much as we do about the cognition of reading (although we know less about comprehension of, and memory for, long non-fiction passages), we should be able to integrate this with user studies of document and media design.

The role of multimedia is also still being explored, and is likely to be overplayed due to novelty for a while longer before its use settles into a convention. With thorough research now (not just the 'look what we've built' kind of study but some deeper, systematic research into the information process), that convention will be one that really educates.

Summary

Reading on a computer screen is probably increasing—although future 'screens' will include electronic paper, and other gadgets very different from the old cathode-ray-tube televisions we've had until recently. Reading from these is no less 'natural' than reading from traditional paper books, but there is still a place for these too.

Information scientists have tended to ignore the process of reading, seeing their own role as stopping when you find the right information source, so most of what we know has come from psychology. I described what we know about the process, which holds some interesting surprises—what we really do is a very long way from following the text letter by letter.

The question of what it means to 'understand' what we read, and whether a computer's 'understanding' could ever help or match this, is a long-running philosophical debate. That debate can make us look harder at how we behave with information that we want to 'understand'. This is particularly important in educational contexts. However, a lot of the work looking at computer-based learning has been flawed, so it's hard to draw clear conclusions.

Scholars fear that the web is 'dumbing down' our reading, or making us less critical, or reducing our attention spans, or all three. These fears actually go back some 200 years, and are not clearly justified by research or by history.

Images 'paint a thousand words' for certain reasons, and in certain ways. They can also help us to learn more when combined with text, but it's hard to do this effectively on current small computer screens.

I showed why, for learning, multimedia must always be carefully designed to focus us on what we're trying to learn, rather than distracting from it.

In text, we often use the spatial layout as a cue to help us go back to bits we've previously read. Visual differences between texts (e.g. fonts) help us to remember which text was which. Online text interfaces need improving to restore these useful features. To encourage proper understanding we might sometimes want to hide the document structure to 'force' people to read linearly, but at other times computers should make it easier to see and use that structure.

Trust, and our tendency to see relevance everywhere, are both difficult personal issues with online information. Once again we need metacognitive skills: critical thinking, self-discipline and awareness.

Further reading

My citations of Andy Dillon's book on electronic text were based on the first edition, but a newly updated second one is now out. This is probably the essential starting point for anyone in this area: Andrew Dillon, *Designing Usable Electronic Text*, 2nd edition (London and New York: Routledge, 2004), ISBN 0-415-24060-3.

To learn more about research into reading, and other relevant work to do with language, read Trevor Harley, *The Psychology of Language: From data to theory* (Hove: Psychology Press, 2001), ISBN 0-863-77867-4.

John Searle's arguments about and beyond the Chinese Room, and other aspects of what he calls the 'false assumptions' of cognitive science, are best described by himself in his books, e.g. this quite readable one: John R. Searle, *The Rediscovery of the Mind* (Cambridge, MA: MIT Press, 1992), ISBN 0-262-69154-X.

Some of the many objections and answers to Searle, and other thought-provoking comments on cognitive modelling of the mind, are in K. A. Mohyeldin, W. H. Newton-Smith, R. Viale and K. V. Wilkes (eds), *Modelling the Mind* (Oxford: Clarendon Press, 1990), ISBN 0-198-24973.

Searle's loudest critic has been fellow philosopher Daniel Dennett, and some of his objections to the Chinese Room argument (among others) are in Daniel C. Dennett, *Consciousness Explained* (London: Penguin, 1991), ISBN 0-713-99037-6.

For inspiring thoughts about visual design of (mostly non-text) information to supplement our texts, Edward R. Tufte's books still inspire, especially *Envisioning Information* (Cheshire, CT: Graphics Press, 1990), ISBN 0-961-39211-8.

I've mentioned Donald Norman at various points in this and other chapters. In this chapter most of his referenced comments are from this always entertaining and useful book: Donald A. Norman, *Things That Make Us Smart: Defending human attributes in the age of the machine* (Cambridge MA: Perseus Books, 1993), ISBN 0-201-62695-0.

Web design guru Jakob Nielsen has some specific advice about online text design, page length, etc. at his information- and opinion-packed website: www.useit.com

A good start as a source of practical research and ideas into the potential for adapting videogames for education is this online NESTA Futurelab (i.e. UK Government-funded) report: John Kirriemuir and Angela McFarlane, *Literature Review in Games and Learning: A Report for NESTA Futurelab*, www.nestafuturelab.org/research/reviews/08_01.htm.

An intriguing and highly readable book on the same topic, drawing partly on cognitive science ideas is: James Paul Gee, *What Video Games Have to Teach Us about Learning and Literacy* (New York: Palgrave, 2001), ISBN 1-403-96169-7.

Chapter 6

Using, remembering and passing on

In Chapter 5 I mentioned the concept of 'roundness' suggested a few years ago in a paper by Paul Solomon. [269] This describes the way that we use whatever sources we find 'situationally relevant'. This reminds us that we don't just seek and read information for the sake of it. We do it in a context, for a purpose. As I'd already said in Chapter 2, this context can be almost any situation from a trivial argument to a terminal disease. So we have myriad ways of using, storing, regurgitating and communicating what we've found and read. The contexts of our lives are too rich and varied even to hint at in this chapter.

Instead, once again, I'll try to draw out some general issues and interesting bits of research that apply across the board in information use, while remaining relevant to the context of computer-retrieved information. All of the previous chapters have already shown that even while we're still wanting, searching, browsing and reading, we're already doing more cognitively to push the information towards 'use'. We've already gone *way* 'beyond the information given'. This chapter can only push a bit further.

What do we use?

We can't go far into this without revisiting what we might mean by information in the first place. I skirted around this earlier in this book, although information as *the process of informing* was discussed in Chapter 5. After all, debates on defining abstract terms don't alter the very concrete tasks of searching, browsing and reading. Even the more cerebral issue of wanting information doesn't depend very much on how we *define* information. As we saw, most theorists have seen 'information need' simply as something to do with a gap or anomaly in what we (think we) know. That seemed a clear enough statement.

However, in this chapter we consider the way that information is used and remembered, in other words the way in which it's transformed into *knowledge*, an even more slippery concept, and then transmitted in some way to form 'information' for others. So what counts as information then?

Throughout this book I've mentioned people's behaviour with information when it comes not just from computers, but also from other sources. Much of what we can learn from that applies to computer-based information as well, although computers are very much a special case. Some definitions of information are even broader than we might imagine, however. Information scientist Robert Losee, in a provocative paper in 1997,[180] stated that *all* activities and processes produce information, even, in his words, baking a cake.

Cynics might say that this is a wonderful way of making information scientists seem all-important and relevant, even to bakeries and village fetes. But to be fair, at least Losee and other information scientists care about information's connection with quality, and with *content*, and that's not something we can take for granted.

Losee quoted the historic work of Claude Shannon, who developed communication theory within engineering in the 1940s, and wrote extensively about it. According to Losee, Shannon somehow avoided defining what information actually was, and stated that its semantic aspects (i.e. the actual meaning of what's transmitted) aren't relevant to the engineer's work in getting it transmitted.[263] This is true, but its content-free approach is obviously the opposite of yours and mine in everyday life; to us almost the *only* thing that matters is what the information says and means.

Other engineers tend to differ from Shannon and use the semiotic approach instead which, as we've seen, does consider the semantic and pragmatic aspects of information along with the means of transmitting it. Yet computer scientists, even those concerned with **HCI**, often try to design information systems without having to worry about what the information they deliver actually *means* to people, and what they'll actually do with it. As we've seen, the integration of content with interface has only finally dawned with the take-off of the web, and even then some developers still try to separate the two.

Losee's cake-baking example made an interesting point. Information, by his definition, is *the values within the output of any process*, and those 'values' indicate something about not only the output itself (i.e. the cake), but also about the process that produced it (the baking). You can bet that when the cake's sagging in the middle, its creator's mother will be on hand to say 'ah, you didn't . . .' or 'you shouldn't . . .'. Whatever causal attributions she makes about how and why the cake became the way it is, she'll base them on the information given to her by the cake itself. So our reasoning and decision-making is based on the information we've taken in already, *and* on the environment directly around us. I'll return to this later.

Losee's description above left us with a very broad and loose idea of information. In the eyes of some authors, such broad sweeps are not scientific enough. Information, to them, has no soul. It is not what we think with, not what inspires or changes society, but it is simply facts, in the same way that the schoolmaster Gradgrind's favoured description of a horse in Charles Dickens's *Hard Times*[72] misses the beauty, usefulness and power of the animal. In a classic comic passage from *Hard Times*, the character Thomas Gradgrind castigates little Sissy Jupe, the daughter of a horse-breaker and therefore highly familiar with horses. Sissy can't think how to define a horse, and is therefore 'possessed of no facts, in reference to one of the commonest of animals!'. A boy supplies a definition that satisfies Gradgrind:

> 'Quadruped. Graminivorous. Forty teeth, namely twenty-four grinders, four eye-teeth, and twelve incisive. Sheds coat in the spring; in marshy countries, sheds hoofs, too. Hoofs hard, but requiring to be shod with iron. Age known by marks in mouth.' ...

> 'Now girl number twenty,' said Mr Gradgrind. 'You know what a horse is.'

Gradgrind's facts contrasted sharply with the obvious deep knowledge of horses possessed by Sissy and her family. According to some authors, this is the same distinction as that between our much-vaunted boom in 'information' and the learning of higher-order *knowledge* and ideas.

One of the most passionate advocates of this downgrading of information was Theodore Roszak, in his 1986 book *The Cult of Information.*[248] An example of Roszak's argument is this passage:

> But I do want to insist that information, even when it moves at the speed of light, is no more than it has ever been: discrete little bundles of fact, sometimes useful, sometimes trivial, and never the substance of thought ... (p. 87)

> That is the great mischief done by the data merchants, the futurologists, and those in the schools who believe that computer literacy is the educational wave of the future: they lose sight of the paramount truth that *the mind thinks with ideas, not with information.* (p. 88)

For cognitive scientists, who spend their research-productive lives trying to establish just 'what the mind thinks with', this distinction is not workable (although some theorists have drawn a roughly similar line between imagery and propositions, as I discussed in Chapter 5). Mr Gradgrind's horse facts and Sissy Jupe's vivid experiences of snorting, stomping, galloping creatures could *all* be among valid responses to the question of what a 'horse' is like. Likewise, a raw dictionary definition, a Yeats poem, a particular sunset, the smell of wet lavender, a beloved or admired person, a snatch of dreamy music or a neat scientific equation might all come to mind when somebody mentions 'beauty'.

Where Roszak was correct was in arguing that the mind does *more* than simply processing the bits of definitions and the concrete sensory memories that it holds. It forms associations, compares patterns, and reasons out causes and solutions. This isn't to say, however, that its raw material is less valuable wherever it consists of a fact. It is to agree with Dickens that the reduction of either information *or* knowledge to simple facts is to siphon all the richness out of the picture.

So, once we've found and read information, it fits into this web of perceptions, knowledge and ideas in our minds, all of which are informative. We then base our thinking, actions and creations on this personal web. Bearing in mind Roszak's passionate denunciation of information as an end in itself, but considering it the basis of all our ideas, we have to ask how we do this. This chapter will just sample a few aspects of it.

What's in there?

How do we organise what we know? Back in the 1970s, the way that the mind stored such such concepts as 'horse' was seen in simple terms. One suggestion was that we held an ideal *'prototype'* notion, and evaluated each horse we came across to see how well it fitted to that prototype.[242] Some things seemed more like the ideal version of the thing than others did (e.g. German Shepherds may seem more doglike than Pekinese), so these were closer to the prototype. Another idea was that we stored multiple *exemplars* of all the items we'd ever come across, and grouped them together only loosely in our minds by their similarity to each other.[214] One reason to call two things similar would be if they had both been labelled 'dog' by someone else, but they could otherwise be very different without causing a problem for exemplar theory.

Both of these models were themselves improvements on the classical model of knowledge developed originally by philosophers, which assumed that we store single and fully defined concepts in hierarchies (so horse would be a subset of mammal, which itself would be a subset of living thing, and so on). That view assumed that at each level of the hierarchy, each concept would have its unique attributes associated with it (e.g. those that Gradgrind's second pupil favoured, such as tooth configurations). But it would also draw on the more general attributes of its parent category (for mammals, hairy coats and four limbs). This was called the *defining feature* model. Each item that you knew of was defined by its set of features and sat on a particular twig in a branching tree of knowledge.

As in other areas of the science, later on cognitivists came to appreciate that these early theories were too simple. Not for the first or last time in psychology, the evidence that supported them had mostly resulted from doing experiments that forced people to respond in ways that fitted the model. Twenty years of further experiments followed, which seemed to be able to shoot down every generalisation cognitivists tried to make about how concepts are organised. So the focus has gradually switched from a notion of neat organization to an idea that we seem to create our own explanatory theories and strategies to solve problems.[201]

It's easy to see how such theory-based categories are more flexible and realistic than older models. We can often (but not always) reuse and reorganise the same information in whatever way suits our current need. For instance, the things in your home can be more or less ideal to have around when visitors come. At other times they're things that attract more or less dust. When moving house, you might group them according to how fragile or valuable they are, and so on (Figure 6.1).

Recent work on concept and category formation has looked at such muddy issues as cross-cultural differences, which show how flexibly we really think about even 'obvious' categories in the natural world.[247] New ideas are emerging based on this need for flexibility. Scientists are using these findings to build 'loose' computational models. These focus on how we use associations and contexts to infer what makes a concept or a category, instead of rigid rules or feature lists.[4]

This work pulls together the traditionally separate areas of memory and reasoning. Our mental models have to be seen as dynamic, rather than some kind of information database waiting to be mined. We can't talk any longer about memory as a static pile of stuff, out of which information is pulled for solving problems and communicating with others. Nor can we pretend that there are rigid rules keeping our memories as tidy as a library on a Monday afternoon. The harder it gets to think about memory as a basis for cognition, the closer we may be to a realistic picture of it.*

Unexpectedly, there's also a vaguely comforting moral aspect to such work. As Geoffrey Bowker and Susan Star pointed out in their

---

*This 'memory as dynamic processes' view was already recognised by neuroscientists working directly on the brain, to test the biological basis of memory. In fact Steven Rose, writing over a decade ago on this, gave the impression of patiently waiting for cognitive science to catch up![243]

No wait! Let's have all the spotty ones first. No, er, the pets. Maybe the mammals? Er...

Figure 6.1. Dynamic and flexible categories.

1999 book on classification, *Sorting Things Out*,[32] classifying things one way often means making any alternative point of view seem invalid. This is exactly the problem we have in racial stereotyping, for instance. It's something of which very few of us are innocent. We may bend over backwards to stress equality and respect for the ethnic groups that others persecute, such as Jews, black people and Asians. In my lifetime, 'Irishman' jokes have gone from normal (even among the second-generation Irish immigrants I grew up with!) to taboo. Yet we may casually pass sentence on 'chaotic' Italians, 'arrogant' Americans, 'corrupt' Nigerians or 'obsessive' Japanese without even being aware of our own prejudices. Because we *type*, we also *stereotype*.

Yet we manage to have much more flexible categories in areas of life where that obviously makes sense to us. This is why sport is so effective at moving us beyond stereotypes. It focuses on athletic ability or football-kicking accuracy regardless of race, and cate- gorises people by team and league instead. The more educated we are to realise the subtleties of every area of life, the harder it is to justify classifying information, people or situations into rigid boxes. In fact, just being a wide and frequent book reader makes it hard to keep the boxes upright.

This, as Bowker and Star suggested, can be worrying for information and library scientists. How can they classify anything if it will never be good enough? But as we start creating workable, useful semantic-based systems for finding and recording information, we won't necessarily need the older systems anymore.

I keep my scientific papers filed in alphabetical order of author, which is useless for finding a paper on 'memory'. That's all right—I just search my literature database which holds my own notes, thoughts, references and keywords. It tells me who wrote the paper I only half-remember, so I can pull it straight from the drawer. It would do it better if I had some semantic linking in there, but in science we're actually not far from that already. Citation cross-searching— who cited whom, i.e. fellow scientists' relevance judgements—gets us halfway there.[52] But only if we trust our fellow scientists' judgement!

However, Bowker and Star's book pointed up an ironic link between the issue of how to classify things and the issue of context I mentioned earlier. One purpose of classification, in their view, is to allow us to transfer information *across contexts*. This means that in a way a rigid formal scheme allows us *more* flexibility because you can use it in many situations, countries and even (after some translation work) languages. Enforcing categories onto things makes them simple and ordered enough for us to think with. The most bigoted people also tend to have the straightest lines of thought. I often envy them, because the alternative is such hard work.

Saving cognitive effort by classifying things is good for our sanity, so far as it goes.[228] Doubtless an evolutionary psychologist is stirring awake to 'explain' it in cave-man speak, even as I write. Rapid decisions and creative processes need it. So it's perhaps a small miracle that in our current very time-pressured society, we are also more aware than ever that life isn't black and white.

A pessimist might have expected the opposite, especially looking at popular tabloid newspapers. There are very clear classifications going on in them. To name just one, a woman will normally be one of these: a desirable sex object, a 'mother of two', or a 'slag' (*un*desirable sex object?). It suits the editors, and some politicians, to keep limiting people's thinking to neat boxes. This is one reason why shallow Christian fundamentalism is the darling of US neo-conservatives.

Some years ago I knew an earnest young activist who always dressed in black, who filled his office wall with political slogan-filled cards. One of these read *The intelligentsia is power's hall of mirrors*. I'm still not sure what he thought this meant, as I never dared ask! To me now, it suggests almost the reverse of the old slogan 'Information is power'. The educated hold and access the most information. With that we can make any bigoted thinking and rigid classification—which are always called on by the powerful at some point in their career—look ridiculous. Which isn't to say that we don't also use them sometimes.

How do we use it?

Tom Wilson has written a number of times on information use in the context of the outcome of information seeking. He's been pointing out for at least 23 years[311, 313] that it is under-researched, relative to other aspects of information tasks.

Doubtless this is partly because, as I said earlier, once information is being used there's nothing to distinguish this situation from the whole of our lives. Also of course, information scientists are most concerned with what predicts why people will come to them (or their systems or libraries) for information in the first place, and how they can be helped. Where the users go after leaving the library or logging off the database is their own concern. Therefore a lot of the time, even when information scientists title a paper with the phrase 'information use', they really mean the context and needs that users bring to using the information *source* to find what they want.

How can we tell what people do with information after that, anyway? Since we can only ask people how they used some information that they retrieved, and they may not be entirely honest or accurate in their response, it's a tricky area to tackle. When researchers try to quantify the amount of information that people use in different ways after a search, they end up with radically different results even within the domain of academic bibliographic searching.[310]

Wilson himself tends to approach this topic by assuming that information use involves some kind of *change of behaviour*, because of a change in people's knowledge structure. Academics may make different decisions about their research based on the studies of others. Marketers may choose a different tactic for advertising their products. You may decide to carry an umbrella today, because rain is forecast. On the other hand, sometimes the only immediate behavioural change is internal—you've learned something and it's altered your mental model of a situation. How that influences your future responses to that situation might be too subtle, and far off in time, to be measurable by researchers. It might also be too personal for you to want to admit. And it may not be possible to trace back the effect to the cause, with so many other influences on our choices.

Thinking about it

Therefore, the most powerful use of information is in reasoning and thought. We may come up with a whole new creative idea, out of putting together the things we already knew in new ways. Cognitive psychology has found it harder to study this type of 'higher-order cognition' than simpler things like perception, attention and reading, and we don't yet have a single, universally agreed set of rules or models for it.

However, clues as to how people think have emerged from strands of research which often seemed, at first, to tell us a simple fact (most commonly, a variation on the 'people are irrational' theme). Scientists then start to test different hypotheses for an explanation of why, for instance, Wason's card task (see Chapter 2) tends to be responded to with an apparent **confirmatory bias**. Eventually, as some experiments emerge in which we still see 'bad' reasoning, while in others people seem to get cued into 'better' logic, some patterns start to emerge.

The result tends to echo the shift in information science over the past decade or two. We find that *context*, in its many aspects, plays a huge role in how we use information in our thinking. As with Losee's badly baked cake, it isn't just the facts in our heads that predict the decision we'll take, but also *the information in the world*.

The most complex and messy aspect of that 'world' is the social relationships within it—our understanding and otherwise of other people. In social psychology, **attribution** studies have looked at our judgements of the causes of events.[163] There seem to be some situations where we attribute causes of things to *people* much more than to facts in the situation itself. This is called the *person bias.**

The old social influence experiments I mentioned in Chapter 2 showed this in frightening ways. People who'd merely been assigned randomly to an acting role suddenly seemed as if that role actually reflected their personality and social value. Less innocuous studies over the years have shown that this happens even in far more neutral, less dramatic situations.

I've often vaguely suspected the person bias occurring in British universities. Scientists and lecturers forced to accept short-term employment contracts through institutional policy are sometimes assumed by permanent staff not to be personally committed to their institution, department, or research group. It's as if their temporary

---

* It's also sometimes been called the 'fundamental attribution error', although calling anything 'fundamental' in psychology is bound to lead to people shooting it down. Sure enough, they have; it looks as though our person bias isn't as common in real life as in some rather forced experiments, but it's still a recognisable phenomenon.

status was an outcome of their own *attitude and ability*, rather than externally caused. We could also commit the person bias if the information supplied to us by a person (or system?—remember the anthropomorphism I mentioned in Chapter 1?) was poor, unreliable or unwelcome. This is what it means to 'shoot the messenger'.

Yet the person bias isn't consistent.[115] Some studies have shown the reverse, where people are biased *away* from judging a person and towards blaming the situation instead, even when a personal attribution would be more logical. Meanwhile, when we're thinking about the reasons for our own actions we generally cite the situation, although we'd ascribe the same actions by others to their personalities. And when we're thinking about what we know of a person, the extent that we know them seems to make us less likely to make person bias errors—we can 'see' how in a given situation, they behaved 'out of character'. Similarly, we can spot when a piece of information in the news doesn't fit our ongoing belief about, say, a political party or a tendency in society, and excuse it as a 'special case'.

Looking at it this way, the person bias then just starts to look like the general confirmatory bias in thinking. We stereotype other people easily, because it saves cognitive effort, and then we try to confirm our beliefs about them. But we know that our loved ones and we ourselves are more complex than that.

However, some cognitive experiments on reasoning about probabilities have added another aspect to the person bias. Probability judgement is one of those 'rational thinking' tasks that we seem in general to be very, very bad at. (However, the way we make people do it in the lab may have a lot to do with this. See my earlier comments on our supposed 'irrationality' in Chapter 2.) One thing that seems to happen in some of these experiments, although the reason for it is hotly disputed by some,[91] is that people seem to get distracted by emotional or social aspects when asked to judge a situation that involves people.[60]

Added to all the other biases we have in that sort of situation, it's hard to figure out whether this really matters. But it does neatly lead us to think about the role of emotion in thinking.

Feeling and thinking

In the past decade, cognitivists have made a long-overdue effort to pick apart the relationship between our cognition and our **affect**. Do emotions, moods and long-term psychological conditions alter the way we think? It's a very complicated area, made worse by our old friends, **demand characteristics**. In too many studies, cynical psychology students are 'put into a happy or sad mood', just by being asked to talk about a past life event for ten minutes. They then have to answer questions or solve problems, to assess their reasoning or memory.

My classmates saw through this kind of study when we were 18. I remember us laughingly debating it in practical class (when the lecturer, who'd become world famous for studies of this kind, couldn't overhear).* Should we sabotage the experiment? Do the opposite of what he wanted? Or just go along with it and give all the 'right' answers, showing a nice big mood difference? Like thousands of other students we just wanted a quiet life, so we did what we thought the guy wanted. So we all went home happy.

Every researcher is a former student. I often wonder what happens to them to make them forget this. Did my degree course give me an unusual overdose of critical thinking training (in which case, maybe students elsewhere are less cynical, and there's no problem anyway)? Can we *really* be sure that in mood-induction experiments, student participants aren't making up their own minds about what types of answers they're expected to give and mostly reaching the same conclusion (luckily, but then it's often so darned obvious)? And anyway, is this type of study really like people's moods and responses in real life? Some studies use hypnotism, but can they be sure it's working (students being very clever actors at times)? And doesn't hypnotism just put someone into an even more artificial cognitive state anyway?

Fortunately there are some more convincing studies of cognition and affect. In the 1980s Gerald Clore[257] ran a telephone survey in which people were asked about their life satisfaction. Checked against the known weather conditions at their location at that time, it turned out that people expressed greater satisfaction *with their lives* (not just the day they were having) if the current weather was sunny. The information you recall and interpret as you think depends on the emotional context, and that in turn actually is affected by the weather. We don't all suffer from Seasonal Affective Disorder, but we are very subtly influenced by the conditions around us.

Psychologists can also induce moods more subtly than via the 'happy event story' bludgeon. In a 1993 study,[202] for instance, subliminal **priming** was used. This just means that a sad or happy face was flashed up on the computer screen so fast (four milliseconds) that the participant had no chance of *consciously* seeing or

---

*Worryingly, this is the only practical class I can remember at all, so perhaps we had more fun than usual that day.

interpreting it.* Then they were shown some Chinese characters and asked to say whether they liked them. The happy/sad manipulation *did* influence people's decisions enough to be **statistically signifi- cant**—not by very much, but quite consistently.

Yet if the faces appeared for a whole second, so that people got a good look at them, there was no significant effect on their preferences. In this case people seem to have realised consciously that there was an extra reason for their feelings, and discounted it.

If I was right above about demand characteristics, of course the participants might have deliberately 'played along' in some way in this condition. Murphy and Zajonc[202] had thought about this and tried to give a neutral 'cover story' about the experiment's purpose. But they still wondered if the 'looming' face pictures might cause resentment, so that people reacted *against* the obvious mood manipulation. After all, they were being asked to give personal judgements.

So a second experiment tried to check for this by asking people if they thought the Chinese characters stood for 'good' or 'bad' things in real life, instead of whether they liked them. Murphy and Zajonc thought that any uncooperative attitudes would be cancelled out by participants' concern not to be *wrong*. Personally I'm not totally convinced, but at least they tried. This kind of careful checking is surely needed in every such study. Anyhow, the main point still stands that mood can be induced enough to alter cognition, even without awareness.

How should we think about the relationship between cognition and affect in the context of handling information? Gerald Clore[53] sees affect as information *in itself*—how you feel tells you something that you use as a factor in your thinking. In his words 'emotion colors cognition'. To him, the evidence shows that emotional effects aren't just a case of warning us to bear in mind that there's something in the situation we don't like. They seem to more *directly* feed into our judgements. He argues that positive affect makes you value your own expectations and interpretations—your internal information. Feeling sad makes you not want to focus on yourself, but on the external information around you, which in many situations (but not all) will make you more rational. However, sad feelings make you less efficient at your tasks, because you never feel you know enough just to make decisions and move on.

---

*This was checked by making the students do a recognition task, at which they did no better than chance. They may also have seen this task as the main point of the experiment, which would help them to stay unaware of the mood manipulation.

So, moods and emotions give you a bias towards different information—what you think you've learned already, or what's actually in front of you. It's also possible, Clore argues, to get similar effects by changing people's approach to a problem *without* manipulating their mood, encouraging them to take a more internally or externally focused approach through more cognitive means.

Donald Norman, the cognitivist and HCI guru, has pointed out that there's a bit more to affect than mere information. Neuroscience has shown clear differences in brain function in different mood states, due to changed dopamine levels in very specific parts of the brain. [14] However, I don't think Norman is really disagreeing with Clore here. Presumably Clore would agree that *something* must happen in the brain to make us take a different information use strategy, so it may as well be dopamine levels as anything else.

It seems, then, that when we want to be decisive and efficient, we need to be in a positive mood. When we want to be rational and accurate, we should sober up. This may seem obvious, but if I'd said that the reverse was true—say, that sad people were more efficient decision-makers but happy people were more willing to look outwards at all the information—you could probably have thought of examples of people and situations you've known which, for a moment at least, would have seemed to fit that too.

Just to complicate it a little further, though, mood also seems to influence our ability to *remember* things. We recall more information if we're in the same mood we were in when we learned it (as with other context effects, e.g. being in the same place, being equally drunk or sober, etc.). [152] This is called *state-dependent* memory. So if we need to recall information before we make a decision or solve a problem, the mood we would ideally 'choose' for ourselves might need to depend on how we were before.

For information-based work, knowing that we are partly creatures of our emotions is not constricting, but liberating. We all know ways of cheering ourselves up or calming ourselves down (unless we suffer from a clinical problem like severe depression). Using tools like music, we can actively choose the right state of mind for what we're trying to do. Our work with information can then be the better for it.

Passing it forward

Where is 'forward' in information use? Obviously the most progressive use of some information is if it helps us create something new—hopefully something with added value from our own ideas. This, of course, is the main purpose of traditional information retrieval from library and bibliographic databases. Students use them to get material for their essays, researchers for their experiments and papers.

I've mentioned the concept of relevance many times above. It's the cornerstone of information science, and of some areas in psychology too. I stressed earlier that relevance is ultimately the user's choice. So, imagine you're a user, let's say a scientist, and have found some things you feel you can call relevant. Do all of those things really get put into the thing you're creating? If not, what makes you choose not to?

In the early 1990s there was a very thoroughly reasoned pair of articles by Patrick Wilson at the University of California at Berkeley.[309] Wilson looked into this issue of information non-use; most information scientists had not explicitly considered it.

In his first paper, Wilson asked whether academic researchers ever fail to take relevant information (generally, other people's research outputs) into account in their own writings and studies. This could be simple ignorance. Perhaps a scientist would be unaware of a publication through overlooking it, or perhaps it wasn't yet published when their work started. Wilson started by citing a couple of earlier surveys where scientists had been asked if this ever happened to them. As Wilson pointed out, only scientists who had had this happen *and had then found out* (i.e. come across the work too late) would be able to say yes. When 27% did, you could expect that there would be others who *never* realised they'd duplicated someone else's work, or that that work had made theirs irrelevant.

Oh dear. So, scientists needed to search better and communicate more openly. Then again, most felt that the late discovery hadn't made a very big difference anyway. But there was more. Wilson's second paper asked whether there could be cases where scientists *deliberately* ignored other people's work. There was some evidence, he felt, that they sometimes did. Why, and was this bad?

This wouldn't always be through a personal decision. A whole discipline (psychology, let's say?) could have a tacit group policy of ignoring other disciplines. This could be for the sake of focusing on the problems that they felt needed solving first. It could be out of some concept of 'purity' of their background science. It could simply be a practical decision to avoid being overloaded with extra information. This in turn would be based on assuming that not very much beyond their own field would make much *causal* difference to their logic or conclusions. It could also be simple social snobbery against the 'out group' who couldn't hope to understand 'our' discipline.

An interesting case of someone braving a dip into another discipline was when information scientist Don Swanson,[286] having done some searches on biomedical literature, noticed that there were a few instances where isolated groups of researchers had found that certain substances affected certain parts of the body. Yet in each case, those researchers hadn't bothered to link up their work with that of a completely separate set of researchers, who studied a medical complaint that affected that body part—and so might be helped by the substance. It's slightly distressing, but not very surprising, to note that the medical research community did not show great gratitude to Swanson for his efforts, and partly ignored or dismissed him.[271] Thus his concern with 'undiscovered public knowledge' (undiscovered by the people who might make use of it) also became true for his own eight articles on it!

Swanson was trying to show that some kind of concept-linking mechanism was needed to help medicine make the most of its own findings. As you can imagine, that sort of 'help' isn't always graciously received! As a cognitive scientist trying to stick my oar into information science areas, I'm taking the same risk. There are plenty of ways that a social psychologist would explain this problem—group biases, loss of face, etc. Ultimately, if we're to be worthy of the name of science, we should be able to learn from a little outside interference.

Also, Wilson pointed out, what would count as relevant to an information scientist—something exactly 'on topic' with another scientist's specialism—the scientist might decide wasn't *logically* related to her or his current strand of thought. Perhaps that other work was on a slightly different aspect of the same problem.

In other words, Wilson seemed rather surprised to conclude, it could actually be perfectly rational to reject some known, relevant information. It may be equally rational to retrieve it and then keep it on one side, aware of it but choosing not to include it 'yet' in your own studies and writings. (Whether you would ever get around to factoring it in later is unknown.) Wilson implied that all this would be heresy to information scientists, but I find that hard to believe—they are overloaded researchers too!

Later Peiling Wang,[302] at the University of Tennessee in Knoxville, actually managed to collect some real data on researchers' document selections from searches and their fate in the researchers' own eventual work. Wang found many individual reasons why documents ended up used or unused, to supplement the rather more brutal rationalisations that Wilson had suggested. Agricultural economists (academics and postgraduate students) did searches in 1992 and were interviewed about which documents they found relevant and useful.

In 1995, 13 of them had written up the work that they'd been researching at the time, but were still around at the university. Wang interviewed them again about the documents they cited in their papers or dissertations. Only 22.1% of the papers from the 1992 searches were cited in the written outputs, and these papers made up only 4.9% of all the papers they cited. Of course, the researchers would have done other searches in the meantime, and been to conferences where they learned of more work, and their own ideas would have evolved so that some 'basic' papers no longer said anything important to their thesis. So perhaps a 'survival' rate of around one in four is quite good.

Wang did not comment on whether the researchers were ignoring or rejecting papers that they *should* have taken note of, but made a careful analysis of their many reasons and criteria for continued relevance. Overall, it seemed that rejections were due to a *narrowing of focus*. At first in a research project, everything on the topic might seem potentially useful, but later your thinking is focused on directly related arguments, theories and data. As their experience of their field also grew, there were more rejections on the basis of whether a journal was 'top' or not, and other judgements of quality and credibility.

This doesn't seem to have been snobbery. It seemed to involve a fear of being associated with less quality themselves. As we've seen, all information sources are not equal. However, all researchers know how hit-and-miss the peer review process can be. Sometimes a very good idea, or some very thorough data, *is* published in a 'lower' journal. The use of this 'social bias' in judging quality would be no surprise to a psychologist, of course, as I mentioned in Chapter 2.

If scientists are ignoring information that they actually possess, which ought to make a difference to the way they do their research, should we worry? Well, we don't have much choice. Since Wilson wrote his articles the 'information overload' that he cited as a major excuse has got worse, although our tools for managing it have got slightly better. I mentioned this in Chapter 1. Researchers are expected to churn out publications as frequently as possible. In the UK most are on short-term employment contracts, so their very future depends on a high 'productivity' level (and arguably, a correspondingly low *thinking* level). Despite all that, new ideas do emerge, new models of physical, biological, medical and behavioural phenomena do get built, and we somehow do manage to tease some nuggets of sense and inspiration out of the mass.

In passing Wilson cited some interesting *1960*s work on people's responses to 'information overload'—yes, it existed even then! The papers he cited were a combination of psychology and information science writers. I'll return to the potential for reviving this in the 'What to do' section later on.

Passing it back

This book has largely been based on our present use of computers. We extract information from their databases and websites. We use them to help us produce some output from this (e.g. an email, report or student essay). Then, at the moment, we leave them in peace. In future we may find ourselves using our knowledge to *teach* computers, so that they can help us better. I've mentioned several times that computers currently don't tend to know the semantics of the information they handle, and they don't have any motivation or intentionality. This has always been presented as a problem. We're getting close to some good solutions on the semantic front. We've got almost nowhere in making the computers care.

However, Yolanda Gil of the University of Southern California, who is an expert in **expert systems** (and, as she puts it, 'interactive knowledge capture'), points out the benefits. Computers also don't *lack* motivation to learn anything. They'll patiently take on whatever you want to teach them. They'll never get distracted or bored, or flick paper aeroplanes across the room. (Another benefit of the motivation lack, of course, is that the computer isn't biased in what it tells you about what it knows, either. It's completely innocent.)

Trying to teach computers about real-life situations and knowledge areas is a long-running obsession of the expert systems area in computer science. Its biggest headache is actually not the computing side at all, but how to extract knowledge systematically from human experts in the first place. Here the relationship between the user and the system is almost reversed, because the system is taking rather than giving information. Yet the expert is still a person with all the non-formal, confused, sometimes irrational and certainly emotional issues I reviewed in previous chapters.

Gil's research group[28] have focused on what it is that users find hard, and tried to build solutions to make it easier. Knowing that people don't 'speak' a formal ontology logic language, they built a user interface that translates into that from English. Knowing that users will often forget to define what they mean by a concept, or won't remember to draw all the relevant associations between things, they made the system cope with that but also encourage the users to fill in the extra blanks. This kind of serious user-centredness was long overdue in this sort of work. It's a key plank in bridging the semantic gap between people and computers.

Gil has also gone further[103] to suggest that mere translation, from users' informal knowledge into formal system ontologies, isn't going to work. In her view, whenever a formal semantic system is built to cover an area of expertise, the formal logic is never good enough to capture everything. Extra descriptive, clarifying information from the experts always has to be added in as well, even with quite rigid domains like the military. As she puts it:

> Although the languages that we use are quite expressive, they *still force knowledge into a straitjacket*: whatever fits the language will be represented and anything else will be left out ... Furthermore, *knowledge ends up represented piecemeal*, compartmentalized in whatever expressions the modelling language supports. Many of the connections between different pieces of knowledge are never stated, nor can they be derived by the system given what it knows. We see no value in representing redundant information or alternative ways to deduce the same facts: if the system can derive something in one way that may be more than sufficient.

A moment's reflection may lead you to agree that this isn't how we store our own knowledge. Quoting Marvin Minsky from 1970, Gil argues that the people developing computerised knowledge bases seem to see themselves as logicians, not as 'educators of intelligent systems', i.e. they seem to want to minimise rather than maximise the rich links between different bits of knowledge. I discussed earlier that in education we want deeper understanding than mere facts. The better educated *we* are, the more connections we can make between things. The more a *computer* is seen to 'know', the more facts it has. But connections and reasoning are what counts as true intelligence. And some of these just don't fit into formal logic.

Does this mean we're kidding ourselves to think we'll ever get a computer to completely map all the meanings of something we know? I'm not sure. We might just not have good enough models yet. A lot of the formal languages that computer scientists have developed for representing knowledge seem a bit archaic, viewed from cognitive science. This is mainly because they tend to focus on classifying things hierarchically, like a library, and on things having specific sets of defining features. This may be partly due to the current vogue for object-oriented programming languages, where 'objects' group into 'classes' and inherit 'properties' from each other. Once you think about the world through that mental model, your approach to semantics will be quite similar. This seems to be part of Gil's point, too.

As a cognitive scientist, I can't scoff too much. It's true that our old hierarchical 'defining feature' model of categories was revamped a little in the 1970s. It was agreed that much of the time, one level of classifying things (e.g. trees as opposed to oaks or living things) seems to be more 'basic'—i.e. used by default in reasoning tasks—than the others. (Later this was refined a little as the 'basic' level was shown to vary with context and knowledge, but the concept has survived.)

Since then, hundreds of papers on concepts and categorisation have been published. Yet for some reason, almost none have seriously pushed the hierarchy issue any further beyond that literally 'basic level'. We now know a lot more about how flexible and theory-based our *individual* concepts need to be. We know little about how valid it still is to assume some degree of hierarchy in the links *between* concepts.

As I said earlier, cognitive models of categorisation have recently become much more 'loose' and based on explanatory reasoning rather than lists of features. At the same time, 'knowledge base' scientists like Gil's group are building less formal, more flexible semantic systems for computers. So it seems that things are coming together. Working towards this, i.e. towards computer models that work more like our human ones (some of which, as I mentioned earlier, are also being simulated on computers now), looks like an exciting future.

What goes wrong with using it?

Emotions and errors

As we saw earlier regarding the effect of **affect**, we don't always think with cool, objective deductive logic when handling information. Sometimes this tendency reflects not just what we happen to think about one topic, but our whole world view, depending on our mood and mental health. Laboratory experiments with people who suffer from depression have shown that even with brief presentations of images and words on a screen, depressed people's eye movements tend to focus more on negative than on positive items.[188]

In another subtle laboratory study, students who had a more anxious personality, when tested on their attention to different stimuli on a screen at various times, tended to look more at words relevant to an exam as it drew nearer, while more laid-back students actually tended to look *less* at such words towards exam time than they had before.[182]

In another study, people who were coaxed into a happier mood by watching a comedy video seemed to tackle reasoning (logic) tasks in a different way from who watched a tragic story (described by one of the researchers as 'Think *Terms of Endearment* [1983 film] condensed into a few minutes'!). Those who were happy performed better at *inductive* logic problems (where we have to make a slight logical 'leap' to reach a conclusion, based on assumptions that haven't actually been stated), but much worse at *deductive* logic (where it's important only to rely on the information that's given, without assuming it means more than it says), than those who were miserable.[221] So we can actually get things *wrong* by being in the wrong mood, not just make decisions in a different *way*.

Of course, demand characteristics may have played a part here, as discussed earlier. (Isn't it pretty obvious that we want you to 'think happy/sad', if we show you a comedy/tragedy?) But it still suggests that mood played some part in reasoning. It seems unlikely that getting wise to the comedy manipulation would somehow stop people wanting to do well at logic problems. But, as we saw earlier, it could make them overconfident (doubly so if they thought they'd got the experimenter sussed!), and more reliant on their intuition than on careful deduction.

So to some extent, our personalities and mental conditions (as far as they are extended tendencies towards particular moods) can affect how we use information. Depressed people have long had a reputation for being more grimly realistic in their cognitive judgements, although most psychologists now think that this view is oversimplified:[120] depressives are more negative about most things, but there are only some situations in which being negative is the same as being more realistic. Also, some of the laboratory tasks on which depressed people seem to be more accurate actually only show better performance for *mildly* depressed people, not worse sufferers.

Similarly, anxious people are known to tend to focus, unfortunately, on problems that will make them feel more anxious. This is not to make themselves feel worse, but because they have a heightened awareness of 'threat' and so 'threats' are what they see and recall. Naturally, whatever information they decide to use will also be affected by this.

Overall, the evidence cited above suggests that anxiety may be a bigger predictor than depression of changes in thought patterns. So emotional influences are not just about being 'happy' or 'sad', but also about the 'fight or flight' panic that anxiety brings on. Since most of us suffer anxiety regularly to some extent, and around one in twenty of us will suffer so badly as to be clinically diagnosable,[215] this may have a serious impact on our ability to use and reflect on the information we gather.

Of course, for someone where one source of our anxiety is actually the computer we use for our information tasks[37] then all the activities I've described in this book will be, as Gerald Clore puts it, 'coloured' by the cognitions arising from perceived threats and obsessive worrying. Carol Kuhlthau has been arguing for years that the affective aspects of information tasks need to be modelled.[164] What is probably needed is for the cognitivists' emerging predictive models (of relationships between emotion and cognition) to be tested out in various applied setting of real information use.

Not passing it forward

I said earlier that we know information has been used when it's been shared with other people. In the business world a great deal of attention has been paid in recent years to the concept of 'knowledge management', i.e. trying to systematically to store and make available the information resources of a whole organisation. This book isn't the place to discuss this area, which is perhaps too young and too laden with optimistic management jargon to make real sense. At present it seems to be confused about its own definition— managing information? managing staff? managing work practices so that people just communicate better somehow? all of the above?

A set of highly critical, and in places almost splutteringly indignant, papers about it in a recent information science journal[5] will give interested readers some pause for thought. But among the perfectly fair questions they raise is this: Can 'knowledge' (as opposed to information sources) ever be managed? Knowledge is surely all about the human meanings that are attached once information has been learned and interpreted. This makes it inherently semantic and complex, not reducible to easily managed 'chunks' as information might be.

Worse, knowledge within an organisation is *shared*. This doesn't necessarily imply complete consensus on its meaning—in fact knowledge that there's a dispute about something is also part of the knowledge itself. This actually makes it harder to express the knowledge in a form that all staff would recognise as fitting their own understanding. Finally, knowledge arises out of many information sources, many (most?) of them humans rather than documents, so it's hard enough to manage the *information* but almost impossible to manage the *knowledge* that results.

Despite the distaste of information scientists about the whole 'knowledge management' concept, I think we can still be optimistic. As we start to add semantics to our information resources, and as we find increasingly flexible ways of structuring them (the web itself showing how far this can go), there *should* be ways to add many different types of item to the mix and link them in semantically, to make it richer and more aligned with the 'knowledge' around the organisation. An example of one suitably flexible technology for this is The Brain.[291] This quite simple piece of software just lets you link almost anything on your computer together (notes, concepts, files, emails, web pages, contact details, etc.). It can be used as a personal non-linear way of organising information, or to link shared information across a group or company.

However, it's not clear that everyone in any organisation would really want this. If so many more of the confidential, internal understandings of a business or public service were recorded in this way, a great deal more could be lost than gained as soon as the first corporate hacker found a way in.

Even if a system was foolproof, people's motivations within an organisation (at least within one that employs them) are such that they might fear reprisals, effects on their appraisal or their job security, accusations of 'bad mouthing', and so on. Some knowledge within organisations is such that people are only prepared to state it explicitly orally, often only outside the building (hence the many jokes about the value of smoking breaks!).

Within academia things aren't a lot better. Steven Rose, the neurobiologist who's done pioneering work on the basis of memory in the brain, wrote an 'interlude' in his 1992 book[243] in which he talked about the fears, competitiveness and formal window-dressing that go on even in his own rigorously scientific (and relatively well-funded) research area. Before the web and email lists really became popular, I was involved in running an online conferencing system for HCI researchers around the UK and beyond. I learned then, early in my career, that many people don't want to share their ideas. They'll wait until they're sure of getting the 'reward' of a published paper, justifiably fearing that others could steal the credit.

Therefore it's not just disorganisation that keeps the typical academic's website out of date. It will list their published and 'in press' publications, and if you're lucky their submitted ones, but will say relatively little about their current ongoing work. Even in a collaborative project, the partners will usually not know everything that's going on in each other's work. Conferences are seen as quick routes to publication and a chance to bounce ideas against learned colleagues, but they're rarely opportunities to find out what's really going on *now* in someone else's lab.

Quite often, then, we pass on information only when it's seen as safe to do so. Before that, it's ours to play with, generally on our own or with those we trust.

Plagiarism and copyright

I discussed images and other multimedia in earlier chapters. One major problem with using these types of information, even if you can find them online, is the question of plagiarism and copyright.

Images, at least those involving any artistic or historical worth, have a value as commodities which, traditionally, would have been paid for by the user. Ownership of the largest collections of photographs (millions of images) is mostly in the hands of commercial or semi-commercial entities such as the Hulton–Getty archive. These are used to dealing with fee-paying customers who require single images for specific purposes such as illustrating a book cover. Their fees have traditionally covered both the time taken by a curator to find the ideal image and the copyright fee for reproducing it.

Now, however, everyone hopes to find everything free online, and copyright is an increasingly cumbersome concept in the 'find it NOW, use it NOW' age we're entering. Somebody owns that image, possibly the person who created or commissioned it, or took a careful photographic copy of it, or possibly the collector who's lovingly preserved and catalogued it. Who are we to expect to get it free and do what we like with it?

This is of course just as big a problem for text as for images, which is why you don't find most bestseller novels available for reading online. However, people generally find it quite easy and worthwhile to throw some summary text together to post online, while encouraging people to buy their books to read further. It's hard to do the same with imagery: what images do you put online that you *really* don't mind somebody else copying and using in their documents and webpages, without even crediting you for them? Images are about a single holistic experience, not a long read or a reference-check, so it's hard to put just 'part' of them online as you can with texts.

So we shouldn't be surprised, perhaps, at the generally limited access to useful online image collections while anybody still has a stake in making a living from them. Who needs to buy a beautiful framed print from an expert photographer when they can print off the digital version for themselves?

One answer to this is that online digital images, at the time of writing, are often still largely inferior in visual resolution to the images produced on film by a camera. Massively high resolutions are now possible in even cheap digital photos, but these can take forever to download. And it's of course possible deliberately to use an even poorer version. This can be seen as a saving grace for people who have images which others will pay to view with a higher level of quality, since they can put low-resolution 'thumbnails' online and then request payment for access to a better copy (on paper or in a larger graphics file). It's hard to see the details in a thumbnail, but then it's hard to know what happens in a book from its Amazon website synopsis.

Yet much of the time this won't stop illicit copying, since people can 'make do' with less than perfect pictures. Our visual perception and attention systems are awesome at decoding what we see, even in poor light and with blurred lines. We are still far, far better at vision than the best image processing algorithms. We can 'fill in the gaps' and ignore the poor quality and jagged edges, just as the illegal down-loaders of bootlegged pop songs can ignore the sound distortions on the recordings because their auditory attention can easily concentrate on the music.

Plagiarism is bad for the consumer or reader, not just for the original creator. It's now a nightmare in education. Students who struggle to create original work can find themselves with worse marks than those who plagiarise from others. Educators have to be more creative themselves to find ways around this, although often plagiarism is obvious. A beautifully written essay is submitted from an normally semi-illiterate student, or else it clearly answers the wrong question about the topic. Universities have tried setting up anti-plagiarism websites and software that can spot inconsistencies of style which might indicate 'lifted' passages. And there are hints that the education system, at least in the UK, is swinging back from its focus on continuous assessment towards exams and large project work, where plagiarism can be controlled (although this isn't the only reason for this).

To really tackle a social problem like plagiarism, perhaps we have to look at the *balance of effort* involved in behaving 'well' or 'badly'. For images and maps, and originally also for text, borrowing someone else's creation used to mean laboriously hand-copying it, which is not much easier than creating your own. It was also quite a bit harder to *find* someone else's relevant work in the first place. Nowadays, we can easily find an image or map of what we want, and we can easily copy and even edit it on a computer. But it's also much easier than it used to be to draw or write our own, thanks to amazingly clever graphics software, animation and web design packages, sophisticated word-processors and cheap digital cameras.

An exception to this, perhaps, is maps, where we can't easily go and survey the landscape ourselves. We can't recreate the basic spatial data this way if we want it to be even vaguely accurate, and our own spatial knowledge is often dreadfully inadequate and patchy. So we may have to buy the mapping data, and use our creativity to extract, edit and add what we need. Or we can rely on our own 'sketch maps' of the places we want to map, as people have done for centuries. The main problem there is in ever showing that map to anyone else. People just tend to assume any map is spatially accurate, and have different ideas of how things are shaped and structured, so other people's digital 'sketchmaps' would always mislead.

The cost of buying accurate mapping data and editing it into the map we want is dropping anyway. But then what do we do with it? Most computers have a word-processor, a calculator and probably a spreadsheet program, and at least a crude graphics package. Yet very few people own or know how to buy any mapping software of their own. Mapping is the only online creative area where creation is still mostly limited to professionals.

However, by 'professionals' I mean people in very many different workplaces. People from the local council, the fire service and the water and electric company, environmental campaigners, super-market chains, police crime investigators and logistics companies are all using geographic information systems (**GIS**) to map the things they work with. Yet most of them work with the raw data, and don't feel the need for 'good' map design on the screen or in their printouts. Cartographers, making a heroic 'last stand' for their centuries of expertise while the GIS world ignores them, point out that surely some better design of these 'working' map images would help people to work better with them, just as better-designed offices help every worker, better-designed user interfaces help every computer-based worker, and better-written text helps every reader.

This is falling on resoundingly deaf ears, so far, and meanwhile cartography degree courses have almost universally closed down. Yet logically, the cartographers must be right. People must be working less efficiently with map-based information because it's not as 'readable' as it should be. This is not (entirely) a problem for the national mapping agencies and commercial companies that sell the raw base data. It needs to be made 'fit for purpose'. But every GIS *can* change the appearance of the map, if its users appreciate how and why to do it.

Unfortunately, cartographers haven't adapted quickly enough to a professional landscape where their skills need to be sold in a new way (literally, and also in terms of 'persuasion' within a workplace). What's needed is some research that actually *shows* lost productivity from poor mapping in workplaces, in the same way that usability of computer systems has been cost-justified by research. But maybe the cartographers and I are wrong, and people cope well with bad mapping. They may be expert enough to get over it, or perhaps even bad maps are somehow easy to read. It's not yet clear if this is true.

Why doesn't the consumer at home get to play with digital map data? The only obvious reason for this is the cost of producing it, but as that cost is dropping, things will change. Imagine a map of your area which only shows the things *you* find useful *personally*, or that shows clearly *why* that nasty industrial port shouldn't be built near your village. A trained cartographer would still (usually) do it better, just as a professional copywriter or academic will (usually) write more eloquently, and an artist or graphic designer will (usually) create better images, but in those fields, everyone can 'have a go' at an amateur level. This will soon be true for mapping, too.

We want to cut down plagiarism and encourage original creativity, which is better for everyone and not just for people who don't want their work copied without credit or pay. But where does computer-based creative work leave us in terms of the 'balance of effort'? For a highly computer-literate person, picking up a computer-based tool and making exactly the right thing for people to 'read' is quite easy. For the average person with little computing education, it's not that simple. Software complexity increases with every new release, and most state-of-the-art software packages are such little worlds of their own that they come with their own jargon language to learn. They may also have their own user interface 'widgets' that may not work like anything else you've seen—despite the basic user interface standards that they 'sort of' follow. The learning curve is very steep.

Most obviously, then, we need to educate people better in the use of creative computing tools, and this should start from a very early age. Kids should be learning in primary school graphics, word-processing and mapping packages that give them the basic conceptual under-standing. By secondary school they could be exploring the very same packages used by adults in professional settings, although perhaps not using all the features. The encouragement to create (anything) from scratch tends to drop off through the education system and beyond, compared to all the frenzy of drawing and story-writing of early childhood, but this should be changed.

Even so, realistically, the 'balance of effort' is never going to swing strongly in favour of everyone making every informative item themselves from scratch, and even if they do they'll probably be copying other people's ideas. Even Albert Einstein is alleged to have said that the secret of creativity was hiding your sources. We'll still need legislation and a strong social taboo on 'cheating'.

To my mind, the latter has been seriously eroded in recent years. The 1980s 'on the make' culture, nurtured by 'new right' politics and economics, seemed to create a whole generation of people whose most common moral statement is that one should 'look after yourself first' (said in a tone of prim self-righteousness). People's attitudes have shifted away from duty and towards 'rights'. This makes it harder to convince people that plagiarism is wrong. So legislation and technical 'anti-piracy' measures are needed too.

Arts organisations suffer endless cuts, schoolchildren are force-fed with a rigid curriculum, and media channels copy each other's ideas (at the time of writing, the main 'idea' being so-called 'reality TV'), creativity seems to have a bad press. Yet out there on the web, **bloggers** and poets publish their own literature, amateur photographers create their own galleries, and rock bands release free original music. The 'great and the good' in our society are also still bent on making the arts accessible to everyone.

On the everyday level, authorised 'clip art' is so readily available that there is now little need to steal when a basic drawing or cartoon is required. Perhaps the panic over plagiarism is unnecessary. Maybe some kind of social dynamic will always give creativity a place (after all, there was plenty of it in past centuries when society was much simpler and poorer). This is not the same as ensuring that all creators can make a safe living from it, but then that has never been the case.

What to do about using it?

For users

Much of the content of this section in previous chapters has focused on improving our **metacognition** during information tasks. In this chapter we've seen that monitoring the effects of our moods and emotions may be helpful, too, since they influence our thinking styles when we finally start applying all that we've found.

On the metacognition front, I discussed above the tendency to stereotype our categories (especially of people) in some situations. Since the underlying reality, as far as we can best model it, is based on our *explanatory theories* of why things belong together, changing those theories should be quite easy once we recognise them for what they are. We should also be able to spot when our choices of action to test theories show the **confirmatory bias** and make it impossible for us to prove ourselves wrong!

When we're working with information, often our social peer group or our own filtering processes may stop us from realising that other disciplines have something relevant to say (or, in the case of the biomedics identified by Swanson,[286] people in their *own* discipline!).

Although we have to have strategies to cope with 'overload', we should always remain conscious of them, and prepare to break them down when it's likely to help. I hope that this book has managed to demonstrate the value of that.

For information providers

In situations where we're in danger of focusing too much on facts, especially where we're producing or designing information content to pass on to others, we need to remember the multisensory, experience-based, image-rich nature of our mental concepts, and try to use this to make information easier to absorb as 'knowledge'.

Information is power, but it is also a brake on misuse of power, because its 'fuzziness' reminds us that situations are not as morally or politically polarised as someone might be trying to tell us. For this to work we need people to get used to hearing less polarised, simplistic information. It doesn't mean we need to lose our 'audience' or 'customers'. For example, every intelligent person respects the BBC's approach to news more than that of more populist, down-market media. This is partly because, by reminding us that current affairs are never simple, the BBC helps to keep our minds open and questioning whenever we hear otherwise. Every other information provider has the same implicit social duty, hard though it is.

Finally, try to be understanding and open with copyright issues, within reason. Make it *very* obvious and easy for people to get permission or pay suitable fees to borrow or copy what they need.

For research

As I've said already, cognitive scientists tend to talk a lot about 'information' without dealing with the types of complex information that information scientists grapple with. In their turn, the information scientists tend only to skim the shallows of the psychological literature, and never get as far in as the (supposedly) predictive computational cognitive science models that are now emerging. With the potentially alarming effects of emotion, particularly anxiety, so much might be achieved for both sides if things were understood in more depth.

If memory for information is dynamic and constantly flexible, can connectionist models that try to mimic this be tested on the outputs of real-world information tasks? If it's too early, then exactly what's missing? We are perhaps not willing to specify often enough at what point an idea or model will ever be ready to leave the lab. Someone should by now be able to measure the true gap between the cognitivists' idea of 'information' and that of information scientists.

Writing about the **confirmatory bias**, it's all too obvious that we scientists fall victims to it ourselves. Do we always *really* design our experiments to give the **null hypothesis** a serious fighting chance? (And shouldn't we be able to test between two positive alternative theories more often, instead of thinking of only one?)

Demand characteristics are especially critical in experiments where we try to manipulate people into completely different mood states. Students (who are still the most usual participants) are not stupid! It ought to be possible to simply *measure* people's mood, or to try to catch them when they already happen to be having a bad/good day. Once a researcher was known to do work on mood, of course, this wouldn't reduce demand characteristics any more. Also, it might take a while before enough people were found in a sad mood but still willing to take part.

But just think what a network of apparently non-mood-research-ing scientists, just quietly collecting data on an *ad hoc* basis, could achieve. If we can get thousands of computer users to join forces to process data for NASA, surely we could get some psychologists to co-operate in collecting more naturalistic, opportunity-sampled beha-vioural data. With the internet everywhere, and mobile devices making it possible for a basic experiment to be run almost anywhere, there's so much opportunity to get our lab theories and tasks out into everyday contexts.

Meanwhile we still don't seem to understand much about the extent to which human concepts are classified hierarchically, or not. This is still a crucial missing piece in our cognitive knowledge models, which are so crucial for linking to the ontological 'knowledge bases' of computer science.

In information science, Wang's[301] valuable findings (based on some real-world use, hardly the norm in this discipline either) could be taken further and reanalysed for cognitive patterns and biases. It may then be possible to adapt some existing cognitive models to help predict the 'long-term relevance' of retrieved information.

There can't be much 40-year-old cross-disciplinary work that's more crucial to revisit than information overload, not just for scientists and professionals, but for all of us.

We know so much more now about **change blindness**, about various concepts of 'relevance', about **semantic** nets and adaptable concepts, about social biases and cultural differences, about different types of logical reasoning and problem-solving, about emotional factors in cognition, about physiological stress responses, and so on, all of which could play small parts in helping us to predict when 'overload' really happens, when it becomes a critical problem and when it's just a risk to our ability to think straight and make the best decisions, and how we'll handle it. And, thus, how to make it better.

Summary

By the time information becomes something we know and can use, it is far more than some transmitted data. It includes rich sensory and image associations, as well as Gradgrind's 'hard facts'.[72] Information science has done relatively little work on information use (although often using the term when really talking about searching or browsing).

The way we 'store' information in our memories (although memory is now being thought of as a more dynamic set of ongoing processes rather than a static 'store') involves flexible concepts which seem to be based on our own explanatory theories of how knowledge is connected in a given situation. However, sometimes we think of concepts as more rigidly defined.

When we reason we often show **confirmatory bias**, i.e. trying to back up what we believe, rather than checking that it's not falsified by the evidence. Social considerations seem to interfere with our reasoning in some situations, but their importance is still hard to gauge.

Studies that try to manipulate people's moods to see if their cognitive processes change seem to have problems with **demand characteristics**. But there is some very convincing evidence that even subtle mood-influencers like the weather can change what we remember and believe. In a positive mood we tend to be more confident, inductive and decisive, while in a negative mood we are more likely to pay attention to evidence, use deductive reasoning properly, and be accurate. One particularly fundamental factor is anxiety, which even affects our subconscious visual attention.

In professional and academic contexts, information is not always taken up, used or disseminated according to what would initially seem appropriate. There are also many other reasons for this, and it does not appear to be due to 'irrationality', but the progress of science is hampered by it, and we don't know how much.

Progress in developing '**expert systems**' that learn from human knowledge may be being hampered by the rigid, narrow and inflexible concepts of computer science developers. Careful user-focused work is starting to overcome this and to create systems that might really reflect the 'messiness' of human concept structures. In the future, we may find ourselves having to teach such systems our own knowledge to make them usable in our information-based work.

Plagiarism and copyright are major issues for the reuse of information. The 'balance of effort' is still tipped too heavily towards it being far easier to cheat than to reward others' creativity. People need more information creation skills, and copyright permissions need to be much easier to obtain (and fees easier to pay, where necessary). Society currently does not stress loudly enough the importance of socially conscious behaviour. Yet the enormous creativity shown across the web suggests that people don't just want to plagiarise—they want to create information themselves.

Further reading

Yolanda Gil's homepage is at www.isi.edu/~gil/

Progress towards the future 'semantic web' is summarised in Dieter Fensel, James A. Hendlers, Henry Lieberman and Wolfgang Wahlster, *Spinning the Semantic Web: Bringing the World Wide Web to its full potential* (Cambridge, MA: MIT Press, 2005), ISBN 0-262-56212-X.

Any recent cognitive psychology textbook will introduce the work on human concepts and categories, and memory in general. The most important theorist and researcher on flexible, adaptive concepts is Doug Medin, whose website is at www.psych.northwestern.edu/psych/people/faculty/medin/medin.html

Attribution theory and the person bias are discussed in most basic psychology textbooks, so long as they cover social psychology. However, thinking has moved on in recent years, and this book is a good summary of it: Bertram F. Malle, Louis J. Moses and Dare A. Baldwin, *Intentions and Intentionality: Foundations of social cognition* (Cambridge, MA: MIT Press, 2001), ISBN 0-262-13386-5.

A good up-to-date book on recent thinking about thinking, i.e. reasoning and how it's influenced by context and biases (including Wason's selection task) is Ken Manktelow and Man Cheung Chung, *The Psychology of Reasoning: Theoretical and historical perspectives* (Hove: Psychology Press, 2004), ISBN 1-841-69310-3.

The most accessible book on the role of emotion is Don Norman's latest punchy bestseller: Don Norman, *Emotional Design: Why we love (or hate) everyday things* (New York: Basic Books, 2004), ISBN 0-465-05135-9. He also cites some of the more relevant academic work. *Cognition and Emotion* is an academic journal that is devoted to the relationship between the two subjects of its title.

I've mentioned **metacognition** at various points in this book—it cuts across every task and situation I've described. Here's one book worth reading (especially Chapters 9 and 10) on the topic: Janet Metcalfe and Arthur P. Shimamura, *Metacognition: Knowing about knowing* (Cambridge, MA: MIT Press, 1994), ISBN 0-262-13298-2.

Glossary

affect, affective: the only time that this word is used as a noun is when it means 'emotion', 'mood', etc.—the way that our emotional selves affect our cognition. (When talking about the *result* of something, it's an *effect*, but it might be *affected* by other factors. Less commonly, when we make something change successfully, we *effect* that change.)

AI: *see* **artificial intelligence**.

algorithm: a computer program that solves a specific problem, usually by looking at an input and transforming it in some way.

anthropomorphism, anthropomorphise: thinking of animals, computers or inanimate objects as if they were human, with minds like ours.

artificial intelligence: the aim of some computer scientists to build systems that behave not just like ignorant-but-rational conventional computers, but more like humans. Some scientists don't care whether the *way* an intelligent system operates is the same *way* that people think, while others do want to make their AI models true *cognitive* models. *See also* **expert systems**.

attribution: when something happens, we tend to *attribute* the cause to something. The reasons why we sometimes blame one thing (e.g. a person), and sometimes another (e.g. the situation), have been studied in detail by social psychologists. Causal explanations for our concepts and categories, in cognitive psychology, are also related to this.

behaviourism, behaviorism: the attitude by a psychologist that we can't observe or measure mental processes, but only the outputs from them (i.e. what people physically say and do). Very few researchers are now strict behaviourists, but most do recognise that many of our concepts are metaphors for how the brain creates the mind, not necessarily real physical variables.

blogger: a person who keeps an online diary on their website, for others to read. The word 'blog' is a corruption of 'web log'.

bookmarks or **favourites**: in a web **browser**, the list of websites that you've asked the browser to remember, so that you can revisit them easily.

Boolean logic: logic used in computer programming, and in traditional information retrieval. If you want to look for some information on gardening, and you're looking at US sites as well as British, you might find yourself wanting '(garden OR yard) AND flowers AND NOT annuals'. Adapted from the way that logic gates work in electric circuits, e.g. switching something on only if both of two other inputs are on (an 'AND gate'). Unfortunately, in English we sometimes say 'or' to mean 'this or this but NOT both', but in computers it means 'this or this or both'. We also sometimes mean 'or' when we say 'and'. So people find Booleans confusing.

browser: software that lets you look through information without changing it. Usually now we just say 'browser' when we mean a web browser, which is a program that lets us both browse *and search* the web (because it gives us access to **search engines** as well as the raw information on web pages).

change blindness: the shocking finding in psychology that we don't process half as much of the visual world around us as we used to think we did. Researchers can show you a video in which something quite ridiculous happens out of context while you're looking at a predictable situation, and you won't notice the anomaly. It's shed some light on the difficult issue of consciousness – the biggest bugbear in science.

chunking: the way that we make it easier to remember and process information by thinking of it as 'chunks'. We might remember a phone number as two separate 'chunks' of three to five digits, for instance.

cognition: such mental processes as thinking, remembering, problem-solving, imagining, creating, interpreting our senses and controlling our responses. Cognitive psychology explores this through experiments and theories. It's now evolved into cognitive science, which also uses studies of the brain and computer modelling techniques, and is close at times to the **artificial intelligence** area. (Tip: unlike 'cognition', 'cognitive' has the emphasis on the *first* syllable, i.e. it's not 'cog*nee*tive' but '*cog*nitive'.)

cognitive artefacts: anything that's designed to help you with how you think about your task, rather than with the physical aspects of work. Your mouse may be designed ergonomically, but was your word-processor?

cognitive dissonance: a concept created by Leon Festinger in the 1950s. The idea is that we try to be consistent with ourselves and with people we care about, so we're motivated to reduce the contradictions between things we believe and do. Nowadays generally viewed as over-simplified, but sometimes valid.

cognitive ergonomics: more often referred to nowadays as **human factors**, this involves applying to **cognitive artefacts** the same principles as **ergonomics** (e.g. design your software to suit a range of people, in the same way that an office chair is designed to adjust for people's heights).

cognitive hysteresis: a term coined by Don Norman for a situation where you're fixed on solving a problem one way. You can't see that perhaps the problem is a different one and your current solution strategy is prolonging it. *See also* **functional fixedness**.

cognitive style: a concept that tries to distinguish between people based on how they usually like to think or learn (also often call 'learning style'). Although difficult to justify in terms of scientific evidence, some researchers find it useful. However, nobody seems to agree on which 'styles' are useful or meaningful, or whether they're reliable enough to be worth measuring (e.g. do people always have the same 'style', or could they be trained or persuaded to change it?). Other psychologists still prefer to focus on *ability* or *aptitude* rather than 'style'; that suffers from all the same problems, but there's a bit more evidence about its stability and basis in the brain.

complex systems: usually used in **HCI** to refer to **process control** systems. In theory, though, any computer system that has a lot of functionality is complex, especially if it has any 'real time' aspect.

computer anxiety, computer aversion: loosely referred to as 'technophobia', this is the emotional response of some people to IT. Even some people who do use a computer may feel strongly that they'd rather not, and avoid it whenever they can. When strong enough, like any emotional reaction, the anxiety can make people less able to cope with computer tasks, which is probably a vicious circle.

conditioning: in **behaviourism** this was the word used for *learning* something. Pavlov's dogs were famously conditioned to salivate at the sound of a bell. You could also have *negative* conditioning: avoiding something because every time you'd gone near it, something bad had happened.

confirmatory bias: the term coined by Peter Wason in 1960 to explain why people don't always use strict deductive logic when trying to prove something. Instead of checking for evidence which, if true, would disprove our theory, we focus on evidence that's consistent with it (but not good enough to prove it).

conjunction: in **visual search** experiments, people take much longer to spot something if it is, say, a blue square among an array of red squares mixed with blue circles. This is because they have to search for both squareness and blueness together.

connectionist networks: also sometimes referred to as 'neural nets'. In cognitive science, connectionism is trying to build computer-based models of how we reason or learn things. It's based on the idea of lots of little units that 'excite' or 'inhibit' each other, like little circuits that turn each other on or off to give a pattern of lights (or in this case, an output, such as a fact or conceptual link). This is roughly, but not exactly, how neurons work in our brains.

cookies: not always as nice as they sound, these are small computer programs that a web server sends to sit quietly on your hard disk, sending back information about you when the server asks for it. Usually they're used harmlessly just to keep track of your preferences or login details, or to remember what you were just doing when you move to a different bit of a website.

declarative memory: simply our memory for facts and beliefs— anything you can *declare*.

demand characteristics: what it is about an experiment that makes you believe you're supposed to behave in a certain way, so that you do. This might mean that your responses are more about this belief, in the context of the study, instead of reflecting how you'd behave outside the lab. An invidious problem in psychology, underestimated by many researchers, despite being shown by M. T. Orne as long ago as 1960.

ecological validity, ecologically valid: a loose term that implies that an experiment isn't too far removed from the real world. If people are given a very artificial task in the lab, can we conclude that they solve problems this way outside it? Normally you get more ecological validity, but less control over what's going on and what extra factors might confound your results, if you get people to do things that are more like their messy reality. It also applies to job assessments: the best way to check someone's suitability for a job is to make them do something very similar to it.

episodic memory: our memory for things that have happened (episodes). We are often quite bad at remembering *when* things happened, but our memory *of* them happening often helps us to recall related information.

ergonomics: the science of designing artefacts (anything that physically exists and is manmade) to support people's work. Known as **human factors** in the United States, although in the UK this term tends to be used more for less physical aspects of design than traditional ergonomics.

error variance: when we do a research study, we often compare two or more different conditions, situations or groups of people. The amount that people vary because of the differences we're examining is the *main effect*; the amount that they vary *anyway* due to other things is the error variance.

experimenter effects: the influence of researchers over their results. Can be indirect, as when expectations of how a person will behave makes you subtly (usually subconsciously) influence them so that they do. Or can be direct, as when you interpret the results in a way that fits what you expected. See also **confirmatory bias**. This was explored by Robert Rosenthal in the 1960s, who showed that we could even influence rats to run mazes more or less efficiently, based on what we believed.

expert systems: systems where the knowledge held by experts in a specialist domain (e.g. medicine) has been represented in the computer's database, so that it can make or suggest decisions without human biases or weaknesses (such as our tendency to overlook or forget some relevant information). They're much harder to build effectively than people first hoped a few decades ago.

font: the typeface used on a computer screen or printout.

functional fixedness: the tendency to be think of a tool as only being usable for one function, so that we can't use it to solve a problem that needs it to be used differently. If I think of a hammer only as something to hit things with, I might not realise that I could use it as a lever, as when removing a nail from a piece of wood. *See also* **cognitive hysteresis**.

Gaussian distribution/curve: see **normal distribution**.

Gestaltists, Gestalt psychology: a movement in psychology in the early twentieth century (mainly in German-speaking countries). Taken from the German word for 'shape', it focused on seeing how we perceived the structure of things even when they seem to consist of separate little bits rather than a whole. This was applied to visual perception e.g. the way we can see a shape even when there are gaps, or even when the shape consists of the gaps in other shapes. It was also applied to problem-solving—the need to look at everything in the problem and avoid **functional fixedness**.

GIS (geographic information systems): computer software to manage spatial data about the real-world landscape. We usually work with digital maps on the screen, but GIS can also calculate where things are without displaying the map. Most GIS can use both **vector** and **raster** data, although some are still specialised for just one or the other.

HCI: human–computer interaction. The research and practice of people's use of computers. Traditionally on the border between psychology and computer science. Also referred to sometimes as 'computer–human interaction'. Also as **usability** research, or 'user interface design'. HCI people get quite cross at the latter phrase, because the problems you have with a computer go way beyond the interface and have to be addressed at the start of a software development project, not as a 'bolt-on' at the end.

history list: in a web **browser**, the function that lists all the websites you've recently visited.

human factors: *see* **ergonomics**.

hypertext, hypermedia: Hypertext was originally suggested by Vannevar Bush in the 1940s, long before computers could do it. The idea is that within one document or page of text, there are links to refer you directly to another one. Hypermedia takes this further by having links between other types of multimedia object: video clips, images, maps, etc. Obviously the web is based on hypermedia.

ill-defined problem: a problem where some aspects aren't clear, so you're not sure how to go about solving it. What isn't clear might be your initial state (where you are now), your goal state (what you want to achieve), the operators (what you can do) or the restrictions (what you can't), or any combination of them. As opposed to a **well-defined problem**.

implicit learning, implicit memory: our ability to pick up on the structure and other information within a (usually visual) image or scene without consciously processing it.

indicative mood: The state of mind where we just want to get a job done: we just look at information that indicates relevance to our task. Proposed by George Kelly as the alternative to an **invitational** frame of mind.

information science: the science of storing, processing, classifying and retrieving information that's outside our heads, e.g. in books or computer systems. As opposed to cognitive science, which is about how we process information *inside* our heads.

intermediary: in libraries, the person who does a computer search for you, based on what you tell them you want.

intersubjectivity: in philosophy, the idea that we see other people as 'subjective' like we are, i.e. having a mind and awareness of it.

invitational mood: the state of mind where we're open to new ideas and information, as distinct from the **indicative** frame of mind. Idea proposed by social psychologist George Kelly.

ISP: internet service provider. The company whose computer you access first on the internet. It then passes on your signals, of what you want or are trying to send, to other computers around the world. Usually all you pay for is the connection to that first computer, no matter where in the world your target information resource is sitting.

learning style: *see* **cognitive style**.

Matthew effect: the more you know already about a topic, the easier it'll be for you to find out more. From St Matthew's Gospel (13.12, 25.29), where Christ says, 'For to everyone who has, more will be given.'

mental models: the idea that when we deal with a situation, we have some cognitive 'structures' in our minds that bring together all the aspects of it. So we might have an understanding of how to make something work (**procedural**), and knowledge of what we think it's meant for (**declarative**). *See also* **schema**.

metacognition: thinking about thinking. 'Meta-'anything is information about that thing, rather than the thing itself. So metacognition is what we know and think about how we're dealing with a situation, such as our strategy while we're talking to someone or solving a problem.

metadata, meta-information: data about data, i.e. information about an information source, but not the 'real' information you wanted. The information held in a library catalogue is metadata, i.e. it tells you about a book, but it doesn't tell you the same things as the book itself.

morpheme: the individual units of meaning within words. Often a word is a single morpheme, no matter how many syllables it has, but many words break down further. 'book' is just one morpheme, but 'booking' is two: 'book' in the sense of reserving tickets, and 'ing' implying that it's an ongoing action.

netiquette: the etiquette of dealing with other people online, especially in email. The two key things that people learn very early are: first, not to use all upper case in messages; second, not to 'flame' people (send messages that are, or seem to be, aggressive or angry). The latter situation can very easily escalate because the two people concerned can't see each other and so 'depersonalise' the other.

normal (or Gaussian) distribution: the sort of bell-shaped curve that most of our human characteristics seem to fit. A few people are very short or very tall, but most are in the middle. I drew a graph in Chapter 2 showing two overlapping normal distributions for two similar groups of people. Psychologists can do better statistics on data that fits a normal curve, because they can make extra assumptions that their sample represents the whole population. But there isn't necessarily something biologically meaningful about a measure just because it happens to fit the curve. (Hence the debate about IQ, where the 'normality' of it is part of the attraction for people who want to believe that different races are differently intelligent.)

null hypothesis: the opposite of what we expect to see happen in an experiment, according to our theory. Well-designed research should always have a clear null hypothesis. It might not just say that 'nothing will happen', but that the reason *why* things happen is different from the reason we're favouring. The experiment should then be able to decide between them.

OCR: optical character recognition. Software that looks at a scanned image of a page of text, e.g. from a fax or a page scanned from a book, and calculates which characters are on the page to create a digital, editable text file.

picture superiority effect: the finding that we are much better at remembering pictures, and names of things that can be pictured, than we are at remembering words. As I discuss in Chapter 5, the effect isn't as simple as it was once thought to be, but it's very robust.

pragmatics: the usually unspoken reasons and assumptions behind the communications we make (or that machines make with each other).

precision: to an **information scientist**, a measure of how many *relevant* things are received back from a search *out of all the things received back in total.*

priming: just as we might 'prime' someone by preparing them for something that's going to happen, priming experiments use this to see when and how thinking is influenced by what's gone before. Very many impressive, surprising priming effects have been found in cognition. Sometimes we can use them to test something else, e.g. to see if **semantic** priming is disrupted by a particular distractor task (which might mean that semantics couldn't be processed while that task went on).

problem space: the sum of all the different aspects of a problem that we're trying to solve. See also **well-defined** and **ill-defined** problems.

procedural memory: simply our memory for how to do things (how to *proceed*).

process control: computer systems that control power plants, factories and other 'real time' situations. Also known as **complex systems**.

propositions: facts or beliefs that can be expressed without any imagery, i.e. in words or a symbolic language.

raster graphics: the results of (e.g.) using a 'paint' program on a computer. Each pixel of the image has a value stored for it to say what colour it should be, but the computer doesn't have any knowledge of how that pixel forms part of a shape or object. Often, though, it can infer that from looking at all the other pixels around that one, to see which ones are similar and what shape that makes. (This is the basis of machine vision techniques.) As opposed to **vector graphics**.

recall: to an **information scientist**, a measure of how many relevant things are received back, *out of all the relevant things that are out there*, as opposed to **precision**. To a psychologist, recall is the process of remembering things without being reminded of them (as opposed to recognition).

resolution: the size of the pixels that make up a screen or a **raster image**. The tinier the pixels, the smoother everything looks to the eye.

saccade: a movement of the eye that's so quick you don't know you did it.

schema, schemata: 'schemata' is the strictly correct plural of 'schema', a Greek word. The main idea of a 'schema' is that it forms a kind of network of interlinked bits of knowledge, based on the observation that human thought seems to involve associations between different ideas and facts. The distinction between a 'schema' and a **'mental model'** is a little vague. Broadly, a schema was traditionally described as a rather passive network of known linked facts, i.e. **declarative** memory, but many cognitive psychologists now feel it's more useful to talk of mental models as something more action-focused, which would also include both **procedural** knowledge of how to do something, and also dynamic knowledge of *how* and *why* things happen or work in certain ways.

search engine: the computer program that looks for information in a database, based on what you've told it you want (usually by typing a few words).

self-efficacy: the level of confidence we have that we can do a particular thing. We can have too much confidence and get sloppy, or we can have too little and go into 'self-fulfilling prophecy' mode. Generally high self-efficacy gets people further in most life situations, within reason. Note: this concept is useful, but, like most such concepts, it hasn't yet been proved to have any real existence in the brain or genes.

semantic, semantics: what things mean. Computer scientists talk of 'semantic nets/webs/reference systems'; they mean the problem of getting computers to have some sense of what words relate to, which we take for granted in our own minds.

semiotics: the study of signs or symbols; the symbolic meaning behind an icon or image.

serendipity: in **information science**, this usually refers to chance discoveries of useful or interesting information while you were looking for something else.

spatial cognition: the way you think and mentally process anything to do with where things are in the real world. This ranges from remembering where things are on a table top or computer screen to being able to find your way home or visualise where Iceland is.

statistical significance: usually psychologists only get excited about anything if the result from a study is so different from random chance that it would happen less than 5% of the time if their explanation for it wasn't true (i.e. if the **null hypothesis** was true instead). If it's not significant, then it could happen more often than that if the explanation wasn't true. Of course, statistical significance doesn't mean the explanation *is* true! It just gives a probability to help us to think about it.

subject gateway a website which consists of a database of other websites, all on a particular subject. Usually there's a little **meta-information** added to explain what each cited website has in it, and often the websites have been checked for reliability and credibility before being listed.

syntax, syntactics: the details of the way something's communicated. With written language, the grammar of the sentence is the main aspect of the syntax.

technophobia: *see* **computer anxiety, computer aversion**.

test-retest reliability: how much the result is the same if, for instance, someone is given the same test (or one with the same type of questions) to do again next month. If they answer differently next time, reliability is low, and you'd question whether the test measured anything useful because you couldn't use it to predict people's behaviour on other tasks (which you might not be able to do anyway, if there isn't much correlation between the two, but that's a separate problem).

topological map: a map of a space (real or imaginary) that doesn't try to show distances or directions accurately, so that the structure or network can be arranged more clearly. The classic map of this sort is the London Underground map.

Turing test: usually 'passing the Turing test' is taken to mean that a human who is hearing or seeing responses from a computer can't tell that it *is* a computer because it seems convincingly human. Alan Turing was a brilliant mathematician whose important code-breaking achievements helped to shorten World War II. Turing's original version of the test was much more specific than the way we usually talk about it.[63]

URL: Universal Resource Locator. A web or other internet address, e.g. http://www.teoma.com

usability: the correct term for what we often casually call 'user friendliness'. A usable system is, by definition, all of these things: easy to use, polite, efficient, reliable, suitable for your tasks and your understanding of them, supportive, and easy to learn.

vector graphics: if you've ever used a 'drawing' program on a computer, as opposed to a 'painting' program, the things you drew were vector graphics. Each separate line, shape or piece of text is stored individually, so that you can edit it or move it around without affecting other things that might be displayed at the same place (e.g. the colour of the area underneath it). In **GIS**, vector mapping lets people add and adjust features, and also to attach database information to them so that clicking on a house brings up (say) a customer record. As opposed to **raster graphics**.

verbal protocol analysis: a useful method of looking into what people do in a situation by asking them to talk you through it. Often they're videoed just doing the task, then the video is played back and they are asked to talk through what happened and what actions they took, and why.

visual search: a type of experiment done by psychologists. Someone sits in front of a computer and an image or array of shapes appears on the screen. They have to hit a button as quickly as possible when a certain shape, the *target*, is in the image. Sometimes the search is more complicated and people have to indicate something *about* the target, e.g. whether it's sloping to the left or the right, but usually they just have to detect it.

webmaster: the person who maintains, and often who built, a website.

well-defined problem: in cognitive psychology, a problem where all of the following are clear to you: the starting point, the goals, the operators (things you can do to get to the goal) and the restrictions on what's possible. As opposed to an **ill-defined problem**.

within-subject: in psychology, we have a 'within-subjects design' if we can compare the same person doing things under two different conditions (instead of having to test two separate people and hope they're similar, which is called between-subjects). People in experiments used to be referred to as 'subjects' but they are now called 'participants'. (This is ironic because originally 'subjects' implied that the people were the most important thing there: it was a reminder that they *were* the 'subject' that was being studied and not just a research tool.)

working memory: the dynamic processes we use for just a short while after hearing, seeing or recalling something, to remember and process its information. First suggested by Alan Baddeley in the 1970s, this replaced the older idea of 'short-term memory', which suggested a fixed temporary store in the brain. Working memory seems to be more complicated than that, with separate components all dealing with different aspects of what's going on.

Yerkes–Dodson law: the idea that when we're stressed in some way, if the stress is too low then we don't perform as well as when it's notched up a bit. But when the stress is too high, we can't do too well either and there's a sharp drop-off of performance. **Self-efficacy** may follow this law.

Bibliography

1. Association for Behavior Analysis (ABA). *Association for Behavior Analysis: An international organization.* 2004. Retrieved 30 November 2004, from www.abainternational.org

2. Adams, D., and Perkins, G. *The Original Hitchhiker Radio Scripts,* 10th anniversary edition. Harmony Books, 1995.

3. agentland. *AgentLand—intelligent agents and bots.* Cybion, France, 2004. Retrieved 30 November 2004, from www.agentland.com

4. Ahn, W.-K., Goldstone, R. L., Love, B. C., Markman, A. B., and Wolff, P. *Categorization Inside and Outside the Laboratory: Essays in honor of Douglas L. Medin.* Washington, DC: American Psychological Association, 2005 (in press).

5. Al-Hawamdeh, S., and Wilson, T. D. (eds). Special issue on knowledge management—the Emperor's new clothes? *Information Research: An international electronic journal* 8 (2) (October 2002). http://informationr.net/ir/8-1/infres81.html

6. Alexander, P. A., Kulikowich, J. M., and Jetton, T. L. The role of subject-matter knowledge and interest in the processing of linear and nonlinear texts. *Review of Educational Research,* 64 (2) (1994), 201–52.

7. Allen, B. Cognitive abilities and information system usability. *Information Processing and Management* 30 (2) (1994), 177–91.

8. Allen, B. L. Cognitive research in information science: implications for design. *Annual Review of Information Science and Technology (ARIST)* 26 (1991), 3–37.

9. Allen, B. L. *Information Tasks: Toward a user-centered approach to information systems.* San Diego, CA, and London: Academic Press, 1996.

10. Amazon. *Amazon.* Amazon.com, Inc. 2004. Retrieved 30 November 2004, from www.amazon.co.uk or www.amazon.com

11. Armstrong, S. L., Gleitman, L. R., and Gleitman, H. What some concepts might not be. *Cognition* 13 (1983), 263–308.

12. Arnheim, R. *Visual Thinking.* Berkeley, Los Angeles, CA, and London: University of California Press, 1969.

13. Asch, S. E. Studies of independence and conformity: 1. A minority of one against a unanimous majority. *Psychological Monographs: General and Applied* 70 (9, whole no. 416) (1956).

14. Ashby, F. G., Isen, A. M., and Turken, A. U. (1999). A neuropsychological theory of positive affect and its influence on cognition. *Psychological Review* 106 (3) (1999), 529–50.

15. Ask-Jeeves *Ask Jeeves.* Ask Jeeves, Inc., 2004. Retrieved 30 November 2004, from www.ask.co.uk or ask.com

16. Barry, C. A., and Squires, D. Why the move from traditional information-seeking to the electronic library is not straightforward for academic users: some surprising findings. In *Online Information '95: 19th International Online Information Meeting: Proceedings, London, 5–7 December 1995.* Oxford: Learned Information Europe Ltd, 1995, 177–87.

17. Barsalou, L. W. Ad hoc categories. *Memory and Cognition* 11 (3) (1983), 211–27.
18. Bartlett, F. C. Thinking (The Clayton Memorial Lecture). *Manchester Memoirs* 93 (3) (1951).
19. Bates, M. J. The design of browsing and berrypicking techniques for the on-line search interface. *Online Review* 13 (5) (1989), 407–31.
20. BBC. *Turning into digital goldfish.* British Broadcasting Corporation, 2002. Retrieved 25 November 2004, from http://news.bbc.co.uk/1/hi/sci/tech/1834682.stm
21. BBC. *Companies learn to live with online fury.* British Broadcasting Corporation, 2002. Retrieved 26 November 2004, from http://news.-bbc.co.uk/1/hi/business/1826964.stm
22. BBC. *BBC—bbc.co.uk homepage—Home of the BBC on the Internet.* British Broadcasting Corporation, 2004. Retrieved 28 November 2004, from www.bbc.co.uk/
23. Belkin, N. J. The cognitive viewpoint in information science. *Journal of Information Science* 16 (1990), 11–15.
24. Berners-Lee, T., Hendler, J., and Lassila, O. The semantic web. *Scientific American* 284 (5) (2001), 34–43.
25. Birkerts, S. *The Gutenberg Elegies: The fate of reading in an electronic age.* London: Faber & Faber, 1994.
26. Blades, M., and Spencer, C. The development of 3- to 6-year-olds' map using ability: the relative importance of landmarks and map alignment. *Journal of Genetic Psychology* 151 (2) (1990), 181–94.
27. Blakemore, C. A mechanistic approach to perception and the human mind. In Said, K. A. M., Newton-Smith, W. H., Viale, R. and Wilkes, K. V. (eds), *Modelling the Mind*, 113–38. Oxford: Clarendon Press, 1990.
28. Blythe, J., Kim, J., Ramachandran, S., and Gil, Y. An integrated environment for knowledge acquisition. In *International Conference on Intelligent User Interfaces—IUI '01, Santa Fe, New Mexico, USA, 14–17 January 2001*, 13–20. Menlo Park, CA: AAAI Press, 2001. www.i-si.edu/expect/papers/blythe-kim-rama-gil-iui01.pdf
29. Booth, P. A., and Sasse, A. (eds). *Mental Models and Everyday Activities: Proceedings of the Second International Workshop on Mental Models.* Cambridge, 1992, unpublished.
30. Borgman, C. L. *Toward a Definition of User Friendly: A psychological perspective. What is user friendly?* Papers presented at the 1986 Clinic on Library Applications of Data Processing, Urbana-Champaign IL, USA, 20–22 April 1986. Urbana-Champaign, IL: University of Illinois, 1987, 29–44.
31. Borgman, C. L. Why are online catalogs *still* hard to use? *Journal of the American Society for Information Science* 47 (7) (1996), 493–503.
32. Bowker, G. C., and Star, S. L. *Sorting Things Out: Classification and its consequences.* Cambridge, MA: MIT Press, 1999.
33. Bowling, A. C., and Mackenzie, B. D. The relationship between speed of information processing and cognitive ability. *Personality and Individual Differences* 20 (6) (1996), 775–800.
34. British-Library. *Turning the Pages.* The British Library, 2004. Retrieved 26 November 2004, from www.bl.uk/collections/treasures/digitisation1.html

35. Brittain, J. M. Information scientists and knowledge. In Meadows, A. J. (ed.), *Knowledge and Communication: Essays on the information chain*, 90–106. London: Library Association Publishing, 1991.
36. Brooks, T. A. Where is meaning when form is gone? Knowledge representation on the Web. *Information Research (online journal)* 6 (2) (2001). www.shef.ac.uk/~is/publications/infres/6-2/paper93.html.
37. Brosnan, M. *Technophobia: The psychological impact of information technology*. London and New York: Routledge, 1998.
38. Bruner, J. Going beyond the information given. In Bruner, J. *et al.* (eds), *Contemporary Approaches to Cognition*. Cambridge, MA: Harvard University Press, 1957. (Reprinted in J. M. Anglin [ed.], *Beyond the Information Given: Studies in the psychology of knowing* (New York: W. W. Norton & Co., 1973, 218–38.)
39. Bruner, J. *Actual Minds, Possible Worlds*. Cambridge, MA: Harvard University Press, 1986.
40. Bryson, B. *The Lost Continent: Travels in small town America*. London: Abacus, 1990.
41. Byrnes, J. P. The nature and development of representation: forging a synthesis of competing approaches. In Sigel, I. E. (ed.), *Development of Mental Representation: Theories and applications*, 273–93. Mahwah, NJ, and London: Lawrence Erlbaum, 1999.
42. Byström, K., and Järvelin, K. Task complexity affects information seeking and use. *Information Processing and Management* 31 (2) (1995), 191–213.
43. Cacioppo, J. T., Petty, R. E., and Kao, C. F. The efficient assessment of need for cognition. *Journal of Personality Assessment* 42 (1984), 306–7.
44. Caramazza, A., McCloskey, M., and Green, B. Naive beliefs in 'sophisticated' subjects: misconceptions about trajectories of objects. *Cognition* 9 (1981), 117–23.
45. Card, S. K., Newell, A., and Moran, T. P. *The Psychology of Human–Computer Interaction*. Mahwah, NJ: Lawrence Erlbaum, 1983.
46. Carroll, J. B. *Human Cognitive Abilities: A survey of factor-analytic studies*. Cambridge: Cambridge University Press, 1993.
47. Caruso, J. C., Witkiewitz, K., Belcourt-Dittloff, A., and Gottlieb, J. D. Reliability of scores from the Eysenck Personality Questionnaire: a reliability generalization study. *Educational and Psychological Measurement* 61 (4) (2001), 675–89.
48. Catledge, L. D., and Pitkow, J. E. Characterizing browsing strategies in the World-Wide Web. *Computer Networks and ISDN Systems* 27 (6) (1995), 1065–73.
49. Chamberlain, R. G. *GIS FAQ Question Q5.1: What is the best way to calculate the distance between 2 points?* US Census Bureau, 1996. Retrieved 24 November 2004, from www.census.gov/cgi-bin/geo/gisfaq?Q5.1
50. Cheng, P. W., and Holyoak, K. J. Pragmatic reasoning schemas. *Cognitive Psychology*, 17 (1985), 391–416.
51. Chisholm, W., Vanderheiden, G., and Jacobs, I. *Web Content Accessibility Guidelines 1.0*. W3C. 1999. Retrieved 24 November 2004, from www.w3.org/TR/WAI-WEBCONTENT/
52. CiteSeer. *CiteSeer.IST: Scientific Literature Digital Library*. NEC/Penn State University/National Science Foundation/Microsoft Research,

2004. Retrieved 29 November 2004, from http://citeseer.ist.psu.edu/cs

53. Clore, G. Emotion colors cognition. Talk given at Northwestern University, IL, 13 March 2003.
54. Cockburn, A., and Jones, S. Which way now —analyzing and easing inadequacies in WWW navigation. *International Journal of Human–Computer Studies* 45 (1) (1996), 105–29.
55. Cole, C., and Mandelblatt, B. Using Kintsch's discourse comprehension theory to model the user's coding of an informative message from an enabling information retrieval system. *Journal of the American Society for Information Science* 51 (11) (2000), 1033–46.
56. Collantes, L. Y. Degree of agreement in naming objects and concepts for information retrieval. *Journal of the American Society for Information Science* 46 (2) (1995), 116–32.
57. Connell, T. H. Subject searching in online catalogs: metaknowledge used by experienced searchers. *Journal of the American Society for Information Science* 46 (7) (1995), 506–18.
58. Convera. *Visual RetrievalWare(tm) SDK: color / shape / texture image retrieval.* Convera, 2004. Retrieved 30 November 2004, from http://vrw.convera.com:8015/cst
59. Cooper, A. *The Inmates Are Running the Asylum: Why high-tech products drive us crazy and how to restore the sanity.* Indianapolis, IN: Sams Publishing, 2004.
60. Cosmides, L. The logic of social exchange: has natural selection shaped how humans reason? *Cognition* 31 (1989), 187–276.
61. Cowan, N. The magical number 4 in short-term memory: a reconsideration of mental storage capacity. *Behavioral and Brain Sciences* 24 (2001), 87–114.
62. Czaja, S. J., and Sharit, J. Stress reactions to computer-interactive tasks as a function of task structure and individual differences. *International Journal of Human–Computer Interaction* 5 (1) (1993), 1–22.
63. Davidson, D. Turing's Test. In Said, K. A. M., Newton-Smith, W. H., Viale, R. and Wilkes, K. V. (eds), *Modelling the Mind,* 1–11. Oxford: Clarendon Press, 1990.
64. Davies, C. Future user issues for the networked multimedia electronic library. In Ramsden, A. (ed.), *ELINOR Electronic Library Project.* British Library Research and Innovation Report 22, 105–30. London: British Library and Bowker-Saur, 1998.
65. Davies, C. When is a map not a map? Task and language in spatial interpretations with digital map displays. *Applied Cognitive Psychology* 16 (2002), 273–85.
66. de Bono, E. *The Use of Lateral Thinking.* Harmondsworth: Penguin, 1983.
67. Dee-Lucas, D., and Larkin, J. H. Learning from electronic texts: effects of interactive overviews for information access. *Cognition and Instruction* 13 (3) (1995), 431–68.
68. Deegan, M., Chernaik, W., and Gibson, A. Introduction. In Chernaik, W., Deegan, M. and Gibson, A. (eds), *Beyond the Book: Theory, culture, and the politics of cyberspace,* 1–10. Oxford: Office for Humanities Communication, 1996.

69. Dervin, B. On studying information seeking methodologically: the implications of connecting metatheory to method. *Information Processing and Management* 35 (1999), 727–50. http://communication.sbs.ohio-state.edu/sense-making/art/artdervinipm99.html

70. Dervin, B. Users as research inventions: how research categories perpetuate inequities. In Dervin, B., Foreman-Wernet, L. and Lauterbach, E. (eds), *Sense-Making Methodology Reader: Selected writings of Brenda Dervin*, 47–60. Cresskill, NJ: Hampton Press, 2003. First published *Journal of Communication* 38 (3) (1989), 216–32.

71. Dervin, B., and Schaefer, D. J. Toward the communicative design of information design: a call for considering the communicating implied in the mandate for information design. Paper presented at Vision Plus 4: The Republic of Information, an international symposium on design for global communication, Carnegie-Mellon University, USA, 26–29 March 1998. http://communication.sbs.ohio-state.edu/sense-making/art/artdervin&schaefer98.html

72. Dickens, C. *Hard Times*. Project Gutenberg, 1997. Retrieved 30 November 2004, from www.gutenberg.org/etext/786

73. Dieberger, A., and Andrews, K. *Spatial User Interface Metaphors in Hypermedia Systems: Workshop at the European Conference on Hypermedia Technology, September 1994, Edinburgh, Scotland.* Dieberger, Andreas, 1994. Retrieved 24 November 2004, from http://homepage.mac.com/juggle5/WORK/archive/Workshop.ECHT94.html

74. Dillon, A. *Designing Usable Electronic Text*. London: Taylor & Francis, 1994.

75. Dillon, A., and Schaap, D. Expertise and the perception of shape in information. *Journal of the American Society for Information Science*, 47 (10) (1996), 786–8.

76. Dillon, A., McKnight, C., and Richardson, J. Space—the Final Chapter, or why physical representations are not semantic intentions. In McKnight, C., Dillon, A. and Richardson, J. (eds), *Hypertext: A psychological perspective*, 169–91. New York: Ellis Horwood, 1994.

77. Directgov. *Directgov home*. e-Government Unit, Cabinet Office, London, 1994. Retrieved 28 November 2004, from www.direct.gov.uk

78. Ditlea, S. The electronic paper chase. *Scientific American* 285 (2001), 50–5.

79. dmoz. *ODP—Open Directory Project*. Netscape Communications Corporation/Open Directory Project editors, 2004. Retrieved 28 November 2004, from http://dmoz.org

80. Dodge, M. *Mappa.Mundi Magazine: Map of the month* (regular feature). media.org, 2004. Retrieved 30 November 2004, from http://mappa.mundi.net/maps/

81. Doublet, S. *The Stress Myth*. Chesterfield, MO: Science & Humanities Press, 2000.

82. Dreyfus, H. L. *On the Internet*. London and New York: Routledge, 2001.

83. Driver, J. The neuropsychology of spatial attention. In Pashler, H. (ed.), *Attention*, 297–340. Hove: Psychology Press, 2000.

84. Duncker, K. On problem solving. *Psychological Monographs*, 58 (270, whole issue) (1945).

85. Eakins, J. P. Automatic image content retrieval—Are we getting anywhere? In *Proceedings of the Third International Conference on*

Electronic Library and Visual Information Research (ELVIRA3), De Montfort University, Milton Keynes, UK, May 1996, 123–35. London: Aslib, 1996.

86. Egan, D. E., Remde, J. R., Landauer, T. K., Lochbaum, C. C., and Gomez, L. M. Acquiring information in books and Superbooks. *Machine-Mediated Learning* 3 (3) (1989), 259–77.

87. Enser, P. G. B. Pictorial information retrieval. *Journal of Documentation* 51 (2) (1995), 126–70.

88. Eppler, M. J., and Mengis, J. *The Concept of Information Overload: A review of literature from organization science, marketing, accounting, MIS, and related disciplines.* Media and Communications Management Research Paper No. HSG/MCM/01. St Gallen, Switzerland: University of St Gallen, 2002. www.knowledgemedia.org/modules/pub/download.php?id=knowledgemedia-25&user=&pass=

89. Ericsson, K. A., and Simon, H. A. *Protocol Analysis—Verbal reports as data*, rev. edition. Bradford Books, 1993.

90. Ethical-Consumer. *Ethical Consumer—The UK's only alternative consumer organisation looking at the social and environmental records of the companies behind the brand names.* Ethical Consumer Research Association, 2004. Retrieved 30 November 2004, from www.ethical-consumer.org

91. Eysenck, M. W., and Keane, M. T. *Cognitive Psychology: A student's handbook*, 4th edition. Hove: Psychology Press, 2000.

92. FamilySearch. *FamilySearch Internet Genealogy Service.* The Church of Jesus Christ of Latter-day Saints/Intellectual Reserve, Inc., 2004. Retrieved 28 November 2004, from www.familysearch.org

93. Festinger, L. *A Theory of Cognitive Dissonance.* Stanford, CA: Stanford University Press, 1957.

94. FirstGov. *FirstGov.gov: The U.S. Government's Official Web Portal.* Federal Citizen Information Center, Office of Citizen Services and Communications, US General Services Administration, Washington, DC, 2004. Retrieved 28 November 2004, from http://firstgov.gov

95. Fischhoff, B. Debiasing. In Kahneman, D., Slovic, P., and Tversky, A. (eds), *Judgment under Uncertainty: Heuristics and biases*, 422–44. Cambridge: Cambridge University Press, 1982.

96. Flake, W. L. Influence of gender, dogmatism, and risk-taking propensity upon attitudes toward information from computers. *Computers in Human Behavior* 7 (3) (1991), 227–35.

97. Fodor, J. *In Critical Condition: Polemical essays on cognitive science and the philosophy of mind.* Cambridge, MA, and London: MIT Press, 1998.

98. Foertsch, J. The impact of electronic networks on scholarly communication: avenues for research. *Discourse Processes* 19 (1995), 301–28.

99. FreeBMD. *FreeBMD Home Page.* Trustees of FreeBMD (registered charity), 2004. Retrieved 28 November 2004, from http://freebmd.rootsweb.com

100. Gee, J. P.. *What Video Games Have to Teach Us about Learning and Literacy.* New York and Basingstoke: Palgrave, 2003.

101. Gelernter, D. *The Muse in the Machine: Computers and creative thought.* London: Fourth Estate, 1994.

102. Gibbs, R. W. Do people always process the literal meaning of indirect requests? *Journal of Experimental Psychology: Learning, Memory and Cognition* 9 (1983), 524–33.

103. Gil, Y. Spinning the Semantic Web. In Fensel, D., Hendler, J. A., Lieberman, H. and Wahlster, W. (eds), *Spinning the Semantic Web: Bringing the World Wide Web to its full potential*, 253–78. Cambridge, MA: MIT Press, 2005.

104. Gilmartin, P. Maps, mental imagery, and gender in the recall of geographical information. *American Cartographer* 13 (4) (1986), 335–44.

105. Gilovich, T. *How We Know What Isn't So*. New York: Free Press, 1981.

106. Girill, T. R. Information chunking as an interface design issue for full-text databases. In Dillon, M. (ed.), *Interfaces for Information Retrieval and Online Systems: The state of the art*, 149–58. Westport, CT: Greenwood Press, 1991.

107. Glenberg, A. M., Meyer, M., and Linden, K.. Mental models contribute to foregrounding during text comprehension. *Journal of Memory and Language* 26 (1987), 69–83.

108. Gluck, M. Understanding performance in information systems: blending relevance and competence. *Journal of the American Society for Information Science* 46 (6) (1995), 446–60.

109. Gluck, M. Exploring the relationship between user satisfaction and relevance in information systems. *Information Processing and Management* 32 (1) (1996), 89–104.

110. Gobet, F. Expert memory: a comparison of four theories. *Cognition* 66 (1998), 115–52.

111. Goel, V., and Dolan, R. J. Functional neuroanatomy of humor: segregating cognitive and affective components. *Nature Neuroscience* 4 (3) (2001)), 237–8.

112. Goldstein, C. *Information Overload: Après le deluge*. Ketchum, 2004. Retrieved 24 November 2004, from www.ketchum.com/DisplayWebPage/0,1003,1901,00.html

113. Goldstein, E. B. *Sensation and Perception*, 6th edition. Thomson, 2001.

114. Grant, A. S. A context model needed for complex tasks. In Booth, P. A., and Sasse, A. (eds), *Mental Models and Everyday Activities: 2nd Interdisciplinary Workshop on Mental Models*, 94–102. Cambridge, 1992, unpublished.

115. Gray, P. *Psychology*, 3rd edition. New York: Worth Publishers, 1999.

116. Green, R. Topical relevance relationships. I. Why topic matching fails. *Journal of the American Society for Information Science* 46 (9) (1995), 646–53.

117. Greene, G. *Travels with My Aunt*. London: Bodley Head, 1969.

118. Greutmann, T., and Ackermann, D. Individual differences in human–computer interaction: how can we measure if the dialog grammar fits the user's needs? In *Human–Computer Interaction: INTERACT '87, Stuttgart, Federal Republic of Germany, 1–4 September 1987*, 145–9. North-Holland: Elsevier Science, 1987.

119. Griggs, R. A., and Cox, J. R. Permission schemas and the selection task. *Quarterly Journal of Experimental Psychology* 46A (1993), 637–52.

120. Haaga, D. A., and Beck, A. T. Perspectives on depressive realism: implications for cognitive theory of depression. *Behaviour Research and Therapy* 33 (1) (1995), 41–8.

121. Harter, S. P. Psychological relevance and information science. *Journal of the American Society for Information Science* 43 (9) (1992), 602–15.

122. Harter, S. P. Variations in relevance assessments and the measurement of retrieval effectiveness. *Journal of the American Society for Information Science* 47 (1) (1996), 37–49.

123. Hatt, F. *The Reading Process*. London: Clive Bingley, 1976.

124. Hawkins, H. L., and Presson, J. C. Auditory information processing. In Boff, K. R., Kaufman, L. and Thomas, J. P. (eds), *Handbook of Perception and Human Performance*, vol. II: *Cognitive processes and performance*. New York: John Wiley & Sons, 1986.

125. Hayes, S. C., Barnes-Holmes, D., and Roche, B. (eds). *Relational Frame Theory: A post-Skinnerian account of human language and cognition*. Dordrecht: Kluwer Academic Publishers, 2001.

126. Hendry, D. G., and Harper, D. J. *Coordinating Information-seeking on Information Displays*. Electronic Library and Visual Information Research: ELVIRA 2, Milton Keynes, UK, May 1995. London: Aslib, 1995, 127–36.

127. Henriksson, A. *Non Campus Mentis: World history according to college students*. Workman Publishing, 2003.

128. Hert, C. A. User goals on an online public access catalog. *Journal of the American Society for Information Science* 47 (7) (1996), 504–18.

129. Hildreth, C. R. Accounting for users' inflated assessments of on-line catalogue search performance and usefulness: an experimental study. *Information Research* 6 (2) (2001). http://InformationR.net/ir/6–2/paper101.html.

130. Hine, C. Representations of information technology in disciplinary development: disappearing plants and invisible networks. *Science, Technology and Human Values* 20 (1) (1995), 65–85.

131. Hockey, G. R. J. Styles, skills and strategies: cognitive variability and its implications for the role of mental models in HCI. In Ackerman, D. and Tauber, M. J. (eds), *Mental Models and Human–Computer Interaction I*, 113–29. North-Holland: Elsevier Science, 1990.

132. Hollnagel, E. Coping, coupling and control: the modelling of muddling through. In Booth, P. A., and Sasse, A. (eds), *Mental Models and Everyday Activities: 2nd Interdisciplinary Workshop on Mental Models*. Cambridge, 1992, unpublished. www.ida.liu.se/~eriho

133. Hollnagel, E. *Cognitive Reliability and Error Analysis Method: CREAM*. London: Elsevier, 1998.

134. Hollnagel, E. (ed.). *Handbook of Cognitive Task Design*. Mahwah, NJ: Lawrence Erlbaum, 2003.

135. Holyoak, K. J., Gentner, D., and Kokinov, B. (eds). *Analogy: A cognitive science perspective*. Cambridge, MA: MIT Press, 2000.

136. Huberman, B. A. *The Laws of the Web: Patterns in the ecology of information*. Cambridge, MA, and London: MIT Press, 2001.

137. Hutchins, E. *Cognition in the Wild*. Cambridge, MA: MIT Press, 1995.

138. Igbaria, M., and Iivari, J. The effects of self-efficacy on computer usage. *Omega, International Journal of Management Science* 23 (6) (1995), 587–605.

139. Iivonen, M. Factors lowering the consistency in online searching. In *Online Information '95: 19th International Online Information Meeting: Proceedings, London, 5–7 December 1995*, 101–7. Oxford: Learned Information Europe Ltd, 1995.

140. IMDb. *The Internet Movie Database (IMDb)*. Internet Movie Database Inc., 2004. Retrieved 30 November 2004, from http://uk.imdb.com

141. Inspiration. Inspiration®: The premier tool to develop ideas and organize thinking. Inspiration® Inc., 2004. Retrieved 23 November 2004, from www.inspiration.com

142. Janosky, B., Smith, P. J., and Hildreth, C. R. Online library catalog systems: an analysis of user errors. *International Journal of Man-Machine Studies* 25 (5) (1986), 573–92.

143. Jansen, B. J., Spink, A., Bateman, J., and Saracevic, T. Real life information retrieval: a study of user queries on the web. *SIGIR Forum* 32 (1) (1998), 5–17.

144. Johnson, C., and Gray, P. Temporal aspects of usability: papers from a workshop. *SIGCHI Bulletin* 28 (2, special issue) (1996), 32.

145. Jopling, D. Cognitive science, other minds, and the philosophy of dialogue. In Neisser, U. (ed.), *The Perceived Self: Ecological and interpersonal sources of self-knowledge*, 290–309. Cambridge: Cambridge University Press, 1993.

146. Jörgensen, C., and Liddy, E. D. An analysis of information seeking behaviors in index use, or opening Pandora's box. In Williams, M. E. (ed.), *15th National Online Meeting: Proceedings (10–12 May 1994)*, 233–42. Medford, NJ: Learned Information Inc., 1994.

147. Julien, H. Where to from here? Results of an empirical study and user-centred implications for system design. In *Exploring the Contexts of Information Behaviour: Proceedings of the Second International Conference on Research in Information Needs, Seeking and Use in Different Contexts, Sheffield, UK, 13–15 August 1998*, 586–96. London: Taylor Graham, 1999.

148. Kahneman, D., Slovic, P., and Tversky, A. (eds) *Judgment under Uncertainty: Heuristics and biases*. Cambridge: Cambridge University Press, 1982.

149. Kehoe, C., Pitkow, J., Sutton, K., Aggarwal, G., and Rogers, J. D. *Results of GVU's Tenth World Wide Web User Survey*. Graphic, Visualization and Usability Center, Georgia Institute of Technology, 1999. Retrieved 21 November 2004, from www.cc.gatech.edu/gvu/user_surveys/survey-1998-10/tenthreport.html

150. Kellerman, K., and Reynolds, R. (1990). When ignorance is bliss: the role of motivation to reduce uncertainty in uncertainty reduction theory. *Human Communication Research* 17 (1) (1990), 5–75.

151. Kempton, W. Two theories used of home heat control. *Cognitive Science* 10 (1986), 75–91.

152. Kenealy, P. M. Mood-state-dependent retrieval: the effects of induced mood on memory reconsidered. *Quarterly Journal of Experimental Psychology: Human Experimental Psychology* 50A (2) (1987), 290–317.

153. Khan, K., and Locatis, C. Searching through cyberspace: the effects of link display and link density on information retrieval from hypertext on the World Wide Web. *Journal of the American Society for Information Science* 49 (2) (1998), 176–82.

154. Kierkegaard, S. *A Literary Review*, trans. A. Hannay. Harmondsworth and New York: Penguin, 2002.
155. Kim, H., and Hirtle, S. C. Spatial metaphors and disorientation in hypertext browsing. *Behaviour and Information Technology* 14 (4) (1995), 239–50.
156. Kirriemuir, J., Dempsey, L., and Brown, C. Meta-guidelines for designing and building world wide web documents/sites. In *Proceedings of the Third International Conference on Electronic Library and Visual Information Research (ELVIRA3), De Montfort University, Milton Keynes, UK, May 1996*. London: Aslib, 1996.
157. Koehler, W. Digital libraries and World Wide Web sites and page persistence. *Information Research* (online journal) 4 (4) (1999). www.shef.ac.uk/~is/publications/infres/paper60.html
158. Kosslyn, S. M. *Image and Brain: The resolution of the imagery debate*. Cambridge, MA: MIT Press, 1994.
159. Kraut, R., Lundmark, V., Patterson, M., Kiesler, S., Mukopadhyay, T., and Scherlis, W. Internet paradox: a social technology that reduces social involvement and psychological well-being? *American Psychologist* 53 (9) (1999), 1017–31.
160. Kreitler, S., and Kreitler, H. *The Cognitive Foundation of Personality Traits*. New York and London: Plenum Press, 1990.
161. Krohne, H. W. Vigilance and cognitive avoidance as concepts in coping research. In Krohne, H. W. (ed.), *Attention and Avoidance: Strategies in coping with aversiveness*, ch. 2. Seattle: Hogrefe & Huber, 1993.
162. Krug, S. *Don't Make Me Think! A common sense approach to web usability*. Indianapolis, IN: New Riders Publishing, 2000.
163. Krull, D. S., and Erickson, D. J. Inferential hopscotch: how people draw social inferences from behavior. *Current Directions in Psychological Science* 4 (1995), 35–8.
164. Kuhlthau, C. *Seeking Meaning: A process approach to library and information services*. Ablex Publishing Corporation, 1993.
165. Kuhlthau, C. C. Accommodating the user's information search process: challenges for information retrieval system designers. *Bulletin of the American Society for Information Science* 25 (3) (1999). www.asis.org/Bulletin/Feb-99/kuhlthau.html
166. Labov, W. The boundaries of words and their meaning. In Bailey, C.-J. N., and Shuy, R. W. (eds), *New Ways of Analyzing Variation in English*, 340–73. Washington, DC: Georgetown University Press, 1973.
167. Landow, G. P. We are already beyond the book. In Chernaik, W., Deegan, M., and Gibson, A. (eds), *Beyond the Book: Theory, culture and the politics of cyberspace*, 23–32. Oxford: Office for Humanities Communication, 1996.
168. Langridge, D. Classifying knowledge. In Meadows, A. J. (ed.), *Knowledge and Communication: Essays on the information chain*, 1–18. London: Library Association Publishing, 1991.
169. Lansdale, M. Modelling memory for absolute location. *Psychological Review* 105 (2) (998), 351–78.
170. Lansdale, M., and Laming, D. Evaluating the Fragmentation Hypothesis: the analysis of errors in cued recall. *Acta Psychologica* 88 (1995), 33–77.

171. Large, A., Tedd, L. A., and Hartley, R. J. *Information Seeking in the Online Age: Principles and practice*. London and New Providence, NJ: Bowker-Saur, 1995.

172. Large, A., Beheshti, J., Breuleux, A., and Renaud, A. Multimedia and comprehension: the relationship among text, animation, and captions. *Journal of the American Society for Information Science* 46 (5) (1995), 340–7.

173. Large, A., Beheshti, J., Breuleux, A., and Renaud, A. Effect of animation in enhancing descriptive and procedural texts in a multimedia learning environment. *Journal of the American Society for Information Science* 47 (6) (1996), 437–8.

174. Larkin, P. *Collected Poems*. London: Faber & Faber, 1988.

175. Lehto, M. R., Zhu, W., and Carpenter, B. The relative effectiveness of hypertext and text. *International Journal of Human–Computer Interaction* 7 (4) (1995), 293–313.

176. Lesk, M. *Practical Digital Libraries: Books, bytes and bucks*. San Francisco, CA: Morgan Kaufmann Publishers, 1997.

177. Lichtenstein, S., Fischhoff, B., and Phillips, L. D. Calibration of probabilities: the state of the art to 1980. In Kahneman, D., Slovic, P. and Tversky, A. (eds), *Judgment under Uncertainty: Heuristics and biases*, 306–34. Cambridge: Cambridge University Press, 1982.

178. Loeb, S. Delivering interactive multimedia documents over networks. *IEEE Communications Magazine* 30 (5, May) (1992), 52–9.

179. Loftus, E. F. *Eyewitness Testimony*. Cambridge, MA: Harvard University Press, 1979.

180. Losee, R. M. A discipline independent definition of information. *Journal of the American Society for Information Science* 48 (3) (1997), 254–69.

181. Lynch, P. J., and Horton, S. *Web Style Guide: Basic design principles for creating web sites*, 2nd edition. New Haven, CT: Yale University Press 2002. www.webstyleguide.com

182. MacLeod, C., and Mathews, A. Anxiety and the allocation of attention to threat. *Quarterly Journal of Experimental Psychology* 38A (1988), 659–70.

183. Macnamara, J., and Reyes, G. E. (eds). *The Logical Foundations of Cognition*. New York: Oxford University Press, 1994.

184. MapQuest. *MapQuest.Com —Maps, Directions and More*. MapQuest.com, Inc., 2004. Retrieved 30 November 2004, from www.mapquest.com

185. Marchionini, G. Information seeking in electronic encyclopedias. *Machine-Mediated Learning* 3 (3) (1989), 211–26.

186. Marchionini, G. *Information Seeking in Electronic Environments*. Cambridge: Cambridge University Press, 1995.

187. Marr, D. *Vision: A computational investigation into the human representation and processing of visual information*. New York: W. H. Freeman & Co., 1982.

188. Matthews, G., and Antes, J. R. Visual attention and depression: cognitive biases in the eye fixation of the dysphoric and the non-depressed. *Cognitive Therapy and Research* 16 (1992), 359–71.

189. McClelland, J. L., and Rogers, T. T. The parallel distributed processing approach to semantic cognition. *Nature Reviews Neuroscience* 4 (4) (2003), 310–22.

190. McCrae, R. R., and Costa, P. T. J. *Personality in Adulthood*. New York: Guilford Press, 1980.
191. McCrae, R. R., and Costa, P. T. J. Conceptions and correlates of openness to experience. In Hogan, R., Johnson, J., and Briggs, S. (eds), *Handbook of Personality Psychology*, 825–47. San Diego, CA, and London: Academic Press, 1997.
192. Meyer, D. E., and Schvaneveldt, R. W. Facilitation in recognising pairs of words: evidence of a dependence between retrieval operations. *Journal of Experimental Psychology* 90 (1971), 227–34.
193. Michel, D. A. What is used during cognitive processing in information retrieval and library searching? Eleven sources of search information. *Journal of the American Society for Information Science* 45 (7) (1994), 498–514.
194. Mikkelson, B., and Mikkelson, D. P. *Urban Legends Reference Pages: Humor (Word Imperfect)*. snopes.com, 1997. Retrieved 21 November 2004, from www.snopes.com/humor/business/wordperf.htm
195. Milgram, S. *Obedience to Authority*. New York: Harper & Row, 1974.
196. Miller, G. A. The magical number seven, plus or minus two: some limits on our capacity for processing information. *Psychological Review* 63 (1956), 81–97. http://psychclassics.yorku.ca/Miller/
197. Mitchell, P. *Introduction to Theory of Mind: Children, autism and apes*. London: Edward Arnold, 1996.
198. Moray, N. Mental models of complex dynamic systems. In Booth, P. A., and Sasse, A. (eds), *Mental Models and Everyday Activities: Proceedings of the Second International Workshop on Mental Models*. Cambridge, 1992, unpublished.
199. Moray, N. Formalisms for cognitive modeling. In *Proceedings of the Fifth International Conference on Human–Computer Interaction, Orlando, Florida, 8–13 August 1993*, vol. 1, 581–86. Amsterdam: Elsevier Science, 1993.
200. Muir, B. M., and Moray, N. Trust in automation. Part II. Experimental studies of trust and human intervention in a process control simulation. *Ergonomics* 39 (3) (1996), 429–60.
201. Murphy, G. L., and Medin, D. L. The role of theories in conceptual coherence. *Psychological Review* 92, 289–316.
202. Murphy, S. T., and Zajonc, R. B. Affect, cognition and awareness: affective priming with optimal and suboptimal stimulus exposures. *Journal of Personality and Social Psychology* 64 (5) (1993), 723–39.
203. Nahl, D., and Tenopir, C. Affective and cognitive searching behavior of novice end-users of a full-text database. *Journal of the American Society for Information Science* 47 (4) (1996), 276–86.
204. Negroponte, N. *Being Digital*. London: Hodder & Stoughton, 1995.
205. Neisser, U. *Cognition and Reality: Principles and implications of cognitive psychology*. San Francisco, CA: W. H. Freeman, 1976.
206. Neisser, U. (ed.) *The Perceived Self: Ecological and interpersonal sources of self-knowledge*. Cambridge: Cambridge University Press, 1993.
207. Newell, A., and Simon, H. A. *Human Problem Solving*. Englewood Cliffs, NJ: Prentice-Hall, 1972.
208. Nicholas, D. (1995). Are information professionals really better online searchers than end-users? (And whose story do you believe?). In *Online Information '95: 19th International Online Information Meeting:*

Proceedings, London, 5–7 Dec. 1995, 383–97. Oxford: Learned Information Europe Ltd, 1995.

209. Nicholas, D., Williams, P., Martin, H., and Cole, P. *The Media and the Internet: Final report of the British Library funded research project 'The changing information environment: the impact of the Internet on information seeking behaviour in the media'*. British Library Research and Innovation Report No. 110. London: British Library Research and Innovation Centre and Aslib, the Association for Information Management, 1998.

210. Nielsen, J. *Features for the Next Generation of Web Browsers*. Sun Microsystems, 1995. Retrieved 24 November 2004, from www.sun.com/950701/columns/alertbox

211. Nielsen, J. *Report from a 1994 Web Usability Study*. useit.com, 1997. Retrieved 21 November 2004, from www.useit.com/papers/1994_web_usability_report.html

212. Norman, D. *The Design of Everyday Things*. London: MIT Press, 1988.

213. Norman, D. A. *Things That Make Us Smart*. Cambridge, MA: Perseus Books, 1993.

214. Nosofsky, R. M. Exemplar-based accounts of relations between classification, recognition and typicality. *Journal of Experimental Psychology: Learning, Memory, and Cognition* 14 (1988), 700–8.

215. Nutt, D. J., Ballenger, J. C., Sheehan, D., and Wittchen, H. U. Generalized anxiety disorder: comorbidity, comparative biology and treatment. *International Journal of Neuropsychopharmacology* 5 (4) (2002), 315–25.

216. O'Hara, K., and Sellen, A. A comparison of reading paper and on-line documents. CHI '97: Looking into the Future [electronic proceedings], Atlanta, GA, USA, 22–27 March 1997. http://sigchi.org/chi97/proceedings/paper/koh.htm

217. Ojala, M. Views on end-user searching. *Journal of the American Society for Information Science* 37 (4) (1986), 197–203.

218. OMNI. *OMNI: The UK's gateway to high quality internet resources in health and medicine*. BIOME, University of Nottingham, 2004. Retrieved 30 November 2004, from http://omni.ac.uk

219. Ordnance-Survey. *Ordnance Survey, Britain's national mapping agency, for best of British maps and mapping data*. Ordnance Survey, 2004. Retrieved 28 November 2004, from www.ordnancesurvey.co.uk/

220. Orne, M. T. On the social psychology of the psychological experiment with particular reference to demand characteristics and their implications. *American Psychologist* 17 (1962), 776–83.

221. Palfai, T. P., and Salovey, P. The influence of depressed and elated mood on deductive and inductive reasoning. *Imagination, Cognition, and Personality* 13 (1993), 57–71.

222. Paré, G., and Elam, J. J. Discretionary use of personal computers by knowledge workers: testing of a social psychology theoretical model. *Behavior and Information Technology* 14 (4) (1995), 215–28.

223. Parkin, A. J. *Memory: Phenomena, experiment and theory*. Oxford and Cambridge, MA: Blackwell, 1993.

224. Penrose, R. *The Large, the Small and the Human Mind*. Cambridge: Cambridge University Press, 1997.

225. Persaud, R. How to cope with a psychological problem. *The Independent*, 2001.
226. Pharo, N. The SST method schema: a tool for analysing Web information search processes. Unpublished PhD, University of Tampere, Tampere, Finland, 2002. http://acta.uta.fi/english/teos.phtml?6719
227. pilotsweb.com. *Pilot's Web, the Aviator's Journal—Direction and Distance*. Pilot's Web, 2003. Retrieved 24 November 2004, from www.pilotsweb.com/navigate/dis_dir.htm
228. Pinker, S. *How the Mind Works*. London: Allen Lane, 1997.
229. Plowman, L. Narrative, linearity and interactivity: making sense of interactive multimedia. *British Journal of Educational Technology* 27 (2) (1996), 92–105.
230. Pocius, K. E. Personality factors in human–computer interaction: a review of the literature. *Computers in Human Behavior* 7 (3) (1991), 103–35.
231. Prabha, C., and Rice, D. Assumptions about information-seeking behavior in nonfiction books: their importance to full text systems. In *ASIS '88: Proceedings of the 51st Annual Meeting of the ASIS, Atlanta, Georgia, 23–27 October 1988*, 147–51. Medford, NJ: Learned Information Europe Ltd, 1988.
232. Project-Gutenberg. *Welcome to Project Gutenberg*. Project Gutenberg (hosted by ibiblio.org), 1971–2004. Retrieved 26 November 2004, from www.gutenberg.org
233. Ratcliff, R., and McKoon, G. Priming in item recognition: evidence for the propositional structure of sentences. *Journal of Verbal Learning and Verbal Behavior* 20 (1978), 204–15.
234. Ratzan, L. Making sense of the Web: a metaphorical approach. *Information Research* (online journal), 6 (1) (2000). www.shef.ac.uk/~is/publications/infres/paper85.html.
235. Rayner, K., and Sereno, S. C. Eye movements in reading: psycholinguistic studies. In Gernsbacher, M. A. (ed.), *Handbook of Psycholinguistics*, 57–81. San Diego, CA: Academic Press, 1994.
236. Rayner, K., Reichle, E. D., and Pollatsek, A. Eye movement control in reading: an overview and model. In Underwood, G. (ed.), *Eye Guidance in Reading and Scene Perception*, 243–68. Oxford: Elsevier, 1998.
237. RDN. *Resource Discovery Network (UK's free national gateway to Internet resources for the learning, teaching and research community)*. Joint Information Systems Committee of the UK Research Councils (with support from ESRC and AHRB), 2004. Retrieved 30 November 2004, from http://rdn.ac.uk
238. Reid, G. *Dyslexia: A practitioner's handbook*, 2nd edition. Chichester and New York John Wiley & Sons, 1998.
239. Reuters. Pentagon explores a new frontier in the world of virtual intelligence. *New York Times*, 30 May 2003, p. A21.
240. Ringelband, O. J., Misiak, C., and Kluwe, R. H. Mental models and strategies in the control of a complex system. In Ackerman, D., and Tauber, M. J. (eds), *Mental Models and Human–Computer Interaction I*, 151–64. North-Holland: Elsevier, 1990.
241. Robertson, S. E. Overview of the OKAPI projects. *Journal of Documentation* 53 (1) (1997), 3–7.

242. Rosch, E. Principles of categorization. In Rosch, E., and Lloyd, B. B. (eds), *Cognition and Categorization*, 27–48. Hillsdale, NJ: Lawrence Erlbaum, 1978.

243. Rose, S. *The Making of Memory: From molecules to mind.* London: Bantam Press, 1992.

244. Rosenfeld, L., and Morville, P. *Information Architecture for the World Wide Web*, 2nd edition. Sebastopol, PA: O'Reilly & Associates, Inc., 2002.

245. Rosenthal, R., and Fode, K. The effect of experimenter bias on performance of the albino rat. *Behavioral Science* 8 (1963), 183–9.

246. Ross, L., and Anderson, C. A. Shortcomings in the attribution process: on the origins and maintenance of erroneous social assessments. In Kahneman, D., Slovic, P., and Tversky, A. (eds), *Judgment under Uncertainty: Heuristics and biases*, 129–52. Cambridge: Cambridge University Press, 1982.

247. Ross, N. *Culture and Cognition: Implications for theory and method.* Thousand Oaks: Sage, 2004.

248. Roszak, T. *The Cult of Information: The folklore of computers and the true art of thinking.* Cambridge: Lutterworth Press, 1986.

249. Ruhleder, K. Rich and lean representations of information for knowledge work: the role of computing packages in the work of classical scholars. *ACM Transactions on Information Systems* 12 (2) (1994), 208–30.

250. Ruhleder, K. Computerization and changes to infrastructures for knowledge work. *The Information Society* 11 (1995), 131–44.

251. Sadoski, M., and Paivio, A. *Imagery and Text: A dual coding theory of reading and writing.* Mahwah, NJ: Lawrence Erlbaum, 2001.

252. Sass, S. A Patently False Patent Myth still! Did a patent official really once resign because he thought nothing was left to invent? Once such myths start they take on a life of their own—1989 article reprinted—Reprint. *Skeptical Inquirer*, May–June 2003. Retrieved 30 November 2004, from www.findarticles.com/p/articles/mi_m2843/is_3_27/ai_100755224

253. Sauer, M. A. C. The mindful conduit: organizational structure, climate and individual characteristics related to stress, communication and decision processes. *Dissertation Abstracts International* 61 (7-A) (2001), 2807.

254. Schank, R. C., and Abelson, R. P. *Scripts, Plans, Goals and Understanding: An inquiry into human knowledge structures.* Hillsdale, NJ: Lawrence Erlbaum, 1977.

255. Scheerer, M. Problem-solving. *Scientific American* 208 (4) (1963), 118–28.

256. Schraagen, J. M., Chipman, S. F., and Shalin, V. J. (eds). *Cognitive Task Analysis.* Mahwah, NJ: Lawrence Erlbaum, 2000.

257. Schwarz, N., and Clore, G. L. Mood, misattribution, and judgments of well-being: informative and directive functions of affective states. *Journal of Personality and Social Psychology* 45 (3) (1983), 513–23.

258. Seagull, F. J., and Walker, N. The effects of hierarchical structure and visualization ability on computerized information retrieval. *International Journal of Human–Computer Interaction* 4 (4) (1992), 369–85.

259. Searle, J. *The Rediscovery of the Mind.* Cambridge, MA, and London: MIT Press, 1992.

260. Searle, J. R. *Intentionality: An essay in the philosophy of mind.* Cambridge: Cambridge University Press, 2004.

261. Self, C. M., Gopal, S., Golledge, R. G., and Fenstermaker, S. Gender-related differences in spatial abilities. *Progress in Human Geography* 16 (3) (1992), 315–42.

262. Shackleford, H. *Healthcare Marketing: Educating the healthcare consumer versus information overload.* HealthLeaders News, 2003. Retrieved 24 November 2004, from www.healthleaders.com/news/feature1.php?contentid=46763

263. Shannon, C. E., and Weaver, W. *The Mathematical Theory of Communication.* Urbana-Champaign, IL: University of Illinois Press, 1949.

264. Sharps, M. J., Welton, A. L., and Price, J. L. Gender and task in the determination of spatial cognitive performance. *Psychology of Women Quarterly* 17 (1993), 71–83.

265. Shepard, R. N. Recognition memory for words, sentences, and pictures. *Journal of Verbal Learning and Verbal Behavior* 6 (1967), 156–63.

266. Sherif, M. *In Common Predicament: Social psychology of inter-group conflict and cooperation.* Boston: Houghton Mifflin, 1966.

267. Shneiderman, B. *Designing the User Interface: Strategies for effective human–computer interaction,* 3rd edition. Reading, MA: Addison-Wesley, 1997.

268. Simons, D. J., Chabris, C. F., Schnur, T., and Levin, D. T. Evidence for preserved representations in change blindness. *Consciousness and Cognition* 11 (1) (2002), 78–97.

269. Solomon, P. Information mosaics: patterns of action that structure. In *Exploring the Contexts of Information Behaviour: Proceedings of the Second International Conference on Research in Information Needs, Seeking and Use in Different Contexts, Sheffield, UK, 13–15 August 1998,* 150–75. London: Taylor Graham, 1999.

270. Song, C.-R. Literature review for hypermedia study from an individual learning differences perspective. *British Journal of Educational Technology* 33 (4) (2002), 435–47.

271. Spasser, M. A. The enacted fate of undiscovered public knowledge. *Journal of the American Society for Information Science* 48 (8) (1997), 707–17.

272. Sperber, D., and Wilson, D. *Relevance: Communication and cognition.* Oxford: Blackwell, 1986.

273. Spink, A., Bateman, J., and Jansen, B. J. Searching the web: a survey of Excite users. *Internet Research: Electronic Networking Applications and Policy* 9 (2) (1999), 117–28.

274. Spink, A., Wolfram, D., Jansen, B. J., and Saracevic, T. Searching the web: the public and their queries. *Journal of the American Society for Information Science* 52 (3) (2001), 226–34.

275. Spool, J. M. *The Search for Seducible Moments.* User Interface Engineering, 2002. Retrieved 24 November 2004, from www.uie.com/articles/seducible_moments/

276. Spool, J. M., Scanlon, T., Schroeder, W., Snyder, C., and DeAngelo, T. *Web Site Usability: A designer's guide*. Middleton, MA: User Interface Engineering, 1997.
277. Springer, S. P., and Deutsch, G. *Left Brain Right Brain: Perspectives from cognitive neuroscience*, 5th edition. New York: W. H. Freeman, 1997.
278. Stumpf, H., and Eliot, J. Gender-related differences in spatial ability and the *k* factor of general spatial ability in a population of academically talented students. *Personality and Individual Differences* 19 (1995), 33–45.
279. Su, L. T. Evaluation measures for interactive information retrieval. *Information Processing and Management* 28 (4) (1992), 503–16.
280. Su, L. T. The relevance of recall and precision in user evaluation. *Journal of the American Society for Information Science* 45 (3) (1994), 207–17.
281. Sullivan, D. *Search Engine Math*. Jupitermedia Corporation, 2001. Retrieved 30 November 2004, from http://searchenginewatch.com/facts/article.php/2156021
282. Sullivan, D. *How Search Engines Rank Web Pages*. Jupitermedia Corporation, 2003. Retrieved 30 November 2004, from http://searchenginewatch.com/webmasters/article.php/2167961
283. Sullivan, D., and Sherman, C. *Search Engine Watch: Tips about internet search engines and search engine submission*. Jupitermedia Corporation, 2004. Retrieved 30 November 2004, from http://searchenginewatch.com
284. Sutherland, K. Looking and knowing: textual encounters of a postponed kind. In Chernaik, W., Deegan, M., and Gibson, A. (eds), *Beyond the Book: Theory, culture, and the politics of cyberspace*, 11–22. Oxford: Office for Humanities Communication, 1996.
285. Sutherland, S. *Irrationality: The enemy within*. London: Constable, 1992.
286. Swanson, D. R. Undiscovered public knowledge. *Library Quarterly* 56 (1986), 103–18.
287. Tan, B. W., and Lo, T. W. The impact of interface customization on the effect of cognitive style on information system success. *Behaviour and Information Technology* 10 (4) (1991), 297–310.
288. Taylor, R. G., and Hinson, N. Individual differences in the use of a pointing device. In *Contemporary Ergonomics 1988: Proceedings of the Ergonomics Society's 1988 Annual Conference, Manchester, England, 11–15 April 1988*, 521–25. London: Taylor & Francis, 1988.
289. Taylor, R. S. Question negotiation and information-seeking in libraries. *College and Research Libraries* 29 (May) (1968), 178–94.
290. Tenopir, C. *Issues in Online Database Searching*. Englewood, CO: Libraries Unlimited, 1989.
291. TheBrain. *BrainEKP(tm) —Enterprise Knowledge Platform: Collapsing the time to knowledge(tm)*. TheBrain Technologies Corporation, 2004. Retrieved 29 November 2004, from www.thebrain.com/
292. Tufte, E. R. *Envisioning Information*. Cheshire, CT: Graphics Press, 1990.
293. Turkle, S. *The Second Self: Computers and the human spirit*. New York: Simon & Schuster, 1984.

294. Turnbull, D. *Augmenting Information Seeking on the World Wide Web Using Collaborative Filtering Techniques.* Retrieved 23 November 2004, from www.ischool.utexas.edu/~donturn/research/augmentis-abstract.html

295. Twidale, M. B. Interfaces for supporting over-the-shoulder learning. In *HICS 2000 Proceedings: The Fifth Annual Conference on Human Interaction with Complex Systems, The Beckman Institute, University of Illinois at Urbana-Champaign, IL, USA, 30 April–2 May 2000*, 33–37. www.lis.uiuc.edu/~twidale/pubs/otslhics.html

296. Twidale, M. B., and Nichols, D. M. Collaborative browsing and visualisation of the search process. *Aslib Proceedings* 48 (7–8) (1996), 177–82.

297. Uttal, D. H. On the relation between play and symbolic thought: the case of mathematics manipulatives. In Saracho, O., and Spodek, B. (eds), *Contemporary Perspectives on Play in Early Childhood Education*, 97–114. Greenwich, CT: Information Age Press, 2003.

298. Veness, C. *Calculate distance and bearing between two latitude/longitude points.* Movable Type Ltd: www.movable-type.co.uk, 2002. Retrieved 24 November 2004, from www.movable-type.co.uk/scripts/LatLong.html

299. Verplanken, B., Hazenberg, P. T., and Palenewen, G. T. Need for cognition and external information search effort. *Journal of Research in Personality* 26 (1992), 128–36.

300. Waern, Y. *Cognitive Aspects of Computer Supported Tasks.* Chichester: John Wiley & Sons, 1989.

301. Wang, P. Wason's cards: what is wrong? In *Proceedings of the Third International Conference on Cognitive Science, Beijing, China, August 2001. Vol. Beijing, China: Press of the University of Science and Technology of China (USTC)*, 371–75. 2001. www.cogsci.indiana.edu/farg/peiwang/PUBLICATION/wang.evidence.pdf

302. Wang, P., and Soergel, D. A cognitive model of document use during a research project. Study I. Document selection. *Journal of the American Society for Information Science* 49 (2) (1998), 115–33.

303. Wason, P. C. On the failure to eliminate hypotheses in a conceptual task. *Quarterly Journal of Experimental Psychology* 12 (1960), 129–40.

304. Waterworth, J. Spaces, places, landscapes and views: experiential design of shared information spaces. *Interfaces* 38 (1988), 4–7.

305. Westerman, S. J., Davies, D. R., Glendon, A. I., Stammers, R. B., and Matthews, G. Age and cognitive ability as predictors of computerized information retrieval. *Behaviour and Information Technology* 14 (5) (1995), 313–26.

306. Weyer, S. A. What can we learn about learners learning from electronic books? *Machine-Mediated Learning* 3 (3) (1989), 289–95.

307. Which? *Which?—Expert advice from an independent source.* Consumers' Association, 2004. Retrieved 30 November 2004, from www.which.net

308. White, H. S. Information technology, users, and intermediaries in the 21st century: some observations and predictions. In Helal, A. H., and Weiss, J. W. (eds), *Opportunity 2000: Understanding and serving users in an electronic library. 15th International Essen Symposium, Essen, Germany, 12–15 October 1992, to commemorate the 20th anniversary*

of the Essen University Library. Festschrift in honour of Herbert S. White, 2–14. Essen: Universitätsbibliothek Essen, 1993.

309. Wilson, P. Communication efficiency in research and development. *Journal of the American Society for Information Science* 44 (7) (1993), 376–82.

310. Wilson, T. Information needs and uses: fifty years of progress? In Vickery, B. C. (ed.), *Fifty Years of Information Progress: A Journal of Documentation review*, 15–51. London: Aslib, 1994.

311. Wilson, T., and Walsh, C. *Information Behaviour: An inter-disciplinary perspective. A report to the British Library Research and Innovation Centre on a review of the literature.* British Library Research and Innovation Centre and University of Sheffield, 1996. http://InformationR.net/tdw/publ/infbehav/prelims.html

312. Wilson, T., Ellis, D., Ford, N., and Foster, A. *Uncertainty in Information Seeking: Final report to the British Library Research and Innovation Centre/Library and Information Commission on a research project carried out at the Department of Information Studies, University of Sheffield.* No. 59 (Grant number LIC/RE/019; ISBN 1–902-39431–3; ISSN 1466–2949). London: Library and Information Commission, 1999. http://InformationR.net/tdw/publ/unis/index.html

313. Wilson, T. D. On user studies and information needs. *Journal of Documentation* 37 (1981), 3–15.

314. Wilson, T. D. Human information behavior. *Informing Science* 3 (2) (2000), 49–55.

315. Winograd, T., and Flores, F. *Understanding Computers and Cognition.* Reading, MA: Addison-Wesley, 1986.

316. Wolfe, J. M. Visual search. In Pashler, H. (ed.), *Attention*, 13–73. Hove: Psychology Press, 1988.

317. Wolfe, J. M. What can 1 million trials tell us about visual search? *Psychological Science* 9 (1) (1988), 33–9.

318. Xie, H. I. Shifts of interactive intentions and information-seeking strategies in interactive information retrieval. *Journal of the American Society for Information Science* 51 (9) (200), 841–57.

319. Yantis, S. Control of visual attention. In Pashler, H. (ed.), *Attention*, 223–56. Hove: Psychology Press, 1988.

320. Yerkes, R. M., and Dodson, J. D. The relation of strength of stimulus to rapidity of habit-formation. *Journal of Comparative and Neurological Psychology* 18 (1908), 459–82.

321. Zimbardo, P. G. *The Stanford Prison Experiment: A simulation study of the psychology of imprisonment.* 2004. Retrieved 30 November 2004, from www.prisonexp.org

322. Zimbardo, P. G., Ebbesen, E. B., and Maslach, C. *Influencing Attitudes and Changing Behavior: An introduction to method, theory, and applications of social control and personal power*, 2nd edition. Reading, MA: Addison-Wesley, 1977.

Index

hypermedia 156, 158, 188–190, 254, 294
hyperspace, *see cyberspace*
hypertext 134, 156, 190, 214, 218, 228, 238, 294

I
ill-defined problems 64, 119, 132, 178, 294
images 4, 97–101, 234–239, 253, 279–280, 297
implicit learning 235, 294
incubating 67
indicative mood 46–47, 294
individual differences 30–34, 72–74, 163–164, 166–169, 171, 173, 175–176, 207
inferences 220–222, 225
information
    as more than facts 56–68, 214–215, 225–230, 234, 239, 251–252, 257–260, 274, 284
    as process 213, 221, 257
information overload 19, 32, 76, 190, 192–194, 196, 207, 247, 272, 284–285
information science 3, 126, 277, 295, 298
    and psychology 8–9, 163–164, 169, 171, 173, 175–176, 183, 218, 284
    user studies 38, 60, 85, 140, 173, 175–178, 180, 182, 184, 186
information seeking, *see searching*
information society 24–27
information use, non-linear 10, 48, 50, 57, 59, 103–104, 178, 180, 182, 193, 257
intelligence 32, 34, 119, 274
intentionality (in computers) 223–226, 229, 233, 273
intermediary 38, 59, 101, 103, 123, 295
internet
    change 18, 20, 71, 73, 187–188
    hoaxes 84, 86
    modelling 4
    nature of 20–23, 25–27, 36–37, 186, 188–190, 192, 197, 232–233
    speed issues 23
    volunteering 26, 232
intersubjectivity 15–18, 295
invitational mood 46–47, 295
IQ 34, 172, 296
irrationality 76–79, 131, 136, 227, 266, 273

J
James, William 160
Jopling, David 15–16
journalists, *see knowledge workers*
Julien, Heidi 182

K
Kelly, George 46–48, 294–295
Kierkegaard, Soren 232
knowledge, types of 56, 117
    see also information, as more than facts
knowledge management 277–278
knowledge workers 31, 55, 62, 85, 135
Kosslyn, Stephen 237
Kreitler, Shulamith & Hans 167, 207
Kuhlthau, Carol 43–49, 55, 57, 60, 73, 104, 178, 277

L
Landow, George P. 212
language 16–17, 23, 34, 57, 70, 83, 98–99, 107, 167, 188, 215–222, 235–236, 255, 273, 297
Larkin, Philip 220
lateral thinking 66
learning 161–163, 166, 214–215, 225, 229, 238–241, 254, 256
learning style, *see cognitive style*
left-brained, *see brain, hemispheres*
Lesk, Michael 106
librarianship 3, 58, 218, 250
    versus computer science 101–105
libraries
    and online resources 20–23, 38, 97, 142, 148–149, 192, 196–197
    catalogues 72, 87, 124–126, 148, 155, 170, 178
linguistics 61
listening 216–217
Loftus, Elizabeth 223
Logic, *see Boolean logic; deductive logic; irrationality; lateral thinking*
Losee, Robert 258
lost in cyberspace 134, 186, 188–190

M
maps 33, 35, 98, 186, 188–190, 234–235, 239, 253, 280–282, 294, 299–300
Marchionini, Gary 3, 12–13, 25, 59, 103, 107, 126–127, 133